Industry in the countryside is a wide-ranging and readable study of manufacturing before the Industrial Revolution. It examines the widely debated theory of 'proto-industrialization', drawing on data from the Kentish Weald – an area which was already a centre of cottage industry in the Tudor era, and was also the earliest rural manufacturing region to '*de*-industrialize'. The book analyses the Wealden textile industry from its workforce to its industrialists, and emphasizes the ubiquity of dual employment among textile workers and the importance of landownership to the entrepreneurs who financed rural clothmaking. It explores the local context of cottage industry: the pattern of landholding and inheritance, the local farming regime, and the demographic background to rural industrialization. Zell outlines what type of local economy became the site of this so-called 'proto-industry' and shows the impact of cottage industry on the people of such regions. He concludes by asking, is there anything in the 'proto-industrialization' model?

Industry in the countryside

*Cambridge Studies in Population, Economy and
Society in Past Time* 22

Series Editors

PETER LASLETT, ROGER SCHOFIELD, and E. A. WRIGLEY
ESRC Cambridge Group for the History of Population and Social Structure

and DANIEL SCOTT SMITH
University of Illinois at Chicago

Recent work in social, economic and demographic history has revealed much that was previously obscure about societal stability and change in the past. It has also suggested that crossing the conventional boundaries between these branches of history can be very rewarding.

This series exemplifies the value of interdisciplinary work of this kind, and includes books on topics such as family, kinship and neighbourhood; welfare provision and social control; work and leisure; migration; urban growth; and legal structures and procedures, as well as more familiar matters. It demonstrates that, for example, anthropology and economics have become as close intellectual neighbours to history as have political philosophy or biography.

For a full list of titles in the series, please see end of book.

Industry in the countryside

Wealden society in the sixteenth century

MICHAEL ZELL

University of Greenwich

CAMBRIDGE
UNIVERSITY PRESS

Published by the Press Syndicate of the University of Cambridge
The Pitt Building, Trumpington Street, Cambridge, CB2 1RP
40 West 20th Street, New York, NY 10011-4211, USA
10 Stamford Road, Oakleigh, Melbourne 3166, Australia

First published 1994

Printed in Great Britain at the University Press, Cambridge

A catalogue record for this book is available from the British Library

Library of Congress cataloguing in publication data
Zell, Michael.
Industry in the countryside: Wealden society in the sixteenth
century/Michael Zell.
p.   cm. – (Cambridge studies in population, economy, and
society in past time; 22)
Includes bibliographical references and index.
ISBN 0–521–44541–8 (hc)
1. Wealden (England) – Industries – History.   2. Wealden (England) –
Economic conditions.   3. Wealden (England) – Social conditions.
I. Title.   II. Title: Industry in the country side.   III. Series.
HC258.W4Z44   1994
338.09422'51 – dc20   93-3978   CIP

ISBN 0 521 44541 8 hardback.

To My Mother and the Memory of My Father

Contents

Figures

Tables

Acknowledgements

The title of this book is only the most explicit recognition of its intellectual ancestry. Joan Thirsk's essay, 'Industries in the Countryside', long pre-dates the proto-industrialization 'model'. Her short article raised the question of manufacture before the Industrial Revolution in a more multifaceted and less jargon-laden way than most of the contributions to the 'debate' that have appeared subsequently. My own curiosity about the early modern Weald was prompted by the combination of Dr Thirsk's paper, my own relative familiarity with Kent (my Ph.D. thesis examined the Reformation in that county) and an interest in studying pre-industrial social and economic history at the local level. It was a happy coincidence that among the regions of pre-industrial rural manufacturing discussed in Thirsk's 1961 paper, only the Kent Weald had not yet found its modern historian. More than a decade ago I decided that this was a niche for me. An indication of just how long this book has been 'in the pipeline' is that I have to acknowledge – with genuine appreciation – the receipt of a small grant from the Social Science Research Council which helped pay for research trips to Kent archives and to parish churches in the Weald. I remember, with diminished vexation, the many hours I spent (sometimes locked) in draughty church vestries – poring over parish registers which had not been deposited in public archives as they should have been. There were the incumbents, proud of 'their' registers, who could not read them themselves, and the appalling case of a Wealden parish where parts of the early registers had been handed over to a number of local worthies – and could no longer be found! My research was not so much 'history on the ground' as 'history out of the bowels of parish churches'. On the other hand, there were the archive staffs, who never failed in their helpfulness and willingness to answer queries and offer useful suggestions of their own. Without minimizing my appreciation of all the archives I have worked in, I must single out the kindness of Kath Topping and Nigel Yates at Maidstone, Anne Oakley at Canterbury and the staff of the Public Record Office, Chancery Lane.

I would like also to acknowledge the help of the University of Greenwich and of its library. Academic research may not have been crucial to one's employment at

Thames Polytechnic (now the University of Greenwich), but at least the University has not stood in the way. More important has been membership of the Institute of Historical Research of London University, home away from home for all historians. Parts of this book, in earlier versions, were presented to seminars at the Institute, as well as to seminars at the universities of Bristol, Oxford and Reading, as well as to the Humanities Research Seminar at Thames Polytechnic. In every case *I* have learned something from those audiences.

If the history of this project can be viewed as a series of movements between London (where I live and teach) and Kent, it can also be traced to gifts and exchanges between London and Cambridge. The gifts have flowed in my direction, and go back to my earliest years in Britain. They began with the unstinting advice and subsequent patronage of Professor Sir Geoffrey Elton. More recently they have come in the form of help from the Cambridge Group for the Study of Population and Social Structure. Roger Schofield has long been a source of ideas, assistance and beneficial criticism, not least over this book. If history – the discipline – is a series of voyages across time taken by historians, my own history has been a series of voyages across space. The most relevant has been my journey from the New World to the Old. In the former my mentor, Professor Joe Slavin, taught me the basic 'tradecraft', as well as the belief that a critical stance towards received wisdom and 'great men's work' should be the keystone of my work, both as researcher and teacher. I may occasionally have taken this advice too literally, but deference and reverence are traits that never properly assisted the study of the past.

Abbreviations

All printed works are published in London unless otherwise stated.

AgHR	*Agricultural History Review*
Arch Cant	*Archaeologia Cantiana*
BIHR	*Bulletin of the Institute of Historical Research*
BL	British Library, London
Bodl. Lib.	Bodleian Library, Oxford
Cal. Pat.	*Calendar of Patent Rolls*
CCL	Canterbury Cathedral Library
CUL	Cambridge University Library
DNB	*Dictionary of National Biography*
EcHR	*Economic History Review*
EHR	*English Historical Review*
Hasted, *Kent*	Edward Hasted, *The History and Topographical Survey of the County of Kent* (10 vols., 1797–1801)
Hist.J	*Historical Journal*
HMC	Historical Manuscripts Commission
IPMs	Inquisitions *post mortem*
J.	*Journal*
J.EcH	*Journal of Economic History*
KAO	Kent Archives Office, Maidstone
LP	*Letters and Papers, Foreign and Domestic, of the Reign of Henry VIII, 1509–47*, (21 vols., 1862–1932)
PCC	Prerogative Court of Canterbury
PRO	Public Record Office, London
Soc.	*Society*
Trans.	*Transactions*
VCH	*The Victoria History of the Counties of England*

1

Introduction

Historians – as Lesley Clarkson recently reminded us – seem to be born with an irrepressible urge to generalize; they regularly set out to construct historical models, and to generate wide-ranging hypotheses about historical change.[1] And surely this situation is beneficial to all concerned, so long as historians exercise their critical skills on new and old historical models with the same acuity as those who have created them. The theory of 'proto-industrialization' is a case in point. Not the least controversial of such models, it attempts to tackle at the most general level certain central questions which will be raised in this study (as well as much else about modern economic development in the West): how did some rural regions or sub-regions become sites of intensive manufacturing during the 200 or 300 years before the English 'Industrial Revolution', and how exactly did these 'industries in the countryside' fit into their surrounding geographical, agrarian and social contexts?

The 'proto-industrialization' hypothesis, as enunciated by Franklin Mendels in 1972, was, however, more than a model of pre-Industrial Revolution manufacturing. It also amounted to a grand, two-stage, theory of Western economic development, in which the evolution of economic institutions and the concentration of capital which occurred in the seventeenth and early eighteenth centuries are as important as the 'industrial revolution' of the next century. The rural, 'domestic' industries of the early modern era were seen by Mendels and his supporters as containing the conditions for the ensuing development of factory-based manufacturing: 'proto-industrialization' leads to 'industrialization'.[2] Explaining the Industrial Revolution, happily, is no part of our task! It is not the second, developmental aspect of the model which is of interest here, but the initial premises of the model: the origins and development of 'proto-industry' in the 'era of transition'.

---

[1] L. A. Clarkson, *Proto-Industrialization: the First Phase of Industrialization?* (Economic History Society, 1985).
[2] F. F. Mendels, 'Proto-industrialization: the First Phase of the Industrialization Process', *J.EcH*, 32 (1972).

It is hardly news that the early industrial development which occurred in southeast England – in the Weald – did *not* lead on to factory-based production. Several explanations for the decline of the Wealden textile and iron industries have been put forward, but there remains room for debate on this question (which will be joined in the conclusion to this study).[3] But for whatever reasons, so thoroughly did the Weald become de-industrialized that today many are surprised by the extent and variety of manufacturing activities which flourished there in Tudor and early Stuart eras. This study examines Wealden society and its 'proto-industry' during its heyday, in the sixteenth century. Therefore only 'part one', as it were, of the 'proto-industrialization' theory comes under the microscope in this project. We have to discover how simple, rural handicraft production for local markets evolved into relatively large-scale manufacturing of commodities for sale in distant markets, and to what extent this intensification of rural manufacturing changed the lives of men and women who lived in the Weald. For, among other things, the theory of 'proto-industrialization' posits that with the development of rural, 'proto-industry' – as opposed to petty handicraft production – came 'proletarianization' leading to the economic and social immiseration of its burgeoning workforce.

The several exponents of 'proto-industrialization' are not in agreement about all aspects of the model, nor are all the assertions about the evolution of rural industrialization internally consistent or logically unchallengeable. But it will be useful nevertheless to lay out in the most simplified way the 'proto-industrialization' thesis as far as it offers an explanation for the origin and growth of rural manufacturing. The theory explains rural industrial growth by reference to two different but not mutually exclusive factors. In explanation one, the origins of rural industrialization are seen to emanate from outside the region in question. Urban capitalists, in search of investment opportunities, located a relatively cheap labour supply in certain rural districts whom they put to work making commodities for sale in non-local markets. In explanation two, certain pre-conditions and circumstances pertaining to the region itself lead to the development of intensive manufacturing activities. Initially this occurs in the form of a higher than average proportion of the region's workforce taking on industrial 'by-einployments' in addition to their basic, agricultural labour. Subsequently, more and more of the 'proto-industrial' region's population turn to (or are forced into) full-time industrial labour for their subsistence. Explanation two combines a number of specific geographical, demographic and social/economic pre-conditions which can be seen both to attract the owners of capital to the region in question, and to induce men and women in such a region to offer their labour to the organizers of cottage industries such as clothiers in the Weald or ironmongers in the West Midlands metalware trades. Such pre-existing, local conditions which permitted or encouraged rural by-employments were emphasized by Joan Thirsk as early as 1961, in an article which foreshadowed many

---

[3] See, for example, Brian Short, 'The De-industrialisation Process; a Case Study of the Weald, 1600–1850', in Pat Hudson (ed.), *Regions and Industries* (1989).

of the key points of the first part of the 'proto-industrialization' model as formulated by Mendels and later by Kriedte, Medick and Schlumbohm.[4] The pre-existing conditions included, among other things, topographical and geographical attributes. Regions ripe for 'proto-industry' tended to be upland areas with fast-moving streams (to power mills, for example), relatively poor soils and possessed of valuable raw materials (such as timber, iron ores and coal) and extensive common grazing.

The physical geography of such regions produced, in turn, agrarian systems which permitted and even encouraged the growth of rural industries: the so-called 'wood-pasture' regions supported predominantly stock-raising husbandry or dairying, neither of which required intensive farm work on as continuous a basis as did the more intensive cereal farming of many lowland districts. The on and off demands of agricultural work characteristic of pastoral farming meant that local labour was under-employed for much of the year – and thus available for cottage industry. In addition, since most families were to some extent producing their own food, they could be employed in the slack periods of the farming year for very low wages. Wood-pasture districts also proved receptive to cottage industry because of their pre-existing structures of landholding, inheritance customs and relatively weak seigneurial control. Wood-pasture regions were often late-settled districts, where both landlords' power and manorial authority had always been weak, compared with the earlier-settled lowlands. In the wood-pasture regions landholding structures were characterized by large numbers of petty freeholders or tenants with copyholds of inheritance and low, fixed rents. In many of these districts farms had always been enclosed, with little or no collective controls over farming. In addition, the typical customs of inheritance in these districts were partible and holdings were often easily alienated or leased out. There was often little or no seigneurial control over settlement and therefore such regions became the destination of poor migrants from lowland regions where household formation was more rigorously controlled by landlords and manorial juries.

All of these circumstances encouraged the proliferation of both small farmers as well as smallholders. In turn these tenurial conditions both permitted and promoted rapid population growth. Most of the proto-industrial regions were relatively densely populated, although whether they were *already* densely populated or *became* densely populated as a result of 'proto-industrialization' is one of the most obvious logical problems with the model in question. But even before proto-industrialization the prevailing inheritance customs encouraged the formation of separate families and households by all sons, while the pattern of landholding resulted in many families with insufficient land to support themselves solely by farming. The resulting local labour-supply conditions were ripe for exploitation by capitalist, putting-out employers: large numbers of under-employed workers, male

---

[4] Joan Thirsk, 'Industries in the Countryside', in F. J. Fisher (ed.), *Essays in the Economic and Social History of Tudor & Stuart England* (Cambridge, 1961); P. Kriedte, H. Medick and J. Schlumbohm, *Industrialization before Industrialization* (1981).

and female, and many smallholding households which desperately needed to supplement insufficient agricultural incomes. Many families turned to cottage industries for mere survival. Increasingly they tended to become wage-workers, dependent on the work given them by the capitalist employers. Yet other households in the proto-industrializing regions combined farming and artisanal work to produce well above average prosperity – although the modern proto-industrialization theorists have little or nothing to say about such economically successful *self*-employment.

This varied combination of pre-existing circumstances tended to provide a cheap and easily expandable rural labour force, as well as to encourage enterprising local artisans and craftsmen to transform themselves from small masters to putting-out employers. It also attracted urban capitalists from further afield to put out raw materials to the small farmers and cottagers of the proto-industrial region. The best examples of industries in the countryside have been drawn from regions of rural textile manufacture – both in England and on the Continent. As early as the sixteenth century these included the West Country woollen district (in parts of Somerset, Gloucestershire and Wiltshire), the Essex–Suffolk textile region, parts of Lancashire and Westmorland and a substantial share of West Yorkshire. More than a century later a characteristic proto-industrial region developed in Leicestershire based on framework-knitting. But equally representative of early modern proto-industry were the metalware districts of the West Midlands and the Black Country, where large numbers of domestic workers were employed in the manufacture of nails and other small metalwares for sale in metropolitan as well as overseas markets.

Certain economic and demographic consequences usually followed the successful planting of proto-industry in a given region, according to the model outlined by Mendels, David Levine and Kriedte, Medick and Schlumbohm.[5] In purely economic terms, successful and expanding rural industrialization generated profits for the putting-out capitalist who organized proto-industry, but brought increased poverty to the domestic outworkers who worked for them. Over time, according to the theory, the numbers of workers employed in rural industry grew: expanding the labour force was the simplest and least capital-intensive means of expanding production in proto-industry. Thus more and more households became wholly dependent on cash wages earned in manufacturing, while a decreasing proportion of households retained their stake in the land. Hence the 'success' of rural industrialization invariably led to proletarianization – according to the model. The expanding labour requirements of the capitalist employers were filled in two ways.

---

[5] Mendels, 'Proto-industrialisation', and Kriedte, Medick and Schlumbohm, *Industrialization*; Hans Medick, 'The Proto-Industrial Family Economy: the Structural Function of Household and Family during the Transition from Peasant to Industrial Capitalism', *Social History*, 1 (1976); David Levine, 'The Demographic Implications of Rural Industrialization', *Social History*, 2 (1977); David Levine, *Family Formation in an Age of Nascent Capitalism* (1977).

A higher proportion of the local labour supply was drawn into cottage industry – both *more* workers and an increasing share of the existing workers' time – and surplus labour from non-industrialized regions was attracted into districts of proto-industry. These changes had the additional consequence of holding outworkers' wages down, even as production expanded. Even as rural outworkers became increasingly dependent on cash income from industrial employment, they were also subject to frequent periods of poverty due to cyclical unemployment. Because putting-out capitalists never hired outworkers on a permanent or annual basis, they could lay them off at short notice for brief or extended periods – in response to short-term interruptions in external demand for their products. The increasing immiseration of proto-industrial workers, according to the model, was due as much to their irregularity of employment as to the low wages they received while in employment.

Given that in most rural areas there was a net surplus of births over deaths, the logical consequence of proto-industry was to drive down rural industrial wages to bare subsistence level, as well as to condemn most proto-industrial workers to the permanent status of wage workers. For, as proponents of the proto-industrialization model point out, the most striking demographic consequence of expanding rural industrialization was to accelerate population growth beyond the levels of predominantly agricultural areas. It did so by undermining the traditional checks which prevented most young men and women from marrying before they were in their mid to late twenties, i.e., before they had built up some capital and/or before the young men had either acquired a farm or completed a relatively extended craft apprenticeship. The possibility of supporting a family by wages earned in cottage industries – much of which was relatively unskilled – and supplemented by seasonal agricultural labour, induced many young people to marry and form households earlier than they would otherwise have done, and also increased the proportion of young people who married at all. So proto-industrialization, it is argued, led to more rapid population growth through higher levels of both nuptuality and fertility. Thus the *demographic* consequences of proto-industrialization accelerated the damaging *economic* consequences of proto-industrialization for rural outworkers – by constantly expanding the local labour supply. Or so the theory goes.

Three decades have passed since Joan Thirsk identified the Weald of Kent as a model region of rural industries, and in many ways her brief descriptive introduction to the area can hardly be bettered. The Weald displayed many of the characteristics which formed part of Thirsk's model of the rise of rural manufacturing.[6] In Anglo-Saxon times 'Andredswald' was an enormous expanse of forest lying between the North and South Downs. It stretched almost a hundred miles from east to west and was

---

[6] Thirsk, 'Industries', pp. 79–80.

from thirty to forty miles broad. The Weald was ancient woodland, although not royal forest. It covered large parts of Kent, Sussex and Surrey, and amounted to an 'upland' island within the English lowland zone. In the early middle ages it was thinly settled, and the Kent Weald was exploited mainly as summer swine pastures for the lathes and then manors of north and east Kent.[7] It has always been notable for its unproductive soils. From a geological point of view the Weald comprises two different zones. Much of the land in the central 'High Weald' region lies at 200 feet or more above sea level, and is formed of Hastings Beds, which comprises three types of strata (Tunbridge Wells Sand, Wadhurst Clay and Ashdown Sand). This is surrounded by the 'Low Weald': a flat plain, mainly less than 100 feet above sea level, but rising to 200 feet in places. Its soils are based overwhelmingly on intractable Weald Clays. The Low Weald in general possessed the poorest soils. Permanent agricultural settlement came late to the Weald: mainly after 1066. Throughout the middle ages and for several hundred years after, the Weald was – in the model suggested by Peter Brandon and Brian Short – a 'dependent interior', dominated by the more prosperous and progressive agricultural economies to the south and north.[8]

The Weald was also exceptional in its man-made structures. Gavelkind tenure (which specified partible inheritance and unrestricted alienation of lands held in gavelkind) applied in the Weald as in other parts of Kent. But the tenurial and agrarian context in the Weald differed from the earlier-settled parts of the county in several crucial ways. In the Weald, land was held and farmed in severalty: there never were open fields (and collective regulation of cropping) in the Weald as there had been in a number of places in north Kent. Wealden landholders farmed their plots of land as they pleased. Secondly – and equally crucially – seigneurial control was weak in the Weald. By the high middle ages north and east Kent manors held feudal sway over groups of dependent 'denns' or swine pastures in the Weald. But they could only turn their notional authority into cash by offering potential tenants extremely favourable terms to settle in the Weald. So Wealden landholders held their land of north Kent manors *freely*. They had to perform few or no labour services, their feudal lords had no control over their marriages or mobility and they only paid small ground rents. They could – and frequently did – freely transfer their holdings to third parties, so long as they registered the transfer in the manorial court of their 'lords of the fee'. Such manorial courts met once or twice a year but exercised little authority over their Wealden tenants. This peculiar settlement history resulted in a large free peasantry in the Kent Weald by the fifteenth century, who farmed holdings made up of many small closes of land, interspersed among a

---

[7] K. P. Witney, *The Jutish Forest: a Study of the Weald of Kent from 450 to 1380 A. D.* (1976); F. R. H. Du Boulay, 'Denns, Droving and Danger', *Archaeologia Cantiana*, 76 (1961).

[8] Peter Brandon and Brian Short, *The South East from AD 1000* (1990), esp. chapter 1; S. W. Wooldridge and Frederick Goldring, *The Weald* (1953); Alan Everitt, *Continuity and Colonization: the Evolution of Kentish Settlement* (Leicester, 1986).

good deal of unsettled (although not unexploited) woodland. There were very few large holdings (over 100 acres) but small farms and smallholders were thick on the ground in the Weald (chapter 2).

Like most other upland areas, the Weald could be described as a wood-pasture district. The local Wealden variety of pastoral husbandry emphasized stock rearing and fattening more than dairying. Most farms, however, did make butter and cheese for their own consumption, and most farms grew some cereals (see chapter 4). On the generally poor Wealden clays crops were small and the grassland was rarely of very good quality. But, given their small outgoings − compared to tenant farmers in many other parts of the southeast − small-scale Wealden farmers were remarkably successful survivors. The Wealden peasantry was neither driven out by 'rising gentry' nor bought out by commercial farmers in the sixteenth century. There were small farms aplenty to purchase or to hire, and thus it was relatively easy to establish a family and a new household in the Weald before the late sixteenth century.

The demographic consequences of the tenurial and agrarian conditions just described became obvious by the early decades of the sixteenth century, and were well-suited to the extension of rural proto-industry. The Kent Weald was a region of fairly rapid indigenous population growth and one which also attracted immigrants from other parts of the southeast (at least until the Elizabethan period). Thirsk in 1961 noted that most parishes in the central Kentish Weald were densely populated compared to other parts of Canterbury diocese (which covers the eastern two-thirds of Kent) in the 1560s.[9] As chapter 3 will demonstrate, the central parishes of the Kent Weald − where rural clothmaking had been established by the fifteenth century − were already densely populated in the 1520s. And, as we shall see, Wealden populations continued to grow throughout the sixteenth century, although by no means evenly throughout the Kent Weald. It will also be possible to investigate if the patterns of nuptuality and household structure predicted by the proto-industrialization theorists actually occurred in the sixteenth-century Weald.

Without doubt a rural textile industry of major significance flourished in the Kent Weald during the Tudor period − alongside the local Wealden iron industry which straddled the Kent–Sussex border. Within the terms of the debate over proto-industrialization, the English textile industry is among the earliest examples of successful *rural* manufacturing; and among the earliest centres of English woollen manufacture for distant markets by a putting-out system was the Kent Weald. It is difficult to discover much about the Wealden woollen industry during its formative stages, but scattered ulnagers' accounts show that broadcloths were being produced in the villages of the central Weald by the mid fifteenth century.[10] By the early sixteenth century the rural industry in Kent was growing rapidly. Expanding Continental demand for English broadcloth was stimulating production in most of the English textile regions during Henry VIII's reign (1509–47). As English cloth

---

[9] Thirsk, 'Industries', p. 79 note.   [10] Public Record Office (hereafter PRO) E101/339/17–20.

exports rose between 1500 and 1550, Kentish Wealden production grew apace, because most of the region's woollen production was destined for foreign markets. After a brief set-back at mid century (due in part to English currency manipulations), Wealden woollen production during the 1560s probably recovered to the levels reached in the 1540s. For the remainder of the Elizabethan period local textile output – and therefore labour demand – remained at its early Elizabethan level. There was certainly some expansion of output during the first decade of James I's reign, but the Wealden industry entered the early stages of its long drawn-out decline during the export crisis which began with the Cockayne project in about 1610 and deepened during the Thirty Years War (1618–48). The decline of rural manufacturing, however, is not crucial to this study. Instead, chapter 5 examines the range of occupational diversity in the Weald during the heyday of rural manufacturing, the sixteenth century. If the first part of the proto-industrialization thesis has anything to recommend it, then we should be able to see a correlation between agricultural regimes (and their different labour demands) and the extent of non-agricultural employment. If wood-pasture regions (including the Weald) lend themselves to large-scale industrial production for distant markets, should they not at the same time have encouraged the proliferation of all manner of by-employments? Given the Wealden tenurial structure and its wide-open land market, to what extent was dual employment typical of the region? Two further chapters explore the Wealden textile industry, its entrepreneurs and its workforce in some detail. Did workers in this proto-industry become proletarianized and cease to maintain their stake in the land? Were the living standards of Wealden textile workers driven inexorably lower and lower as the logic of the proto-industrialization model would appear to dictate? Were all textile craft workers driven into complete dependence on the capitalist clothiers – from independent small masters into mere wage workers? Was there, in reality, a single 'economic ecology' of rural, capitalist manufacturing, or did proto-industry develop within a variety of economic contexts and spawn a number of different outcomes in terms of the social relations of production? In short, here is a chance to compare theory with reality, during the first century of expanding proto-industry in the English countryside.

In what follows the Kent Weald is represented by a sample of thirty-nine parishes covering some 200,000 acres (313 sq. miles or 810 sq. km.). These include all twenty High Weald parishes in Kent, and nineteen Low Weald parishes, out of perhaps two dozen, depending upon which parishes are assigned to the Weald. (see figure 1.1). In the mid sixteenth century the population of the sample parishes was about 24,000. The region of intensive rural industry, however, was considerably smaller (see figure 6.1). Although the role of rural manufacturing within the region's agrarian and economic structures is the ultimate object of this investigation, this study nevertheless attempts to answer many of the general questions asked by recent generations of local historians. But rather than trace the 'origin, growth, decline and fall' of a 'local community' in the Weald, the present work concentrates on certain themes or topics over a relatively short period of time. Like Victor Skipp's 'ecological' case study of the Forest of Arden in the late sixteenth and seventeenth centuries, the present work is primarily concerned with the material and social aspects of the region under investigation, rather than the reconstruction of the 'total history' of the region.[11] It is therefore both the most recent offering in a long tradition of English local and regional history and, at the same time, an effort to engage in an on-going theoretical debate about the origins and nature of early industry in the West.[12]

[11] Victor Skipp, *Crisis and Development: an Ecological Case Study of the Forest of Arden, 1570–1674* (Cambridge, 1978). And now see David Rollison, *The Local Origins of Modern Society: Gloucestershire, 1500–1800* (1992), which reached me too late to be given the consideration it rightly deserves.

[12] For which also see Myron Gutmann, *Toward the Modern Economy: Early Industry in Europe, 1500–1800* (Philadelphia, 1988).

2

Landholding, inheritance and the local land market

At the very heart of the pre-industrial – and proto-industrial – economy was the land. Even though the Kentish Weald was a manufacturing region during the sixteenth and seventeenth centuries, it nevertheless is crucial to understand the basic structures of landholding and land use. Therefore this study must begin by considering land ownership and the local land market. For if the connections between rural industry and contemporary agriculture are to be understood, historical analysis must move from the latter to the former: Wealden clothmaking and ironworking operated within a pre-existing framework of landholding and farming.

Small landowners were thick on the ground in the sixteenth-century Weald. And, although many estates tended to grow larger through a process of amalgamation by purchase and through marriages, consolidation was constantly being reversed by the stubborn adherence of most owners to the Kentish custom of dividing their lands among their heirs. Only at the very top of the landholding hierarchy – among the gentry – and at the bottom – the smallholders – was partition not the normal response of Wealden landowners on their deathbeds. This cyclical process was strengthened in the course of the sixteenth century as rural prosperity allowed those with land, and perhaps with a craft as well, to purchase additional parcels in what was an active land market, especially from the 1540s. At the same time the demographic trends (discussed at greater length in chapter 3) were such that an increasing share of these small estate builders and inheritors had more than one male heir. Therefore more of the small- and medium-sized holdings were divided in successive generations. For the holders of very large estates, of course, the process of estate building was not checked by such inheritance strategies, and for a variety of reasons gentry estates in the Weald grew steadily throughout the century. A minority of gentry estates were, however, divided when their owners died without sons and their lands passed to daughters or collateral male heirs. A handful of very large estates – that is, large by Wealden standards – did survive into the seventeenth century. But perhaps more characteristic of the sixteenth century was the appearance of additional medium-sized gentry estates in all parts of the Weald, the result either of successful estate building by local entrepreneurs or of purchase by newcomers to the Weald, including a number from London.

Estates in the Weald shared certain characteristics, regardless of their size. Land was held freely of some lordship, in return for small quitrents, suit of court and a relief of one half to one year's rent when the holding was transferred by death or alienation. Holdings were of inheritance; they were also freely alienable without the permission of the 'lord'. All cultivable land was enclosed; no collective rights obtained over individual holdings. The court of the manor – which theoretically met once or twice per year – had only the minimal functions of collecting the small quitrents and reliefs and of recording changes in ownership after a death or sale. Everyone, from smallholders to squires, held land by such terms, although many of the latter also held part of their estates in chief from the Crown. None could be considered copyholders or customary tenants in the normal, sixteenth-century sense.

All arable and pasture land, and almost all woodland, was individually owned. In the first half of the century there remained several large tracts of relatively undeveloped parkland and open forest – as in the huge parish of Tonbridge. But these too were owned – by a succession of aristocratic estates including the Crown – and not open to anyone who might decide to settle. All that remained outside of individual private ownership were small areas of rough common, and even some of these were restricted to local landholders rather than to all residents. In sum, the mythic days when the Weald was a vast, partially-settled open forest – with land available for the taking to men from the appropriate parts of north Kent – were long gone before the sixteenth century dawned. But the legacy of the Weald's medieval past, with its summer swine pastures associated with north and east Kent manors, its complex pattern of distant lordship associated with free peasant farming within the Weald and its geographical history of dispersed settlement rather than nucleated villages, remained the framework within which sixteenth-century inhabitants ordered their lives. That same heritage – of individual settlement, a multiplicity of lordships each of which held sway over a number of dispersed patches of Wealden territory and the consequently weak manorial authority – left a variety of knotty problems for historians.

Land in the Weald can alternately be described as being 'held of the manor of A', where A is a manor in north or east Kent; as 'on the den of B in the parish of C', but where the seigniorial attachment of the 'den' (or medieval swine pasture) in question sometimes cannot be determined; or as 'the manor of D' where D is clearly in the Weald, but whose lands are dispersed across one or more Wealden parishes; or as 'held of the manor of D' but not necessarily lying in the same parish as the manor of D; or simply as 'three pieces of land in the parish of E'. In short, 'manors' did not exist in much of the Weald in the way that manors did in many other parts of England. Wealden 'manors' as well as land held of real manors in north and east

Kent were usually not consolidated blocs of land. Rather, they were collections of
sometimes widely dispersed enclosed fields. The fields were usually referred to as
'pieces' of land in sixteenth-century records.

Not only were 'manors' in the Weald geographically fragmented; ownership
also could be divided. The manor of Chingley (mainly in Goudhurst) owned wholly
by Boxley Abbey until the Dissolution, was by the middle of Elizabeth's reign
partitioned. It was granted by the Crown to the Culpepers of Goudhurst, who sold
it to the Darrells, another Wealden gentry family. Thomas Darrell sold off parts of
the manor in about 1575, mainly to William Campion, a London lawyer. It and the
larger 'borough' of Chingley were described by an early seventeenth-century
surveyor thus:

[The borough of Chingley] containeth the manor of Chingley, containing 766 acres, besides
the waste of Kilndown – whereof Mr Darrell is owner of 399 acres (whereof Chingley Wood
is 240 acres) and Sir William Campion is owner of 360 acres; and Mr Metham owns 7 acres.
It [the borough] containeth also other lands of Sir William Campion called Stonecrouch
(108a.); also Pelmans (80a.) whereof Mr Richard Thomas is owner. Also other lands owned
by Mr Thomas of 206 acres. Also it contains Great Sharnwood (68a.) owned by Mr Bathurst
and 12 acres owned by Robert Fuller.

Equally typical of landholding in the Weald were the lands 'held of the manor of
Wye' (owned by Battle Abbey in Sussex until the Dissolution): they existed in
Bethersden, Biddenden, Cranbrook, Hawkhurst, Smarden, Tenterden and Woodchurch, all in the Kent Weald.[1] In those same parishes other lands were held of other
lordships, and in most cases it is impossible to ascertain the acreage of land
associated with each lordship. All that survives are occasional lists of the small
quitrents or rents of assize payable by named landholders in the Weald to specific
'manors'. In theory, of course, all land in the Weald should have been held of some
lordship or directly of the Crown. But it is by no means certain that all landholders
in the Kent Weald were paying ground rent in the sixteenth century. Without
contemporary rentals from all the lordships which held sway over land in the parish
or parishes under investigation it is impossible to reconstruct the distribution of
landholding in a given parish or set of parishes. Predictably, rentals covering all the
land in a given parish tend not to survive from the same year or even decade. Even
if they did, they could not readily be correlated because most rentals list the
quitrents payable rather than the size of holdings. Quitrents were not always
charged at a standard rate per acre for lands held of the same manor, much less of
lands held of different 'manors'. From a number of rentals which record both
acreage and the quitrents due, it can be shown that Wealden landowners normally

[1] Hasted, *Kent*, vii, p. 78 and KAO U1006/M17; PRO E 315/433, 434; H. E. Muhlfeld, *A Survey of
the Manor of Wye* (New York, 1933); Wye court rolls at PRO SC 2/182/48, 57, 61 ff.

paid between one-half penny and 2d. per acre and that these levels remained stable throughout the sixteenth century.

Occasionally rentals have survived which appear to cover quite extensive tracts of land in the Weald – although never whole parishes – and which record the size of holdings as well. These offer a glimpse of the range of small estates, and of the large numbers of different landowners in relatively small areas. But they do not, it must be emphasized, provide a real breakdown of the distribution of landownership in a particular district. A large – although unknown – proportion of landowners in the Weald held land of more than one lordship, even if their estates were little more than twenty or thirty acres in a single parish. More substantial holdings might owe ground rents to a dozen or more lordships.

One well-documented but typical example is Richard Lellisden of Benenden. He inherited seven pieces of land equalling twenty-four acres on his father's death in 1519. But the only surviving seigniorial record we have of his holding is the entry in the court roll of the 'manor' of Benenden in October 1520 that Richard succeeded to four acres of land, owing a ground rent of 6d. per annum and a relief of 3d. which he paid. The other twenty acres of Richard's inheritance were held of one or more other lordships. Equally illustrative is the large estate of Thomas Sheffe, surveyed in an inquisition *post mortem* of 1604. He held almost 1,000 acres, dispersed across fifteen parishes, nine in the Weald and six in the Marsh to the east and south of Tenterden. Three-quarters of the estate lay in the Weald (749 acres) and was made up of thirty-seven messuages and scores of separate parcels of land. The lands were held of twelve different 'lords of the fee' ranging from the Crown to the Dean and Chapter of Canterbury to a number of gentry-owned 'manors' within the Weald. For all of this Sheffe owed just under 49s. quitrent. The amounts could be ludicrously small: twenty-two acres of land lying in Brenchley and Pembury were said to be held of Sir Thomas Culpeper's 'manor' of Beancrouch for a ground rent of 11d. per annum, and just 4d. was owed for two messuages and eighteen acres of land in Biddenden, held of the 'manor' of Kencham. Even Sheffe's 'principal messuage' in Cranbrook was an amalgam of lands held of three different lordships: seventeen acres on the den of Cranbrook, forty-two acres on the den of Turnden and another eleven acres in Cranbrook where the den was not specified.[2]

The crazy patchwork of lordship in the Kent Weald, illustrated by the Sheffe estate, was common to holdings of all sizes but was rarely recorded in such detail. Most landowners held nothing of the Crown directly and thus there would have been no inquisitions *post mortem* on their decease. Wills tended to describe lands in the vaguest of terms, and even most deeds and indentures record no more than the location and acreage of the land being conveyed. A systematic analysis of landownership in the Weald is therefore precluded by the very weakness of seigniorial institutions and by the practical reality of dispersed estates. Many small

---

[2] Lellisden: KAO PRC 17/14/25 and U 49/M26; Sheffe: PRO Wards 7/37 no. 11.

landowners did not possess compact farms, and holdings greater than thirty acres invariably contained parcels which were distant from the main holding – and thus likely to be held of a different lordship.

A further complication is introduced by the Wealden dens, land originally associated with pre-conquest manors in north and east Kent during the centuries before permanent settlement in the Weald. Almost 700 dens are mentioned in surviving medieval records, although many of those can no longer be precisely identified. However, the brilliant detective work of K. P. Witney has gone a long way to pinpoint and identify many of the Wealden dens, and, more importantly, he has provided an explanation of their evolution and function during five centuries before and after the Norman Conquest. To quote Witney,

the dens owned by an individual manor – which may number anything from two to a dozen or more – are usually to be found spaced in depth along the line of what must once have been a forest drove ... and manors in the same area of north Kent used the same or adjoining droves, so that their dens were all closely clustered together.[3]

By the sixteenth century most of the Weald was permanently settled and no longer used as seasonal pasture for the livestock of north Kent manors. But in a large swathe of the central and eastern Weald – roughly the parishes of Yalding, Brenchley and Horsmonden and all others to the east – parcels of land are often identified on deeds, wills and inquisitions as being on a certain den and in a named parish. Identification by den is by no means invariable and tends to appear less frequently in later than in early sixteenth-century deeds. In the western Weald such traditional identification of land had all but disappeared by this period. The dens themselves can usually be given a rough location on the map, but their size is frequently a mystery. Since the rentals covering lands paying quitrents usually record only the names of holders and the annual rent, for most of the dens only the number of free tenants paying rents and the total amount payable give a rough indication of the size of a given den.

In a few cases the records are more instructive. A Crown survey of about a dozen dens associated with the manor of Aldington records the acreage of landholders as well as the ground rents payable.[4] The dens were situated in four adjacent parishes – Sandhurst, Benenden, Rolvenden and Tenterden – and varied considerably in area and in the number of landowners paying rents. The largest was the den of Fordisham in Rolvenden parish, which, according to the survey, covered 470 acres divided between two large owners. By contrast, the second largest den, Iden in Benenden, was held by twenty different landowners with holdings ranging from one acre to forty-two acres, for a total of 255 acres. The den of Sandhurst, in the

[3] K. P. Witney, *The Jutish Forest* (1976), p. 37; also pp. 211 ff. See also F. R. H. Du Boulay, 'Denns, Droving and Danger', *Arch Cant*, 76 (1961).   [4] KAO U 1220/M25.

parish of that name, contained only a messuage and eighty acres owned by John Foule, gent., who also owned a further 220 acres in two other Sandhurst dens. In this case the round numbers are somewhat suspicious, but the point remains that even in the sixteenth century the dens had a real if somewhat sketchy existence. The nine Aldington dens located in Sandhurst parish contained about 1,600 acres according to the survey, which amounts to about 35 per cent of the parish's area. This is a fairly high concentration of land owing quitrents to a single lordship, for the Weald. But, even in the case of Sandhurst, it is quite likely that some of the local landowners who appear in the Aldington survey merely as smallholders, held additional lands in the parish owing suit to a different lordship. It is also the case that a number of names which appear in the Aldington lists as owners of small parcels also owned land in other parishes. The historian can easily recognize Sir Henry Baker for example, one of the greatest landowners in the county, who appears in the survey of Sandhurst dens as the owner of just seven acres on the den of Chellenden. Tracking down the less familiar names would be a more formidable task.

The same possibilities and problems emerge from a survey of the same date of three dens owing ground rent to the Archbishop's manor of Northbourne. These were the den of Basden (in Hawkhurst) covering 276 acres and held by twenty different free tenants; the den of Bursile or Boars Isle in Tenterden with fifteen holders owning 300 acres in all; and the den of Munden in Halden, whose seven free tenants held 127 acres between them. The survey notes that the den of Basden lay along the King's highway from Flimwell to Rye, with the den of Sysley on the west, the den of Pipsden on the east and the dens of Ockley and Hartnop on the north.[5] In parts of the Weald at least there was an awareness of the location of the old dens in one's own neighbourhood, even if their exact size and their boundaries remained imprecise.

What records like these unfortunately do not explain is whether there was land in Wealden parishes which was not considered part of a den, and therefore paid no quitrents. That is, as the Weald filled up in the later middle ages, as more and more rough forest and scrub land was settled and converted to farming, did the new assarts simply become part of an expanded existing den? Were new dens created? Or, did recently settled farms remain outside of the older system of land division? The surveys and rentals of lands on the dens will not provide the answer. The fact that many parcels are recorded in sixteenth-century deeds without reference to any den, though dens are regularly referred to in the same parish, and that in many sixteenth- and seventeenth-century inquisitions lands are said to be liable for ground rent to a manor within the Weald, both suggest that a substantial part of the settled land in the Weald was not part of the ancient system of dens.[6]

---

[5] PRO LR 2/219 fo. 136 ff.
[6] See e.g. the IPM of Alex. Courthop (1608), who held a messuage and thirty-five acres of land in Cranbrook which owed quitrents of 3s. 4d. to Sir Henry Baker's manor of Morehouse (in Hawkhurst): PRO C 142/693 no. 7.

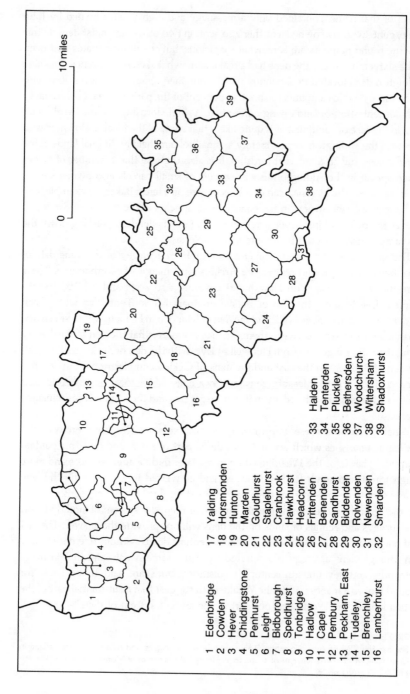

1	Edenbridge	17	Yalding	33	Halden
2	Cowden	18	Horsmonden	34	Tenterden
3	Hever	19	Hunton	35	Pluckley
4	Chiddingstone	20	Marden	36	Bethersden
5	Penhurst	21	Goudhurst	37	Woodchurch
6	Leigh	22	Staplehurst	38	Wittersham
7	Bidborough	23	Cranbrook	39	Shadoxhurst
8	Speldhurst	24	Hawkhurst		
9	Tonbridge	25	Headcorn		
10	Hadlow	26	Frittenden		
11	Capel	27	Benenden		
12	Pembury	28	Sandhurst		
13	Peckham, East	29	Biddenden		
14	Tudeley	30	Rolvenden		
15	Brenchley	31	Newenden		
16	Lamberhurst	32	Smarden		

Fig. 2.1   Map of Kent showing sample Weald parishes.

The typical Wealden estate remained small throughout the sixteenth century. It is described in thousands of wills and in numerous deeds. Figure 2.2 illustrates the layout of a typical Wealden farm. Although the extant records do not permit a systematic analysis of all these small- and medium-sized landowners at different periods in the century, or even at one point, there is sufficient evidence to argue for the continuity of these kinds of holdings throughout the period and into the next century. The evidence can be likened to pieces of a jigsaw puzzle, but in this case all the pieces never existed. The evidence includes last wills, manorial rentals and surveys, inquisitions, deeds and occasionally legal proceedings. From these sources it is clear that landownership was quite widely dispersed in the Kent Weald. And leasing produced a greater number of occupiers than there were landowners. If the nature of farming in the Weald is to be understood, then the distribution of land occupation is at least as important to our understanding as knowledge of landownership.

It is often best to begin with a concrete example. When William Goodgrome of Biddenden made his last will in 1502, he was more explicit than most small landowners, perhaps because his one child was under age. William left his main messuage with sixteen acres of land to his wife for her lifetime. He also owned another parcel of five acres, purchased during his lifetime, making a total farm of twenty-one acres. All was to pass to his son on his wife's death, but if he died without heirs of his body the lands were to be sold. Goodgrome further advised his executors and overseer what he thought the lands were worth: the messuage and original sixteen acres should fetch at least 21 marks (£14), and the other five-acre piece would be worth at least 10 marks (£6 13s. 4d.) on its own, in all just over £20. Apparently the purchased field was better land than his inherited farm, perhaps meadow rather than pasture or arable. The estate left by William Goodgrome was similar to hundreds of others described in less detail in wills made throughout the century. Their usual form is to leave 'my messuage and lands' or 'my messuage and three or four pieces of land' to my son A, with a remainder to son B or to my daughters or my brother C. Rarely did a testator state the total area of his holding, and almost never its value or the lordships of which it was held. Normally a holding as small as fifteen or twenty acres was not partitioned. Instead two procedures were most commonly followed: either the holding was left to both sons jointly, or it was left to one son, who was obliged to pay a cash sum, say £5 or £10, to his brother.[7]

---

[7] Goodgrome: KAO PRC 17/8 fo. 176v. A typical inheritance strategy was that of Thos. Ellis of Brenchley, a small farmer, who in 1544 left his 'house and lands' to his wife for life, then to both sons jointly. The widow was rated £1 per annum in lands in 37 Henry VIII, suggesting a quite small estate: PRO E 179/125/307 and KAO DRb/Pwr/10 fo. 52v. The other alternative, a variation of gavelkind, was followed by Robt. Fisshenden of Brenchley (1546): he left lands to his wife until his eldest son was twenty. Then all lands went to him, but he was to pay his mother £1 per annum during her widowhood and 1 mark per annum to his two brothers in turn until each had received 8 marks (£5 6s. 8d.): KAO DRb/Pwr/10 fo. 196. A wealthier neighbour, Wm. Dann (rated at £22 in goods in 35 Henry VIII) followed the same strategy: he left his 'messuage, lands and tenements' in Brenchley and

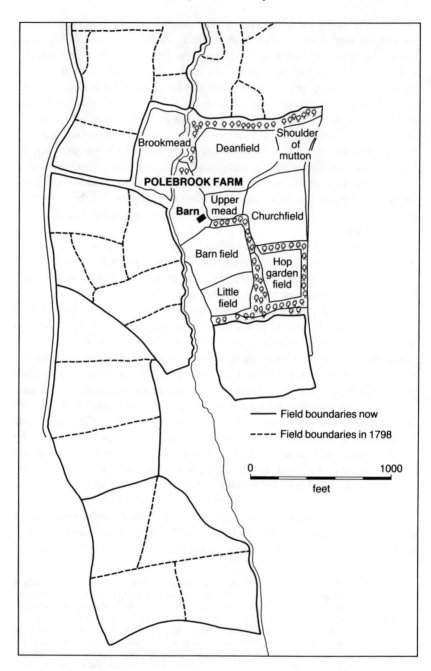

Fig. 2.2   Plan of typical Wealden farm.

Holdings slightly larger than William Goodgrome's were usually divided among a landowner's sons, although not invariably in equal shares. Robert Edmede of Horsmonden (d. 1528) left his main messuage with gardens and four pieces of land to his second son, who already farmed it for his father. An older son was left just one piece of land; probably he had already received land from his father. A third son was left two pieces of land and two younger sons were given one piece each. The will therefore distributed a central messuage and nine pieces of land, representing between twenty-five and thirty-five acres. The original holding – if land had passed *inter vivos* to the eldest son – may have totalled fifty acres or more. Prosperous yeoman landowners, with more than one farmstead and its attached lands, could make a variety of arrangements to transmit their estates. But almost all divided them if they had more than one son. Matthew Haler of Brenchley (d. 1532) left his principal messuage and lands to one son; another messuage and lands would pass to a second son at age twenty-two; the third son was to have a group of lands called Wykes at twenty-two and a fourth son was left six other pieces of land and the lease of a property called Bulbrokes.[8] Thomas Bourege of Capel (d. 1535) owned lands in three different parishes, and had three sons and two daughters. He willed that one son be given £40 ('to arise out of my lands'), a second son was left a messuage, four gardens and thirty acres of land, plus several pieces of meadow, and a third son received six pieces of land and three pieces of meadow. Both sons who received land were given fields in all three parishes.[9]

There is no hint here of any desire to consolidate holdings: Wealden landowners were so used to fragmented farms that even when offered an opportunity to create more compact holdings they rarely did so. The examples cited here are merely indicative of the range of estates held by the majority of Wealden freeholders, randomly selected from the wills of testators with two or more sons. Naturally wills made by men with a sole heir tend to be less informative, but the cases quoted above typify the normal practice of testators. The historian can do little more than calculate what proportion of testators – who after all represent an unknown and possibly varying proportion of adult males and widows – at different times and in different parishes had land to leave to their heirs. And what share of these appear to be substantial holdings (two or three separate messuages and associated lands) of fifty acres or more, and what proportion seem to be small farms (usually described as a messuage and lands or 'my house and lands').

The testators from the two adjacent parishes of Brenchley and Horsmonden in the central Weald, between 1491 and 1610, can serve as a sample.[10] The wills have been divided into four thirty-year periods, and into four categories of male and

Nettlestead to his eldest son, who had to pay £10 each to his two brothers and £1 p.a. to his mother for life: PRO E 179/125/ 268 and KAO DRb/Pwr/10 fo. 61.
8 KAO DRb/Pwr/8 fo. 148v; 9 fo. 44.   9 KAO DRb/Pwr/9 fo. 203v.
10 Brenchley and Horsmonden wills from Rochester consistory court and from the Prerogative Court of Canterbury (KAO DRb/Pwr and PRO PROB 11): 1491–1520 (69 wills); 1521–50 (74 wills); 1551–80 (127 wills); 1581–1610 (105 wills).

female testators, with and without lands mentioned in their wills. There was an absolute increase in the numbers of extant wills between the earliest period, 1491–1520 and the third period, 1551–80. The last period showed a slight drop but was still well above the total for 1491–1520. The chronological distribution of wills indicates not only the growth in willmaking in the early sixteenth century, but even more obviously the periods of increased mortality. This latter explains the very large increase in Brenchley and Horsmonden wills in the period 1551–80: much of the increase was due to a big jump in wills proved between 1557 and 1560, the brief period which Wrigley and Schofield have shown to have been the most serious and widespread mortality crisis between 1541 and 1871.[11] In Brenchley and Horsmonden the early sixteenth-century growth in the numbers of last wills continued, but reached something of a plateau in the second half of the century. After 1560 they no longer increased in line with overall population growth. The sample also exhibits another common characteristic of wills from the Kent Weald: more and more were being made by people with no land of their own to devise. In the first thirty-year period, 1491–1520, 87 per cent of all testators had real estate to leave to their heirs. The proportion of testators with land drops in each successive period, to a low of 43 per cent in the years 1581–1610. The fall in the share of testators without land is less in the case of male testators only: from 89 per cent to 50 per cent in the last thirty-year period.

To test the Brenchley–Horsmonden evidence, the wills from another parish, Staplehurst, were also analysed. Wills were divided into two equal periods, 1501 to 1550 and 1551 to 1600. There were actually more extant wills in the first than in the second half of the century (seventy-six to sixty-seven). In the first half 68 per cent of testators left land in their wills; in the second half 58 per cent did so. The decrease in the proportion of testators who were freeholders is noticeable but much less steep than the decline of landowners among Brenchley and Horsmonden residents who made wills.[12] These figures suggest that by the early sixteenth century it was normal for people with land to leave to make a will, but much less so for those without real property. By the middle of the century it was becoming more common among the landless to make a will, although they must still have represented a small proportion of all adults who died owning no land.

The wills of landowners offer impressionistic evidence about the size of holdings, depending upon whether a testator refers simply to his messuage and lands, or describes several messuages and lands or perhaps a long string of named fields. The figures based on this kind of evidence can only be rough approximations given the wills' lack of specificity, and probably understate the number of testators with more than a small farm. This is because of the many cases where testators leave 'all my

---

[11] E. A. Wrigley and R. S. Schofield, *The Population History of England, 1541–1871: a Reconstruction* (1981), pp. 332–40, 649–56.

[12] Staplehurst wills from Canterbury archdeaconry and consistory courts and the Prerogative Court of Canterbury: KAO PRC 17 and 32; PRO PROB 11.

lands' to a single heir. The 225 wills from Brenchley and Horsmonden which include land nonetheless give some indication of the size of estates. For the three thirty-year periods beginning in 1491, about two-thirds of wills mentioning land appear to refer to relatively small farms, or mere smallholdings. About a third describe holdings which appear to be larger than a family farm. Only a few of the latter were gentry estates. Many of these more substantial landowners refer to themselves as 'yeoman' in their wills. During the last sample period, 1581–1610, the share of obviously small estates decreases to about 55 per cent of all testators with land. The sample size is admittedly small, with no more than seventy landed testators in any thirty-year period, and will hardly carry the weight of serious statistical analysis. It suggests that in this area of the Weald at least, some consolidation of freeholders' estates was taking place, although the bulk of holdings remained under fifty acres. It may also be a reflection of smallholders' declining enthusiasm for making a will.[13]

It may be concluded, therefore, that in Brenchley and Horsmonden, and to a lesser extent in Staplehurst, a slightly smaller share of the population owned land at the end than at the beginning of the sixteenth century. Common sense suggests that it was more likely that those with land would make a will than those who had none. But we shall have to see if other evidence bears out this indication of a decline in the proportion of freeholders in the Wealden population.

Lists of quitrents or rents of assize paid by landowners offer another route to discovering the reality of landholding in the Weald. Many have survived from the late fifteenth to the late seventeenth centuries. Some, as noted earlier, are lists of free tenants who held lands on ancient dens and paid ground rents to non-Wealden manors. Others, often in the same parishes, owe ground rents to Wealden 'manors', which in many cases did not exist in the thirteenth or fourteenth centuries. By the mid sixteenth century, most of the Wealden 'manors' were owned by locally resident gentry families. Some of the Wealden 'manors' had demesne lands which were directly farmed by their gentry owners or leased out at market rents, but these were rarely consolidated blocs. Others seem to have been little more than rent-collecting institutions, with no demesne lands, only free tenants paying rents of assize. Occasionally such rentals have survived for different dates over substantial periods and in a form which would allow for a comparison over time. Less common are rentals which record the size of holdings. We shall examine several of each type, along with a number of rentals which exist for one date only but are nevertheless valuable for the information they contain.

The manors of Pembury Magna and Parva, which held lordship over about 500 acres of land in Pembury and the adjoining parishes of Tudeley and Capel, were originally owned by Bayham Abbey in Sussex. The monastery was one of several

---

[13] Share of wills mentioning land which refer to small estates only: 1491–1520 (68 per cent); 1521–50 (69 per cent); 1551–80 (66 per cent); 1581–1610 (55 per cent), including wills proved in local and prerogative courts.

which were dissolved to endow Cardinal Wolsey's Oxford college in the 1520s. At
Wolsey's fall, the college's possessions returned to Crown hands, but the two
manors were soon granted to Sir Edward Guildford, a Wealden landowner and royal
councillor. In the course of the 1530s the manors passed to Guildford's daughter and
her husband, Sir John Dudley, who in turn sold them to Sir Thomas Cromwell. At
the latter's demise in 1540, they returned to the Crown, only to be sold again in
1545 to a local gentleman, William Wybarne, who lived just across the county
border at Bayham.[14]

There was not much to the manors. A survey of what looks like the demesne of
the manor of Pembury, from about 1514, shows no more than 160 acres, and when
the manor was valued for sale to Wybarne it was rated at under £9 per annum clear
– and that included the ground rents which came to £4 per annum.[15] Several rentals
have survived listing the landowners who held of the manors of Pembury Magna
and Parva from the early sixteenth to the late seventeenth centuries. A Bayham
Abbey rental of the 1520s, which specifies neither the location nor the size of
holdings, shows that there were thirty-three free tenants, several of whom held of
both manors. Pembury Magna alone received ground rents from twenty-six
different freeholders, for a total of £3 8s. per annum. Rents for lands held of Pembury
Parva came to just 11s. per annum. Already in the 1520s a relatively small number
of owners were responsible for a majority of the ground rents – and presumably
held the bulk of the land. The top seven holders were responsible for 53 per cent
of the total ground rent. But there were also a further seven holdings which paid
rents of 2s. per annum or over, as well as a number of quite small holdings.[16] The
next surviving rental, made in 1587 for the 'lord of the manor, John Wybarne, Esq.'
showed that the distribution of landholding had changed little during the preceding
sixty years.[17] The total quitrents due to the two manors were £4 4s., paid by thirty-
one different holders. Now the top five holdings paid 53 per cent of the rent, the
next six, medium-sized holdings were responsible for 26 per cent, and the twenty
smaller holdings paid the remaining 21 per cent. Gentry landholders were
conspicuous both in the 1520s – when two of the largest holders were the local
squires, the Wybarnes, and the Culpepers of Goudhurst – and in the 1580s, when
the larger holders included the wealthy Fanes as well as Thomas Culpeper, Esq. and
John Wybarne. Well-known local yeoman families like the Bourages and the
Amhersts appeared as substantial holders in both rentals; by the early seventeenth
century the latter were reputed to be gentlemen.

The owners of small parcels held of the court of Pembury, however, were just as
much in evidence in the 1580s as they had been in the 1520s. And the survival of
small holdings is confirmed by a detailed rental of the manors drawn up in 1618.[18]
The number of tenants remained at thirty-one, seven of whom held land of both

---

[14] On the manors see Hasted, *Kent*, v, pp. 261–3. Grant to Wybarne: *LP*, xxi, i, 846 (17).

[15] Survey: KAO U 249/M13 fo. 5v; particular for sale: PRO E 318/23/1265.

[16] PRO E 36/164 fo. 9v.   [17] KAO U 1061/M1.   [18] KAO U 249/M13.

Table 2.1 *Size of holdings in the manors of Pembury, 1618*

10 holders of under 10 acres	57.5 acres (9%)
12 holders of 10–29 acres	214 acres (33·5%)
9 holders of 30 acres or more	367 acres (57·5%)

manors. The 1618 rental also records the exact acreage of almost all the holdings. The great majority were under thirty acres, although the nine holdings of thirty acres or above accounted for about 58 per cent of the land.

The distribution of landownership in the region of Pembury at large may not have been identical to that of holdings which paid quitrents to the manors of Pembury. The 640 acres which owed suit to those manors were only a small part of the settled land of the three parishes in which they lay. Some of the holders who appear to be no more than smallholders in these rentals undoubtedly held land elsewhere in the same parishes, and certainly the gentry estates which held thirty to eighty acres of the Pembury manors were far larger than these rentals suggest. And by 1618 many of the sixteenth-century freeholders had gone, to be replaced by a variety of up and coming landowners. But the small estates had not been gobbled up by gentry landowners during the century. A large share of the land continued to be held by local yeomen, in many cases as part of estates of 100 to 200 acres.

A few miles to the east of Pembury, in the parishes of Marden and Goudhurst, a similar structure of landholding can be found. There, a significant proportion of the land was held of the manor and hundred of Marden, itself an appendage of the north Kent manor of Milton Regis. A late fourteenth-century document recorded the names of twenty-eight dens in this area which were said to owe ground rents to Milton Regis. By the time of the first detailed rental to survive, 1574, the holders were listed by parish and no mention was made of the dens on which their lands lay.[19] The Marden rental unfortunately does not record the size of holdings, listing only the rents payable by each owner. A rough indication of the location of lands held of Marden is given by the division of the quitrents: about two-thirds of the £14 plus was paid by lands in the parish of Marden, with most of the other third paid by lands in Goudhurst parish. In all there were 136 different landowners owing suit to the lordship of Marden, over half of whom paid quitrents of under 1s. per annum. As in Pembury, a number of local gentry families appear here as major landowners: Sir Thomas Fane, Sir Richard Baker and the Maplesdens in Marden parish, and Sir Alexander Culpeper and Edward Horden, gent. in Goudhurst. The distribution of holdings can be constructed on the basis of quitrents due.

---

[19] Marden rental: KAO U 2087/M1. A later rental, of 1647, records the acreage of many holdings and shows a wide variation in quitrents per acre. On Marden manor see Hasted, *Kent*, vii, p. 53–4 and Witney, *Jutish Forest*, p. 240–2.

Table 2.2 *Holdings owing quitrents to Marden, 1574*

71 holdings (52%) owing under 1s.	29s. 1d. (10%)
27 holdings (20%) owing 1s. to 1s. 11d.	36s. 5d. (13%)
29 holdings (21%) owing 2s. to 5s. 11d.	106s. 9d. (38%)
9 holdings (7%) owing 6s. to 18s. 8d.	109s. 9d. (39%)

If the assize rents averaged about 1d. per acre – in fact they varied widely around that figure – the holdings above included about 3,400 acres, spread across two parishes which cover over 17,000 acres. Again, a caveat must be entered. Many of the landholders who appear for quite small parcels in the rental of Marden lordship owned additional lands in the same parishes, and many holders on the Marden rental owned lands in other parishes as well. An obvious example is Thomas Sheffe, mentioned earlier. He appears among the hundred-odd small owners in the Marden rental, with a quitrent of 1s. 1d. That property can be identified in his inquisition *post mortem* of 1604: two messuages and thirty-four acres of land were said to pay rent of 1s. 2d. to the Crown as of its manor of Marden. But of course this small owner in the manor of Marden also owned another 940 acres in fourteen other Kent parishes.[20]

Moving to Thomas Sheffe's home parish, Cranbrook, manorial records associated with the Roberts family of Glassenbury in Cranbrook shed light on the pattern of landholding in the populous, central Weald parishes. The Roberts's were already major local gentry in the second half of the fifteenth century, and by 1603 their large collection of properties known as the manor of Glassenbury included well over 1,000 acres spread across Cranbrook, Goudhurst and Hawkhurst. They were also the recipients of quitrents from at least nine Wealden dens in the same region, and it is possible to compare the landholders of at least two Cranbrook dens at widely separated points in time. The 1603 rental of the dens of Cranbrook and Badlingden can be compared to a rental of 1483 for Cranbrook den and one of 1501–2 for Badlingden. In 1483 the den of Cranbrook was in the hands of fifty-seven different free tenants, who owed quitrents totalling about £2 10s. At that time the land was very widely distributed, with only the Hendley family responsible for more than about 2s. in rents (their holdings owed 9s. per annum). Over a century later there were still fifty-one separate holders, now responsible for £2 17s. in ground rents. The Hendleys had gone, to be replaced by a handful of families, most of whom were

---

[20] Cf. KAO U 2087/M1 *sub* 'The Rent of Goudhurst' with PRO Wards 7/37 no. 11. Other landholdings in Marden parish can be identified: the 'manor' or den of Whitehurst (owned by the Wottons of Boughton Malherbe) received quitrents worth 12s. 10d. per annum from a dozen holders in 1638: BL Add. MS. 33,899 fo. 151 sqq; the 'manor' or den of Sheephurst (owned by the Bakers in the late sixteenth century): KAO U 24/M24; the 'manor' of Mountain, with a dozen free tenants in the 1620s: KAO U 514/M1; the den of Chillenden (held of manor of E. Peckham, owned by Christ Church Priory and then the Wyatts until 1554) had six free tenants paying 18s. 6d. in quitrents in the 1540s: PRO SC 12/9/39.

Table 2.3 *Holdings on the dens of Cranbrook, Swatlingden, Thornden, Hartley,*
Badlingden and Hockeridge, 1603

41 holdings (51%) owing 1s. or less	17s. (14%)
15 holdings (19%) owing 1s. 1d. to 2s. 9d.	26s. (23%)
16 holdings (20%) owing 3s. or more	75s. (63%)

associated with Cranbrook's most important industry, clothmaking. There remained
plenty of smallholdings, but the largest share of the land was now owned by
members of the Hartrege, Sheffe and Weller families. The local squirearchy was
represented only by its wealthiest member, the Bakers of Sissinghurst, who held
land in this den paying only 8d. ground rent. The much smaller, neighbouring den
of Badlingden had eleven different holders in 1502 and the same number in 1603;
the total rent had risen from 13s. 8d. to 19s. 4d. per annum. Around 1500 no single
family controlled a major share of land in Badlingden, but the largest holders were
minor local gentry: the Bettenhams, the Hendleys again and the Tuftons. Also
among the bigger landholders was John Brickenden, a clothier. A hundred years
later two of the larger holders were Sir Thomas Hendley and Sir Nicholas Tufton.
But alongside them were Alexander, John and Stephen Weller and the by now
familiar Thomas Sheffe. During the preceding century a large share of the land of
Badlingden den had been in the hands of the Courthops, prosperous clothiers since
the early sixteenth century. They sold out to the owners of 1603, not because of
financial collapse, but simply as part of the ongoing buying and selling in the
Wealden land market.[21]

A more detailed, if static, view of the distribution of land in the Cranbrook area
can be established from the 1603 Roberts rental, covering lands on the den of
Cranbrook and five nearby dens. There were eighty different landholders in the six
dens, who paid in all £6 per annum in quitrents. Dues varied from a penny a year
to 9s. 3d., the last paid by Sir Richard Baker to his decidedly less well-off 'landlord',
Sir Thomas Roberts.

The names of the largest landholders in this sample of the Cranbrook area
provide a useful reflection of the location of wealth at the end of the sixteenth
century. The half dozen biggest property owners (if brothers, fathers and sons are
grouped together by family) neatly represent the most important local gentry
families: the Bakers (11s. 10d.), the Hendleys (4s. 8d.) and of course the recipients
of these rents, the Roberts'. But also they include some of the most important
families in clothmaking and trade: the Wellers (17s. 6d.), the Courthops (7s. 4d.,

---

[21] Rentals of 1483 and 1501–2 in KAO U 47/11/M8; 1603 rental in KAO U 47/11/M9. Two deeds
of 1583 and 1629 suggest that the manor of Glassenbury alone covered 2,000 acres (KAO U
708/T14), but inquisitions after Thos. Roberts's death in 1580 show that the whole Roberts estate
in Kent came to just 1,600 acres: PRO C 142/189 no. 97 and C 142/221 no. 104.

Table 2.4 *Size of holdings in nine Sandhurst dens, 1608*

17 holders of under 20 acres	148 acres (9.5%)
8 holders of 20–49 acres	281 acres (18%)
3 holders of 50–99 acres	225 acres (14.5%)
5 holders of 100–300 acres	905 acres (68%)

although John Courthop is now labelled 'gent'), the Brickendens (4s. 1d.) and the Sheffes (8s. 8d.). As will be emphasized in later chapters, the most successful Wealden tradesmen and putting-out manufacturers usually were also substantial landowners. Cranbrook was not typical of the Weald as a whole. But the pattern detected there – the concentration of a majority of land in the hands of a small number of owners and the continued presence of numerous smallholdings – occurred in many places besides Cranbrook.

In Sandhurst, mentioned earlier, lands in the nine dens of the manor of Aldington were owned by thirty-three different persons in 1608, fourteen of whom held land in more than one den. In all the dens covered 1,560 acres; the three largest holdings totalled 668 acres (43 per cent). Seventeen holdings of under twenty acres each accounted for less than a tenth of the land in the nine dens.[22]

The continuity in the number of holdings – although not in the surnames of the holders – is striking, whenever a comparison across time can be made. Not only was this true of holdings paying quitrents to Pembury and to Aldington. The same pattern is visible in two widely separated rentals of five dens in Marden and Goudhurst, appendant to the manor of East Peckham. In the 1540s, when the Wyatts owned East Peckham, there were twenty-two different holders, paying quitrents totalling 50s. 1d. per annum. In 1632, when the manor was in Crown hands, there were twenty-five separate owners, who owed 51s. 5d. in all.[23] In the interval the majority of holdings had changed hands, although two or three surnames appear in both rentals, but not necessarily for the same holdings in 1632 as their ancestors had held in the late 1540s.

A similar blend of continuity and change can be found in four dens in Bethersden and Smarden held of the manor of Hothfield, in rentals of 1564 and 1627. The rentals covered about 400 acres, mainly in Bethersden. At the earlier date there were eighteen different owners, including five Glovers and two Witherdens, who owed 32s. 6d. in quitrents. Over seventy years later rents totalling 33s. 3d. were due from sixteen tenants; there were still two called Glover and two Witherdens. Of the thirteen different surnames appearing in 1564, only five remained in 1627.[24]

---

[22] KAO U 1220/M25.

[23] Rental of 1540s: BL Add. MS. 34,154 fo. 20v ff; 1632 rental: PRO SC 12/23/54; another 1540s rental at SC 12/9/39.

[24] KAO U 455/M13/6 and M15. Hothfield also held rights over two dens in Biddenden (Ewehurst and Ibornden) with about 165 acres and one den of under 100 acres lying in Benenden and Cranbrook.

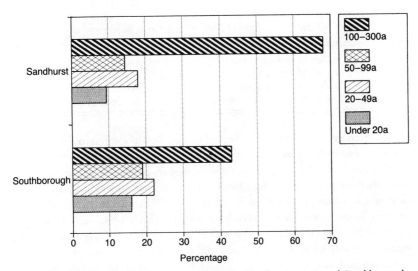

Fig. 2.3a   Distribution of land by size of holding: Sandhurst (1608) and Southborough (1621).

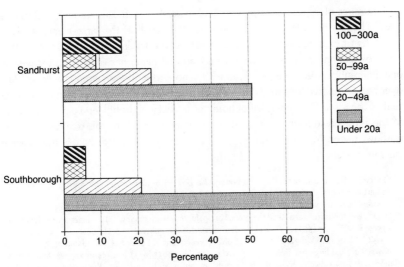

Fig. 2.3b   Distribution of landholders: Sandhurst (1608) and Southborough (1621).

Moving further west in the Weald brings us to a region where the ancient organization of settled land into dens was no longer recognized. Peasant settlement generally occurred later here than in the central and east Weald and in the early sixteenth century it was also less densely populated. Landowners in this region were more likely to hold of a manor which was itself within the Weald, or of a chartland

Table 2.5 *Size of holdings in Southborough and Bidborough, 1621*

56 holders of under 20 acres	339 acres (16%)
17 holders of 20–49 acres	465 acres (22%)
5 holders of 50–99 acres	406 acres (19%)
5 holders of 100–300 acres	889 acres (43%)

manor which in the middle ages extended its jurisdiction south into the Weald by spawning a subordinate manor.[25] Landowners held their land (often dispersed over a wide area) for small ground rents and notionally owed suit of court and a relief of one half or one year's ground rent. Heriots are occasionally mentioned, either in the form of a small money payment or a live animal.[26] From a scattering of rentals covering lands in the western Weald, it appears that ground rents often were slightly higher than in the central Weald parishes. But there is no uniformity in this regard, even with lands held of the same lordship. There is the vague impression too that seigniorial authority was slightly more in evidence in this part of the Weald. Again, the historian is frustrated by the small number of rentals which recorded the actual size of holdings.

A number of typical examples of landownership in the western Weald can be cited. The manor of Hadlow, with lands in the parish of the same name, received about £23 per annum in quitrents from fifty-seven landholders in 1587. A further £21 16s. per annum was received from manorial demesnes rented out to twenty-one different persons, nine of whom were among the fifty-seven freeholders.[27] Just over half of the free tenants (twenty-nine) owed quitrents which amounted to 9 per cent of the total. The upper half of holdings (twenty-eight holders) paid 91 per cent of the rent, presumably representing about nine-tenths of the free land held of Hadlow manor. In fact the six biggest holdings accounted for half of the quitrent income.

[25] On the western Weald see F. R. H. Du Boulay, *The Lordship of Canterbury* (1966), Witney, *Jutish Forest* and articles by H. W. Knocker in *Arch Cant*, 44 (1932).

[26] Quitrents per acre were quite high in, for example, the manor of Southborough (in Tonbridge): KAO U 442/M67. But free tenants of the manor of Speldhurst were paying only 1d. per acre or less in the 1550s: KAO U 934/M10–11. Reliefs of a quarter of the quitrent at Speldhurst and Yalding (KAO U 934/ M10–11; U 787/M15–16), but of one year's rent at Sundridge Weald and in the manor of Bowsell in Chiddingstone (KAO U 1000/M14–15; U 1996/M8/3). Heriots also appear to have been more regularly collected by west Weald lordships, although in some cases the manor accepted 'dead heriots' in lieu of live beats: Broxham manor in Edenbridge and Westerham (£1 charged as the price of a cow in 1569): KAO U 789/M1; manor of Leighton in Cowden (a heriot required after a death or alienation, but several compounded for at £1 and £1 10s.): KAO U 908/M86; manor of Chiddingstone Cobham (heriot due, either best beast or a 'dead heriot' of 3s. 6d., in 1575): KAO U 908/M50; Sundridge Weald ('heriots' of 3s. 6d. paid, but a horse valued at 10s. also taken in 17 Eliz. I): KAO U 1000/M15; manor of Speldhurst *alias* Harwarton (between 1 and 30 Eliz. the court collected seven dead heriots of 3s. 6d. each plus eight cows, three oxen and two horses): KAO U 934/M27.

[27] Rental of 1587: KAO U 38/M1 (the top three tenants owed almost 40 per cent of all quitrents).

Moving to the southwest corner of the Weald, the manors of Southborough (in the parish of Tonbridge) and Bidborough held suit of court over more than 2,000 acres in the parishes of Tonbridge, Bidborough and Capel. A particularly detailed rental of 1621 recorded the acreage of most holdings. It reveals a pattern which has been noticed before. The great majority of free tenants owned under twenty acres each but a large proportion of the land paying rents of assize to the two manors was in the hands of a small minority of property owners.[28]

The largest holdings, as in other parts of the Weald, were owned by resident gentry families including the Fanes and the Wybarnes, by a descendant of a prosperous sixteenth-century ironmaster and by local yeomen.

Enough examples have been cited to demonstrate a general trend. The pattern that emerges — and it describes the situation in 1600 as well as in 1500 — is one of a large number of small estates, many not big enough to survive as subsistence peasant holdings, intermixed among the dispersed holdings of a much smaller number of yeoman and gentry estates. The latter tend to be multiples of the former, agglomerations of scores and sometimes hundreds of enclosed parcels of land and wood.

At the bottom of the landownership ladder were the numerous smallholders whose property was insufficient to support a family by farming alone. Many would have been craftsmen or labourers. One such freeholder was Thomas Dyne of Staplehurst (d. 1533), a wheelwright, whose smallholding comes to light because his will was challenged in the court of Chancery by one of his two daughters and her husband. According to their bill Dyne held a tenement, one orchard and seven acres of pasture, and it should have descended to her. The defendants who were in possession, Dyne's other daughter and her husband, answered with Dyne's will which indeed left his 'house and lands' to the defendant, the son-in-law Richard Drowley, if he would pay Dyne's legacies and debts. It appears from the will that Dyne favoured one of his daughters over the other — in the matter of his seven acres anyway — because she and her husband Richard Drowley already had two sons.[29] A typical Wealden parish contained dozens of smallholdings like that of Thomas Dyne: some were occupied by their owners, others could easily be rented out to local farmers for short or longer terms.

Next up the property ladder were the owners of what we have been referring to as small estates. The small, owner-occupied farm of twenty or thirty acres was normally composed of half a dozen to a dozen enclosed fields, usually within a quite limited area although not invariably in a compact bloc. The less numerous yeoman

---

[28] KAO U 442/M67: total quitrents were £16 5s. per annum. The figures in this table are not exact because the acreage of about fifteen of the eighty-three holdings was not given; estimates have been made for these.

[29] PRO C1/750/25–7; KAO PRC 17/19 fo. 293. The case was dismissed in 1537. Another wood-pasture region also boasted large numbers of small freeholders, the Forest of Dean in Gloucestershire: see J. C. K. Cornwall, *Wealth & Society in Early Sixteenth Century England* (1988), pp. 150–1.

estates – probably no more than a few hundred in the Kent Weald at any single point in the century – varied in size from sixty or seventy acres up to about 200 acres. They frequently included lands in more than one parish and usually included several parcels of woodland, which were a rarity among the smaller estates.

The gentry estates were larger still and even more likely to be dispersed over a wide area. Nevertheless, the majority of these were relatively small, 300 or 400 to 1,000 acres, with lands in two or three adjacent parishes. They were distinguished from the larger yeoman estates not by the extent of their home farms, but by their possession of extensive woodland and parks, as well as by additional land that was rented out. Many of the gentry estates also included quitrents among their possessions, although in very few cases were such feudal dues more than a very minor element in the income of a gentry estate. Gentry landowners, of course, were paying out quitrents as well. About the middle of the century there were roughly forty to fifty gentry estates situated wholly or predominantly in the Kent Weald. By 1600 their number was slightly higher. At least a score of non-Wealden gentry and noble families also owned some land in the Weald, but it rarely amounted to more than 100 acres and was almost always let to local farmers. Of the forty or fifty gentry estates, only a handful at any time extended to more than 1,000 or 1,500 acres.

The very few aristocratic estates which included land in the Kent Weald did not dominate the region because much of their property lay outside it. In the early part of the century the foremost example was the estate of the Duke of Buckingham, with extensive holdings in the Tonbridge area. It fell to the Crown with the third duke's attainder in 1521. The Nevilles, Lords Abergavenny, held substantial estates in the Kent Weald throughout the century, but far more of their lands lay to the north, and to the south – in Sussex. In the later sixteenth century there were the Sackville and Sidney estates, but they too were as much Sussex as Kent landowners. The Sidneys did acquire extensive acreage in southwest Kent, but not enough in the region to dominate more than their home parish. The only other estates of equivalent size – though their owners possessed no titles in the sixteenth century – were those of Sir Edward Guildford of Benenden and Rolvenden, which were split up in Henry VIII's reign; the Fanes of Hadlow and Tudeley; and the Bakers, whose estate centred on Cranbrook but extended into many parishes. Such magnate gentry, often with connections at the royal court, were anything but typical of the Wealden squirearchy of the period.

Neither was the church a major landowner in the Kent Weald, as the entries in the *Valor Ecclesiasticus* of 1535 demonstrate. Monastic lands, which before 1540 amounted to at least a quarter of all land in many parts of England, were far less prominent in the Weald. There were no major abbeys situated there, and Combwell Priory in Goudhurst owned property worth only about £80 per annum, and much of that was rectorial tithes rather than land. The greater abbeys of Kent (along with Battle and Robertsbridge in Sussex) owned only scattered parcels in the Kent

Weald. Most of their income from the Weald – and it was not much – came from quitrents owing to their north and east Kent manors. Christ Church Priory, Boxley Abbey and Malling nunnery owned a good deal of land on the fringes of the Weald, the archbishop's bailiwick of Otford included some Wealden property (but it passed to the Crown in 1537) and Westminster Abbey owned the considerable manor of Westerham on the northern edge of the Weald.

Compared to north and east Kent, lay landowners were overwhelmingly dominant both before and after the Dissolution. Most Wealden parishes contained the seats of resident gentlemen, despite the recent historical myth that the Weald was one of the least governed regions in England, a veritable 'dark corner of the land'. Of about forty Kent parishes mainly or wholly in the Weald, only ten or eleven do not appear to have had at least one resident squire during most of the sixteenth century – and most of those were quite small parishes. The proportion of Wealden parishes without resident gentry was no higher than in most of England, and lower than in many counties.[30] The few larger parishes in the Weald without resident squires nonetheless contained many properties owned by gentlemen resident in adjoining parishes. Marden, for example, without a resident gentry family, included estates owned by gentry resident in Cranbrook, Goudhurst and Staplehurst. A good deal of Rolvenden was owned by the Guildfords, whose seat was next door at Hemsted in Benenden. Most of the other Wealden parishes had at least one, and several more, resident gentlemen for much of the century and beyond, although many of these were small fry indeed. But if there was a gentry seat in most parishes, only a minority contained a resident justice of the peace, especially before the 1560s. In the second half of the century 'parish gentry' proliferated in the Weald. Using the commissions of the peace, the subsidy rolls and Hasted's *History* to plot the Wealden gentry at different periods during the century, it is clear that there were considerably more men known as gentlemen in Elizabeth's reign than in Henry VIII's.

By Lambarde's day there were a number of newcomers who had acquired small gentry estates, as well as local families – either successful yeoman families or prosperous merchants and clothiers – who were beginning to assume the style of gentlemen as their landholdings grew large enough to justify their new status. In Benenden, for example, the Guildfords were joined by the Gibbons, who had prospered as farmers and clothiers in Henry VIII's reign. In Brenchley, which had no resident gentleman in the early sixteenth century, an incomer, Paul Sydnor, bought land from the Crown and settled in the 1540s. But the family sold out in the 1570s to William Lambarde and left the county. In Goudhurst, the leading landowners, the Culpepers of Bedgebury, were joined by the Campions (ex-London merchants), who bought the Combwell Priory estate in the 1590s. In Penshurst, the Willoughbys

---

[30] Parishes with no regular resident gentry were mainly small: Bidborough, Capel, Cowden, Frittenden, Hever (except during the 1520s and early 1530s when the Boleyns presided at Hever Castle) and Newenden.

(ex-law) were joined by the Sidneys, who obtained a variety of former Crown lands from Henry VIII's reign onwards. At Chevening (just north of the Weald), the major property owners, the Lennards's (ex-law and royal service) estate extended into the Weald.

In Biddenden, the Allards, who had prospered as merchants and clothiers, joined the 'older' gentry family, the Maynes, by the late sixteenth century. At Hawkhurst, the Boys's, scions of a prosperous and large clan of East Kent gentry, arrived in the late sixteenth century. In Horsmonden, the only resident gentleman at mid century was a nephew of the Darrells of Scotney in Lamberhurst next door. The Darrells were soon replaced by William Beswick, the son of a London merchant, who bought the Darrell property in Horsmonden in the 1580s. In Smarden, the resident gentry were the Draners, who earlier in the century were Cranbrook clothiers. Staplehurst had no resident gentry until one of the Maynes of Biddenden established himself there in Henry VIII's reign. During the same era, the Bathursts, who had prospered as merchants and clothiers both in the Weald and at Canterbury, also set up as mini-squires in Staplehurst. And, finally, a good example of the rising yeoman family are the Streatfields of Chiddingstone. Among their number in the Elizabethan era were a woollen draper, an ironmaster and several big farmers. They were buying land in several adjacent west Weald parishes, investing in mortgages and by the early seventeenth century were reputed 'gentlemen'.[31] Information about the size and character of gentry estates can be gleaned from inquisitions *post mortem*, Court of Wards surveys and schedules, deeds and wills. But detailed records have not survived for all gentry estates. Both IPMs and wills are often disappointingly unspecific about property. Despite the many gaps, enough evidence survives to indicate the nature of these large estates, particularly in the later sixteenth century. It is relatively easy to pinpoint gentry residences within the Weald. But it is altogether more complicated to locate their holdings, since all but the most minor of parish gentry owned property in more than one parish. Given the size of most Wealden parishes – usually 5,000–10,000 acres – a gentleman with a few hundred, or even 500 acres in a single parish owned only a small percentage of the land.

In no case where the size of a gentry holding in a parish can be calculated was it ever as much as a third or a half of the parish. Sir Anthony Mayne's lands in Biddenden, around 600 acres, amounted to just 8 per cent, while his cousin John Mayne of Staplehurst owned 500–50 acres in that parish, again no more than 8 or 9 per cent. In parishes with several local gentry estates, however, their combined holdings could well be of the order of half the land in the parish. Cranbrook, for example, contained large chunks of the Baker estate, the main holdings of the Roberts and Hendley families. By the late sixteenth century the same parish included the lands of the lawyer-turned-gentleman, William Plummer, as well as

---

[31] See especially Streatfield deeds and wills in KAO U 908.

some of the estates of the Courthops, formerly clothiers but now 'gentlemen'. Goudhurst included the seat and much of the estate of the Culpepers of Bedgebury. But it was also for most of the sixteenth century the home of a lesser gentry family, the Hordens of Fishcocks. In Hadlow, too, by the later sixteenth century, a majority of the land may have been owned by two families, the Fanes and the Rivers. But the apparently overwhelming size of the major gentry estates must be seen in context. When it is possible to analyse gentry holdings in more detail, it often turns out that they were not as valuable as their sheer size might suggest. The 1,600 acre estate of Walter Roberts, Esq. contained a park of over 400 acres as well as other woodland, while Sir William Campion's 1,000 acres, mainly in Goudhurst (c. 1620), included 300 acres of woods. These same Wealden parishes contained scores of lesser landowners, most of whose land was neither wood nor waste.[32]

The extent and nature of medium-sized gentry estates can be illustrated by specific examples. John Mayne of Staplehurst (d. 1588), just mentioned, owned under 700 acres in all. He held 136 acres in Romney Marsh and about 550 acres in Staplehurst and Frittenden (mainly the former). John Drayner of Smarden (d. 1567) was another typical lesser gentleman. Of his total 580 acres, over 500 lay in his home parish, with another thirty acres each in Bethersden and in the Marsh.[33] Sir Henry Isley of Sundridge on the northern fringes of the Weald (attainted 1555), owned a typically fragmented estate. Only about one half of the £193 clear annual value of his property derived from lands in or on the borders of the Weald. His 'manor' of Brasted amounted to quitrents and perquisites of court valued at just £19 per annum, while his home manor of Sundridge was worth only about £70 per annum clear. Of the gross income of £95 per annum from Sundridge, about a third came from quitrents owed to that manor, the remainder from the farm of the demesne lands. The Sundridge estate consisted of only about 550–600 acres of land plus a small park which was leased out for £2 per annum.[34]

More extensive gentry estates in the Weald did exist, but there were few at any given moment. Sir Anthony Mayne of Lynton and Biddenden, who died an old man

---

[32] Anthony Mayne: PRO C 142/693 no.26; John Mayne: PRO Wards 7/22 no. 92 and a schedule, unnumbered in Wards 4/10; Walt. Roberts: PRO C 142/189 no. 97, C 142/221 no. 104; Campion: KAO U 814/P1. Another example is the manor of Combwell (in Goudhurst and Staplehurst). It covered about 700 acres, of which lands in hand came to 467 acres: of that 'demesne' 380 acres was woodland, the other 230 acres were farmed out: KAO U 513/E2/1-2. The manor of Bockingfold (in Goudhurst, Marden and Yalding), owned by the Culpepers, totalled 685 acres, but 290 acres were woods: PRO SC 12/3/34. Hendleys: PRO C 142/230 no. 61 and KAO U 1044/F1; Plummers: KAO U 1406/P1; Fanes: PRO C 142/223 no. 84; Wards 7/20 no. 138; an unnumbered schedule in Wards 4/9; KAO U 282/M14 and T76; Rivers: PRO Wards 7/21 no. 97.

[33] PRO Wards 7/22 nos. 92, 96 and another in Wards 4/10; C 142/146 no. 116.

[34] KAO U 1000/8/M32 which varies slightly from a valor of 1553: PRO LR 2/258 fos. 154–64. Brasted manor had some demesne land but it had been conveyed to Isley's son William. After Isley's execution, his son was re-granted much of the estate for £1,000 (*Cal. Pat. Rolls*, 1554–55, pp. 170–2). The family never fully recovered: Wm. Isley, Esq. was still at Sundridge in 1569 (PRO KB 9/625 no. 147), but by the 1570s was deeply in debt to the Crown. Land was sold and the local beneficiaries were the Lennards, and the Seyliards of Brasted (KAO U 908/L1).

in 1611, owned about 1,200 acres in six Wealden parishes, as well as 700 acres in Romney Marsh. Walter Roberts, Esq. of Glassenbury in Cranbrook (d. 1580) owned some 1,640 acres in Cranbrook and the two neighbouring parishes of Goudhurst and Hawkhurst, along with sixty acres in the Marsh.[35] But the larger the estate, the less likely was it to be concentrated in a single parish or group of adjoining parishes. The Twysden estate, surveyed in 1604, contained about 2,400 acres. The core of the estate extended in all directions from their seat in East Peckham, Roydon Hall. There were over 900 acres in the vicinity, but it was spread across the parishes of East Peckham, Nettlestead, Hadlow and Wateringbury, with another 100 acres lying in Yalding and Brenchley. There was another large group of lands (1,200 acres) situated mainly in Great Chart, Bethersden and Woodchurch in the eastern Weald, and finally about ninety acres in Romney Marsh.[36] The Lennards of Chevening (on the northern border of the Weald) built up an even larger estate than the Twysdens, but much of it lay far beyond the Kent Weald. John Lennard, Esq. (d. 1591) owned extensive holdings in Brasted and Chevening, but he also held estates in other parts of Kent, and in Cambridgeshire, Somerset, Wiltshire and Yorkshire! Lennard had managed to parley the profits of office in the court of Common Pleas into an enormous landed estate.[37]

As in the case of the Lennards, service to the state lay behind most of the biggest gentry estates in the Weald. Another successful lawyer, Sir Thomas Willoughby, amassed substantial holdings in the western Weald through marriage and the profits of his legal practice during the first half of the sixteenth century. But the debts piled up by his grandson forced the sale of a large part of the estate in the later decades of the century. In Henry VIII's reign, however, by far the largest gentry estate was that of the Guildfords of Benenden and Rolvenden. The family was already of county gentry rank when Richard Guildford cast his lot with Henry Tudor in 1483. His two sons Henry and Edward followed him into Crown service in their turn: Sir Edward rose to be Lord Warden of the Cinque Ports, served as a Kent M. P. and increased his estates considerably. A younger brother, George, inherited a smaller estate in Benenden. There is no detailed record of the estates of Sir Edward and George Guildford, but by the 1530s the family lands included major holdings in Halden, Rolvenden, Benenden, Cranbrook and Tenterden in Kent, as well as marshland in Sussex, and valued at over £300 per annum. Sir Henry and Sir Edward died within two years of one another in the early 1530s, the latter intestate. Sir Edward's young son died soon after, and there emerged two claimants to the property: Sir Edward's son-in-law and former ward, John Dudley, and his nephew

[35] Anthony Mayne: PRO C 142/693 no. 26; Roberts: C 142/189 no. 97; C 142/221 no. 104. See also *Accounts of the Roberts Family of Boarzell, Sussex*, ed. Robert Tittler (Sussex Rec. Soc., 71).

[36] Bodl. Lib. MS. Top. Kent c.11–12, after the death of Robert Twysden in 1603.

[37] PRO C 142/229 no. 143. The Lennards' arrival among the county elite seems to be confirmed by a marriage of about 1590 to a daughter of Sir Ric. Baker of Cranbrook (noted in IPM of Sampson Lennard, 1616: PRO Wards 7/54 nos. 138a, 139).

John Guildford, son of George. In the end the estate was broken up. Much of the land in Rolvenden and Tenterden passed to Dudley and thence to the Crown in 1553, while the Benenden and Cranbrook property and all the Sussex land went to John Guildford, the heir male, who remained at Hemsted in Benenden. Based on the values given in IPMs and the surveys of the 1530s, the Guildfords' Wealden property alone must have exceeded 2,000 acres. But by the 1550s the Guildford estate was no greater than that of several other local families already mentioned. Only in the lifetime of Sir Thomas Guildford, in the 1560s and 1570s, did the estate begin to expand again.[38]

Another pre-sixteenth-century gentry family which prospered mightily in the sixteenth century were the Fanes (later changed to Vane) of Tudeley and Hadlow. From the early decades of the century their lands were divided among several branches of the family, sons of a John Fane of Tonbridge (d. 1488), who owned lands in at least half a dozen parishes. By the 1530s the Fanes of Badsell in Tudeley were the wealthier branch, but there remained Fanes of Tonbridge and of Hadlow. The Fanes of Hadlow, in the person of Henry Fane (d.1580), owned lands in Hadlow, Shipborn, Tudeley and Capel, which were formally valued at £35 per annum in his IPM. A more realistic assessment of his estate would be three or four times that figure, but the properties listed in the inquisition point to holdings of 1,000 acres or less.[39] The property of Sir Thomas Fane of Badsell (d. 1589), by contrast, was valued in a Wards schedule of 1604 at over £275 per annum and included lands in at least sixteen Kent parishes. The central group of estates extended from Tudeley into Tonbridge, Hadlow, Capel, Yalding, East Peckham and Brenchley. There was also land in Romney Marsh as well as several hundred acres in northwest Kent at Crayford and Plumsted. Two generations of the Tudeley branch of the family had built a medium-sized gentry estate into one of magnate gentry rank. That status was recognized by the marriage of Sir Thomas Fane to the daughter and heir of Henry, Lord Abergavenny. Their son, Sir Francis Fane, was promoted to the old Neville title, earl of Westmoreland, early in the seventeenth century.[40]

The outstanding example of a minor Wealden gentry family rising to county gentry status during the sixteenth century is that of the Bakers of Sissinghurst in Cranbrook. Their ascent was quite rapid, and again involved a legal education and a career in royal service. By 1600 Baker children were marrying into the leading

---

[38] Willoughby: *The Reports of Sir John Spelman*, ed. J. H. Baker (Selden Soc., 1977); *The House of Commons, 1509–58*, ed. S. T. Bindoff (1982); Hasted, *Kent*, vol. iii; PRO E 179/240/273 (£106 per annum in lands in 1524); KAO U 1000/3/E35/1–15; Nottingham U. Lib. Middleton MSS. Guildfords: *DNB* sub Ric. and Hen. Guildford; Edw. Guildford's estate in PRO SC 11/Roll 851; SC 12/9/46 and 12/18/55; Sir John Guildford (d. 1565) will: PRO PROB 11/48a/25; Sir Thos Guildford (d. 1574) will: PROB 11/57/32 and schedule in Wards 4/8, unnumbered.

[39] See Fane pedigrees in 1574 and 1592 Visitations of Kent (Harleian Soc.). The family's success was due in part to the activities at the court of Edward VI of an illegitimate son, Ralph Fane. See PRO E 318/10/425–6; Wards 7/20 no. 138 and C 142/246 no. 128.

[40] Thos. Fane: KAO U 282/T76 and PRO C 142/223 no. 84. It is impossible to reconstruct the size of the estate from these sources.

gentry of Kent and beyond, among them the Lennards and the Guildfords. It must be stressed, though, that the estates of many local gentry families expanded without recourse to direct grants or purchases from the Crown. Royal service was, for the minority who benefited from it, a source of revenue first and foremost. It could be used to buy Crown lands but just as frequently was laid out on purchases from neighbouring landowners.[41] There were several minor gentlemen from Wealden families who made their careers during the peak decades of Crown land sales, who did purchase directly from the state. Sir John Baker was the most notable, but two other local examples were Sir Walter Hendley (d. 1552) and Sir Thomas Moyle (d. 1560). Both bought extensively from the Crown, including land in the Weald, but at their deaths the bulk of their estates passed to other families through co-heiresses.[42] The Baker estate, on the other hand, remained intact for five generations from the death of Sir John in 1558, and in the late sixteenth and early seventeenth centuries was the greatest in the Kent Weald.

John Baker was the son of a minor Cranbrook gentleman who was trained in the common law. He rose from the post of Recorder of London, through a number of Exchequer offices, to become a privy councillor. He regularly conformed to each successive religious change under Henry VIII, Edward VI and Mary Tudor, and even died at an opportune moment. When his son Richard obtained livery of lands in 1559, a schedule recorded an estate valued at about £675 per annum, of which £150 per annum came from outside Kent. Although Sir John owned land in over twenty Kent parishes, the core of the estate lay in the central Weald parishes of Cranbrook, Hawkhurst, Frittenden, Biddenden, Staplehurst and Halden. There were also substantial holdings in six parishes just to the north: Hunton, West Farleigh, Loose, Teston, East Barming and Wateringbury. There was so much land, and the tenurial obligations so complicated, that the Court of Wards official was reduced to inventing a lord of the fee – a certain Ralph Beauclere – for much of the Wealden property that was not clearly held in chief of the Crown.[43] Neither this schedule nor

---

[41] See Zell, 'The Mid-Tudor Market in Crown Land in Kent', *Arch Cant*, 98 (1981). The best documented example is Sir Edw. Wotton of Boughton Malherbe, who owned lands in the Weald at Brenchley, Hadlow, Marden, Headcorn and Lenham, along with much else. A survey of the Wotton estate in 1560, which records how each property came to the family – and much was added in the sixteenth century – shows almost no purchases of Crown land: BL Add. MS. 42,715 fo. 190 ff. Others who bought locally include the Fanes, the Lennards and the Willoughbys along with most of the clothmaking and trading elite of Cranbrook. Even Sir Walt. Hendley, who bought much from the Crown, also bought small parcels locally: KAO U 1044/F1, pp. 27–9, 37–40, 71–2, 80, 218–19.

[42] Hendley, of Coursehorne in Cranbrook, was a Court of Augmentations official, and Moyle of Eastwell (north of Ashford) was one of the General Surveyors of Crown Lands. The latter's two daughters married Sir Thos. Finch and Sir Thos. Kempe (both JPs). Hendley's three daughters married major Wealden landowners: Wm. Waller, Esq. of Speldhurst (and secondly Geo. Fane of Tudeley), Thos. Culpeper of Goudhurst, and Ric. Covert, a Sussex landowner.

[43] For Baker see *DNB* and *The House of Commons, 1509–58*. There are particulars for several of Baker's purchases of Crown land at PRO E 318/189/80, E318/3/75, E 318/24/1405–6 and E 315/336 fo. 57, but a full list must be retrieved from the patent rolls. He spent at least £2,000 and probably much more. The schedule is KAO U 24/T426.

the later IPMs or Wards schedules for the Baker estate attempted to specify the acreage of the properties involved. However, a deed of 1559 which covers much of the estate in six central Weald parishes including Cranbrook gives a rounded-off total: 2,100 acres of land, 1,600 acres of wood, 120 acres of marsh and 100 acres of heath. Although the acreage given on many deeds, especially on fines, is not to be trusted, the area listed on this deed of recovery may not be a wild exaggeration. If this is correct, then the whole estate would have been several times that large. Very little of it was sold off until after 1596.[44]

The Baker estate was exceptional. Most esquires and even knights owned less than 2,000 acres in the Kent Weald, while ordinary 'gentlemen' commonly held under 1,000 acres. The *combined* acreage controlled by gentry and aristocratic families in the Weald probably grew slightly in the course of the century, but the number of men calling themselves 'gentlemen' increased at a much faster pace.

Landowners, be they magnate gentry, prosperous clothiers or yeomen farmers, all faced the problem of how to manage their property. Obviously the issue was not peculiar to the Weald, but, because of the geographical arrangement of so many estates in the region, the problem was magnified. The most common response in the Weald was to rent one's land out. The area's burgeoning population in the sixteenth century, and the disappearance of any unsettled land worth farming, ensured that there was no lack of tenants. Information about leasing can be drawn from inquisitions and schedules of larger estates which came to the attention of royal officials, from surviving leases themselves, from scattered estate records and from wills. Together they reveal an almost universal tendency on the part of landowners to lease out a major share of their holdings.

The leasing behaviour of smaller landowners can often be inferred from the terms of their wills. Parcels of land which have been farmed out are not mentioned as a matter of course, but specific parcels or messuages are often identified by their tenants when a yeoman estate is being divided between heirs. Thus James Hersett of Staplehurst (d. 1488), who owned lands in two other parishes besides Staplehurst, left his wife part of his estate, referring to it as his messuage and lands 'farmed to John Rydden'. And Peter Hoo, 'husbandman' of Staplehurst (d. 1563), referred to his Lower Lands as 'now occupied by Thomas Scranton'. James Austen of the same parish, who appears to have owned four messuages and lands in 1567, had leased two of the farms while keeping in his own hands two other messuages and lands. All were in Staplehurst yet he chose not to farm directly all his property. In 1576 John Harold of Staplehurst authorized his wife to sell a tenement and lands which he had recently purchased from a Horsmonden man; they were said to be occupied

[44] Recovery: KAO U 24/T278; other Baker schedules and inquisitions are PRO C 142/244 no. 10; C 142/246 no. 114; Wards 4/9 unnumbered and a copy at KAO U 24/T426. Some lands were sold about 1596 by trustees of John Baker's will, to pay his debts and raise marriage portions: PRO Wards 7/70 no. 159.

by a tenant farmer. The profits from his other lands were to go to his wife until his two daughters were twenty-one, at which time they would inherit.[45]

This last provision highlights a commonplace practical situation which frequently resulted in small farms becoming available to let. Many landowners died before their heirs were of age, and the most common direction of testators in the Weald was to leave their property to their wives until their heir(s) reached twenty-one. Richard Sharpe of Staplehurst (d. 1498) owned lands in Staplehurst, Marden, Cranbrook and Frittenden, and his ultimate heir was his daughter's young son. By his will he directed his executors to lease his lands until his grandson was twenty-two. Another Staplehurst man, William Goldham (d. 1530), had two sons, one of whom was only a child. Part of his lands were left directly to his older son, but a messuage and lands destined for his younger son were left to Goldham's wife for four years (to keep the boy at school), and then were to be farmed out until he was twenty-two. Thomas Osborne, 'yeoman' of the same parish (d. 1534), planned to divide his lands between his two sons. But the younger was under age, and so his lands were to be farmed out by a neighbour until the younger son came of age. Most wills of men with underage heirs are not so specific, but in the absence of older children it is likely that the intention of most testators who left property in their wives' hands until their heirs attained their majority was that the widow should farm out the lands. Examples of the uses of leasing have been drawn from the wills of a single parish. In fact any group of Wealden wills will show that owners of small estates frequently leased out part of their holdings during their lifetimes. In some cases it was because of retirement from farming, in others because they chose not to farm directly outlying parcels they owned. Many other properties were temporarily farmed out during the minority of heirs.[46]

The scattered evidence of leasing in freeholders' wills yields almost no information about rents or fines, the terms of leases or even if formal indentures of lease were normally drawn up. It may be that during minorities small estates were let to friends or kin at below market rates. But leasing of small parcels of land was never confined to such interim situations. The dozens of tiny holdings so noticeable on the manorial rentals were readily leased out to local farmers if their owners were not local residents. The very profusion of such scattered smallholdings — whether owned by larger estates or not — would have resulted in numerous fields and closes being available to let in most Wealden parishes. As a consequence, a prosperous Wealden farmer could readily increase the size of his farm, at certain points in the family life-cycle, by hiring additional fields in the vicinity of his own lands. Later in

---

[45] Hersett: KAO PRC 17/5 fo. 72v; Hoo: PRC 17/37 fo. 116; Austen: PRC 17/40 fo. 33; Harold: PRC 17/42 fo. 321.

[46] Sharpe: KAO PRC 17/7 fo. 71; Goldham: PRC 17/19 fo. 124; Osborne: PRC 17/20 fo. 69v. There is least evidence of leasing *inter vivos* in wills of owners of very small estates. There is some evidence of petty freeholders in other areas commonly leasing lands in J. C. K. Cornwall, *Wealth and Society*, pp. 113 ff.

life, the same farmer who had rented extra land might farm out some of his own property if he felt unable to continue farming all of it himself. The fragmented character of Wealden estates — whatever its disadvantages — in this way permitted flexibility in the size of farming units. Equally important, the landless could easily find smallholdings to rent — if they could pay market rates.

Leasing the bulk of their lands was the normal practice among large landowners, whether resident or non-resident in the Weald. Collections of deeds relating to gentry estates and almost all the detailed schedules and valors of major landowners reveal that much of their farmland was in the hands of tenants. Considering the dispersed nature of large estates, the decision to rent out is readily understandable. Where evidence is available about the direct farming operations of the major gentry landowners, it too shows that only a small proportion of such estates were retained in hand: usually a home farm of up to 200 acres, plus some woodland and perhaps a park. The bulk of the tenements and farms were let. Unfortunately, the proportion of estates which was farmed out cannot be known with any accuracy for many of the larger holdings. Very few are the subject of detailed surveys in this period, while many of the IPMs, schedules and valors fail to specify which parcels are in hand and which leased. So, conclusions must be drawn from a sample of well-documented estates.[47]

There is reasonably full evidence for a number of lesser gentry, yeoman and tradesman estates. If any of the larger properties were likely to be directly farmed, it should be these. Their owners were normally resident on their estates and their property was less likely to be spread over a very wide area. But the records suggest nevertheless that among these groups leasing was commonplace. A well-endowed yeoman, Christopher Newenden (d. 1599), owned just over 100 acres in two adjoining parishes. In Headcorn he had a 'capital messuage' and sixty acres occupied by one tenant, and another messuage and twenty-three acres of meadow and pasture, also let to a tenant. In Staplehurst he held twenty-three acres of land. This is not to argue that most yeoman farmers leased the majority of their lands as Newenden did; only that leasing was a possibility for owners of estates of all sizes when personal circumstances recommended it. The 'yeoman'-sized farms of fifty to 150 acres which typically appear in the rate books of Wealden parishes may represent owner-occupied farms, but they may equally be the farms of major lessees or farms composed of both rented and freehold property. A well-off yeoman of Goudhurst, Richard Baker, held about 250 acres of land when he died, probably an

---

[47] The limited evidence about gentry farming operations in the Weald, discussed in chapter 3, shows farms of this size. Rating assessments, also, when they are recorded in acres, suggest the same thing. In Pluckley, in 1628, the largest occupied holding was just 280a (KAO P 289/5/1 fo. 7); at Horsmonden in 1619 Wm. Beswick, Esq. had in hand just 115 acres, about the same amount as several yeoman farmers (KAO U 71/01); a full rating of Chiddingstone (1625) showed that Bernard Hyde, Esq. (who bought Bore Place from the Willoughbys) occupied just 200 acres (KAO TR904 at July 1625); and a church rate for Bethersden (1614) shows the largest occupier as holding 250 acres (Churchwardens' account book, dated '1576–1647' at fo. 104: held in Bethersden church).

old man, in 1606. Most of his property was in Goudhurst, but sixty acres lay in Ticehurst, across the Sussex border. Several messuages were said to be occupied by his two sons, but the majority of the estate was in the hands of tenant farmers.[48]

A typical 'middling' gentleman, John Draner of Smarden (d. 1567), owned a reasonably compact estate: 520 out of 579 acres of it lay in his home parish. And yet he had in hand just sixty-three acres in Smarden and twenty-nine acres in the Marsh. The rest, 487 acres, was let to fourteen different farmers. The Cranbrook clothier, Alexander Dence (d. 1574), owned a moderate-sized estate in Cranbrook and four adjacent parishes, with another forty-six acres of marsh at Rucking. The IPM values the whole at £145 per annum. Exact acreages are not given for much of the estate, but from the descriptions it would have come to at least 300 or 400 acres. His Cranbrook lands were let to eighteen different tenants. A messuage and forty acres in Benenden were occupied by a tenant, as were his lands in Goudhurst and Frittenden. Only the marshland appears to have been in hand.[49] Old Thomas Hendley, Esq. (d. 1591), of the Cranbrook gentry family, lived in retirement at Otham outside the Weald, but left a large estate in Cranbrook, Benenden and Biddenden and in Romney Marsh. According to the patchy information in his IPM, his various Cranbrook holdings were occupied by sixteen separate tenants, almost all in quite small parcels. But even back in 1565 he recorded that the 'house and all the lands in my own occupying' were worth just £14 per annum, as compared to his cash income of that year of about £130.[50]

Minor gentlemen, especially newcomers to the Weald, seemed to have kept very little of their estates in hand. The Plummers settled in Cranbrook in the last decades of the century. A plan of William Plummer's holdings in Cranbrook at the time of his death in 1622 shows an estate of about 160 acres in the parish, of which only sixty acres were in hand. The rest was occupied by six tenants. A much more detailed survey of the estate of Thomas Plummer in the 1630s shows a total estate of some 750 acres, including 159 acres in the Marsh. The Wealden property – in Cranbrook and five neighbouring parishes – was occupied by eighteen different farmers. No tenant held more than eighty-six acres, and most held under thirty acres.[51] The estate of Thomas Sheffe, 'gent' (d. 1604), which had been amassed by several generations of Cranbrook merchants and clothiers, included about 750 acres in nine central Weald parishes. In this part of the estate Sheffe had no less than three dozen tenants, some of whom leased no more than a tenement, while others occupied farms of up to seventy-four acres.[52] But not only newly risen gentlemen leased out the lion's share of their property. Thomas Wilford, Esq. of Cranbrook

[48] PRO Wards 4/8 (unnumbered); Baker: Wards 7/30 no. 53. Entries of the baptisms of children of Ric. Baker in the 1570s and 1580s, and of his wife's burial in 1593, in the Goudhurst parish register, suggest a man of at least fifty-five in 1606.
[49] PRO C 142/146 no. 116; C 142/169 no. 91.
[50] PRO C 142/230 no. 61; KAO U 1044/F1 fo. 171.   [51] KAO U 1406/P1.
[52] PRO Wards 7/37 no. 11. The arrangement of holdings by lordship in the IPM prevents a calculation of how much land Sheffe held in hand.

(d. 1553) was the latest of several generations of gentry landowners. He left an estate lying mainly in Cranbrook, Frittenden and Staplehurst. Of the Wealden property, valued at about £157 per annum in a Wards schedule, lands worth just £38 per annum were not occupied by tenant farmers.[53]

Magnate gentry and aristocratic estates, as one might expect, were even more likely to be largely in the hands of tenants than the property of their less far-flung gentry neighbours. The manor of Penshurst offers a good example. The manor and several of the nearby parks were originally part of the Stafford estate, which fell to the Crown in 1521. The manor remained in Crown hands until a grant to Sir Ralph Fane in 1550, who farmed out most of it. After Fane's attainder, as a close supporter of Protector Somerset, Penshurst was granted to Sir William Sidney, a royal servant of Henry VIII and already a Sussex landowner. Up to that time the Sidney estate in the Kent Weald was worth little more than £15 per annum, and consisted of the 'manor' of Lamberhurst (£14 per annum) and some quitrents. The manor of Lamberhurst was already leased out. The Sidney estate of the late 1540s included Kent properties producing about £59 per annum, Sussex lands worth close to £200 per annum and property in Hampshire bringing in about £130 per annum. The new Penshurst estate – in all about 2,500 acres – extended over several adjacent parishes and included well over 1,000 acres of parkland and woods. It was worth between £75 and £100 per annum in the 1550s, most of which was paid by leaseholders. By the 1560s and 1570s it was yielding between £100 and £200 per annum, apart from wood sales which in some years were quite substantial.[54]

No other major Wealden landowner of the 1560s or 1570s was as wealthy or as well-connected as Sir Henry Sidney. In the late Elizabethan period several major gentry families controlled almost as much land in the Weald as the Sidneys, and less of theirs was in the form of unremunerative parks. The Baker estate has been mentioned. Another was that of Sir Anthony Mayne of Lynton and Biddenden (d. 1611), who owned at least 1,200 acres in the Weald. The exceptionally informative IPM taken at his death shows that almost all his Weald lands were rented out: to eighteen different tenants in Biddenden, nine for lands in Smarden and Headcorn, five in Halden and three more for property in Tenterden. Almost all of his Wealden farms were less than 100 acres and most under fifty.[55]

If to farm out part of one's lands was commonplace, so too was it to become another man's tenant. Farmers were to be found at all levels of society. Richard

---

[53] PRO Wards 9/136 fos. 321v–322v; C 142/100 no. 50. A rough league table of accuracy in official valuations can be suggested: IPMs are less under-valued than Wards schedules, and IPMs made before 1560 are less under-assessed than those made later.

[54] Grant to Fane: *Cal. Pat.* 1550–53, p. 13. At Fane's attainder the Penshurst farms brought in £64 per annum in rents, and only the capital mansion of Penshurst and 250 acres of parkland were not leased out (KAO U 1475/M58). Sidney estate pre-Penshurst accounts in KAO U 1475/A2/1–6. Lamberhurst leased to Thos. Darrell, gent: U 1475/E19. Penshurst estate survey: U 1475/M59, M34. Income in 1560s and 1570s: U 1475/E2, 3, 5. Their manor of Halden was also farmed out; it included 197 acres of land, 124 acres of wood and a 429-acre park: U 1475/E3 and E23/1.

[55] PRO C 142/693 no. 26.

Dering, the leading gentleman of the parish of Pluckley, took a twenty-one-year lease of land in his home parish from the Bakers in 1568. Robert Clampard of Horsmonden, a clothier, became the farmer of William Lambard's manor of Brenchley *alias* Criels (of 400 acres including 134 acres of wood) in a lease for forty-five years at £34 6s. 8d. per annum in 1574. By 1577 Lambard noted that Clampard had sold the lease for £130. Another clothier, Robert Scotchford, became Lambard's tenant of a 112 acre farm in Brenchley, at a rent of about £15 per annum. A third tenant was Richard Willard of Brenchley, who took a lease of an 82 acre farm in Brenchley in 1574 for 45 years, at just £7 per annum. Willard's will shows that he was a freeholder as well as a tenant farmer. He left his lease to one of his sons and his 'messuage and lands' to another. The manor of Halden, which was actually in Rolvenden and Benenden, was let to Sir John Baker by the Crown in 1544 for £37 per annum. The ownership of the manor was granted out later, and as a result the Bakers became tenants of Sir Henry Sidney. A Crown lease of a large portfolio of lands, involving former Tonbridge Priory property, the manors of Hadlow and Knole and much else, was purchased from its original tenant by Alexander Culpeper, Esq. of Goudhurst in the early years of Elizabeth's reign. Most of the land would have been occupied by sitting tenants and the lease had under ten years to run. But the purchase is entirely understandable in view of the fact that Crown rents could be very low indeed.[56]

Most of the larger farms, and sometimes woodlands, were leased to resident yeomen and entrepreneurs. We have already noticed the clothiers who were tenants of William Lambarde, the lawyer and local historian. But an equally interesting case is the Tonbridge ironmaster Davy Willard. He had an interest in a number of furnaces and forges in the Kent and Sussex Weald, and in the 1560s was a partner of Sir Henry Sidney in a steelmaking venture at Robertsbridge, Sussex. But he was also actively hiring farmland in the western Weald. He rented about fifty acres of the Penshurst demesnes in the early 1550s and a decade later he can be found as the farmer of parts of the Tonbridge Castle demesnes and of Cage Park (400 acres) in Tonbridge. He also rented lands worth 5 marks per annum from the free tenants of the hundred of Wachlingstone, in the same area. Yet another ironmaster, Michael Weston, held the lease of the extensive manor of Ashurst from the local squires, the Wallers of Groombridge in Speldhurst, for £100 per annum.[57]

Despite these suggestive examples of prosperous entrepreneurs taking agricultural leases, the bulk of the tenants of the larger farms appear to have been local yeoman farmers. A representative example of conventional leasing arrangements can be seen in the parish of Cowden, at the southwestern corner of the Kent Weald.

[56] Dering: KAO U 350/T6; Clampard and Scotchford: Drapers' Co., London MS. Q. E. C. H/Add. 1–2; Willard: *ibid.* and KAO DRb/Pwr 17 fo. 297; Baker: PRO E 315/216 fo. 108v; Hasted, *Kent*, vii, p. 187; KAO U 1475/E3, 5; Culpeper: KAO U 1475/E24.

[57] Davy Willard: Jeremy Goring, 'Wealden Ironmasters in the Age of Elizabeth' in *Wealth and Power in Tudor England*, ed. E. W. Ives *et al.* (1978); KAO U 1475/M58, E24; Weston: *Sidney Ironworks Accounts, 1541–1573*, ed. D. W. Crossley (Camden Soc., 4th ser. 15, 1975) and KAO U 1475/M71.

There were two manors, 'Cowden' and Leighton, neither of which were very large. When Cowden manor was granted out by the Crown in 1557, the lands were occupied by one William Wickenden. The grantees subsequently sold the estate to Wickenden. Leighton manor, owned by Thomas Lord Burgh in 1585, had demesne lands of 269 acres. It had just two tenants: 104 acres were leased to John and Henry Saxpes, and the rest to a Thomas Wickenden. Leases of substantial parcels owned by major estates often went to local yeomen who were clients of the owner. But patronage had its limits in the late sixteenth century as prices – and land values – rose rapidly. Sir Henry Sidney's manor of Ensfield, with about 300 acres in Leigh, Tonbridge and Bidborough, was first farmed to John Terry of Leigh, yeoman, 'servant unto Sir Henry', for twenty-one years at £13 6s. 8d. per annum in the 1560s. In 1580 the same property was re-leased to William Terry of Leigh, yeoman, at £20 per annum and for a fine of £40. Finally in 1595, after Terry had surrendered his lease, Sir Robert Sidney farmed the manor to an Edmund Videan of Leigh, yeoman, for twenty-one years at £30 per annum.[58]

Farms to rent came in all sizes. Formal indentures of lease may not have been drawn for single fields or small farms, and there is no systematic way of measuring what proportion of tenanted land was held at will as opposed to being leased for terms of years. An impressionistic conclusion based on a wide variety of evidence about the size of parcels leased is that the central and east Weald parishes contained relatively more individually let bits and pieces than the western Weald. This is more likely a consequence of the historic pattern of estate-building in the former areas, than any policy of consolidation of holdings into larger farms on the part of sixteenth-century landowners in the western parishes. The larger holdings, even those called 'manors', in the more densely populated east and central Weald, were collections of small farms and numerous individual fields. Aside from extensive parcels of woodland, they were usually let out to farmers, craftsmen and manufacturers in the same small units.

This can best be seen in the valors and surveys of the larger estates in parishes like Biddenden and Cranbrook. Thomas Sheffe's estate had been built up by the purchase of many small parcels from neighbouring landowners, among them major gentry. They were either already occupied by small leaseholders, or Sheffe himself farmed them out after he acquired them. There appears to have been little or no effort on the part of major Wealden landowners like these to consolidate holdings into bigger, compact properties. This is partly because the parcels were dispersed in the first place, but equally because they were so readily rented out as they were. Where a landowner's holdings were less fragmented – such as the demesnes of the manor of Leighton in Cowden – landowners appear to have been happy to lease larger blocs to the wealthier local yeomen. The widespread practice of leasing by Wealden landowners of all sizes was not unique. In a comparable wood-pasture

---

[58] Cowden manor: Hasted, *Kent*, iii, pp. 204–5; Leighton: *ibid.*, pp. 205–6 and KAO U 908/M86; leases: KAO U 1475/T9/7, T58/1–2.

region, the Forest of Arden, a majority of holdings under sixty acres were in 1605 leased to sub-tenants.[59]

The value of land in the Kent Weald rose throughout the sixteenth century; rather slowly during the first three decades, and rapidly in the last three or four. And the price rise continued during the early decades of the next century. Insufficient estate records survive to allow the reconstruction of series of rents taken on the same holdings over many decades. Instead we have to depend on examples of the rents paid for parcels of known size at specific dates and on scattered records of sale prices of land to illustrate the inflation in land values. The range of rents taken on different types of land can be given for different periods.

When land was purchased in the sixteenth century, the most common method of arriving at a sale price was to establish its present rental value and multiply that by a number which the current market dictated. In Henry VIII's reign the normal multiplier was twenty, hence land was said to sell for '20 years' purchase'. The crucial bargaining thus took place over what the annual rental value of the property being conveyed was or should be. As far as can be gathered, land in the Weald was sold without reference to quitrents, perhaps because lessees were usually made responsible for their payment.[60] Therefore, if the upward trend in the price of land is to be charted, the best place to begin is the level of rent, on which purchase prices were normally based. The movement of rent has particular significance for the Weald because hiring out land was so common.

Potential buyers and sellers had plenty of information about the current rental values of different types of properties, since much of what was passing through the land market was in fact occupied by tenant farmers. From scattered comments in wills it seems that even petty freeholders knew what the going rate for land was and had a rough idea of how much theirs was worth. There clearly was, at any given time, a current market rent for the main types of land, and therefore a current price if the land was to be sold. This might vary, of course, depending upon the quality of the land or whether or not a property for sale included houses and barns. An obvious exception to the 'market price' of land, either for lease or for sale, were especially large properties – which usually included a good deal of woodland and waste – and which sold at a lower price per acre than the current market average. Another was attractive small parcels of land near population centres like Cranbrook, Tenterden or Tonbridge, which often fetched well above the going rate.

Early sixteenth-century rents were already a good deal above those taken in the mid fifteenth century. Back in 1466 a messuage and sixty acres in Edenbridge were

---

[59] PRO Wards 7/37 no. 11. The manor of Leighton's 269 acres were divided into thirty-six 'pieces' of land, which suggests that the typical field or close was larger here than in the central Weald, where 'pieces' of land were mostly within the range of two to four acres. V. H. Skipp, *Crisis and Development*, 1570–1674 (1978).

[60] Lambarde's tenant of a messuage and 100 acres in Cranbrook was expected to pay the quitrents: Drapers' Co. MS. Q. E. C. H/Add. 18.

leased for seven years at just two marks per annum – under 6d. per acre. By the first few decades of the sixteenth century pasture and arable land was being let at between 8d. and 12d. per acre, and as elsewhere meadow land commanded about double that. As late as the early 1530s part of the Combwell Priory demesnes in Goudhurst was farmed at only 8d. an acre, while mead was rated at 16d. or 20d. per acre. But these values were already out of date, compared with the rents recorded in other documents and leases made in the mid and late 1530s and early 1540s. Most of these leases are for a tenement and lands, and perhaps not strictly comparable with the Combwell example. Nevertheless, a majority of the extant leases with all the necessary information are in the form of a messuage with X acres of land. The rent given for such farms of up to 100 acres in the 1530s and early 1540s range from about 1s. 4d. to 2s. per acre, and sometimes even higher.[61]

The chantry certificates for Kent offer useful information about the rents charged for small- and medium-sized parcels as they stood in 1547. The rents paid for chantry-owned lands within the Weald varied considerably, but almost all fell within the range between 1s. and 3s. per acre. Most of the chantry property was let in quite small parcels and thus relatively high rents per acre would be expected, irrespective of the length of leases. The lands of Milkhouse Chapel in Cranbrook amounted to about seventy acres, including seventeen acres of woodland. They were leased to nine different tenants in leases going back to 1520, the shortest of which was for thirty years! The rents varied from 1s. to 3s. 4d. per acre, but the majority were at 2s. per acre or above. The lands of the more well-endowed Kent's Chantry in Headcorn were divided into fourteen tenancies: the largest was of 180 acres, though the vast majority were parcels of thirty acres or less. The rents being charged here were even more varied, from 10d. per acre to 4s. 9d. However, the bulk of the land was fetching between 1s. 6d. and 2s. 6d. per acre. Rents did not rise uniformly in the 1540s. In about 1547 the politician John Gates, the new owner of the manor of Bockingfold (with lands in Marden, Yalding and Goudhurst), was informed that the arable and pasture was worth only 1s. an acre, the meadow just twice that rent.[62]

By the Elizabethan period the rise in rents was apparent all over the Weald. A 1574 survey of Sir Thomas Fane's lands in half a dozen Wealden parishes showed a wide range of values from just over 2s. an acre to over 10s. Most of the farms were let at between 2s. 9d. and 6s. per acre. A parcel of eighty-six acres occupied by Fane himself was valued at 4s. 8d. per acre. Not all landowners were equally canny. William Lambarde purchased over 800 acres of land in Brenchley and Yalding between 1570 and 1574. Most of it was leased out in four large farms in 1574. The leases were for forty-five years, far longer than most Elizabethan leases, but it is possible that Lambarde extracted heavy fines at the time of the lease. All were let for under 3s. per acre, the low rent perhaps reflecting the large amount of woodland

<hr />

[61] KAO U 908/T49/6; U 1513/M15; U 1044/F1 pp. 25, 31; U 1450/T7/103.
[62] *Kent Records*, xii (1936) *sub* Cranbrook and Headcorn; PRO SC 12/3/34.

in each farm. One other part of the estate, 100 acres of land not including woodland, had been farmed by the previous owners in 1568, for ten years, at a rent of nearly 4s. per acre. When it was surveyed for Lambarde in 1577, the marginal comment of the surveyor is instructive. He noted that high rents could be expected for this property, because of the 'fair house ... meet for a gentleman's dwelling', and the nineteen acres of meadow should be worth 10s. or more per annum. The medium-sized estate of William Lambarde typifies all the wrinkles in the market for farms in the region. The larger properties usually included woodland – in which the 'timber trees' were reserved for the landowner – and which was worth considerably less than farmland. A desirable house, a mill or a well set-up dyehouse suitable for a clothier or the existence of marl pits on the property could add substantially to the average rent per acre. And scarce meadow boosted the overall rent of a property.[63]

Wealden rents continued to rise in the 1580s and beyond. Lambarde purchased a farm of 100 acres called Turk's Place in Cranbrook in 1587, and immediately leased it for forty years at £25 per annum. The average rental of 5s. per acre was not high by then, and it is difficult to explain Lambarde's long leases. The wardens of the Tonbridge town lands were able to farm the thirty-four acres in 1586 for about 7s. 9d. per acre, on three-year leases. Other surviving leases tell the same tale. A messuage and twenty-five acres in Chiddingstone were let for ten years in 1587 at £8 per annum plus a £10 fine, a composite rent of over 7s. per acre, and a two-acre meadow in the same parish was let for 10s. an acre in 1584. Even at the end of the century, however, many Wealden tenants were not paying as much as 8s. or 10s. per acre. A 15-year lease of a house with 102 acres of land and thirty-four acres of wood in Hever commanded a rent of £26 13s. 4d. per annum in 1592, or about 4s. per acre in all, or 5s. 3d. per acre if only the land is counted. Larger farms continued to be let for quite low rents per acre. The Sidneys were receiving under £38 per annum for their manor of Hadlow in 1574. It contained 323 acres, of which 124 were woodland. The rent worked out at only 2s. 4d. per acre, or 3s. 10d. if the woods are ignored. In the same year Lambarde's manor of Brenchley *alias* Criels (total 400 acres, of which 134 acres was woodland) was let at just £34 6s. 8d. per annum, or less than 2s. per acre in all or just over 2s. 6d. per acre if the woods are excluded. In comparison, small parcels of usable arable and pasture were usually leased at between 3s. and 6s. per acre. And lands in or near towns still tended to command a premium over the current market rates. The Tonbridge town lands, mentioned earlier, fetched a higher rent than was common in that decade, and a survey of leases, valors and IPMs suggests that land in Cranbrook was generally rated higher than land in the predominantly rural parts of the Weald. In the IPM on the estate of Peter Courthop (1568) a messuage with fifty acres of land and wood was valued at £10 per annum or 4s. per acre, while a house and thirty-one acres of land was valued at the same amount, i.e., 6s. 6d. per acre. But high quality grazing land in the

[63] KAO U 282/M14; Drapers' Co. MSS. Q. E. C. H/Add. 1; H/Add. 13/1; H/Add. 15; H/21; H/5; and a plan of two farms at KAO U 2315/P/2–3.

Weald could always be let at a big premium. In the course of a tithe dispute in 1614 at Staplehurst, deponents noted that local farmers were willing to hire pasture on short leases at rents of 10s. to £1 per acre![64]

In the course of the sixteenth century rent levels had risen about four-fold, if this survey of scattered evidence from small- and medium-sized farms is at all representative. The inflation in rents would have been irregular; most of the surviving leases are for terms between ten and twenty-one years, and very few stipulate rises in rent during the term of the lease.[65] The trend in rents over the century, nevertheless, was steeply rising, not far below the rise in corn prices.

The sale price of land reflected the upward curve in the value of leased land. The Wealden land market was anything but a sudden development of the 1530s in response to the booming sales of Crown land. In fact quite a large number of fifteenth-century deeds survive in various collections of family manuscripts. But many of these early records are deed polls or quitclaims which record only the parties to a conveyance and a brief description of the lands. Prices are not often found. From the mid sixteenth century private deeds and indentures survive in some quantity. The other main sources are the final concords, or feet of fines. They register the conclusion of a fictional suit in the Court of Common Pleas in which the purchaser 'wins' against the vendor, and thus permanently records the buyer's title to the land being conveyed. But fines in Common Pleas are notoriously problematic. In many cases what appears on the face of a fine as a straightforward sale may in fact have been a mortgage, a settlement or an enfeoffment. The nature of a conveyance can only be known for certain when the full set of title deeds has survived.[66] In addition neither the acreages nor the purchase prices given in fines can be taken at face value: both are usually suspiciously rounded figures, and can only be taken as rough approximations of the real values. The smaller the size of the parcel being conveyed, the more likely is the acreage recorded on a fine to be nearly accurate. But where larger properties are being sold, the common formula for acreage found on the fines, e.g., '150 acres of land, fifty acres of meadow, 100 acres of pasture and fifty acres of wood', is usually an overstatement. In many cases the first figure given, '150 acres of land', is a good approximation of the actual size of the property.

Feet of fines, since they survive in almost complete series from the fifteenth century, have been used by historians as a rough index of the numbers of transactions in the land market. But this strategy cannot be pressed too far. After all, a rise in the numbers of feet of fine may indicate an increase in the volume of the

[64] Drapers' Co. MS. Q. E. C. H/Add. 18; Nottingham U. Lib. Middleton MS. 5/161a/31, 17; KAO U 1408/T2; U 1475/E23/1 and E5; Drapers' Co. MS. H/Add. 1; PRO Wards 7/12 nos. 66, 11; C 78/148 mm. 10–16.
[65] Several of Lambarde's leases stipulated modest rent increases after the first five to ten years: Drapers' Co. MS. Q. E. C. H/Add. 1 fos. 4, 4v, 5, but the policy is exceptional as are his forty-five-year terms.
[66] On final concords see A. A. Dibben, *Title Deeds* (Historical Assn., 1971) and C. A. F. Meekings (ed.), *Abstract of Surrey Feet of Fines, 1509–1558* (Surrey Rec. Soc., 19, 1946).

local land market. But it might equally indicate nothing more than the increasing use of final concords to register conveyances of land, in place of or in addition to other forms of conveyance. Despite these caveats, the figures are worth noting. Counting all final concords other than those which specifically declare themselves enfeoff-ments and settlements, there was a rising number of fines from early in Henry VII's reign into the Elizabethan period. In the late fifteenth century there were, on average, about five fines per annum registered in Common Pleas involving lands in Kent Weald parishes. The annual average doubled during the first ten years of Henry VIII's reign through the 1520s. In the 1530s the annual average rose to about 15, then doubled again in the five years 1538 to 1543 – the period when Crown land sales began in earnest. The annual average then rose again slightly, to a peak of forty-two in the late 1540s, but levelled off at just under forty per annum in the 1550s. The numbers of fines rose slightly at the beginning of Elizabeth's reign, but remained at about forty-five per annum throughout the 1560s and 1570s.[67] By the later sixteenth century there were a wide variety of alternative methods of recording conveyances, including the common recovery. Hence the feet of fines are increasingly less valuable as an indicator of land market activity.

The great majority of both feet of fines and privately drawn deeds record the sale of quite modest properties. Only a small minority pertain to transactions involving more than 100 acres of land. Many fines include land in more than one Wealden parish. An idea of the character of the transactions registered by final concords in the early part of the century can be gained from an examination of the fines involving Kent Weald land recorded in the first two years of Henry VIII. Only three of the thirteen were of transactions where the notional purchase price was above £100, and one of those looks suspiciously like an enfeoffment. The fourth highest figure (£100), said to have been paid by George and Edward Guildford to Sir Andrew Windsor for a moiety of their own manor of Hemsted, is also suspect. There remain two probable medium-sized sales, both set down with purchase prices of 200 marks (i.e. £133 6s. 8d.). One was for the sale of about 100 acres of land and three messuages in Headcorn, the other ostensibly for two messuages, a mill and about 175 acres of land in Sandhurst. In both cases the acreage is probably exaggerated, since it is likely that only the figures given for 'land' and 'wood' are even approximately accurate. But these two fines at least record real transactions, typical of the larger sales of that period. The great majority of fines (nine of thirteen) involved sales of small amounts of land, and were given purchase prices between £10 and £40. One involved a rent charge of £1 5s. per annum, said to have been sold for £20, or somewhat under the going rate of the 1530s.

A typical early sixteenth-century private sale was the purchase by Richard Mugge from Thomas A Lye and his wife of three gardens and sixteen acres of land in Goudhurst for £30. Both parties were from minor freeholder families in that

---

[67] Weald sample drawn from Kent fines in PRO CP 25(1)/117a/343–52 (covering Henry VII); CP 25(2) 19/102 to 72/615 (covering 1509–58) and CP 25(2) Files 2398–479 (covering 1 to 24 Eliz. I).

parish, the figure given for the amount of land on the fine is credible and the price of the property – at just under £2 per acre – is what one would expect for land in the central Weald in 1510. Another was the sale by Robert Bromley, his wife and her son to John Courthop of Cranbrook of a messuage, two gardens and ten acres of land in Staplehurst; the price is given as £20, again just under £2 per acre.[68] In all, the eleven probable sales involved property in nine different Weald parishes, and none of these involved lands in more than one parish. Also, it's likely that none of the thirteen – despite the wording of the fines – involved more than 100 acres of land. There were, certainly, far more than eleven private land sales in the Kent Weald during these two years. The majority of transactions simply were not registered in the Common Pleas.

The character of the Elizabethan land market in the Weald can be shown by another two-year sample of final concords, this time for the years 1578–9. There were about ninety transactions in these years – compared to the thirteen of 1509–10 – if family settlements are excluded. But though the numbers had changed, the kinds of properties being conveyed are familiar. At least a few of the ninety 'bargains and sales' were in fact mortgages, but that cannot be established from the final concords. Two-thirds of the fines concerned properties with listed prices of between £40 and £100. (The court officials by this period apparently set £40 as the minimum price to be used on concords, even if only a house and garden were being sold.) A quarter of the fines reported purchase prices between £101 and £250, while five were for higher amounts; the highest price listed was 760 marks or £506. The properties were predominantly messuages and associated lands, usually less than thirty acres in each conveyance. The most substantial deal, in which Thomas Darrell, Esq. sold Thomas Dyke, the ironmaster, lands in three parishes, involved under 200 acres. Representative bargains included the sale of a messuage and eight acres in Goudhurst with a recorded price of £40; a messuage, barn and twenty-four acres in Brenchley for £100; and a messuage with thirty-four acres of land and three acres of wood in the same parish, at 200 marks (£133 6s. 8d.).[69] The parties to most of these transactions were local yeomen, with a scattering of local gentry landowners. Lands lying in almost all the sample Wealden parishes were involved in transactions during 1578–9, and the going rate for small and medium-sized properties now hovered around £4 per acre compared to the £2 of seventy years earlier.

Small, private purchases involving local residents remained the staple of the Wealden land market throughout the sixteenth century, even as the numbers of sales may have doubled or trebled between the 1510s and 1560s and 1570s, and despite the Crown land sales of the 1540s to 1560s. The large majority of properties being conveyed also remained of relatively small size: most were for less than 100

---

[68] Fines mentioned are in PRO CP 25(2)/19/102–3.
[69] Two-year sample is PRO CP 25(2) Files 2461–8; examples at File 2462 no. 25; 2463 no. 51; 2466 no. 39.

Table 2.6a *Wealden land prices: parcels up to fifty acres each*

Period	No.	Median price/acre	Mean price/acre
1510–39	10	£1 10s.	£1 17s.
1540–54	13	£2 16s.	£3 10s.
1555–69	7	£4 16s.	£5 1s.
1570–9	8	£5 5s.	£5 1s.
1580–9	10	£6 6s.	£6 11s.
1590–1600	7	£6 17s.	£7 17s.

Sources: KAO deeds in the following collections: U 24, U 78, U 106, U 195, U 280, U 301, U 383, U 409, U 455, U 513, U 705, U 769, U 813, U 908, U 1000, U 1006, U 1044/F1, U 1094, U 1299, U 1542, U 1823, U 2026, U 2140; BL Add. Chs. 41,740, 41,751; Add. MS. 42,715; PRO C 54/801 m. 13,836 m. 48; Nottingham U. Lib. Middleton MSS. 5/161a, 161b, 162.

Table 2.6b *Decadal means of grain prices*

Period		Oats	Wheat
1510–19	Index no.	119	114
1520–9	Index no.	148	144
1530–9	Index no.	155	140
1540–9	Index no.	191	171
1550–9	Index no.	356	285
1560–9	Index no.	322	293
1570–9	Index no.	343	336
1580–9	Index no.	457	385
1590–9	Index no.	638	499

Note: 1450–99 means of oats [1.92 s./qtr.] and wheat [6.32 s./qtr.] = 100.

acres of land. Of course the later period saw a big absolute increase in the sales of larger estates, often involving 500 or 1,000 acres. But such sales remained exceptional, even if Crown land sales are counted as part of the local land market. Most parishes would have been unlikely to see more than one or two sales of a large property in the parish during the whole of the Elizabethan period. It may be argued that the market rate for land was a function of the much busier trade in small properties that was so characteristic of the Weald. The impact of the sales of large estates on the local land market was probably felt more in terms of the volume of properties being sold subsequently than on the price of land. It was common for big purchasers to sell off small bits of land to local buyers within a few years of their purchases. Undoubtedly land prices rose to unheard of levels by the 1550s and 1560s.

The price rise indicated by the notional amounts recorded on the feet of fine can be confirmed by the trend of prices recorded in private deeds and indentures of bargain and sale, shown in tables 2.6a and b. Nevertheless, neither the types of properties purchased nor the kinds of people buying and selling changed radically in the course of the century. If anything, the increased availability of small farms and parcels of land to purchase was the most significant development of the period. The local gentry retained their place as the biggest landowners in the region – and some individual estates increased in size – but there is no indication that the number of small and 'middling' landowners was diminishing. But, against the background of a rapidly expanding population, the proportion of families who owned no land was steadily increasing. As the century drew to a close more and more Wealden families had no 'stake in the land'.

3

Demographic movements, household structure and geographical mobility

The Weald was a wood-pasture island within the sea of lowland England, set apart from the prevailing landscape of nuclear villages which were mainly settled before the Norman conquest. The wood-pasture regions were very thinly settled in the Middle Ages and contained extensive forests and wastes. The emphasis of wood-pasture farming was, as the name implies, biased towards livestock husbandry rather than cereal production. Such regions – and the Weald is typical – had weak structures of seigniorial authority, and thus were attractive to immigrants from other parts of the country when demographic expansion began afresh at the end of the fifteenth or early sixteenth century. Applied specifically to the Kent Weald, this model would assume that the region was underpopulated in the fifteenth century, but became crowded in the following period as the 'surplus' population of lowland England in general migrated to the Weald (and other wood-pasture districts) in search of the land which historians have often assumed was there for the taking. But, as we have seen, there was little 'free' land in the Kent Weald, in the sense of being open and available for migrant settlement.

One other element has to be added to our model: rural industries. The wood-pasture districts became the sites of a variety of manufacturing trades, ranging from metal crafts to textile manufacture, normally organized as domestic production, and frequently controlled by entrepreneurs through a putting out system. The regions' attractiveness to rural manufacturing is usually explained in terms of a combination of natural and social factors. There was an abundance of fast-running streams which were useful to a variety of industrial processes, whereas their generally poorer soils rendered these areas less valuable for arable agriculture. At the same time, the wood-pasture districts have been seen as regions of available and relatively cheap labour, both because of their relative 'over-population' by the sixteenth or seventeenth centuries, and because their less labour-intensive agricultural regimes resulted in considerable seasonal under-employment. A further refinement of the model adds the additional variable of inheritance customs: where in wood-pasture areas partible inheritance prevails, the availability of non-agricultural employment is presumed to be an additional cause of population growth.

However, the model's scenario would seem to require a specific economic and demographic chronology in which industrialization follows demographic expansion, although neither that scenario or a different one precludes the likelihood that existing rural industrialization would encourage additional population growth. It will be interesting to see if the demographic and economic history of the Kent Weald conforms to the model generated by previous historians, or whether it may need to be modified in the light of local evidence. In doing so we must take into account the local custom of inheritance: Kentish gavelkind custom encouraged partible inheritance, as well as a more fluid land market. All other things being equal, if the custom was adhered to – and it has already been suggested that all but smallholders and gentry owners tended to divide their land among their sons – the presumption must be that a relatively higher rate of family formation is to be expected in Kent than in areas of impartible inheritance. The same result might also be predicted in a region of established rural industry: even if farms were not available for all sons of existing families, the alternative of combining a smallholding with regular industrial employment would allow the formation of new families which in different economic circumstances might not have occurred.[1]

The aim of this chapter will be to test some of these theoretical propositions against the reality of demographic trends and family structures in the sixteenth-century Kent Weald. Among other things, it will investigate whether the region shared a common demographic experience during the century, or whether there were differences between one part of the Weald and another. Did, for example, those parts of the Weald which supported extensive rural manufacturing display demographic characteristics peculiar to themselves, and which therefore cannot be traced to a common Wealden topography, inheritance custom or farming regime? A number of different techniques will be used to analyse population movements and family/household structure. For the pre-parish register era – which for most of the Weald means the period up to about 1560 – last wills and testaments can be used as indirect evidence of demographic trends, although a simple count of the surviving wills is not a reliable indicator of population trends. For the Elizabethan period all the surviving parish registers of baptisms and burials (about thirty-five out

---

[1] On wood-pasture regions see Joan Thirsk (ed.), *The Agrarian History of England and Wales, iv, 1500–1640* (1967), p. 57–9. On rural industries see Joan Thirsk, 'Industries in the Countryside' in F. J. Fisher (ed.), *Essays in the Economic and Social History of Tudor and Stuart England* (1961); F. Mendels, 'Proto-industrialization: the First Phase of the Industrialization Process', *JEcH*, 32 (1972); Rab Houston and K. D. M. Snell, 'Proto-industrialization? Cottage Industry, Social Change and Industrial Revolution', *Hist.J*, 27 (1984); L. A. Clarkson, *Proto-Industrialization: the First Phase of Industrialization?* (Economic History Soc., 1985); and cf. G. L. Gullickson, 'Agriculture and Cottage Industry: Redefining the Causes of Proto-Industrialization', *J.EcH*, 43 (1983) who shows that rural industry was not limited to pastoral regions. Also David Levine, *Family Formation in an Age of Nascent Capitalism* (1977).

of thirty-nine mainly Wealden parishes) have been consulted.[2] Aggregative methods have been applied to the registers to produce an estimate of the total population of the region in the 1560s as well as the trends in the numbers of christenings and burials in individual parishes from about 1560 to 1600. The estimates derived from parochial registration can be compared with estimates based on the numbers of communicants or numbers of households (or both) given in a diocesan survey of communicants taken in 1563. The latter, however, is available only for parishes in Canterbury diocese and thus leaves out the western half of the Kent Weald, the area also with more missing registers and no surviving bishops' transcripts.[3] From such materials we can estimate the overall demographic trends, the existence of mortality crises and the relative density of population in different districts of the Weald, at least for the period after 1560.

Then, to analyse demographic experience in greater depth and to examine household structure, several sample parishes have been selected, both because they are well documented and because they lie within the Wealden manufacturing area. The families of three parishes with reasonably accurate and full registers – Brenchley and adjacent Horsmonden combined, and Staplehurst – have been reconstructed to provide data on infant mortality, birth intervals, age at first marriage and geographical mobility and population turnover. In addition to parish registers, there are household lists extant for two parishes, Staplehurst and Cranbrook (although the latter involves communicant lists from just after 1600). From this evidence some findings can be offered about the number and distribution of resident servants, the size of households and the persistence and turnover of households and individuals. Combining the various types of evidence will allow us to gauge if this region of intense rural industry displayed demographic characteristics unique to itself, similar to those reported in other 'proto-industrial' areas or similar to the national trends reported by E. A. Wrigley and R. S. Schofield.[4]

Demographic trends during the decades before the earliest parish registers of the 1540s cannot be reconstructed in any detail. For the half century before that decade last wills and testaments must be the major source, other than the indirect evidence of price and rent movements. The price trends of agricultural commodities during the last decades of the fifteenth and first few decades of the sixteenth centuries are broadly upwards but not consistently so. The acceleration in prices was not strongly established until the 1520s, but that may well be a lagged reflection of population expansion which began several decades earlier.[5] As suggested in the

---

[2] See table 3.12 at end of this chapter.

[3] 1563 survey: Corpus Christi College, Cambridge MS. 122 is in most cases superior to the more widely used text, BL Harl. MSS. 594, fo. 63 ff. These do not cover parishes in Rochester diocese or Shoreham peculiar.

[4] Wrigley and Schofield, *The Population History of England, 1541–1871: A Reconstruction* (1981).

[5] See E. H. Phelps Brown and Sheila Hopkins, 'Wage-rates and Prices: Evidence for Population Pressure in the 16th Century', *Economica*, 24 (1957), p. 306; Thirsk, *Agrarian History, iv*, pp. 857, 863.

previous chapter, land values in the Kent Weald were already well above their mid fifteenth century levels by 1500, but then stuck at that level for several decades. Last wills may be used as a rough indicator of population trends, although it must be shown that changes in the numbers of wills reflect changes in mortality rather than simply variations in the tendency of people on their deathbeds to make wills, or even just variations in the enrolling of original wills by the church courts. In any case fluctuations in the numbers of testaments more accurately reflect short-term peaks in mortality – mainly due to epidemic disease – than they do secular trends in the size of the overall population. This chapter draws on the extant, enrolled wills and testaments from twenty-nine sample parishes, and highlights the problematic nature of this source.[6]

There was a rapid growth in the numbers of enrolled wills in the last three decades of the fifteenth century and the first ten years of the sixteenth. Far too rapid, in fact, to reflect any real demographic movement. What these sources show was either a growth in the popularity of will-making, or in the practice of enrolling existing wills – or both. The fluctuations in the total numbers of wills per decade shown in table 3.1 would seem to indicate a fairly stable will-making population from around 1500 to the 1540s. The variation between decades points up the periods of higher than 'normal' mortality – the 1520s and the 1550s – which historians have shown from other sources to have been periods of frequent epidemics, and the relatively healthy decades, the 1530s and 1540s. Since the will-making population was drawn predominantly from the well-off and middling strata of Tudor society, it is not likely that short-term peaks in the number of wills proved were the result of additional deaths due to harvest failure and famine. Disease was no respecter of social class; but famine was socially selective.

The trends in wills from the Kent Weald do not demonstrate on their own that population was growing before 1500, or even in the first decades of the sixteenth century. Therefore, rather than totting up the numbers of testaments, an attempt was made to study replacement rates based on the sample wills. This has only been partially successful because of the verbal conventions of will-makers: in a large proportion of the wills drawn up for married persons, the exact number of children cannot be known. Many late fifteenth- and early sixteenth-century wills are extremely brief: they frequently refer only to 'my children'. Even testators who refer to one or more children by name, do not invariably list all their children. Hence the references to children/heirs in wills must be interpreted: the percentages shown in the table under 'one child' and 'two or more children' are minima, rather than the

[6] See Robert Gottfried, 'Bury St Edmunds and the Population of Late Medieval English Towns', *J. British Studies*, 20 (1980). Wills from all sources, of married and widowed males from Benenden, Bethersden, Biddenden, Brenchley, Capel, Cranbrook, Edenbridge, Frittenden, Goudhurst, Hadlow, Halden, Hawkhurst, Horsmonden, Lamberhurst, Leigh, Marden, Pembury, Pluckley, Rolvenden, Sandhurst, Smarden, Speldhurst, Staplehurst, Tenterden, Tonbridge, Westerham, Woodchurch and Yalding.

Table 3.1 *Numbers of children mentioned by married male testators*

Decade	None	1 child	2 or more children	Totals
1480s	4 (2%)	54 (27%)	141 (71%)	199
1490s	37 (12%	50 (17%)	211 (71%)	298
1500s	53 (14%)	56 (15%)	273 (71%)	382
1510s	59 (17%)	68 (19%)	230 (64%)	357
1520s	58 (14%)	54 (13%)	301 (73%)	413
1530s	32 (10%)	46 (15%)	238 (75%)	316
1540s	25 (7%)	46 (13%)	289 (80%)	360
1550s	51 (9%)	60 (11%)	441 (80%)	552

'real' number. Our inference may be that if at least two-thirds of married males were survived by 'two or more children', then the replacement rates were at least positive: how positive cannot be shown. What can be demonstrated from these data is that the proportion of parents leaving two or more children on their deaths was growing. As the table indicates, the upward trend was not continuous from the 1480s, but only clearly established in the decade of the 1520s. The combination of a high proportion of men with two or more surviving children and a relatively low proportion succeeded by no children seems well established by the 1530s and 1540s, when this kind of evidence can first be compared to parish register data.

It is likely that the Wealden population was expanding from the very early sixteenth-century at least, even if the testamentary evidence cannot prove it unequivocally. The indirect evidence of the rise in local land values suggests that, even in the Weald, population pressure was forcing up rents and land prices by 1500. In addition, the national evidence of the buoyant demand for English woollen textiles – and the growing volume exported – from the end of the fifteenth century makes it likely that in the central Wealden clothing parishes – if not in other parts of the Weald – demographic expansion began before the 1520s and 1530s.[7]

A glance at the lay subsidy returns for the central Weald hundreds (Cranbrook, Barclay and Barnfield) that covered most of the main clothmaking parishes shows a region as densely populated as any area in north or east Kent at that time.[8] From two parishes with registers surviving from the 1540s there is evidence of substantial demographic expansion in that decade and most of the next. Both Biddenden and Staplehurst – the first predominantly and the second partly, clothmaking parishes – recorded mean annual baptism totals in the 1540s as high or higher than during several five- or ten-year periods in Elizabeth's reign. During the years between the beginning of registration and 1557, there was a substantial surplus of christenings

---

[7] See E. M. Carus-Wilson and Olive Coleman, *England's Export Trade, 1275–1547* (1963), p. 139.
[8] PRO E 179/125/324.

over burials in both parishes. The only other parish with early coverage of both baptisms and burials, Tenterden (begins 1544), recorded average annual baptisms as high as during the 1570s. However, Tenterden parish, with its urban core, was already recording the net surplus of burials over baptisms which was to characterize the late sixteenth century. Its average annual christenings suggest a total population of 1,300 or 1,400 people both in the 1540s and at the end of the century.[9] The patchy evidence of early registration therefore hints at substantial growth in the rural population from the 1530s to the 1550s, probably reaching a peak in 1557. The already densely populated region around Cranbrook in particular saw continuing increases in numbers, but the pattern in the western Weald remains uncertain.

The steady upward trend was suddenly interrupted by the influenza outbreaks of 1557 to 1559. Between the beginning of registration in 1538 and the end of the century (and beyond), these years witnessed the only widespread mortality crisis in the Weald (as Wrigley and Schofield have shown for England at large). Every extant register for Wealden parishes shows an exceptional peak in the numbers of burials in those years, although in a number of parishes only the tail end of the crisis is visible, just at the point when many of the copy registers begin. The crisis was not limited to urban areas, and can be detected in both the east and west Weald. In Staplehurst, where average annual burials in the early 1550s was about twenty, the harvest year 1558–9 saw the total rise to over fifty. A number of registers, including that for Staplehurst, have gaps at some point between 1557 and 1559. In Biddenden, where the normal number of burials each year varied between twenty and thirty, there were thirty-seven burials in the six months between March and August 1559. At Horsmonden to the west, whose register recorded burial totals continually under twenty per annum in the 1560s, the first twelve months of the register (beginning in November 1558) counted forty-nine burials. Northwest of Horsmonden, at Hadlow, burials during the harvest year 1558–9 reached an astounding eighty-four, against the normal totals of between fifteen and twenty during the 1560s. Next door, at East Peckham, the crisis was equally devastating: eighty-three people were buried during 1558–9, five times the average yearly burials in the 1560s. Further west, at Tonbridge, the burial register begins well before the epidemics, and thus we are able to follow the crisis as it developed. The normal annual total of burials was in the range of thirty to thirty-five. But in the three successive harvest years 1556–7 to 1558–9 the burial totals were fifty-four, sixty-eight and 148! On the other side of the Weald, at Tenterden, a similar although not as extreme crisis occurred. Whereas in the 1560s the average total of burials varied between forty and fifty-five, the harvest years 1557–8 and 1558–9 saw seventy-seven and 106 burials respectively.

The crisis of 1557–9 struck the Weald at approximately the mid point of the

---

[9] KAO original registers for Biddenden and Tenterden; Staplehurst registers in parish church, but also an accurate transcript: *The Registers of Staplehurst, 1538–1695*, ed. J. S. F. Chamberlain (4 vols., Canterbury, 1907–14). The Woodchurch register begins in 1539 but there are large, early gaps.

sixteenth-century population expansion. By coincidence, Harpsfield's visitation of the archdeaconry of Canterbury in 1557 contains notes of either the number of 'parishioners' (?communicants) or the number of families (or both) in most of the Wealden parishes of the diocese. This can be compared with the totals given in the 1563 ecclesiastical survey and the episcopal visitation of 1569 – although whether the 'parishioners' of 1557 cover the same age group as the 'communicants' of 1569 remains unproven. Nevertheless, in many Wealden parishes the figures recorded in 1563 or 1569 were below those of 1557, a measure of the seriousness of the mortality crisis of 1557–9. Benenden, for example, was said to have 600 parishioners in 1557, but only 547 communicants in 1569; Goudhurst had 900 parishioners in 1557 and only 759 in 1569; Hawkhurst, 800 in 1557 but just 680 twelve years later; and Tenterden recorded 700 in 1557 but only 586 in 1569. In fact only Cranbrook showed a real increase between the two visitations, from 1,500 to 1,908.[10] It appears that many parishes in the Weald may have had larger populations in the 1550s than in the 1560s, and that a decade or more would pass before the earlier peak in the population was reached and then surpassed in the 1570s.

The parish register era in the Weald begins properly in 1559, the date at which most of the extant parchment registers (copied out in 1598–1600) begin. The Canterbury diocese bishops' transcripts also survive from about 1560. The forty-odd Wealden parishes examined here account for just under 20 per cent of the land area of the county. The population of Kent can be estimated only very roughly, on the basis of the ecclesiastical surveys of 1563, 1569 and 1603. Only the last of these covers the whole county, and suggests a total of 120,000–130,000 persons, of whom between 60 and 65 per cent lived in Canterbury diocese.[11] Applying that same proportion to the surveys of the 1560s (and using a 4.75 multiplier for the number of persons per 'family') produces a rough estimate for the late 1560s of 80,000 – 85,000 for the county. By this era the Weald was relatively densely populated, although that population was far from evenly spread across the Weald from east to west. The sample Wealden parishes contained around 25,000 people in the 1560s, that is about 30 per cent of Kent's population in less than a fifth of its land area. The total has been reached by calculating the mean annual totals of baptisms for all the parishes with surviving registers during the 1560s, and by assuming that the crude birth rate approximated thirty-five per thousand persons. Population estimates for a handful of parishes with no extant registers have also been made, to produce the estimate of about 25,000. Of course, if the Weald were

[10] Parish registers in KAO, except Tonbridge and Staplehurst, in their parish churches. The 1557 visitation transcribed in *Archdeacon Harpsfield's Cantebury Visitations (1556–8)* Catholic Rec. Soc., 45–6 (1950–1). On the crisis see Wrigley and Schofield, *Population History of England*, pp. 332–40, 649–56; Paul Slack, 'Mortality Crises and Epidemic Disease in England' in Charles Webster (ed.), *Health, Medicine and Mortality in the Sixteenth Century* (1979).

[11] Surveys: 1563 (Corpus Christi College, Cambridge MS. 122 and BL Harl. MS. 594); 1569 (Bodl. Lib. Tanner MS. 240 fo. 29 ff.); 1603 (BL Harl. MS. 280 fo. 157 ff.). C. W. Chalklin, *Seventeenth Century Kent* (1965), p. 27.

defined more loosely to include more parishes, the total population of 'the Weald' would be greater. But in any case, the Weald, however defined, was more densely populated than the average for the county as a whole.[12]

The geographical distribution of population within the Weald in the 1560s can be tackled first. Comparative figures have been calculated to give the number of persons per thousand acres for each parish, based on the parish register totals for that decade. Quite clearly, this measure of population density leaves a great deal to be desired. It takes no account of topographical diversity between one parish and another, nor the extent of privately held woodland or enclosed parks and forests in particular parishes. Goudhurst, for example, contained extensive woodland in this era, and a large proportion of the vast parish of Tonbridge was unavailable for general settlement in the 1560s: thousands of acres were still enclosed within Postern, North and South Frith parks. The estimates of population density based on parish register data should normally be compared with the totals of taxpayers per thousand acres (or square miles) recorded in the subsidy rolls of the 1520s and 1540s. But both these important sets of tax lists are arranged by hundreds rather than by parishes for Kent. Not only do the Wealden hundreds contain parts of several parishes, but the actual area of the Wealden hundreds is in many cases uncertain.

The most striking aspect of Wealden population densities is the extent of the variation between regions: from as little as seventy-two persons per thousand acres (Tonbridge) to over 190 per thousand acres (Cranbrook). In the Kentish Weald as a whole (as defined in this study 202,000 acres or 316 sq. miles or 818 sq. km.) the average density in the 1560s was about 119 persons per thousand acres (or seventy-six per sq. mile or twenty-nine per sq. km.). Aside from Shadoxhurst (eighty-eight) and Woodchurch (seventy-nine) in the east, most of the parishes with low population densities are in the western Weald: Tonbridge (seventy-two), Leigh (about seventy), Cowden (seventy-seven), Edenbridge (ninety) and Sundridge (102). At the opposite extreme the parishes with the highest densities are to be found in the central Weald, and most of them were clothing parishes: Cranbrook (192), Hawkhurst (180), Brenchley (154), Goudhurst (153), Biddenden (146) and Benenden (142). The only other densely populated parishes were East Peckham (152), Pluckley (137) – which had some country clothmaking – and Tenterden (141), an incorporated town with special privileges as a limb of the Cinque Ports. Parishes just outside the clothmaking centres could have only average or below average population densities: Sandhurst (ninety-one), Halden (107) and Rolvenden – which supported some clothmaking (126). The only departures from the association between high population density and rural clothmaking are Marden (100),

[12] See table 3.12 for details of parishes, the state of registers and individual parish population estimates. Surface area of parishes taken from early Ordnance Survey maps and nineteenth-century printed gazetteers. Alan Everitt's Weald is more extensive than the Weald of this study: at 260,000 acres, his amounts to a quarter of the county's surface area: *Continuity and Colonization* (1986), p. 45.

Staplehurst (110) and Frittenden (114), in all of which some textile manufacturing took place in the sixteenth century. One possible explanation for such anomalies is hinted at by the relatively large size of farms in these parishes (especially Marden and Staplehurst).[13] There may well have been greater resistance to smallholder and cottager settlement by the larger landholders of these parishes.

The general picture is clear though, notwithstanding the exceptions: high population densities in the parishes with rural industry and relatively low densities in the predominantly agricultural parishes, especially those between Tonbridge and the Surrey border. The existence of ironmaking in a parish, by itself, made little difference to the population density (e.g., Tonbridge). Horsmonden, which supported ironworks as well as some rural clothmaking, still registered only an average density of population. Only in the course of the seventeenth century would this stark contrast between a densely populated district centred on Cranbrook and a much more thinly populated region in the southwest of the county be diminished. The change was the result of the opening up of many areas of the western Weald for permanent settlement, as well as the slow demise of the Wealden broadcloth industry.[14]

Having established the broad geography of the Weald's population at the outset of the Elizabethan period, the demographic trends of the succeeding forty years can be charted. So far as can be gauged from aggregative methods, the demographic experience of the Weald mirrored quite closely the national population trends outlined by Wrigley and Schofield. This region, like many other rural areas of England, was producing a 'net natural increase' from the 1560s onward (following, as we have seen, the earlier period of sustained population increase beginning at least by the early 1530s, but briefly interrupted at the end of the 1550s). If one arranges the baptism and burial returns in five-year periods beginning about 1560, the net 'surplus' or 'deficit' population in each parish for every quinquennium can be calculated. The procedure obviously ignores migration which, as will be shown below, is crucial to our eventual conclusions about the population history of the Weald of Kent as a whole. But, for the moment, it is a necessary first step to look at the figures generated by counting christenings and burials alone. Taking the Weald as a unit, and working from the twenty-five-plus parishes with reasonably full and accurate registers, the region was definitely generating a net 'surplus' of births over deaths. Only a very few parishes had a net 'deficit' in population between 1560 and 1600. And yet the population of many Wealden parishes seemed not to have grown very much between the 1560s and the 1590s, if estimates for

---

[13] See chapter 4 below.
[14] In general cf. the map (figure 38) in A. R. H. Baker, 'The Field Systems of Kent', unpublished Ph.D. thesis, University of London, 1963. For the seventeenth century see C. W. Chalklin, 'The Rural Economy of a Kentish Wealden Parish, 1650–1750', *AgHR*, 10 (1962) and his *Seventeenth Century Kent* (1965).

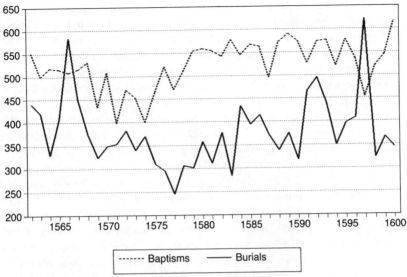

Figure 3.1   Aggregated baptisms, burials: fifteen Weald parishes, 1562–1600.

total population based on the average annual baptism totals for the two decades are compared.

Analysis of the registers shows that there were three different demographic districts within the Kent Weald in the later sixteenth century, one of which experienced a far from expansive demographic history. Beginning in the east there was a region of demographic stagnation in the Wealden parishes adjacent to Romney Marsh and surrounding Tenterden. Figures can be adduced from the following parishes in the eastern region: Bethersden, Halden, Woodchurch, Tenterden, Rolvenden and Wittersham. The demographic pattern here was one of either a net 'deficit' of burials over baptisms, or, in a few cases, a tiny net 'surplus' over the forty-year period. The numbers of people living in these parishes were no greater at the end of the century than they had been in the 1560s, and in some cases there was probably a slight decline in parish populations. At the heart of this eastern region was Tenterden, the most populous parish among the group. It produced a net 'deficit' of baptisms compared with burials through most of the decades under review. Between 1544 and 1556 there was a net 'loss' of eighty-five, in an era when most of the Weald saw considerable population growth. In the short crisis of 1557–9 there was a further net 'deficit' of 111, and the succeeding decade also saw a surplus of burials over baptisms. Only two decades showed net 'surpluses', the 1570s and the 1590s, while the intervening decade recorded a small deficit. Over the whole period 1544 to 1601, there was a net 'natural decrease' in Tenterden's population, which was just about offset by immigration from nearby areas of 'natural increase'. Tenterden was therefore the only Wealden parish to experience an 'urban' demographic pattern in the sixteenth century, in spite of the fact that Tenterden Town could only be counted as among the lowest rank of the urban hierarchy in the early modern period. Many other English towns of similar size did not experience this type of 'negative growth' which depended on immigration rather than 'natural increase'. By contrast, in the Weald itself Cranbrook appears to have grown through both 'natural increase' and migration.

High Halden, adjacent to Tenterden, also experienced no growth, and possibly a decline in population during the Elizabethan period. Of the group only Rolvenden recorded a net 'natural' increase, albeit a very small one. The numbers of christenings there held up strongly until the 1590s, when the average annual total of baptisms fell considerably below the averages for the previous three decades. The six parishes in this group were all predominantly agricultural. Tenterden parish contained several hamlets and was by no means wholly urban. Tenterden Town appears to have functioned mainly as an agricultural market centre, although a small volume of long-distance trade reached it via the small riverine port of Smallhythe in the south of the parish. The surrounding parishes seem to have been affected by Tenterden's dismal experience. Like Tenterden, for example, Bethersden, Halden, Rolvenden and Wittersham all suffered heightened mortality in the harvest year 1565/6. And, since Tenterden's indigenous population was for much of the period declining, migration into Tenterden may have sapped the strength of the neighbouring villages. In addition, only the eastern Weald contained substantial areas of marsh. As Mary Dobson has demonstrated for both Kent and Essex, marshland parishes were subject to endemic fevers, including malaria in this era, and in consequence suffered higher levels of mortality than was common in upland and true Weald parishes.[15] Thus the eastern part of the Weald was singularly out of step with the prevailing demographic pattern of positive growth which characterized the Kent Weald as a whole.

The central Weald presents a stark contrast to the demographic experience of the eastern parishes. The central area covered about a dozen parishes to the north, east and west of Cranbrook, and was defined by a common population history in the Elizabethan period. Though reliable registers have not survived for all of them, the prevailing pattern of rapid population growth in the second half of the sixteenth century can be charted from the record of vital events in at least seven of them: Benenden, Biddenden, Brenchley, Cranbrook, Goudhurst, Hawkhurst and Staplehurst. The central district was already the most densely populated part of the Kent Weald in the early sixteenth century, if the tax lists of the 1520s are a reliable indicator. The heart of the district lies in the High Weald country and includes parishes stretching from Brenchley in the west to Sandhurst and Benenden in the east. Several parishes further north, including Yalding, Marden and Staplehurst,

---

[15] Mary Dobson, 'Marsh Fever – the Geography of Malaria in England', *Journal of Historical Geography*, 6 (1980).

would not be linked by geographers to the High Weald core, but appeared to have shared a common economic and demographic history in this period. The central Weald was the focus of rural manufacturing in Kent. It was most intense in the southern tier of High Weald parishes: from Brenchley and Horsmonden in the west, taking in Goudhurst, Hawkhurst and Benenden, and bending slightly north to encompass Biddenden. Parishes on the fringe of this area also supported some rural industry: Marden, Staplehurst, Frittenden and Headcorn on the north and Lamberhurst and Sandhurst to the south. The predominant non-agricultural industry within the whole region was clothmaking, but ironmaking and metal crafts figure strongly in Horsmonden and Goudhurst. The district's economic centre was Cranbrook with its populous urban core; there was a smaller market centre at Goudhurst.

All seven sample parishes in the central Weald area recorded sizeable net surpluses of baptisms over burials: Benenden and Biddenden (about 450 each between 1560 and 1600), Brenchley (almost 700), Cranbrook (about 1,070), Goudhurst (about 700), Hawkhurst (about 675) and Staplehurst (about 380). The 'net natural increase' for the four decades in most of these parishes amounted to about half of their total populations of the 1560s. And yet many of these parishes were not significantly more populous in the 1590s than they had been thirty years earlier. If estimates of total populations in the 1560s and in the 1580s and 1590s are calculated by the same method – the mean annual baptisms in each period divided by thirty-five and multiplied by 1,000 – they show that the large 'natural increases' were not incorporated into the permanent populations. In most of the seven parishes the estimated total populations in the 1580s–90s was only 10–15 per cent larger than in the 1560s. In reality the difference may have been somewhat larger because parish populations in the early 1560s had still not recovered from the mortality crisis of 1557–9, while family formation may have been exceptionally high and thus the assumed birth rate of thirty-five per thousand may be too low for that decade. Only Cranbrook showed a substantial increase in its total population between the 1560s and 1580s–90s: upwards of 40 per cent! It seems that this densely populated region of the Weald was approaching its demographic limits by the last decades of the sixteenth century; not because of any natural ecological barrier but as the result of what might be termed the human-made ecology of the region. Its limits are a function of the social and economic circumstances which favour or discourage family formation and in-migration: the nature of regional husbandry, the pattern of landholding and ownership and the level of prosperity of local manufacturing industries. By the end of the century these factors were no longer encouraging the population expansion which had characterized the area since at least the early 1500s. The 'natural increase' in population was not being maintained.

Further to the west there was a third and different demographic experience during the second half of the century. The picture here is obscured by the absence of parish registers for five parishes and the deficiencies of several others. Nevertheless, taken broadly, the dozen or so parishes from Hadlow and Pembury west to the Surrey border were growing substantially during the latter half of the century. It must be recalled, of course, that the population of this region was starting from a much lower base than the central Weald area, and that in terms of land there was plenty of room for expansion. Several parishes with reliable registration show a significant net 'surplus' of baptisms over burials, among them Chiddingstone and East Peckham. Several others – including Tonbridge, Speldhurst, Edenbridge and Penshurst – recorded average annual totals of christenings 15–25 per cent higher in the 1580s and 1590s than during the 1560s, another indication of growth. Finally, at least one west Weald parish (Pembury) which probably generated a net 'surplus' during the period, appears not to have held on to those additional people. There the level of baptisms in the 1580s–90s was not much higher than it had been in the early years of Elizabeth's reign. In the western Weald population growth was based on expanding agriculture: outside of a few ironworks there was no significant rural manufacturing. Growth in farming occurred through the intensification of land use: more woodland and rough grazing land was turned into permanent farmland, although the balance of husbandry remained tipped towards livestock. Behind the expansion lay the demands of the growing London market for beef and hides. The region appears to have retained its indigenous population growth as well as attracting some migrants.

The population of the Weald in general, and the central Weald in particular, should have – on the figures and trends identified – grown rapidly in the latter half of the sixteenth century. Unfortunately, there are no detailed totals of parish populations (or communicants) in the 1603 ecclesiastical survey against which we could test our estimates of total population based on parish register data. All that can be certain is that many Wealden parishes showed major net 'surpluses' of baptisms over burials while at the same time the average annual numbers of christenings in the 1580s–90s were frequently no higher than or only slightly above the averages of the 1560s. The available evidence suggests that the Wealden population grew *less* rapidly than that of Kent in general (about 50 per cent between the 1560s and 1603).[16]

Several explanations present themselves to explain the apparent discrepancy. First, the sizeable 'natural increases' of the 1570s and 1580s had not yet made an impact on total numbers (as calculated from the level of baptisms) before 1600 or 1620; but then what of the probably substantial growth of the 1540s and 1550s? Secondly, that the relatively low average annual baptism figures for the 1590s are a reflection of a temporary check to family formation caused by the exceptionally poor economic conditions of that decade. Thirdly, could occasional outbreaks of disease or famine have wiped out most of the 'natural increase' recorded in so many

[16] See p. 58 above and n.11.

of the registers? Fourthly, was infant mortality so high that the effect of surplus baptisms was rapidly nullified? And finally there is the possibility that many Wealden residents were emigrating to the metropolis and to other parts of Kent.

The first possibility – that the big increase in population simply did not show itself until the early seventeenth century – will not hold water. If most of the people born in the 1560s–80s had remained in their parishes (or in the Wealden region) there should have been a correspondingly large increase in baptisms by the first decade of the seventeenth century. The mean annual number of christenings in the decade 1601–10 were calculated for twenty parishes and compared to the means for each parish during the 1560s, a decade which may have had an exceptionally high level of family formation. In twelve cases (Benenden, Biddenden, Brenchley, Cranbrook, Goudhurst, Hadlow, Headcorn, Lamberhurst, East Peckham, Penshurst, Sandhurst, and Tenterden) baptisms were higher than in the 1560s, but significantly higher (over 20 per cent) in only four: Cranbrook (38 per cent), Goudhurst (23 per cent), Lamberhurst (35 per cent) and Penshurst (27 per cent). There was no change between the 1560s and the 1600s in two parishes (Pluckley and Staplehurst), and absolute decreases, albeit small ones, in three others (Halden, Pembury and Rolvenden). As a whole, the mean annual baptism total of the decade 1601–10 was just 12 per cent higher than the total of these parishes in the 1560s: a much smaller rise than the 'net natural increase' might suggest. These data indicate that the estimated totals of parish populations in the 1590s are not statistical illusions and that the rate of family formation was not exceptionally low in the 1590s. The fourth possible explanation, high infant mortality, will be considered in greater detail below, but it too appears to be a non-starter.

What then of the possibility of crisis mortality? Did short outbursts of epidemic mortality erase most of the obvious natural increase? The answer is almost certainly no. The only widespread mortality crisis, during which the normal level of burials was doubled or trebled, occurred in 1557–9, before the substantial net surpluses of the Elizabethan period. In the decades after 1560, when most parishes are represented by full registers, there is a scattering of 'crisis' years (defined as a doubling of burials compared to the average of the preceding five years) visible in a minority of parishes, but nothing again approaching the crisis of the late 1550s. The years 1565/6 and 1566/7 were bad years in at least two or three parishes (especially in the eastern Weald). In Brenchley burials doubled in 1586/7, and in Staplehurst the number of burials in 1591/2 was about double that of the recent past. However, the only serious plague outbreak of the later sixteenth century in the region was that which struck Cranbrook in 1597/8. During the Old Style calendar year 1597 there were 224 burials recorded of which 180 were listed as plague victims. In all, probably 8 per cent of Cranbrook's population died that year. But Cranbrook, it should be recalled, had a large urban core, and the parish's other hamlets were also densely populated. Plague deaths here occurred not only during the terrible year 1597/8: the Cranbrook parish register records several smaller outbreaks. Eighteen died of the plague during September to December 1581, and there was a further outbreak the following year: forty-one plague burials took place between August 1582 and January 1583. The winter of 1583/4 saw another outbreak of disease with eleven burials (January to March 1584) labelled 'plague' by the parish clerk – although the timing of these sudden deaths hardly suggests plague. Finally, after the devastation of 1597/8, there were ten burials marked 'plague' in October–December 1603, no doubt an echo of the major outbreak in London that year. In the rest of the Weald occasional plague burials are recorded, but the regions seems generally to have escaped the major outbreaks seen in Elizabethan and early Stuart London and several other towns (including Maidstone) in this era.

Mortality during the 1590s was certainly higher, on average, in most Wealden parishes than during the previous two or three decades. Most parishes recorded one or two years of exceptionally high (but not necessarily 'crisis' level) burials during the decade, although in some it occurred in the early 1590s rather than during 1594–8, the years of national harvest failure and dearth. There is no evidence of famine in the region, even though a number of registers note the burials of a handful of 'poor travelling men' or women and of demobilized soldiers during the 1590s. In the end, therefore, crisis mortality cannot provide the explanation to our conundrum. All that remains is migration, a phenomenon notoriously difficult to document from the normal demographic sources. We shall return to this question later in the chapter, but before that it is necessary to look beneath the averages and trends produced by aggregative methods into the lives of families and individuals.

To put some flesh on the bare bones of aggregative description – and to explain it – the experiences of a few parishes have been studied in greater detail. Those selected are not necessarily the ideal choices from every point of view; but the state of the parish registers and the availability of other, associated evidence dictated that Brenchley, Cranbrook and Staplehurst should be chosen. Biddenden, too, could have been used but there is no great advantage in adding another clothing parish to the two already included. Ideally, a west Weald parish should have been analysed in the same detail, but those parishes either were not populous enough to generate meaningful statistics, or their registers were deficient. Also, there are no surviving census-type records for that area, which could compare with the household communicant lists available for Cranbrook and Staplehurst. Therefore much of what follows will be of particular relevance to the study of the demographic and family experience of wood-pasture regions which developed rural manufacturing.

The three parishes varied in size, population and the extent to which they were centres of non-agricultural production. Cranbrook was the largest of the three (10,400 acres), the most populous (at least 2,000 persons in the 1560s, probably 2,500 to 2,800 in the 1590s) and the most densely populated (192 persons per thousand acres in the 1560s). Cranbrook's inhabitants lived in at least eight separate

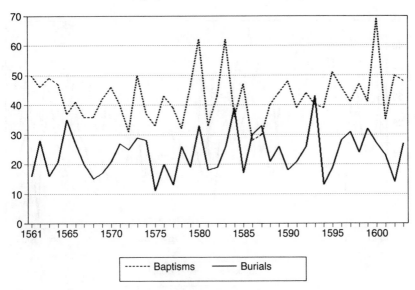

Figure 3.2   Aggregated baptisms, burials: Brenchley, 1561–1603.

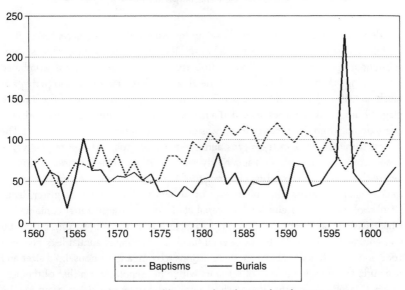

Figure 3.3   Aggregated baptisms, burials: Cranbrook, 1560–1603.

hamlets in addition to 'Cranbrook Town', which, though unincorporated, was the only sizeable market town between Tonbridge and Tenterden and Ashford. Cranbrook was also the centre of the Wealden broadcloth industry; clothmaking was carried on in the town and in the surrounding hamlets. The parish supported

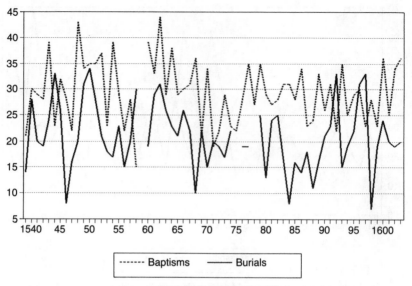

Figure 3.4   Aggregated baptisms, burials: Staplehurst, 1540–1603.

a wide variety of occupations (as shown in the wills and probate inventories of its inhabitants), several inns and many alehouses. It contained the seats of at least three substantial gentry families (Baker, Roberts and Hendley), whose combined landholdings in the parish certainly made up a very large minority (and perhaps as much as half) of land within the parish. Even with the terrible toll of the 1597/8 plague outbreak, Cranbrook recorded a net 'surplus' of christenings over burials in every decade from the 1560s (when it was only about eighty-five) to the 1590s. The largest surpluses were in the 1570s and 1580s (about 300 and 560 respectively). Cranbrook's register, although apparently accurate, is not suitable for reconstitution before the seventeenth century. For much of the late sixteenth century the parish clerks failed to record the full names of fathers in the baptism register. Thus Cranbrook is mainly useful for its overall statistics and the material contained in what may be a unique communicant register or Easter book. Organized by households and divided into the several hamlets, it contains annual lists between 1608 and 1612. It is possible from these listings to compare the household sizes and structure, and the distribution of servants within households, with that of the next parish, Staplehurst. Information on short-term mobility and persistence can also be drawn from the Cranbrook communicant lists.

Staplehurst was the smallest of the three parishes (5,900 acres), the least populous (about 650 in the 1560s) and the least densely populated (about 110 persons per thousand acres). There was some clothmaking in Staplehurst, but it was much less prominent than in Cranbrook or Biddenden. There was no dominant aristocratic landowner, although one recognized gentry family resided and held land in the parish, and other Wealden gentry estates included lands in Staplehurst. Its agriculture was prosperous and it had no real urban centre. Like Cranbrook, its inhabitants lived in a number of separate settlements but we have no information about their relative sizes. The Staplehurst wills and probate inventories show the expected spread of rural occupations plus one draper, a few tanners (common in most Wealden parishes) and a number of weavers and clothiers. By the standards of some other parts of Kent, it was a wealthy parish, lacking only the top layer of rich men which could only be found in Cranbrook. Staplehurst's register begins in 1539 and, apart from a frustrating but short gap in 1558–9, is complete and usually records fathers' full names. Staplehurst produced net 'natural' increases in population of over a hundred in the 1560s, 1570s and 1580s, with a reduced net 'surplus' in the 1590s. Its families have been reconstructed as far as they can, given the high degree of geographical mobility, and these data can be related to an almost perfect household communicant list compiled in late 1563 and early 1564. Data from this list can be compared with equivalent material from Cranbrook, and the vital data, generated from reconstituting Staplehurst's families, can be compared with analogous figures and trends from our third parish, Brenchley.

Brenchley was an extensive parish (7,800 acres), relatively populous (about 1,200 in the 1560s) and one of the more densely populated (154 persons per thousand acres). It too had no significant urban core, its population was involved both in agriculture and clothmaking, but its clothiers were mainly much smaller operators than many of those in Cranbrook. There were no major resident gentry families. Being in Rochester diocese, there are no extant probate inventories, so its occupational structure cannot be known in any detail. However, its parish register is apparently accurate and full enough to reconstitute families in the Elizabethan period. According to the register Brenchley produced a large and steady net 'natural increase' in population in all decades from 1560 to 1600. There may be some doubt, however, about the size of these surpluses because the ratio of baptisms to burials is exceptionally high. Undoubtedly there was a significant natural increase but it may have been less than the register suggests because of inadequate registration of burials.

The accompanying graphs illustrate the overall trends in the totals of christenings and burials in the Weald in general and in the three sample parishes, showing the gap between them that was normal throughout most of the central and western Weald.[17] Certain other selected measures of family formation are shown in the tables that follow. Age at first marriage was relatively low in both Brenchley and Staplehurst. The figures may be slightly lower than was actually the case, because they include data taken from the early years of the parish registers and thus miss the

---

[17] Fifteen parishes: Benenden, Bethersden, Biddenden, Brenchley, Cranbrook, Goudhurst, Halden, Hawkhurst, Headcorn, Marden, East Peckham, Penshurst, Rolvenden, Staplehurst and Tenterden.

Industry in the countryside

Table 3.2 *Age at first marriage*

Parish	Females		Males	
	Mean	Median	Mean	Median
Brenchley/Horsmonden				
(persons baptized in	23.7	23 yrs	25.3	25 yrs
the 1560s–70s)	(N = 79)		(N = 92)	
Staplehurst (persons	23.5	23 yrs	26.3	26 yrs
baptized in the 1540s–70s)	(N = 64)		(N = 45)	
Some comparable data:				
Terling, Essex (1550–1624)	24.5	23.8 yrs	25.9	25 yrs.
Thirteen English Parishes	25.6 yrs	(Mean)	28.1 yrs	(Mean)
(1600–49)				

Note: 30 of 92 examples from Brenchley and Horsmonden are based on the date of the first child's baptism minus one year; if the interval between the two events was longer, then average age would be higher: just under 26 years.
Sources: K. Wrightson and D. Levine, *Poverty and Piety in an English Village* (1979), p. 68; Wrigley and Schofield, *Population Studies* (1983), pp. 157–84.

baptisms of some who may have married at a relatively late age during the first decades of registration (and therefore would not be included in these averages). There was some inter-registration of vital events between Brenchley and its smaller neighbour, Horsmonden, and so the families in both were reconstructed.

There remains one crucial variable which cannot be obtained from parish registers or the other sources used in this chapter: the proportion of young men and women who did not marry. It might be predicted that the number of adults in the Weald who never married should have been quite small, given a number of economic and social circumstances which might have had some bearing on the issue. The existence of a variety of employment prospects, a fluid market in small parcels of farmland both to rent and to purchase and the normal practice of partible inheritance among most landholders bar the gentry – all these should theoretically have encouraged a very high proportion of young adults to marry. But we cannot demonstrate that this was in fact the case. And it may well be that the proportion (however small) never marrying rose by the end of the sixteenth century and the early decades of the next.

If the age at which women first married is, in the early modern period, one of the two most important determinants of fertility – and therefore of overall demographic change – as Wrigley and Schofield argue – then the relatively low ages seen in these sample Wealden parishes help to explain the substantial net increase recorded in so many of them. An average age for women's first marriage of about twenty-three is among the lowest cited anywhere for sixteenth- or seventeenth-century England. And, since most of the data summarized in table 3.2 relates to marriages occurring in the last two decades of the sixteenth and the first decade of the

Table 3.3 *Birth (baptism) intervals (in months)*

Parish	Marriage to 1st Baptism	1st–2nd Baptism	2nd–3rd Baptism	3rd–4th Baptism	Mean of intervals 1 to 4
Brenchley &					
Horsmonden	14.7	25.5	27.4	29.6	27.3
(1560–1600)	(N = 166)	(254)	(222)	(177)	
Staplehurst	14.9	26.5	28.6	30.5	28.3
(1540–1600)	(N = 105)	(171)	(146)	(126)	
Some comparable data:					
Colyton, Devon					
(1560–1640)	11.3	25.2	27.4	30.1	
Terling, Essex					
(1550–1724)	14.9	29.5	37.0	38.1	

Sources: Colyton, quoted in R. Finlay, *Population and Metropolis* (1981), p. 136; Wrightson and Levine, *Poverty & Piety*, p. 52.

seventeenth century, it is probable that the average age at first marriage was even lower during the 1560s and 1570s.

Another measure of marital fertility is the length of intervals between marriage and first baptism and then between subsequent baptisms: the shorter the intervals the higher number of children likely to be born, everything else being equal. The figures for several Wealden parishes are given in table 3.3, and again there is little difference between the two areas, although the Staplehurst sample is drawn from a wider time span. These can be compared to the experience in other English parishes.

The birth intervals calculated for the sample Wealden parishes are definitely on the low side, although quite similar to those recorded in Colyton. They definitely point to relatively high marital fertility levels in the Weald. The average intervals between christenings was not as low as in many London parishes, where many children were put out to nurse soon after birth (and therefore the contraceptive effect of lactation was nullified). The practice was apparently not common in the Weald. Wealden birth intervals were comparable to those found in Arden, Warwickshire, during the period when employment in rural manufacturing was becoming available. There, in 1600–24 the mean interval between births one to four was 27.7 months, very close to the average in the Weald in the late sixteenth century.[18]

Illegitimate births did not make a significant contribution to the rising population in Wealden Kent. Some registers record so few illegitimate christenings that they

[18] Victor Skipp, *Crisis and Development: an Ecological Case Study of the Forest of Arden, 1570–1674* (Cambridge, 1978), p. 14. On short birth intervals in London, see Roger Finlay, *Population and Metropolis* (1981), p. 137.

cannot be considered as valid evidence. Those registers which regularly appear to list the baptisms of bastards show that the illegitimacy rates were quite low in the period 1550 to 1600. In Brenchley, for example, there were just thirty-six illegitimate baptisms during 1560–1600, or 2.2 per cent of all infants baptized. There the rate was highest in the 1570s (2.7 per cent) and lowest in the 1590s (1.8 per cent). Likewise in Cranbrook, illegitimacy remained only a marginal phenomenon in the sixteenth century although it was growing in the 1590s. The Cranbrook register shows a big jump in base births in the decade 1601–1610, as does that of Goudhurst:

> Cranbrook, 1591–1600: 13 illegitimate baptisms (1.5%)
> 1601–10: 23 illegitimate baptisms (2.4%)
> Goudhurst, 1591–1600: 9 illegitimate baptisms (1.8%)
> 1601–10: 23 illegitimate baptisms (3.3%)

The levels of illegitimacy found in these sample Wealden parishes, therefore, were not dissimilar to those reported in a national sample of ninety-eight parishes. In England at large the illegitimacy rates varied between 2 and 3 per cent from 1570 to 1600, then rose to a peak of about 3.4 per cent in the years 1600–4.[19] Even these low ratios exaggerate the real demographic impact of extra-marital fertility. In the Weald, at least, the likelihood of illegitimate children surviving beyond infancy was much lower than the chances of infants in general. The christening of a bastard followed by the entry of its burial within a few days or a few weeks is a common feature of many Wealden registers. In these cases where the birth of a base child was known and recorded, their early deaths were more likely the consequence of intentional neglect than of infanticide as defined by statute in the sixteenth century.

The seasonal distribution of vital events can also be measured, with the year-to-year fluctuations ironed out. It would be exceptionally interesting if the Weald, with its concentration of non-agricultural employment, displayed seasonal patterns (especially of baptisms) different from the norm of contemporary rural England. The tables below show the monthly distributions of christenings and burials in eighteen and fourteen sample parishes respectively, during the period 1560–1600. The raw numbers have been converted to monthly index numbers, whereby 100 represents the number of events which would have occurred had the baptisms (or burials) been evenly distributed throughout the year. In the first table the time of conception is assumed to be nine months before baptism, since there is no evidence that christenings took place more than a week or so after birth in the case of most families.

The seasonal distribution of baptisms (and therefore of conceptions) was similar in all the sample parishes, with a long plateau of baptisms in February, March and

---

[19] Cited in Peter Laslett, *The World We Have Lost–Further Explored* (1983), p. 159.

Table 3.4 *Seasonality of births (baptisms): monthly indexes*

(Conception):	A	M	J	J	A	S	O	N	D	J	F	M
Baptism:	J	F	M	A	M	J	J	A	S	O	N	D
In 18 Kent Weald parishes, 1560–99												
	107	117	123	119	98	85	77	87	94	97	96	100
In 404 parish national sample												
1540–1599	111	123	123	111	89	81	78	89	105	100	101	91
1600–1649	110	125	124	112	92	82	77	88	97	100	99	97

Note: total number of Weald events is 22,178, from Benenden, Biddenden, Brenchley, Chiddingstone, Cranbrook, Goudhurst, Hadlow, Hawkhurst, Headcorn, Marden, East Peckham, Pembury, Penshurst, Rolvenden, Speldhurst, Staplehurst, Sundridge, Tenterden. *Source:* Wrigley and Schofield, *Population History of England*, p. 286.

April – indicating a high level of conceptions in the late spring and early summer months. The Wealden pattern was broadly similar to that shown in a sample of 404 English parishes reported by Wrigley and Schofield, except that the peak period in the Weald was one month longer than that in the national sample. The seasonal distribution of conceptions (and baptisms) had not, at least in the sixteenth century, departed from the traditional English rural regime, even though some have argued that proto-industrialization (like urbanization in later periods) produced a more even spread of conceptions as sexual relations and marriage become less tied to the rhythms of the farming year. In the Weald, the industrialized parishes did not exhibit a different seasonal distribution of baptisms from that recorded in mainly agricultural parishes, nor did the region as a whole differ from the 404 parish national sample (which was drawn from predominantly agricultural communities). The explanation is straightforward enough. Most families in the Weald still had a toe-hold in farming. The inventories of numerous Wealden weavers and other artisans – which will be discussed at greater length in chapter 4 – show that most of them at least were smallholders, and that many ran substantial farms alongside their craft occupations.

Death, too, in the Weald occurred in its traditional season, as table 3.5 indicates. In all but one of the fourteen sample Wealden parishes the peak of burials occurred in either March or April. More generally, there was an extended plateau of heightened mortality between January and May, very similar to the national sample, except that the period of high mortality in the wider sample lasted only until April. The March–April peak is more extreme in the Kent Weald sample, but that may only be a reflection of the smaller number of events. In the much larger national sample, the peaks tend to be reduced. In the Weald, as in England in general, far fewer deaths occurred in the summer and autumn, which suggests several points. First, plague, with its late summer and autumn peak, had very little

Table 3.5 *Seasonality of burials: monthly indexes*

	J	F	M	A	M	J	J	A	S	O	N	D
14 Kent Weald parishes, 1560–1600	115	111	124	130	114	90	84	75	80	85	89	103
In 404 parish national sample												
1540–99	107	111	121	120	99	87	81	89	92	97	97	99
1600–49	112	114	115	116	102	90	83	85	91	93	98	102

Note: total number of Weald events is 14,798, from Benenden, Biddenden, Brenchley, Cranbrook, Goudhurst, Hawkhurst, Headcorn, Marden, E. Peckham, Penshurst, Rolvenden, Staplehurst, Tenterden, Tonbridge, but excluding 1597–8 for Cranbrook.
Source: Wrigley and Schofield, *Population History of England*, p. 294.

impact in the Weald, as in most other rural areas by the late sixteenth century. Infections and illnesses of the winter and early spring months were far more important causes of death. Second, to the extent that infant (and maternal) mortality was a part of mortality in general, the greater number of spring births were reflected in the rise of burials in the spring. But this point must not be over-emphasized: adult burials made up a sizeable majority of all burials. As between parishes in the Weald sample, there was a good deal more variation in the monthly distribution of burials than of christenings. In two parishes, Headcorn and Marden, burials were also high in November (index number 113 and 110), while in East Peckham burials were unexpectedly low in February (index number 80). Taking all the variations into account, the seasonal pattern of both births and deaths in the Weald was quite similar to that found in less industrialized regions of rural England.[20]

The level of infant mortality, alluded to earlier, could be a significant factor in the overall demographic pattern. Infants buried within twelve months of their baptism have been counted for Staplehurst and Brenchley, and the numbers divided into successive ten-year periods from the beginning of registration. In Staplehurst there was much greater variation between decades than in Brenchley, and yet the infant mortality rates were surprisingly similar – and quite low for the sixteenth century.

In both parishes infant mortality was somewhat lower in the later decades than during the middle of the century. The rates recorded in these semi-industrialized Wealden parishes compare favourably with the results of Schofield and Wrigley's study of infant mortality in sixteen widespread English parishes in the 1580s. In

[20] On seasonality in general see Wrigley and Schofield, *Population History*, pp. 285–305, and now Irene Greatorex, 'Seasonality and Early Modern Towns: the Timing of Baptisms, Marriages and Burials in England, 1560–1750, with Particular Reference to Towns', unpublished Ph.D. thesis, CNAA (Thames Polytechnic), 1992.

Table 3.6 *Infant mortality ($1{,}000q_0$) in two Weald parishes*

	1538–48	1548–58	1558–68	1568–78	1578–88	1588–98	1598–1608
Staplehurst							
Rate	175	162	222	97	131	75	114
Baptisms	228	296	306	259	282	280	316
		Overall rate, 1538–1608: 140 per thousand					

	1560–70	1570–80	1580–90	1590–1600
Brenchley				
Rate	158	158	142	119
Baptisms	398	387	387	438
	Overall rate, 1560–1600: 144 per thousand.			

their sample, the mean infant mortality rate was 149 per thousand. In another study, based on family reconstitution in twelve English parishes which separated male from female infants, the rates for the period between 1550 and 1599 were similar to those obtaining in the Weald: 143 per thousand males and 127 per thousand females.[21]

Parishes in the sixteenth-century Weald – like elsewhere in England – were in a very important sense collections of families and households. Given the dispersed nature of settlement within Wealden parishes, families might be expected to have been even more important institutions of social and economic life than in regions with nucleated villages and strongly collective parochial institutions. What can be known about family structure and mobility in the Weald? And, was there anything exceptional about family and/or household structure in a region of 'proto-industry'? Any special characteristics in regions like the Weald, of course, cannot be ascribed solely to the impact of rural manufacturing. Distinguishing cause from effect may not be a simple matter. Other factors, which should be taken into account, include the prevailing agrarian regime, the typical customs of inheritance and the issues briefly surveyed in chapter 1: the distribution of landholding, the availability of land for hire and the openness of the local land market. All these could theoretically have had an impact on family structure – and vice versa. The availability of non-agricultural employment is not the only – nor perhaps the most important – influence in family formation and household structure.

The theory of 'proto-industrialization' might lead to two different – and possibly contradictory – expectations about household size and family structure. Since the proto-industrial family allegedly tried to maximize its total income by utilizing the

---

[21] Schofield and Wrigley in Charles Webster, *Health, Medicine and Mortality in the Sixteenth Century* (1979), p. 82; Laslett, *World We Have Lost* (1983), p. 112.

labour (and earning) capacity of both wife and husband and their economically productive offspring, we should expect larger households in regions of rural industry. On the other hand, because young adults in proto-industrial areas did not depend on the inheritance of a holding before forming their own households upon marriage, and could sustain themselves through non-agricultural employment (in addition to wage work in farming at certain times of the year), we should expect them to leave the parental home earlier than their counterparts in predominantly farming regions. Thus households should, on average, be more numerous and smaller than elsewhere. Needless to say, the theory takes little account of the widespread English tendency for economically productive young people to leave their own homes to go into service or apprenticeship in the households of neighbours. Such 'life-cycle' servants were ubiquitous in both farming communities and in regions of mixed agriculture and commodity production – including, as we shall see, the Kent Weald.

It has already been shown that the average age at first marriage in several Wealden parishes which supported rural industry to one degree or another was lower than that found in England in general. What then were Wealden households like, and how stable were they? The materials to answer these questions include two census-type listings of communicants (from Staplehurst, 1563–4, and Cranbrook, 1608–12) as well as the parish registers. The Staplehurst listing is not quite complete: it records 114 households containing 399 persons of communicant age. The document, as it exists today, breaks off before the concluding totals, which would have shown that there were between 120 and 125 households in the parish. The extra five to ten households can be deduced from entries in the parish register.[22] No very large households are missing from the list. The remaining 114 had an average of 3.5 communicants per household. If at this date communicants made up about 65 per cent of all persons, the mean household size in Staplehurst was of the order of 5.3 or 5.4 people; if the age of communion was slightly lower – and communicants made up 70 per cent of the population, the average household included about five persons. In either case, Staplehurst households were larger than the conventionally accepted average, 4.5 or 4.75 persons. Dyer's suggested multiplier of about five for the sixteenth-century household is more convincing. But so too is it probable that Staplehurst's households were slightly larger than elsewhere in Kent. In twenty-three Kent parishes where the numbers of communicants and households are both recorded in the 1557 archdeaconry visitation, the mean number of communicants is 3.3, compared to Staplehurst's 3.5.[23] Staplehurst had no significant urban area, and as the listing does not divide

[22] The listing: KAO PRC 43/13/31.
[23] The 1569 ecclesiastical visitation gives 440 communicants in 120 households for Staplehurst, which would produce an even larger mean number of communicants per household: Bodl. Lib. Tanner MS. 240. Traditional multiplier in Peter Laslett, 'Mean Household Size in England', in *Household and Family in Past Time* (Cambridge, 1972); Alan Dyer, '"The Bishops" Census of 1563', *Local Population Studies*, 49 (1992).

Table 3.7 *Household size in Staplehurst, 1563–4*

Household Size	No.	Share	No. of persons	Share
1 communicant	6	(5%)	6	(1.5%)
2 communicants	39	(34%)	78	(19.5%)
3 communicants	24	(21%)	72	(18%)
4 communicants	13	(11.5%)	52	(13%)
5 communicants	19	(17%)	95	(24%)
6 or more	13	(11.5%)	96	(24%)
Totals	114		399	

households into the different hamlets within the parish, it must be assumed that household size was relatively similar in the various settlements.

In Staplehurst a solid majority of households contained three communicants or less, but the majority of communicants were members of households with four or more communicants. Almost half of the parish's inhabitants lived in households of five or more communicants. Only in Cranbrook is it possible to examine differences in household size in different parts of the parish.

Cranbrook was vastly more populous than Staplehurst. It had a large urban core and six to eight subsidiary settlements. The comparison is not ideal since the Cranbrook listings record the names of communicants almost forty years after the Staplehurst list was drawn up. Our preliminary figures for Cranbrook are based on the list for 1608, and distinguish two residential areas: Cranbrook 'Town' on the one hand, and on the other all the remaining hamlets. The urban area had a higher share of smaller households, and a much smaller share of very large households – like other English towns. In the 'Town' the mean household size was 2.9 communicants per house; in the rural settlements the average size was 3.4 communicants (very close to Staplehurst's of 1563–4). The overall parish mean was 3.2. The Cranbrook urban households can be compared to households in a number of other sixteenth- and seventeenth-century towns. In urban Romford, Essex, the average number of communicants in 1562 was three, remarkably close to Cranbrook in 1608. Other comparisons exist but for complete households, rather than just communicants. Mean household size in the poor suburban parishes of Canterbury in 1563 was 3.4 persons. In early seventeenth-century Cambridge the average household size was 4.1 persons, but that fell to about 3.9 in the poorer parishes. Assuming that communicants represented two-thirds of total population, the mean household size in Cranbrook was significantly larger: about 4.3 persons in Cranbrook 'Town', and just over five persons per household in the rural hamlets.[24]

[24] The listing: KAO P100/28/1. Romford: M. McIntosh, 'Servants and the Household Unit in an Elizabethan English Community', *Journal of Family History*, 9 (1984), pp. 7–8; Canterbury households: A. Detsicas and N. Yates (eds.), *Studies in Modern Kentish History* (Maidstone, 1983), p. 69; Cambridge households: N. Goose, 'Household Size and Structure in Early Stuart Cambridge', *Social History*, 5

Table 3.8 *Household size in rural Cranbrook, 1608*

Household size	No.	Share	No. of persons	Share
1 communicant	34	(9%)	34	(3%)
2 communicants	121	(33%)	242	(19%)
3 communicants	95	(25%)	285	(22.5%)
4 communicants	45	(12%)	180	(14%)
5 communicants	28	(8%)	140	(11%)
6 or more	49	(13%)	384	(30.5%)
Totals	372		1,265	

Table 3.8 shows the distribution of households by number of communicants for the non-urban settlements, and is thus comparable to the case of Staplehurst displayed earlier. The rural settlements in Cranbrook parish, recorded forty years later than Staplehurst, showed a similar distribution of household sizes: a large number of relatively small households, but a majority of the population living in the less numerous, larger households. The only real difference between the two areas was that Cranbrook had an exceptionally large group of very large households. The biggest households in Staplehurst – there were four – contained nine communicants. In Cranbrook there were seven with nine communicants each as well as thirteen others with ten to eighteen communicants in each. At the other extreme, the local tendency towards a relatively low age of marriage seems to be reflected in the strikingly high proportion of small households of one or two communicants each (39 and 42 per cent respectively in the two parishes). At the same time, the concentration of small households in both Staplehurst and in Cranbrook (47 per cent in Cranbrook parish as a whole) may also be a reflection of the large number of poor families in both these central Wealden parishes.

The composition of rural households in both parishes can also be inferred from the two listings, although neither gives ages or the exact relationship of all other residents to the householder. Not surprisingly, a very large majority of the households were headed by a married couple: about 89 per cent in Staplehurst and 79 per cent in Cranbrook (the whole parish). Most of the rest were headed by widows: 8 per cent in Staplehurst and 12 per cent in Cranbrook. The single male householders were mainly widowers. The Cranbrook case is most similar to that of suburban Canterbury in 1563, where just over 80 per cent of households were headed by married couples. There were no complex or three-generation households in Staplehurst; in Cranbrook just one or two. The substantial bloc of two-communicant households were predominantly composed of nuclear families. The listings, unfortunately, cannot tell us what proportion of these small households contained two or three children under the age of communion (which in Staplehurst seems to have varied between thirteen and fifteen, if the examples tracked down in the register are typical), and what percentage were families whose teenage children had already left home.

While the great majority of these households were based on nuclear families, many were not nuclear family households in the twentieth-century sense. In Staplehurst sixty-three households out of 114 contained at least one inmate described as a servant (55 per cent). Sixty-one households there included communicants with a surname different from the head of household; a number of 'servants' were relatives of the householder. The Staplehurst list does not distinguish apprentices or journeymen from other servants. In the rural areas of Cranbrook parish at least 40 per cent of households included residents with surnames different from the householder, most of whom were probably servants. In both Weald parishes, therefore, a significantly larger share of households contained resident servants than was common in sixteenth- and seventeenth-century England at large, where on average less than a third of households had resident servants. In poor, suburban Canterbury in 1563, for example, under 27 per cent of households contained servants, in Cambridge (the whole town) in the 1620s the proportion with servants rose only to 35 per cent, and in Romford, Essex, about 40 per cent of households contained servants.[25]

The annual lists of Cranbrook communicants frequently describe servants more specifically: many are listed as apprentice ('pr') or journeyman ('ior'). The practice varies from year to year in the series, but the fullest of the listings from this point of view, that for 1612, records 208 apprentices and journeymen living in 110 households (19 per cent of households listed that year). Resident servants (including domestic and farm servants, apprentices and journeymen) appear to have been almost the norm in this area of the Weald both in the 1560s and the first decade of the seventeenth century. Staplehurst's exceptionally high percentage of households with servants – compared with Cranbrook's or the poor Canterbury suburbs – hints at a relatively widely distributed prosperity. Cranbrook, with its much more concentrated industrial activity, clearly had a higher proportion of poor households. But even there resident servants were commoner than in most English parishes. In the Weald the larger households are full of residents with different surnames from the householder; some undoubtedly were teenage children of the householder's wife by her previous marriage(s), and perhaps a few were more distant kin. But the majority must have been resident servants. Some households did contain sons and daughters of communicant age, but the majority of teenagers seem to have been life-cycle servants in households other than their parents': the fact that almost half of all households contained servants underlines this conclusion. The listings, on their own, do not provide much information about the economic status of all these

[25] Laslett, *World We Have Lost* (1983), p. 296; Detsicas and Yates, *Studies in Modern Kentish History*, p. 73; Goose, 'Household Size', p. 374; McIntosh, 'Servants and the Household Unit', p. 13.

'servants'. It is likely that only the wealthy minority of households, those operating a substantial craft enterprise or large farm, or both, had resident servants working for wages. The great majority of servants were most likely teenage life-cycle servants and apprentices who received little or no money wages. In a few cases, servants can be readily identified as the sons and daughters of near neighbours, but far more, especially in Cranbrook, would have come from further afield, although mainly from within the Weald.

In Cranbrook the very large households were of two types. A few were gentry establishments: the households headed by Sir Thomas Hendley and Sir Thomas Roberts contained twelve and twenty-one communicants, respectively. Sir Henry Baker's house had nine adults and Mr William Plummer's eight. The remainder of the exceptionally large households were headed by wealthy clothiers and a few other tradesmen or master craftsmen. Stephen Weller, a clothier. and his wife headed a household containing four journeymen, two apprentices, one other male servant and three maids (and possibly underage children as well). John Holden's house included four journeymen, two apprentices, a maid and his unmarried daughter. There were at least a dozen other households like these in Cranbrook, but only a small minority contained teenage children of the householder. A larger number included inmates with the same name as the householder, in many cases specifically described as journeyman or apprentice. Almost all the large households and most medium-sized households included at least one maidservant. There was, undoubtedly, a transfer of young people from poor households into the establishments of the better off. At the same time, however, many wealthy parents also sent their offspring into friends' or relatives' households for a number of years before they were old enough to marry and set up on their own.

How stable were Wealden households and how mobile were the men and women who lived in them? A number of different measures of stability and turnover are used in this chapter; the results suggest that a very large share of the Wealden population did not spend their whole lives in the parish of their birth. Nor did they usually remain in their parents' household until they were married. Individuals moved frequently between different households – especially as teenagers and young adults – and, to a lesser extent, they moved from one parish to another even after they had formed their own families. Using the communicant listings and parish registers, examples of both the levels of persistence and of mobility can be calculated for different groups of the population. Other measures suggest by inference the high levels of geographical mobility in our period. The most obvious of these tests has been appreciated by historians for many years: the majority of persons born in a given parish cannot be shown to have married there, even in the case of women who were more likely to marry in their parents' parish.

A clear majority of the resident adults in Staplehurst in 1563–4 were not buried there. Although a few women who were unmarried at the time of the listing and who subsequently married in another parish but returned to live in Staplehurst may have escaped notice, only 37 per cent of the 1563–4 communicants can be traced to a burial in Staplehurst. Some categories of people were more likely to move than others. Older people were less likely to move: almost two-thirds of heads of households (including widows) were buried in the parish. About 40 per cent of the wives of male householders were buried in Staplehurst, but only 20 per cent of all other communicants of 1563–4 (mostly unmarried young men and women) were buried there. Householders and their wives made up just over half the total number of communicants in the parish. They were, not surprisingly, older and less likely to move away, but even householders' wives were as likely to move from the parish before their deaths as householders were to stay.

The series of annual communicant lists for the parish of Cranbrook can be used to test for the level of persistence over a much shorter period. The procedure is simple: what proportion of people listed as communicants in 1608 were still in the parish in 1612? Of the 596 households of 1608 only 420 were identifiable just four years later (70 per cent). Four hundred and four were headed by the same householder, sixteen by the widow of the 1608 householder. In the same time there had also been a good deal of movement between settlements within the parish, besides the disappearance of 30 per cent of households altogether. The turnover among servants and other non-householders between 1608 and 1612 was much higher. Of 530 named servants (out of about 1,900 named communicants) in 1608, only 171 (32 per cent) were on the listing of 1612. Only a third of these persisting 'servants' were in the same households in 1608 and 1612. Over half the 171 were residents of different households in 1612 from their residences of 1608. Some moved to other households within Cranbrook, others left the parish. Thirty of the persisting 'servants' had become householders themselves by 1612. As in Staplehurst, young people moved frequently.

The mobility of the Weald's population can also be shown by calculating the turnover in the names of fathers of children christened in a given parish over a period of time. The numbers of such 'reproducing surnames' in stated time periods can be compared. If new surnames continue to appear in later periods then the presumption is that new families are arriving in the parish. If at the same time the total number of reproducing surnames remains substantially the same, the inference is that other families are moving away (or dying out) – see table 3.9 on Staplehurst as an example.

The relatively high proportion of new reproducing surnames in the 1590s and early seventeenth century implies not just the arrival of new families in the parish but, since the total number of families in Staplehurst was only slightly higher at the end of the century than in the 1560s, the disappearance of many active families of the Elizabethan period as well. But the high turnover of families at the end of the century was nothing new; the same high level of migration into the parish was

Table 3.9 *Turnover of surnames in Staplehurst, 1538–1608*

	1538–48	1548–58	1558–68	1568–78	1578–88	1588–98	1598–1608
(a) Number of surnames	121	119	127	107	112	118	127
(b) Surnames appearing first time	54	67	44	31	41	52	
(c) (b) as a % of (a)	(45%)	(53%)	(41%)	(28%)	(35%)	(41%)	

Table 3.10 *Numbers of baptisms per father in same parish*

	1	2	3	4	5	6 or more
Staplehurst, 1548–98:	153 (35%)	86 (20%)	55 (12.5%)	28 (6.5%)	45 (10%)	69 (16%)
Brenchley, 1560–90:	106 (29%)	53 (14.5%)	47 (13%)	38 (10%)	35 (9.5%)	87 (24%)

already occurring in the 1550s and 1560s. Data like these imply that not only the young and unmarried were mobile, but that married householders were also quite likely to move from one parish to another, even if the distances travelled were quite short.

The turnover of families can also be highlighted by counting the number of children of the same father in one parish. The figures above include children of more than one wife. Something approaching a third of families had only one child christened in the sample parishes, and almost half were resident in those parishes only long enough to have had two offspring baptized. A glance back at table 3.3 shows that the average period between marriage and the baptism of a second child was under four years, and between second and fourth baptisms under five years: thus nearly a half of fathers with children baptized in the two sample parishes were resident there for less than five years. Of course reality was probably not so simple. Not all of the nearly 400 families with just one or two baptisms recorded moved out of the parishes. A certain number represent men who died relatively young, or who failed to remarry after the deaths of their wives. A few were probably residents of neighbouring parishes who happened to have a child baptized away from their home parish. But whichever way these figures are interpreted, they suggest a high level of family mobility. Most of the men either arrived in the two parishes after fathering children elsewhere, or left the parishes, still quite young, presumably to have additional children in the parish they migrated to after leaving Staplehurst or Brenchley. There was some difference in the levels of turnover between the two sample parishes: a higher degree of mobility in Staplehurst and a somewhat higher level of family persistence in Brenchley. The real difference may have been slightly larger: because the Brenchley sample begins very soon after the start of the surviving register, it artificially increases the percentage of fathers with just one or two children baptized, since a number of families would already have had several children before the register begins. Having said all this, the relatively small number of families with five or more children baptized in the same parish (26 per cent in Staplehurst and 33 per cent in Brenchley) points to a high level of adult mobility – and mortality.

The 'movers' were to a certain extent balanced by a minority of stable households in both parishes. Even in those, however, 'stability' was hardly identical to the 'stable' families of nineteenth- or early twentieth-century Britain. Many of the families who figure in the last two tables as most persistent were long-lived because of remarriage. Numerous cases of fathers with five to ten children baptized in a single parish represent, in fact, changing families. Many men produced a string of children by two, three or even four wives; and young widows frequently remarried, and might give birth to children by several husbands. In both cases, 'households' persisted but 'families' were far from stable and unchanging.

The impression of an extremely mobile Wealden population is reinforced by one final set of data: the level of individual geographical mobility shown by adults who were witnesses in ecclesiastical courts. The ideal, full deposition of a witness was proceeded by a short, potted biography, in which some or all of the following information might appear: name, age, occupation or status, place of residence, place of birth, the number of years spent by the witness in each parish of residence. Such evidence has become the standard source for studies of migration by historians in recent decades. Unfortunately many depositions do not include all the relevant information about deponents. Nevertheless, the depositions given in the Canterbury diocese church courts offer a large sample to work with, and the chance to measure geographical persistence among adults living in a large number of Kent Weald parishes. It is sufficient to ask a very few simple questions about these witnesses: how many were resident in their parish of birth at the time of their deposition, and how many were living in a parish other than where they were born? And, of those living in their native parishes, how many had been there all their lives? The sample is based on all the enrolled depositions made between the early 1560s and 1609 by witnesses who at the time of their statements were residents of fourteen Kent Weald parishes in Canterbury diocese.[26]

The deposition evidence shows that a clear majority of adult witnesses, at the time they gave evidence, were no longer residents of the parishes of their birth.

---

[26] Migration studies using depositions include Peter Clark, 'The Migrant in Kentish Towns, 1580–1640', in P. Clark and Paul Slack (eds.), *Crisis and Order in English Towns* (1972). Sample parishes: Benenden, Bethersden, Biddenden, Cranbrook, Frittenden, Goudhurst, Halden, Hawkhurst, Marden, Newenden, Rolvenden, Smarden, Staplehurst and Tenterden, drawn from: CCL X.10.7–21; X.11.1 and PRC 39/4–13 (covering the 1560s to 1589); and PRC 39/13–29 (covering 1590–1609). Most suitable depositions came from PRC 39.

Table 3.11 *Residential persistence, Kent Weald witnesses*

	1560–89	1590–1609
Residing in native parish	71 (35%)	133 (42%)
Residing in parish other than native parish	134 (65%)	181 (58%)
Totals	205	314
Always resided in native parish	38 (19%)	84 (27%)

And, that a quarter or less had always lived in their native parish. This evidence of geographical mobility is all the more convincing because it can be assumed that there was a bias in favour of selecting long-term residents as witnesses in many ecclesiastical court cases. The bias in favour of 'stayers' was reinforced by the additional tendency of litigants and court alike to select older, more 'respectable' persons as witnesses. And yet, even with this artificially skewed population of adults, the high level of mobility is demonstrable. It is equally apparent from the depositions that most movement was quite localized. A substantial proportion of people who moved from their native parish for one reason or another later returned. Unfortunately the deposition evidence rarely goes into detail about a person's motives for migration, and the full itinerary of the few long-distance migrants is only rarely given.

Typical of the scale of normal mobility was Richard Waterman, 'husbandman', aged twenty-three in 1594. He had been living in Bethersden, his native parish, for the past three years only. Before he had been in neighbouring Halden for a year, following a spell of one month back in Bethersden. The previous one year he had lived in Great Chart, another parish adjoining Bethersden, and before that he had always lived in Bethersden. It looks as if Waterman, a farmer, had moved from his native parish on two occasions of one year each, perhaps to work as a farm servant. In each case he had moved less than five kilometres. Another exceptionally well-documented case history was that of John Hopper of Staplehurst, age sixty-five when he made his deposition in 1595. He stated that he was born and brought up in Staplehurst, 'saving about seven years in his youth when he went to school'.[27] Local migration histories like the two quoted were typical of the majority of deponents living in the Weald: most had moved residence no more than once or twice, often returning to their native parish, and most had migrated within Kent. The vast majority of deponents had been born in Kent: in the 1560s–80s, only 16 per cent of the Wealden witnesses were natives of other counties (over 40 per cent of those were Sussex-born); in the period 1590–1609 just 18 per cent of the witness sample were born outside of Kent (55 per cent in Sussex). Most of the Sussex-born

27 CCL PRC 39/17 fos. 196v, 114v.

witnesses were natives of parishes in the Sussex Weald, and thus could hardly be counted as long-distance migrants. And a number of the other witnesses of non-Kent origins were clerics, and in that sense atypical in their migration habits. Nevertheless, there were more migrants to the Weald from outside Kent than native-born witnesses who had spent time outside the county. In the two periods only seven and eight native-born witnesses recorded an earlier residence beyond the county boundaries, in each case the majority had been in Sussex. To summarize, it appears that the Kent Weald was the destination of only a very small number of migrants from beyond the county and its southern neighbour, Sussex. The Wealden population was extremely mobile, but within very short distances. The great bulk of intra-county movement was between parishes within a radius of ten to twenty kilometres of one another, and there appears to have been almost negligible movement into the Weald from north Kent during the period covered by these depositions.

The population of Wealden parishes – especially those in the clothmaking region – was continually changing, both through emigration and immigration. Given the high rates of 'natural increase', particularly in the central and west Weald parishes, and the quite low levels of infant mortality, there may well have been more people moving out than moving into the Weald by the late sixteenth century. That situation may have had a great deal to do with the fluctuating level of prosperity of the Wealden broadcloth industry. As will be seen in chapter 5, the expanding industry of the late fifteenth and early sixteenth century probably attracted significant numbers of immigrants, as well as encouraged a high rate of family formation among the indigenous population. From the sixth decade of the sixteenth century the export trade in traditional woollens stagnated, while the 'new draperies' were not introduced into the Weald. The long-term increase in employment in textile manufacturing came to a halt. Although Wealden agriculture remained prosperous, the countryside had simply filled up in many parts of the Kent Weald. With opportunities expanding neither in the cloth trades nor in farming, many young people moved elsewhere: to the less densely populated parishes of the west Weald, to Maidstone and to other regions of Kent, and probably also to London. There remained, in 1600, parts of the Weald able to accommodate larger numbers, but they were not the areas that had seen the most rapid demographic growth in the preceding century. Rural industry, it seems, encouraged population growth only so long as there was a reliable and expanding demand for its products. By the same token, the availability of a pool of cheap, rural labour by itself could not sustain a region's prosperity. The rate of family formation appears to have held up for at least a generation after employment prospects in local industry had ceased to grow. The century after 1560 was not one of continuous decline in broadcloth manufacture, and historians are familiar with the significant lag between the onset of declining economic prospects and real wages, and the demographic response in

Table 3.12 *Sample Weald parishes: basic data*

Parish (acreage)	1560s population	Density per 1,000 acres	Parish register	Map ref.
Benenden (6,700)	950	142	Good	27
Bethersden (6,400)	700	109	Good	36
Bidborough (1,300)	?200	?	None	7
Biddenden (7,200)	1,050	146	Good	29
Brenchley (7,800)	1,200	154	Good	15
Capel (1,500)	?200	?	None	11
Chiddingstone (6,000)	475	79	Good	4
Cowden (3,200)	250	77	?Burials	2
Cranbrook (10,400)	2,000	192	Good	23
Edenbridge (5,300)	475	90	?Burials	1
Frittenden (3,500)	400	114	Transcript only	26
Goudhurst (9,800)	1,500	153	Good	21
Hadlow (5,950)	600	101	Gaps	10
Halden (3,750)	400	107	Usable	33
Hawkhurst (6,500)	1,170	180	Good	24
Headcorn (5,000)	600	120	Good	25
Hever (2,650)	?300	?	None	3
Horsmonden (4,600)	550	120	Good	18
Hunton (2,100)	?250	119	From 1585	19
Lamberhurst (5,200)	475	91	Gap, 1587–95	16
Leigh (4,500)	?300	?	None	6
Marden (7,750)	770	99	Good	20
Newenden (1,000)	150	150	Good	31
Peckham, East (3,350)	500	152	Good	13
Pembury (3,500)	525	150	Good	12
Penshurst (4,550)	550	121	Good	5
Pluckley (3,100)	425	137	Gaps	35
Rolvenden (5,750)	725	126	Good	30
Sandhurst (4,400)	400	91	Good	28
Shadoxhurst (1,980)	175	88	Gaps	39
Smarden (5,400)	600	111	Transcript only	32
Speldhurst (4,000)	475	119	?Burials	8
Staplehurst (5,900)	650	110	Good	22
Tenterden (8,500)	1,200	141	Good	34
Tonbridge (15,350)	1,100	72	Gaps	9
Tudeley (1,600)	?200	?	None	14
Wittersham (3,600)	375	104	Few gaps	38
Woodchurch (6,950)	550	79	Gaps	37
Yalding (5,850)	725	124	Good	17
Totals c.202,000 acres	24,140	119		

the form of lower levels of fertility (the product of both an increase in the age of marriage and the numbers who never married) which Wrigley and Schofield have described for England as a whole. The more immediate response in the Weald appears to have been emigration rather than a rapid decline in the rate of family formation. That would come later, in the seventeenth century.

4

The Wealden agrarian regime

In every local region or *pays* in sixteenth-century England, even those areas characterized as 'proto-industrial', the basic industry was farming. The fundamental theme of this study is the link between agriculture and rural industry, and before it is possible to contemplate the nature of manufacturing in the Weald, the region's agrarian system must be examined. Not only did the agricultural regime of the Kent Weald antedate the arrival of clothmaking by at least several centuries, but, as will become obvious in later chapters, the bulk of the labour supply deployed by Wealden manufacturers and much of their capital depended on the region's farms. In recent decades historians have looked with increasing sophistication into the regional variations of British history. So historical geographers and agricultural historians have exposed the enormous variety in landscapes and in agricultural and tenurial structures to be found in early modern England. The most fundamental division between 'highland', wood-pasture regions on the one hand and lowland, 'champion' districts has been accepted for many years. Since the 1960s, and the publication of Thirsk's first early modern volume of *The Agrarian History of England and Wales*, numerous historians have set to work researching smaller areas within the broad upland and lowland divisions. Revision has proceeded apace and historians have pointed out the wide variation between different landscapes and agrarian systems within the two conventional zones, and suggested that the old classification into just two contrasting zones requires amendment. Many students of farming systems and landscapes now think in terms of two, four, six (or more) basic regional types. This chapter looks at one of the types of wood-pasture districts which happens to be well within 'lowland' England. The Weald can be compared on some criteria to the region composed of northern Essex and southern Suffolk, and on other grounds with districts like south Staffordshire or the Warwickshire Arden. What these all had in common is the absence of communally organized farming in open fields and an emphasis on livestock husbandry rather than on corn production. But not all became centres of flourishing rural manufacturing in the sixteenth or seventeenth centuries.[1]

In the pamphlet *The Inrichment of the Weald of Kent* of 1625, the author advocated a systematic programme for improving the productivity of the 'unapt' soils of the region. It was to be based on the regular spreading of marl (which was commonly found in the Weald) to enrich the ground, and, equally important, the introduction of ley farming to the enclosed fields which had previously been used for either pasture or arable. A complete dressing of marl – the author recommended 300 to 500 loads per acre – would serve for twenty to thirty years: 'your marleable grounds being ordered in this wise ... will continually stand fruitfully either for corn or pasture '.[2] The improver did not go into much detail about the cost of systematic marling, but gave the game away when he referred to the farms he had in mind. Under his scheme a 'husbandman' of 100 or 125 acres would plough a fifth or sixth of his land, leaving the rest to pasture, and after a few years the former arable would become pasture again, as former grassland was ploughed up for corn in turn. In the sixteenth century, however, the farm of 125 acres in the Weald was exceptional, and the improver's prescription, had it been widely known, was beyond the budget of most Wealden farmers. Nevertheless, such grandiose schemes for dressing both the arable and pasture land of whole farms speak loudly of the recurring reality of Wealden farming: most Wealden soils were poor and unproductive compared to nearby arable regions like northeast Kent. Many farmers in the Weald used marl and other dressings in much smaller quantities in the sixteenth century and probably earlier, but since we know little or nothing about arable yields in the Weald, it is impossible to suggest with what success their efforts to improve the soil were rewarded. The question facing this chapter, then, is what was Wealden farming like in the age before the seventeenth-century agricultural reformers with their gospel of convertible husbandry? And, was the Wealden agrarian regime well suited to operation in tandem with artisanal or manufacturing activities?

The most important sources for investigating the agrarian system of the Weald are the surviving probate inventories of farmers. The inventory sample referred to in this chapter is composed of all the inventories of persons who died between 1565 and 1601 and who resided in fourteen wholly Wealden parishes in Canterbury diocese, covering the Weald from Marden and Goudhurst to the east.[3] Because inventories from Rochester diocese have not survived for the sixteenth century,

---

[1] See Joan Thirsk (ed.), *The Agrarian History of England and Wales, iv, 1500–1640* (Cambridge, 1967), chapter 1; Pauline Frost, 'Yeomen and Metalsmiths: Livestock in the Dual Economy of South Staffordshire', *AgHR*, 29 (1981); Victor Skipp, *Crisis and Development: an Ecological Case Study of the Forest of Arden, 1570–1674* (Cambridge, 1978); Joan Thirsk, *England's Agricultural Regions and Agricultural History, 1500–1750* (1987).

[2] *The Inrichment of the Weald of Kent* (1625), frequently attributed to Gervase Markham, p. 19.

[3] Inventories in KAO PRC 10/1–29; PRC 21/1–16; PRC 28/1–4. Sample parishes: Benenden, Bethersden, Biddenden, Cranbrook, Frittenden, Goudhurst, Halden, Hawkhurst, Marden, Rolvenden, Sandhurst, Staplehurst and Tenterden.

much less can be known in detail about the farms of the western Weald. If the farming of that part of the Weald was distinctive in any way, it must have been for reasons other than differences of landscape or soils. For the elevation of land in the Weald, its geology and its soils are not different in the west from the east; instead the main topographical and geological divisions within the Weald run in several belts across the Weald from east to west. The conventional division between the more southerly 'High Weald' landscape and the wider belt of land to the north known as 'The Vale of Kent' or Low Weald, occurs in the west as well as in the central and eastern Weald.

The High Weald – including our sample parishes of Benenden, Sandhurst, Hawkhurst and Cranbrook – consists geologically of alternating sands and clays known as the Hastings Beds, and elevations of 500 feet or more are frequently broken by deep valleys cut by the many streams. At the higher elevations the soils are generally poor and there is extensive woodland and waste. In the valleys, by contrast, there are fertile alluvial meadows and on the hills above them the soil is relatively rewarding to farmers. The Low Weald or Wealden Vales to the north – including such sample parishes as Marden and Staplehurst – is made up of rather low-lying Weald clays. The heavy clay soils are usually described as wet and cold, 'ungrateful to handle' and mostly in need of artificial drainage if cereal crops are to be successful. Marden, according to Hasted in the eighteenth century,

lies very low and flat, the soil a stiff clay, a very heavy tillage land; in winter the lands are exceeding wet, and much subject to inundations, and was it not for the manure of their native marl, and the help of chalk and lime brought from the northern hills, would be still more unfertile than they are at present.[4]

There was much woodland in this region as well. But most writers agree that in general the Low Weald contained a higher proportion of relatively fertile land than in the adjoining district to the south.[5] If the agriculture of the western parishes varied from the Wealden norm described in this chapter, it can only have been in superficial ways due to the somewhat greater impact of manorial lordship and – as stressed in chapter 3 – the sparser population.

The probate inventories cover the great majority of farms with the exception of the largest, gentry-owned estates, and can be supplemented by wills and estate records for some points. Manorial records in the main, as was noted in chapter 2, are of only limited use, because most of the records which survive are concerned with the quitrents payable by free tenants and the registration of land sales and inheritances, rather than with the farming operations of the gentry or aristocratic home farm. They mainly serve to demonstrate how un-manorialized Wealden agriculture was. Equally unrepresented in most manorial records was the wide availability of land on short and medium-term leases at market rents which was

---

[4] Hasted, *Kent*, vii, p. 53.
[5] See map 1 in K. P. Witney, *The Jutish Forest* (1976); R. W. Gallois, *British Regional Geology: The Wealden District* (1965); map, p. 272, in Joan Thirsk (ed.), *The Agrarian History of England and Wales, v, 1640–1750* (Cambridge, 1985).

discussed in chapter 2. The real dearth of continuous series of estate accounts from the few large gentry estates, however, precludes any systematic study of who – gentry landowners or their big tenants – was benefiting most from the secular rise in farm commodity prices. What all the extant records agree about, however, is that landowners wealthy and not so wealthy regularly leased out a large share of their holdings. It is significant for a study of farming practice that the gentry landowners never farmed directly more than a fraction of their estates. Most of the agricultural land they owned, which was as we have seen often widely dispersed, was leased to a variety of tenants in parcels of varying sizes. When the large estates appear in exceptionally detailed inquisitions *post mortem* or Wards schedules, they show few gentry farming more than 100 or 150 acres on their own account. And farms for lease were provided not only by gentry estates. The wealthier Wealden clothiers, as will be shown in more detail later in the study, were also landowners who tended to lease out a substantial share of their holdings. And, of course, there were numerous owner-occupier farmers, but they too seem to have been limited to farms of 100 or 150 acres.

In terms of agricultural practice, then, the student of Wealden farming is dealing predominantly with small- and medium-sized farms: those that are described in the surviving probate inventories. Unfortunately it is next to impossible to match up farms described in inventories with holdings shown in manorial rentals, both because land is never described in wills as being held of such-and-such manor, and because most medium and large owner-occupier farmers held land of several lordships. In addition many farms seem to have included both freehold and leased land.

The numerous smallholdings and relatively small farms are the most characteristic feature of Wealden agriculture. In an age when in many parts of England the numbers of family farms was apparently declining, at least relatively, in the Weald they existed in profusion. The reasons for this prevalence of small farms in the late medieval Weald – and their survival into the late sixteenth century and beyond – have been alluded to in chapter 2: the tenurial peculiarities of gavelkind tenure, the original settlement in which land was held and farmed in severalty, and the absence of large fields. All these circumstances encouraged a busy land market in which the small closes of two to five acres could easily be sold or leased when surplus to requirements or when cash was urgently needed. The survival of hundreds of deeds which pre-date the Dissolution show an active market in these small parcels of land, whereas the sale of larger holdings was much less common before 1540. Partible inheritance acted as a brake on the consolidation of larger holdings, without preventing them altogether. Using probate inventories as one indicator, table 4.1 shows that a clear majority of deceased persons represented by inventories had carried on some farming activity just before they died. The figures would be higher if the numbers of retired farmers could be deducted from the total numbers of surviving inventories. This is not to postulate that a majority of adult males in the

Elizabethan Weald held a farm, for it is likely that most of the adults whose deaths went unnoticed by the probate courts were landless artisans or labourers. Nevertheless, the large number of inventories which show a small farm (whether in conjunction with a craft, or not), or which suggest a smallholding (the 'Smallholder Plus?' category in the table), together enforce the conclusion that agriculture in the Weald was not dominated by the large producers.

The surviving rate books and lists which record the occupiers of land in a given parish reinforce the results of an analysis of the size of farms based on probate inventories. The values displayed in tables 4.2 and 4.3 and figure 4.1 show that in most Wealden parishes there were scores of smallholders, substantial numbers of small and medium-sized farms and a limited number of larger holdings of sixty to at most a few hundred acres. Both of these sources, of course, exclude woodland held by occupiers. Together, the different sources show that farm land was widely, but not evenly distributed. They clearly indicate that the more substantial farmers (of sixty acres or more) controlled over forty per cent of farm land in many parishes, but that, also, small farmers (of ten to fifty-nine acres) held forty to fifty per cent of agricultural land. And, of course, in numerical terms, the typical farm was well under sixty acres.

The rate books (table 4.2) demonstrate that smallholders comprised a substantial share of Wealden households, and thus represent a very real element in the agricultural structure of the region, even if their output was commercially negligible. Their inventories show that many smallholders were labourers or artisans who supplemented their money wages with their own produce. They must have depended to a much greater degree than the farmers on the limited parish wasteland and commons for their pasture. For many, the only farming activity consisted of keeping a couple of cows, a few sheep and usually a few swine, and they would have been rivals of the totally landless for the small area of Wealden commons. As we have seen in chapter 2, the heroic days of Wealden settlement, when thousands of acres remained unclaimed and available to all for wood or for grazing, was long since past by the sixteenth century. Most woodland areas, except in the Lowy of Tonbridge, were privately held and not open to squatters (except on leases or at will, at market rents). With growing demand for wood by clothmakers and ironmasters, forests were far too valuable to be left open to all and sundry. The thousands of small parcels of woodland which were a part of most medium and larger estates played their small but not negligible part in the agricultural system. A tithe dispute from Staplehurst in 1613 reminds us that much woodland in the Weald was used to graze cattle. The parishioners insist that they should not be asked to pay tithe on their woodlands, 'for we do pay tithe for our cattle which do feed in our woods'.[6]

Parochial and manorial wastes existed in the Elizabethan period but they were

[6] PRO C 78/148 mm. 10–16.

Table 4.1 *Farming activity in Wealden inventories, 1565–99*

Parish	Farmer	Farmer/ tradesman	Smallholder plus?	Tradesman	Labourer or retired	No.
Benen.	33%	28%	7%	14%	18%	118
Beths.	47%	17%	14%	6%	15%	105
Bidd.	29%	20%	8%	24%	19%	98
Cranb.	22%	20%	5%	31%	22%	143
Goudh.	26%	24%	12%	20%	18%	105
Hald.	61%	10%	6%	4%	19%	48
Hawh.	21%	22%	16%	14%	27%	95
Mard.	47%	17%	11%	4%	21%	84
Rolv.	52%	15%	14%	6%	13%	109
Sandh.	63%	9%	7%	7%	14%	56
Smar.	41%	24%	14%	8%	13%	91
Stapl.	44%	16%	1%	13%	26%	70
Tent.	38%	13%	11%	11%	27%	158

Source: Canterbury diocese inventories cited in note 3, including all inventories from sample parishes except those of widows not practising a trade nor farming. The first three categories show some farming activity in inventories. Total number = 1,280.

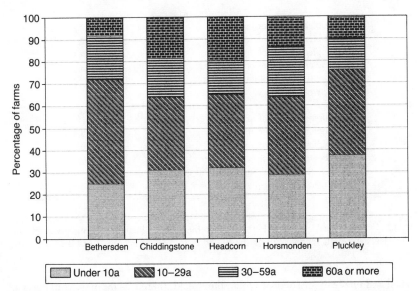

Figure 4.1 Distribution of farms by size in five sample parishes, from rates.

Table 4.2 *The occupiers of land in five Wealden parishes*

Chiddingstone, 1625

40 occupiers (31%) of under 10a.	188a.	(5%)
43 occupiers (33%) of 10–29a.	686a.	(17%)
23 occupiers (17.5%) of 30–59a.	888a.	(22%)
24 occupiers (18.5%) of 60a. or more	2195a.	(56%)
(Largest holding: 200a.)		
130 occupiers	*3957a.*	

Horsmonden, 1619

28 occupiers (29%) of under 10a.	125a.	(4.5%)
34 occupiers (35%) of 10–29a.	636a.	(23%)
22 occupiers (23%) of 30–59a.	848a.	(30.5%)
12 occupiers (13%) of 60a. or more	1171a.	(42%)
(Largest holding: 120a.)		
96 occupiers	*2779a.*	

Pluckley, 1628

31 occupiers (37.5%) of under 10a.	165a.	(8%)
32 occupiers (38.5%) of 10–29a.	540a.	(26%)
12 occupiers (14.5%) of 30–59a.	488a.	(23.5%)
8 occupiers (9.5%) of 60a. or more	884a.	(42.5%)
(Largest holding: 280a).		
83 occupiers	*2077a.*	

Bethersden, 1614

35 occupiers (25%) of under 10a.	165a.	(4.5%)
68 occupiers (47%) of 10–29a.	1063a.	(29.5%)
29 occupiers (20%) of 30–59a.	1134a.	(31.5%)
12 occupiers (8%) of 60a. or more	1256a.	(34.5%)
(Largest holding: 250a.)		
144 occupiers	*3618a.*	

Headcorn, 1640

37 occupiers (32%) of under 10a.	178a.	(5%)
38 occupiers (33%) of 10–29a.	683a.	(18.5%)
17 occupiers (15%) of 30–59a.	719a.	(19.5%)
24 occupiers (20%) of 60a. or more	2116a.	(57%)
(Largest holding: 184a.)		
116 occupiers	*3696a.*	

Sources: Chiddingstone: microfilm of parish register at KAO, at fos. 49–50; Horsmonden: KAO U 71/01; Pluckley: KAO P 289/5/1; Bethersden: vol. labelled 'Churchwardens and Overseers Accounts, 1576–1647' in the church, at fo. 104; Headcorn: KAO P 184/4/1 fos. 2–3.

small and unevenly distributed within the Weald: there was far more common and wasteland in the western Weald and along the Sussex border than in the populous central Weald parishes. In villages in and around Cranbrook it is unlikely that the limited commons could have accommodated the livestock of the thousands of poorer inhabitants of those parishes. Indeed it is doubtful if all inhabitants, as opposed to all landholders, had equal access to commons and wastes. While some parish wastes appear to have been open to all residents, certain 'commons' seem to have been restricted to landholders (i.e., the free tenants). The court of the 'manor' of Whiteherst in Marden asserted that the common there known as Marden Thorn was the property of the manor, although in 1610 it accepted as a free tenant the son of a man who in 1597 had built a cottage and enclosed a garden on the common without the licence of the lord or consent of the tenants.[7] Although evidence about access to commons is slender, it looks as if common land did not play a very important role in sustaining the region's burgeoning population. Nevertheless, to the extent that smallholders produced some of the foodstuffs they consumed, the numbers which depended wholly on the market were reduced. This was of real significance in a region which even at the best of times never produced food surpluses (other than beef), and normally imported a proportion of the cereals it consumed from north Kent.

The Wealden smallholders were distinguishable from the labourers and poor artisans whose inventories show neither livestock nor gardens. Both groups – smallholders and landless labourers and craftsmen – are seriously under-represented in the probate records, but in the relatively few inventories which were recorded for the Wealden poor the difference between those with some land and those with none are clear. The smallholders are usually slightly wealthier, because the value of a few livestock bulk large in a total inventory of less than £15. But the slight difference in money terms must have meant a real difference in living standards. It is the landless whom some parish registers are most likely to label 'poor householder' at the occasion of their burial.[8] The smallholders were certainly agriculturists of a sort, but none were 'farmers' within the definition used for the remainder of this chapter.

The analysis of farming practices which follows is based on the farms of those above the smallholders on the social ladder, and all will be referred to as 'farmers'

---

[7] See, e.g., the dispute over access to commons in Hawkhurst and Cranbrook, 1567–8, with access given only to certain landholders: PRO C 78/38 no. 12; C 3/27/5. A list of commons and wasteland can be assembled, but in most cases their size cannot be determined. Some examples are Cranbrook: Wilsley common, 1611 (KAO QM/SIq/40); Frittenden: Frittenden Brook, 1570 (PRO C 54/836 m. 48), Singsted Green (Hasted, *Kent*, vii, map of Cranbrook); Horsmonden: Horsmonden Hoath, 1639 (KAO U 86/P2; U 180/P1); Hawkhurst: Seacock's Heath and open land between the two main villages of the parish (KAO U 1050/T1; Hasted, *Kent*, vii, p. 146, map of Great Barnfield and Selbrittenden hundreds); Goudhurst: Kilndown Common (Hasted, *Kent*, vii, map of Marden hundred, and as a waste, 1638, KAO U 1006/M17); Marden: Marden Thorn, 1590s (BL Add. MS. 33,889 fo. 154, and Hasted, *Kent*, map of Marden hundred); Brenchley: Pearson's Green and Low Waste (KAO U 86/P2); Lamberhurst: Lamberhurst Down, Hock Green and Freeheath Common, all in Sussex (KAO U 200/P1); Hadlow: Hadlow Common, 1621 (KAO U 31/P3); Hunton: Cockshoath, 1563 (KAO U 282/M9); Leigh: Blackhoath *alias* Newberyhoath, 1519 and 1570 (KAO U 908/T16, 12, 19, 21). In this period the only unsettled woodland and waste was in Tonbridge parish: C. W. Chalklin, 'The Rural Economy of a Kentish Wealden Parish, 1650–1750', *AgHR*, 10 (1962).

[8] Robt. Bronger of Staplehurst was called 'poor householder' when buried in Jan. 1577: parish register; his movables came to £8 5s. in the inventory, and show no farming at all: KAO PRC 10/9 fo. 93.

or 'farmer/tradesmen', irrespective of their tenurial position. In both cases the probate inventories of such persons (including widows) show substantially greater farming activities and goods than those of the smallholders. The line between peasant or family farmers or husbandmen and smallholders may be occasionally difficult to draw, but logically it should be between those with farms extensive enough to maintain a small household, and, on the other hand, farming which is no more than supplementary. The farms of many tradesmen and artisans are also included in most of the tables, if their farms, taken on their own, might have supported a small family. Most of the farms on which the chapter is based were mixed arable and livestock enterprises. Only a small minority were devoted wholly to livestock. The purely livestock units were not limited to very small farms, or the farms of tradesmen and craftsmen, but are to be found among all levels of farmers, albeit in quite small numbers. Though they are not included in some of the tables, they should not be lost sight of; if anything they are pointers to the future, more specialized, husbandry best suited to the Weald.

The predominance of small- and medium-sized farms is apparent in both High and Low Weald parishes (tables 4.2, 4.3, figure 2.2), even when smallholders are ignored. More than two-thirds of farmers in both High and Low Weald parishes had under ten acres in crop (and hence well under fifteen acres of arable land). At the same time, six out of ten Wealden farms had under twenty acres of pasture. And, if many of the smaller farmers grazed some of their stock on parish wastes, then their pasture acreage was somewhat less than the averages shown in table 4.3. These estimates of 'arable' and 'pasture' acreage are calculated on the assumption that most farmers were not practising convertible husbandry, which is unproven but likely to have been the case. Even if some ley farming was going on, with farmers using their fields in rotation for cereals and grass, the total of their 'arable' and 'pasture' acreage is still likely to provide a reasonable estimate of their farming land.

The number of large farms was minute. In seven sample parishes covering High and Low Weald districts, between 1565 and 1601 only twelve inventories showed either ten acres or more of winter cereals or twenty sown acres or above in the summer. The few gentry estates would add only a handful of additional large farms at any one time to those included in the extant probate records. Measured in terms of pasture area, only about 15 per cent of farms (between 1565 and 1601) in the same seven parishes had forty acres or more of meadow and pasture, fifty-three farms to be precise. And farms with over 100 acres in all were quite rare: only fifteen farms had pasture estimated at seventy-five acres or over, which suggests a total farm size of more than 100 acres. At any one time a medium-sized Wealden parish of 4,000–7,000 acres would boast no more than two or three farms of more than 100 acres (excluding woods); the same hypothetical parish might also contain ten to twenty medium-sized farms of sixty to 100 acres, and many more small farms of under fifty acres. This hypothetical portrait of a parish's farms is over-simplified of course: as stressed in chapter 1, almost any reasonably large holding in the Weald

Table 4.3 Size of farms from probate inventories (1565–1601)

High Weald parishes

Parish	Arable Acreage[a] Mean	Median	Range of acreage in crop (%) Up to 4a.	Up to 6a.	Up to 10a.	Up to 20a.	Over 20a.
Benenden	10a. (48 farms)	7.5a.	38.5%	15.4%	23.1%	18%	5.1%
Cranbrook	14a. (30 farms)	12.5a.	34.5%	6.9%	13.8%	34.5%	10.4%
Hawkhurst	9.5a. (31 farms)	6.5a.	41.9%	25.8%	12.9%	12.9%	6.5%

Parish	Pasture Acreage[b] Mean	Median	Range of pasture acreage (%) Up to 10a.	Up to 20a.	Up to 40a.	Over 40a.
Beneden	24.9a (69 farms)	17a.	33.3%	23.2%	28.9%	14.5%
Cranbrook	27.2a. (53 farms)	18a.	22.6%	32.1%	22.6%	22.6%
Hawkhurst	17a. (39 farms)	13.5a.	38.5%	41%	10.3%	10.3%

Low Weald parishes

Parish	Arable Acreage[a] Mean	Median	Range of acreage in crop (%) Up to 4a.	Up to 6a.	Up to 10a.	Up to 20a.	Over 20a.
Bethersden	10.5a. (44 farms)	8a.	30.2%	20.9%	23.3%	23.3%	2.3%
Biddenden	11a. (39 farms)	11a.	25.6%	15.4%	33.3%	23.1%	2.6%
Marden	15a. (37 farms)	12a.	10.5%	21.1%	21.1%	42.1%	5.3%
Staplehurst	13a. (34 farms)	11.5a.	14.7%	20.6%	35.3%	26.5%	3%

Parish	Pasture Acreage[b] Mean	Median	Range of pasture acreage (%) Up to 10a.	Up to 20a.	Up to 40a.	Over 40a.
Bethersden	28.3a. (39 farms)	17.5a.	17.3%	40.4%	23.1%	19.2%
Biddenden	21.4a. (44 farms)	17a.	25%	38.6%	31.8%	4.6%
Marden	25.8a. (40 farms)	20.5a.	22.5%	32.5%	25%	20%
Staplehurst	23.7a. (40 farms)	15.5a.	37.5%	22.5%	20%	20%

Notes:
[a] The first two columns include an estimate for fallow at 25% of total arable acreage.
[b] Based on stocking estimates of 1.5 acres per head of cattle or horses, 0.5 acre per sheep or colt, and not counting calves, lambs or other livestock.

was likely to contain fields in more than one parish, and that degree of dispersion would have been commonplace among farms of 100 acres or more. The greatest distance between outlying fields in such a farm might still be under five kilometres. What percentage of these large farms was operated by tenants of the gentry and what proportion by yeomen freeholders cannot be estimated, but it is certain that at least some of the large farms were owner-occupied. It should also be borne in mind that some of the larger leaseholders were also substantial freeholders in their own right.

To what extent were the High Weald and Low Weald distinct agricultural regions in the sixteenth century? Kerridge thought they were, in part because of the differences in soil and in part because he detected distinct agricultural regimes (although both were broadly speaking pastoral systems). The High Weald, he argued, specialized in cattle-rearing, while Wealden Vale farmers were primarily concerned with cattle-fattening. The volume of the *Agrarian History of England and Wales* dealing with the century following 1640 also treats the Weald as containing two agrarian regions. But it must be said that sixteenth-century records show little evidence of different emphases in pastoral farming between High and Low Weald parishes. There were small numbers of large, commercial farms in both areas, and stock rearing and fattening seem to have been the practice of big farmers in both High and Low Weald parishes. Clearly distinct agricultural systems had not yet emerged in the Weald. But, there were visible differences in the agrarian regimes of the two districts, which can be studied in tables 4.3 and 4.4. Most importantly, farms were somewhat larger in the Low Weald than in the High Weald (at least in Canterbury diocese whose inventories have survived). This correlates logically with the evidence presented in chapter 3 that the central High Weald parishes were relatively densely populated. The sample farms in three High Weald parishes (Benenden, Cranbrook and Hawkhurst) had median arable acreages of under nine acres, compared to a median of 11.5 acres in three Low Weald parishes (Biddenden, Marden and Staplehurst). The median pasture acreage on farms in the three Low Weald was also slightly larger than farms in High Weald parishes, eighteen acres compared to sixteen acres. This pattern is confirmed by the ratios between livestock and corn values shown in the inventories of the two sets of High and Low Weald farms. In both summer and winter inventories the livestock to corn ratios were greater in the High Weald than in Low Weald parishes, indicating also that somewhat more land was devoted to cereals on Low Weald farms than on those further south. This tallies with the conventional view that there was more extremely poor (for cereals) soil in the High Weald than in the Low Weald.

Despite this detectable difference, the emphasis was strongly towards pastoral husbandry in both areas. Kerridge's contention that High Weald farms carried three sheep to every head of cattle (and that farmers in the Wealden Vales kept far fewer sheep) is not borne out in the sixteenth-century inventories. In the High Weald parish of Benenden, for example, out of fifty-seven sixteenth-century inventories describing working farms, there were medium-sized or substantial sheep flocks in just seventeen. Many small farms in the High Weald kept few or no sheep. In the sixteenth century, at least, the only significant difference between Low and High Weald parishes was the greater proportion of small farms in the most densely populated High Weald parishes. Farmers may indeed have been practising up-and-down husbandry, whereby individual fields or closes which had carried a cereal crop for a number of years were then laid down to grass for long periods, while other closes which had been used for pasture were ploughed up for arable crops. The dispersed and enclosed nature of Wealden farms – in both the High Weald and in the Vales – easily allowed for a transition to convertible husbandry, especially for the bigger farmers. But there is little evidence for Kerridge's sweeping assertion that up-and-down husbandry rapidly became the norm in the Wealden Vales from 1540. Woodland clearances there certainly were, but in 1600 substantial areas of woods remained in most Wealden parishes, not only those of the High Weald. The more refined agricultural specialization detected in the different parts of the Weald by the eighteenth century had not, before 1640, been established.[9]

The typical Wealden farm (figure 2.2), including many run by tradesmen, had no more than six to nine acres in crop, representing eight to twelve acres of arable. From one sample parish to another there was a considerable range, with mean summer sown acreage varying from six acres in Benenden to over a dozen in Sandhurst with its quite small sample. From the few inventories which record fallow acreage, it would appear that most Wealden farmers planted about 75 per cent of their arable each year. The inventories show no direct evidence of ley farming, but the information found in inventories would be unlikely to give such evidence even if convertible husbandry was being practised. On almost all Wealden farms the pasture acreage considerably exceeded arable. Though averages again varied from one parish to another, the 'typical' farm contained fifteen to twenty acres of grassland, somewhat less than twice the arable acreage. The majority of farms therefore totalled twenty-five to thirty-five acres, with a sizeable minority ranging up to seventy-five acres or so. In addition, of course, there would have been dozens of smallholdings in most Wealden parishes, ranging in size from a mere garden to holdings of two or three pieces of land containing five to ten acres in all.

The Weald in the broadest sense was a pastoral farming district. Nevertheless, most farms had some arable land. Wealden farmers tended to stick to a traditional balance of cereal crops, with little indication that novel cash crops or fodder crops had made any impact before the end of Elizabeth's reign. By and large, about half the sown acreage was devoted to a winter grain – usually wheat – and most of the other half was sown with the most appropriate spring-sown cereal for the heavy, poorly drained clays, oats. In a few of the sample parishes oats actually accounted for more than half of the cropped acreage in all the summer inventories combined.

[9] Eric Kerridge, *The Agricultural Revolution* (1967); Thirsk, *Agrarian History*, v, pt. 1, pp. 270–3.

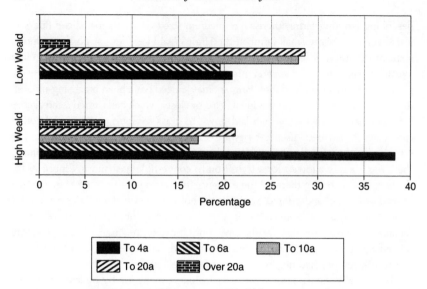

Figure 4.2　Arable acreage in Weald farms, 1565–1601.

In none of the parishes did wheat comprise as much as fifty per cent, but in five of them there was nevertheless more wheat planted than oats. The crop acreages found in inventories covering the 1560s to the 1590s have been grouped together, because there appears to have been no change in the choice or balance of crops which farmers planted during the whole period. Wheat and oats were dominant throughout the Weald, with the exception of Tenterden, a parish that was also exceptional in the amount of marshland within its bounds. Peas and beans were the next most common crops, with many farms showing one or two acres of these pulses, planted presumably as fodder crops. Only in Goudhurst and Hawkhurst (both High Weald) were peas and beans a major component of the spring-sown arable. Why these two parishes should differ in this regard from neighbouring Benenden and Sandhurst is not clear. Rye appears occasionally in farm inventories, usually sown in small quantities alongside wheat. Barley only very rarely occurs, in very small amounts, and hops do not figure in the inventories. Crops planted in gardens are not covered in most inventories, and since hops were first planted in gardens, it may be that hops had already been introduced in a small way before 1600. The predominance of wheat and oats is the region's hallmark, as has also been shown in studies of Sussex farming.[10] It followed then that of necessity malting barley was imported into the Weald from downland Sussex or from east Kent.

[10] C. E. Brent, 'Rural Employment and Population in Sussex between 1550 and 1640', *Sussex Archaeological Collections*, 114 (1976), esp. pp. 38–48; G. H. Kenyon, 'Kirdford Inventories', *ibid.*, 93 (1955); Julian Cornwall, 'Farming in Sussex', *ibid.*, 92 (1954); C. E. Brent, *The Rural Economy of Eastern Sussex, 1500–1700* (E. Sussex Records Office, 1978). An early reference to hops is in a nuisance case over damage to the 'hop garden' of Alex. Brickenden, gent. in 1606: KAO QM/SB/1350.

Table 4.4 *Arable and livestock on Wealden farms, 1565–1601*

| | Summer inventories w/known acreage | | | | | Winter inventories | |
Parish (No.)	Wheat	Oats	Peas/B.	Other	Ratio	No.	Ratio
Benen. (16)	47%	46%	1%	6%	3.4:1	20	3.0:1
Beths. (20)	46%	53%	1%	–	3.0:1	10	4.2:1
Bidd. (18)	48%	52%	–	–	2.5:1	16	3.2:1
Cranb. (12)	43%	49%	2%	6%	3.7:1	13	3.2:1
Goudh. (6)	44%	39%	15%	2%	2.1:1	9	3.0:1
Halden (13)	42%	57%	–	1%	3.7:1	13	4.6:1
Hawkh. (13)	48%	41%	11%	–	2.1:1	12	3.9:1
Marden (26)	47%	48%	3%	2%	2.3:1	12	2.2:1
Rolv. (20)	47%	43%	4%	6%	3.7:1	30	3.3:1
Sandh. (10)	42%	54%	3.5%	0.5%	3.5:1	13	3.6:1
Staple (12)	47%	47.5%	4%	1.5%	2.7:1	13	2.3:1
Tent. (16)	48%	32%	14%	6%	5.3:1	18	4.4:1

Note: 'Other' grains covers rye and barley. The 'ratio' is the inventory values of all livestock to all corn (excluding hay) in each estate: the ratios for each farm in a parish have been averaged for both summer and winter figures, so the 'ratio' is a composite picture of the comparative values in each parish. Very small farms have been excluded. *Source:* inventories cited in note 3.

There is little evidence about crop rotation in the sources for this period. It is probable that the small arable fields were cropped in the most simple rotations, including a fallow, but fields on the very best, well-drained soils may have been cropped more intensively than the norm. The one Elizabethan lease which has anything at all to say about farming methods specifies only that the farmer must not sow oats in two consecutive years in the same fields. Hardly a remarkably advanced demand![11]

Arable farming, however, was by no means the main business of the Wealden farmer. In this region of heavy clays and frequent hills and valleys, the balance of the agrarian regime was tipped heavily in the direction of livestock husbandry, more especially towards cattle rearing and fattening. This can be demonstrated from a variety of sources, from sixteenth- and seventeenth-century husbandry treatises to estate records and probate inventories. Almost without exception, the inventories which show any type of farming invariably include cattle. It is exceedingly difficult to find an inventory with crops but no livestock, but relatively common to find small farms with livestock but no corn. At the other end of the scale, the wealthiest farmers were rich in cattle, not in cereals.

The balance between livestock and corn can be measured in a number of ways, and these are shown in the tables. One method is to compare the money value

[11] KAO U 409/78.

assigned to livestock in inventories with that placed on all corn, whether in the barn or on the ground. This can be presented either as a livestock to corn ratio, or as the percentage share of, say, livestock to the value of animals and corn combined. Another method is to compare the estimated amount of land devoted to crops with the amount of pasture necessary for the livestock listed in the inventory. Table 4.4 allows a comparison of the livestock to corn ratios (in money values) in both summer and winter inventories. It might be hypothesized that the livestock to corn ratio would be relatively lower in the spring and summer since it included the value of both winter and spring sown crops. On the other hand, the reverse might also be expected: that there would be more animals to be valued in spring and summer than in the valuations made in autumn or winter. The sample inventories from Wealden farms show that both in the winter and in the months between spring sowing and harvest the value of farmers' livestock was at least twice that of their corn. The variations among the ratios, both as between seasons and as between parishes, suggest a good deal of local variety in farming, but also puts paid to the old chestnut that farmers regularly sold or slaughtered most of their cattle at the beginning of winter. In half the parishes the mean livestock to corn ratio was higher in the summer than in the winter inventories; in the other half the situation was reversed. But in all the parishes the mean ratio of livestock to corn was at least two to one. The mean ratio of all the parochial averages was over three to one. If the value of hay had been included, the margin between livestock and corn would have been further increased. In percentage terms the predominance of livestock can be shown just as strongly.[12]

Wealden meadows were regularly mown, and the resulting hay along with the cheaper grain grown by farmers sufficed to feed most of their livestock during the winter months, and allowed them to sell their real cash crop, cattle, when the return was highest. Only two parishes show a consistently lower ratio between livestock and corn, Marden and Staplehurst. Both are in the less hilly, Low Weald area, and farmers there seem to have planted somewhat larger cereal crops than their counterparts in other Wealden parishes. But even in those two parishes, the livestock to corn ratios of the appraised values in inventories were over two to one.

Land use on Wealden farms, as estimated from the probate inventories, clearly demonstrates the bias towards livestock. In both High and Low Weald parishes the average arable acreage is only about half the estimated pasture acreage (table 4.3). In fact the livestock to corn ratios correlate quite well with the equivalent ratios between pasture and arable land. Marden's farms appear again to have had a somewhat closer balance between corn and livestock, while Hawkhurst had, in

---

[12] Livestock as a percentage of corn and livestock combined (but excluding hay) in seven sample parishes: High Weald: Benenden (sixty-nine farms), 75 per cent; Cranbrook (fifty-four), 77.5 per cent; Hawkhurst (thirty-five), 71 per cent; Low Weald: Bethersden (fifty-six), 75.5 per cent; Biddenden (forty-four), 73 per cent; Marden (forty-three), 66 per cent; Staplehurst (forty-one), 69.5 per cent. See the useful study of James Yelling, 'The Combination and Rotation of Crops in E. Worcestershire, 1540–1660', *AgHR*, 17 (1969).

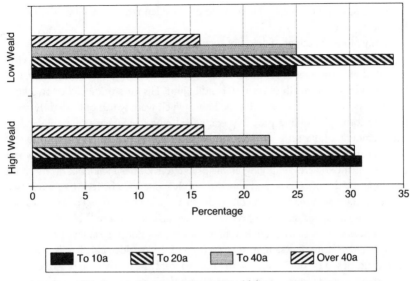

Figure 4.3   Pasture acreage in Weald farms, 1565–1601.

general, exceptionally small farms. Hawkhurst was also the most densely populated rural Wealden parish (see table 3.12). The general rule appears to be, the greater the share of small family farms in the sample, the greater the likelihood that farmland will be more evenly divided between arable and pasture (and the livestock to corn ratio lower).

Wealden farmland was not suited to cereals. However, in this period before the 'agricultural revolution' and before convertible husbandry had made any widespread impact, specialization had not advanced to the point when clayland farmers could give up arable farming. As yet no national – or even regional – market structure was advanced enough for that to have been a practical possibility. The small farmers who planted wheat at least insulated themselves from the vagaries of the market, for their bread, even if yields on Wealden soils were lower than elsewhere. For many farmers wheat was a useful cash crop, especially in a region with so many landless mouths to feed, and where wheaten bread seems to have been the norm for rich and poor alike in most years. Oats actually grew well in Wealden soils, and although worth only about half as much as wheat per acre, it could be fed to animals and served as a bread grain for the local poor in years of dearth. The Wealden farm therefore remained a mixed enterprise for a number of good reasons, but livestock probably provided the lion's share of the cash income. In general, as the size and value of farms moved upwards, so the ratio between livestock and corn grew larger. The big commercial farms in the Weald were notable for the size of their herds, while their cereal acreage was only two or three times that of the typical small farmer's. A few examples, chosen from the more informative inventories, will illustrate best the range of Wealden farms as well as the typical farming regime.

Family farms abounded. Typical of such small mixed farming units was the estate of Thomas Turner of Marden (June 1571), worth in total under £25. His crop consisted of three acres of wheat, four acres of oats and a half an acre of barley, and he still had £1 12s. worth of corn on hand in June. His livestock included two kine, two heifers, a calf, one mare and three hogs, which were worth only slightly more than his corn. His holding probably comprised nine to ten acres of arable and an equal amount of pasture. A different balance was struck by Richard Allen of Goudhurst (April 1573), whose chattels were worth just over £25. His winter wheat crop was just two acres (implying arable of five to six acres in all), but his livestock were appraised at £14 10s., and consisted of five kine, two heifers, two buds, two bullocks, one calf, a mare and a colt, eight sheep and three hogs. For his livestock Allen would have needed twenty to twenty-two acres of pasture.[13] Neither of these farmers possessed his own plough or plough team, nor did most small- and medium-sized Wealden farms. In a sample of farms from seven Wealden parishes, based again on inventories, 113 out of 295 farms (38 per cent) had two or more oxen. The percentage varied from 28 per cent (Benenden) to 58 per cent in wealthy Cranbrook.[14]

Representative of the medium-sized farms was that of Edmund Baker of Rolvenden (April 1572), whose goods totalled £69. He owned eleven kine or heifers, a bull, three buds, plus a mare, six sheep and three hogs. The livestock to corn ratio for his farm was 2.7:1, and his holding had nine to ten acres of arable and twenty-five to thirty acres of grass. Equally typical was the farm of John Smith of Benenden (April 1593), whose chattels came to £54 in all. He had five acres of wheat and four acres of oats, and his livestock included four steers, three one-year bullocks, three kine, two heifers and a calf, as well as a mare, eight ewes with lambs and some swine. His arable lands would have come to twelve acres and his stock grazed on twenty to twenty-five acres. The livestock to corn ratio was 2.9:1.[15]

A small number of large, commercially-oriented farms dotted the Wealden countryside. They must have played a leading role in the commercial life of the parish, as well as being a significant source of domestic and agricultural employment. Christopher Vynie, 'yeoman' of Staplehurst (d. 1577) farmed on a large scale. His inventory total was over £190, and it showed that he had planted twenty-three acres of cereals that year. His livestock were valued at £106, and his will records that he owned land in six other parishes as well as in Staplehurst. Unfortunately the will doesn't divulge how many of his outlying properties were leased out and how

---

[13] KAO PRC 10/5 fo. 240; 10/6 fo. 308v.

[14] From the total sample of farm inventories. Parish totals were: Benenden (sixty farms), 28 per cent; Cranbrook (thirty-six), 58 per cent; Hawkhurst (thirty-two), 31 per cent; Bethersden (forty-seven), 30 per cent; Biddenden (forty-one), 41 per cent; Marden (forty), 45 per cent; Staplehurst (thirty-nine), 41 per cent.   [15] KAO PRC 10/6 fo. 224v; 10/20 fo. 213.

many he farmed himself. But it does mention specifically three male servants. Vynie's 1572 subsidy assessment of £26 in goods made him one of the three highest-rated taxpayers in the parish.[16] It is likely that the large farms like that of Christopher Vynie produced the bulk of the livestock that entered the flows of long-distance trade, in this case the trade with London.

The scale of operation of an extensive, gentry-owned farm in the early sixteenth century can be seen from the few surviving accounts of the bailiff of husbandry to Thomas Willoughby, Esq. of Bore Place, Chiddingstone, in the western Weald. For the year ending 25 March 1519 the stock remaining on Willoughby's home farm amounted to twenty-six oxen, five steers, thirty-one kine, three bulls, nineteen ewes, fifteen wethers, one ram, nine horses and mares and six colts. During the year the bailiff sold eighteen oxen, fourteen steers, twenty-five kine, eight calves, two bulls, seventeen lambs, a colt and two horses. In addition nine oxen, six steers, fourteen kine, nineteen calves, thirty-two ewes, nineteen wethers, two rams and nine lambs were accounted for by household consumption! Just to carry the stock remaining a year's end would have required upwards of 130 acres of grassland: considering that neither calves nor lambs were included in the March account, Willoughby's pasture was probably closer to 150 acres. In the 1518 account is a note of the farm's arable crops: sixteen acres of wheat and twenty-four acres of oats, indicating arable land of fifty to fifty-five acres. So the pasture on Willoughby's farm was about three times the acreage of the arable. In 1518–19 Willoughby's bailiff realized about £60 from livestock sales, which probably made it the second most important source of rural income, after rent from Willoughby's tenanted lands.[17]

A rare Prerogative Court of Canterbury inventory of the goods of Dame Constance Culpeper, dated 1542, gives one other example of gentry farming operations. The farm goods on the Culpeper estate in Goudhurst were valued at almost £100 – this at a date just before the mid century price rise. The sown arable was fourteen acres of wheat and thirty-four acres of oats, representing about sixty-five acres of arable land. Like the Willoughby home farm in the western Weald, the Culpepers planted far more oats than wheat; enough wheat to serve a large household, but sowing oats over a large acreage to take advantage of its relatively higher yield on Wealden soils. The livestock on the Culpeper farm was mainly cattle – in fact a herd of almost 100 cattle – along with forty adult sheep. On my estimate the pasture required for the stock would have come to about 160 acres, well over twice the arable acreage. In all the Culpepers' home farm totalled about 220 acres, which from late sixteenth- and early seventeenth-century evidence based on rate assessments was about as large as any farm in the Kent Weald.[18]

Estates like the Willoughbys' and the Culpepers' were exceptional in the Weald during any part of the century. Lower down the social scale, although often equivalent in terms of their direct farming operations, were the estates of the minor

---

[16] KAO PRC 10/9 fo. 125; PRC 17/43 fo. 66; PRO E 179/126/423.
[17] KAO U 1000/3/E11–12. [18] KAO U 660/F1.

gentry and prosperous yeomen like Christopher Vynie. Only a very few of these were comparable to the farms of the wealthy East Kent arable farmers, many of whom owned agricultural goods worth 300–500 pounds and more. Nevertheless, there were a few Wealden farmers who were as well off as any of their neighbours except the most successful clothiers or the leading gentry. Robert Willard died late in 1572, leaving chattels worth £161. His winter wheat alone extended to thirteen acres, and he also had £14 worth of corn in store. But his livestock were worth almost half the value of his whole moveable estate: four oxen, nine kine, six young steers, eight one-year bullocks, ten weaners and a bull, as well as sixty-eight sheep, three mares and a colt. His farmland therefore consisted of about thirty-five acres of arable and approximately seventy-five to eighty acres of pasture. In neighbouring Benenden, Thomas Sharpe's total estate came to £323 in December 1586. His winter wheat covered twelve acres, and his livestock included four oxen, four steers, fourteen 'two-years', eight 'one-years', eleven Welsh bullocks, twelve kine, a bull and ten weaners, plus 62 sheep and lambs, four horses and four colts. Sharpe's farmland would have comprised about thirty acres of arable and at least 100 acres of grass; the livestock to corn ratio was 4.3:1. A final example is Stephen Gibbon of Rolvenden, whose family would soon be recognized as gentlemen. His 1570 estate totalled £339, including debts due worth £85. He had 8 acres of wheat in the ground, and £13 worth of corn in his barn, itself more than the total value of corn harvested by most Wealden farmers. But that was small beer compared to his livestock, rated at more than £110. He owned fifty-four head of cattle and a large sheep flock by Wealden standards, eighty-one animals. Gibbon's farm was thus made up of about twenty to twenty-five acres of arable and 125 acres of pasture.[19] A much more detailed account of the commercial agriculture of the Weald cannot be given, because runs of estate accounts from any of the large farms have not survived; but the inventory evidence suggests certain generalizations.

Raising and fattening cattle for the market was the mainspring of Wealden agriculture, and involved most farmers in exchange transactions even if only within the local market sphere. For those with access to substantial acreage and cash, fattening store cattle purchased either in the metropolitan markets or at the main Kentish cattle markets was as important as rearing their own stock. The inventories of many wealthier farmers include non-local breeds, the most favoured being 'Northerns' and Welsh. Stephen Gibbon, mentioned above, had ten 'Northern runts', and another prosperous grazier, Thomas Boone of Biddenden, had both Northern heifers and bullocks in his herd. Boone also owed £17 to 'the Welshman' for cattle, while Thomas Sharpe of Benenden counted eleven Welsh bullocks among his stock.[20] Many of the specialist graziers not only occupied scores of acres of grass in the Weald, but also owned or hired summer grazing in Romney Marsh or in the

[19] KAO PRC 10/6 fo. 311; 10/15 fo. 281v; 10/5 fo. 55.
[20] KAO PRC 10/7 fo. 197: Boone's total was £227. Cf. a case concerning a Yorkshire drover and the Northern steers he attempted to sell in Kent and Sussex in 1601: KAO QM/SB/376.

parish of Tenterden.[21] It has already been shown in chapter 2 that many large freehold estates included outlying land in the Marsh; it appears from many inventories that the big commercial farms used such marshland as part of their overall livestock operations, mainly as summer grazing. Marshland grazing was suitable for sheep as well as cattle, and was still being used by Wealden farmers in the 1840s.[22]

But even at the level of the family farm, the emphasis was on beef even if the farmer was selling only half a dozen beasts a year at a Kentish market. The small farmer – like the smallholder – usually kept one or two dairy cattle, but what distinguished the farmer from the cottager was the presence of bullocks and steers. Dairying, especially cheese and butter making, is in evidence on most farms, but there is little indication of commercial dairy production or sales to London. It seems that by the late sixteenth century if not earlier some pastoral districts leaned to dairying while others, including the Weald, were more specialized beef producers.

A large share of the Wealden herds was probably destined for the London market, although cattle may have passed through several hands in the course of that journey. Kentish steers and bullocks were driven on the hoof to the London and Southwark markets, but since the internal trade in cattle was unregulated until it reached the capital's official markets, there is no documentary evidence on which to estimate the volume of cattle sent by various regions to London. It is also likely that Wealden cattle were sold to butchers and graziers from Ashford, Maidstone and the north Kent towns. A simple flow chart of agricultural commodity movements within Kent would show livestock from the Weald moving north and east, while grain – especially barley – moved in the opposite direction. Within the Weald itself there was a market for livestock too, probably drawing heavily on the animals reared by the lesser farmers who never considered sending their stock to London. Certainly the local butchers of the larger Wealden towns and villages had a convenient market for their surplus hides, for most parishes supported one or two well-off tanners. In fact there was a significant concentration of the leather industry in the western Weald and in the several parishes just to the north around Brasted, a phenomenon which will be treated in greater detail in the next chapter.[23]

The ubiquity of cattle in the Weald – as compared to other livestock – is graphically demonstrated in table 4.5, based on probate inventories of farmers from both High and Low Weald parishes. Cattle were universally kept, with moderately large herds owned by between forty and fifty per cent of farmers. Most farmers owned at least one mare: the sale of her offspring would have been a useful addition

---

[21] E.g., Boone, note 20 above; also Pet. Piers of Tenterden (1572), total estate £350: the appraisers mentioned three leases of marshland, and much of his stock, especially the sheep, was pastured in Romney and Guildford marshes: KAO PRC 10/6 fo. 151v.

[22] Roger J. P. Kain and Hugh C. Prince, *The Tithe Surveys of England and Wales* (1985), pp. 235–7.

[23] Most of the tanners informed against for infractions of penal statutes who lived in Kent came from the west Weald and the four parishes west of Sevenoaks: PRO KR Memoranda Rolls (E 159) Recorda section, *passim*.

Table 4.5 *Livestock on Wealden farms, 1565–1601*

		Cattle		Sheep		Horses	
		1 or	10 or	1 or	30 or	1 or	3 or
Parish	No.	more	more	more	more	more	more
Benenden	73	100%	38%	59%	19%	89%	26%
Cranbrook	57	100%	56%	40%	14%	84%	35%
Hawkhurst	41	100%	37%	32%	7%	81%	15%
Rolvenden	55	100%	60%	71%	29%	82%	40%
Bethersden	54	100%	46%	80%	11%	89%	39%
Biddenden	46	100%	36%	56%	7%	84%	31%
Marden	43	98%	44%	77%	14%	88%	42%
Staplehurst	41	100%	49%	51%	12%	83%	46%

Notes: 'Cattle' includes calves, oxen; 'sheep' excludes lambs; 'horses' includes colts.

to the income from cattle sales each year. The more specialized, large-scale breeding of horses, however, remained an avocation for gentlemen and royal officials.[24] Although horses were not used for ploughing, they were in constant demand for carrying goods and timber and for personal transport. A mare could be had for about £1 in the 1560s, within the reach of many householders and all 'farmers'; fine geldings were valued at £2–3 or more in the same period. Finally, a majority of Wealden farmers owned some sheep. In most cases they seem to have been kept for household use, for the table and for the domestic spinning of wool. Well under a fifth of farms carried flocks of as many as thirty sheep, and it is rare indeed to find flocks of a hundred or more. In the more important sheep-breeding regions of Kent, both in the north and in Romney Marsh, flocks numbering in the hundreds were commonplace. Wealden grassland was not ideal sheep country, and even the considerable market offered by the Wealden broadcloth industry could not alter the agricultural ecology of the region. Indeed the few Wealden graziers who owned large flocks tended to acquire marsh grazing for them. To sum up then, the region's commercial agriculture was basically pastoral, and cattle were the prime commodity.

The backbone of the Wealden economy more generally was agricultural in the widest sense, despite the presence of both cloth and ironmaking. The distinction often seen in occupational studies between 'craftsmen and tradesmen' on the one hand and 'farmers' on the other, is not a useful one for the Weald, nor probably for other similar regions. A more useful distinction might be drawn between families with farms, and families without. The widespread combination of active farming with artisanal or trade employment may well be emphasized even more strongly

[24] Joan Thirsk, *Horses in Early Modern England* (University of Reading, 1978). Best documented are the Sidneys at Penshurst.

than the comparatively large share of the Wealden population which lived by some non-agricultural occupation. In the sixteenth century all manner of craftsmen and tradesmen combined farming with their trade or handicraft. This applies not only to domestic workers in the cloth industry, but to people involved in most crafts from the metal and leather trades to tailors and carpenters. More than half the tradesmen identified by their inventories were also farmers, and that does not include the poorer rural artisans who kept a couple of cows or swine only. Higher up the social and economic ladder, most of the wealthier tradesmen and clothiers also ran farms, and – it may be guessed – financed their commercial operations in part from the profits of farming. Many of them were rentiers as well, as an examination of their wills discloses.

The Wealden agrarian regime – which provided the setting and the opportunities for clothmaking and other rural industry – was fundamentally different from the farming systems of the manorialized and champion districts of England which normally occupy the attention of historians. In much of England farmers operated within a system of communally organized agriculture. The holdings of most farmers, especially the copyholders, were spread over two or three village fields, each man's strips interspersed among those of other holders. His choice of crops and rotations and his access to pasture were normally fixed by village agreement and manorial custom, and his lands were subject to communal grazing after harvest and when fallow. The real rents of copyholders at least were not negligible and were beginning to rise in the second half of the sixteenth century. By contrast, in the Weald (and in a few similar regions) the farmer's holdings were separate and enclosed, mainly in small, irregular fields. The only limitations on land use were the natural advantages and disadvantages of each separate piece. The manor or manors of which an owner-occupier farmer held his lands freely – for only a minuscule, fixed ground rent and very limited reliefs – had no part to play in the practice of farming. There appear also to have been no seigniorial restrictions on the leasing of land by Wealden freeholders, and because each large estate was in practice a conglomeration of a number of enclosed parcels of land, the landowner could easily vary the proportion of his estate which he kept in hand and the parts which were leased out for long or short periods. This meant that an ambitious farmer could quite easily obtain additional fields to lease in the vicinity of his existing farm, whether it was based on freehold or leased land. The structure of local landholding, and the ease with which fields could be obtained on leases or at will, made it possible for individual working farms to grow or contract at relatively short notice.

The contrast with the Midlands and much of south central England is equally noticeable in the balance between arable and pastoral farming. Wealden agriculture was different from both the sheep–corn husbandry of Norfolk and the Downlands, and the mainly arable, champion husbandry of the Midland and eastern regions. The Wealden system was predominantly pastoral, but with its own particular emphasis on cattle. In contrast to what appears to have been the national trend towards larger farms and the disappearance of subsistence holdings, both smallholders and small, family farms abounded in the Weald and showed no signs of extinction in the late sixteenth or early seventeenth centuries.[25] The explanation for their survival has to do both with local gavelkind custom and weak seigniorial control, and with the economic possibilities of combining farming with a craft or trade and/or the availability of part-time wage labour in the broadcloth industry. It may also be the case that the economic crises which struck small farmers in other parts of England during the disastrous harvests of the 1590s, were much less damaging to Wealden farmers whose arable crops were relatively less crucial to their survival.

Wealden farming could accommodate itself to different types and degrees of non-farming employment. By the sixteenth century the mixed agricultural and manufacturing economy in the central Weald was a success, if population growth and immigration are measures of economic success. The possibilities of dual employment encouraged the formation of more families. In turn, Wealden industry, as we shall see, flourished on the basis of relatively cheap labour based on an expanding rural population – at least so long as the overseas markets for Kent broadcloth were buoyant. By the late sixteenth century, however, that prosperity was under threat. Those families with land could readily supplement farming with another trade or with part-time work in clothmaking, if their holdings did not produce a marketable surplus. And running a full-size farm did not prevent families from carrying on other trades in addition. But the number of landless was growing. For them the ability to combine part-time spinning, a craft or trade and work as agricultural labourers was crucial to their survival. And here, of course, the nature of most Wealden farms, generally small scale and not heavily dependent on inputs of hired labour, worked against the landless in search of work.

Sweeping conclusions cannot be drawn on the basis of the appraised values of farmers' personal estates, shown in table 4.6. The most that can be essayed is that farmers in the Weald were at least holding their own, in the face of rising prices in the sixteenth century. The average values of their chattels was certainly rising, when the estates of the 1580s and 1590s are compared to those of the 1560s and 1570s. In the first fifteen-year period the poorer estates – those up to £40 – made up almost half the total, whereas in the 1580s and 1590s, they made up just 29 and 25 per cent of all farmers' inventories, respectively. The better-off farmers, those with chattels assessed at £50 or above, comprised 44 per cent of all farm inventories in the first fifteen years, but almost two-thirds of the farmers' inventories in the 1580s and 1590s. Farmers – as opposed to smallholders and the landless – were it seems at least keeping up with inflation. But farmers, of course, probably made up a smaller percentage of families in the Weald at the end of the century than they had in 1550 or 1560. The number of poor families was rising.

---

[25] For two examples among many of the disappearance of family farms see Margaret Spufford, *Contrasting Communities* (Cambridge, 1974) and Cicely Howell, *Land, Family and Inheritance in Transition* (Cambridge, 1983).

Table 4.6 *Inventory values of full-time farmers, 1565–99*

Total estate	1565–79	1580–9	1590–9	1565–99
£10–20	21 (10.1%)	6 (4.1%)	9 (5.4%)	36 (6.9%)
£20–30	45 (21.6%)	13 (9%)	19 (11.4%)	77 (14.8%)
£30–40	32 (15.4%)	23 (15.9%)	14 (8.4%)	69 (13.3%)
£40–50	19 (9.1%)	13 (9%)	19 (11.4%)	51 (9.8%)
£50–60	18 (8.7%)	13 (9%)	18 (10.8%)	49 (9.4%)
£60–80	22 (10.6%)	10 (6.9%)	23 (13.8%)	55 (10.6%)
£80–100	13 (6.3%)	19 (13.1%)	22 (13.2%)	54 (10.4%)
Over £100	38 (18.3%)	48 (33.1%)	43 (25.8%)	129 (24.8%)
Totals	*208*	*145*	*167*	*520*

Sources: As in table 4.1.

Without significant increases in agricultural productivity – and there are few signs that sixteenth century Wealden farmers were practising the kinds of techniques advocated by *The Inrichment of the Weald of Kent* – or renewed expansion of the demand for Kentish cloth, the economic system of the Weald could not provide a satisfactory living for its growing population. The limit seems to have been reached in the early seventeenth century. The evidence for this is the steadily rising level of poor relief in the 'proto-industrialized' central Wealden parishes. The Cranbrook churchwardens' accounts show payments to the local poor of over £100 per annum in 1611 and the six succeeding years, with a peak of £146 expended in 1615–16.[26] This is significantly higher than during the 'crisis' decade of the 1590s. There was a safety valve for some – migration – as described in the previous chapter. But it was not available to all, as the Cranbrook poor law accounts testify. The farming regime itself, however, was more resilient, and at the same time not resistant to agricultural improvement on a small scale. The professional survey of the demesnes of the manor of Combwell (in Goudhurst) in 1587 designated most of the fields as either 'to sow' or 'to mow', but one field of fourteen acres had obviously been adapted to up-and-down husbandry: it was available 'to mow and sow'.

By Charles II's reign, it appears that most of the larger farms on the Weald clay had made the transition to up-and-down farming. The return to the Royal Society which described farming practices in the Low Weald district south and west of Ashford speaks of the local soil as 'cold, weeping ground'. By this time the normal procedure is to plant cereals for four years (in the rotation oats or 'small beans', wheat, oats or beans and then a final wheat crop) after which 'we lay it down for pasture or meadow for ten or twelve years, then we convert it to tillage'. The correspondent reported sowing rates of three bushels of wheat and six bushels of

[26] Cranbrook: KAO P 100/5/1 fos. 142v, 148v, 156, 160, 161v, 166, 170. See below, chapters 6–7.

oats per acre as the norm, with wheat being sown in the fortnight after Michaelmas, oats in early March. He assumed that local farmers treated their up-and-down land with both dung and marl, the latter at the rate of 300 or 400 loads (of nine bushels each) for each acre. The report records farming methods uncannily similar to those recommended by *The Inrichment of the Weald of Kent* forty years earlier. In 1625 the combination of up-and-down farming and heavy soil dressing was a novelty taken up by a few innovative, large farms; by the 1660s it was apparently the norm. Through the adoption of convertible husbandry and extensive planting of cash crops like hops, and buoyed by the growing food demands of the metropolis, Wealden agriculture flourished as it became more specialized in the seventeenth and eighteenth centuries.[27]

[27] Cf. C. W. Chalklin, 'The Rural Economy of a Kentish Wealden Parish, 1650–1750', *AgHR*, 10 (1962). The freeholders of one Wealden manor (Pembury Magna) were as numerous in the 1660s as in the 1520s: 26 in the 1520s (PRO E 36/164 fo. 9v); 28 in 1666 (KAO U 1823/37/M2). See also Joan Thirsk, *Agrarian History*, v, pt. 1, chapter 9. Combwell: KAO U 1513/E2/1; Royal Soc. of London Classified Papers X(3) no. 28, cited in R. V. Lennard, 'English Agriculture under Charles II', *EcHR*, 4 (1932–4).

5

Occupational structure and levels of wealth in the Weald

The crucial role of agriculture in the Wealden economy – and in the family economy of its inhabitants – has been emphasized in chapter 4. But the same could be argued for any region of England and Wales in the sixteenth and seventeenth centuries. The contention of this, and succeeding chapters, is that the Weald was an agricultural region with a difference: its farming regime co-existed with – and complemented – an extremely diverse non-agricultural economy. The burden of the present chapter is two-fold: first, to describe and analyse the occupational structure of the Kent Weald, and secondly, to examine the levels of wealth within different occupational groups as well as in different parts of the Weald. The region's key non-agricultural industry, clothmaking, will only be treated cursorily here, and is the subject of more detailed examination in chapters 6 and 7. Two other branches of manufacturing – ironmaking and the associated metalware trades, and the leather industry – were in the sixteenth century concentrated in a limited number of rural areas. The Weald was one such region. Neither was as important to the people of the Kent Weald as textiles, but both will be discussed in this chapter.

The occupational structure of rural areas in early modern England is comparatively poorly documented, in contrast with what can be discovered about urban occupations. Certainly there is anecdotal evidence aplenty of men and women practising a variety of trades in many rural parishes. But systematic evidence – in which all persons of a given parish or region are recorded with an occupation or status addition after their names – is normally missing. There are only rare exceptions; a few of the returns to the 1522 militia survey include occupations; the 1608 muster return for the county of Gloucestershire lists male occupations as does the 1599 census of the village of Ealing, Middlesex. No 'perfect source' like this has come to light for sixteenth-century Kent, or for any substantial district of the Weald. Equally disappointing, no extant sixteenth-century register for a wholly Wealden parish records occupations, like the record books of the parish of St Botolph without Aldgate in London in the late sixteenth century. Nor does any Kent Weald parish register list the occupations of men in the burial register as did those of Tottenham High Cross, Middlesex, between 1574 and 1649. Nevertheless, mention will be made of the occupational listings in the Cranbrook parish register during the 1650s, and of the recording of occupations between 1559 and 1569 in the register of Westerham, a Kent parish which extended into the Weald. But neither can serve as a secure base for our inquiry into Wealden trades and occupations.[1]

Of necessity, we must turn to sources which cover incomplete samples of the rural adult population. One possibility would be to use the deponents in ecclesiastical court cases – where occupations are regularly recorded – as a surrogate for the whole adult populations of all the parishes concerned. But unfortunately there are not enough depositions with occupational information in the records for the sixteenth century to be able to claim that they constitute a valid sample of the Wealden population. Only probate records remain to be considered. One successful study of non-agricultural occupations in East Anglia analysed all the extant sixteenth- and seventeenth-century rural wills which named the testator's occupation. It calculated the changing proportion of parishes in which a given trade or occupation is named by at least one testator during three successive long periods. But the number of wills with the appropriate occupational information must have been quite small. Patten found, on the basis of wills, that only 15 per cent of Norfolk and Suffolk parishes in the sixteenth century had tailors, and less than 3 per cent had shoemakers! Of course, Patten did not argue that in reality less than a fifth of East Anglian parishes had resident tailors or carpenters during the century. Circumstantial evidence suggests that tailors, carpenters and shoemakers were commonly to be found in most rural villages of southern England in the sixteenth and seventeenth centuries. The point of Patten's research was to show that over time, the proportion of parishes with a variety of non-agricultural occupations increased substantially.[2]

But this mode of analysis cannot show which parishes supported the conventional tradesmen who serviced local populations only (such as tailors, blacksmiths and carpenters) and which supported significant concentrations of artisans and outworkers who supplied goods and services to more than the immediate local market. If the surviving sixteenth-century wills from the Kent dioceses of Canterbury and Rochester are at all typical, a majority of testators did not specify their occupations. The number of surviving wills is indeed large, but the number with the appropriate occupational information is not. Because of this it is not

---

[1] Julian Cornwall, 'The People of Rutland in 1522', *Trans. Leics. Arch. & Hist. Soc.*, 37 (1961–2); A. J. and R. H. Tawney, 'An Occupational Census of the Seventeenth Century', *EcHR*, 5 (1934); K. J. Allison, 'An Elizabethan Village Census', *BIHR*, 36 (1963); Thomas R. Forbes, *Chronicle from Aldgate* (1971); David Avery, 'Male Occupations in a Rural Middlesex Parish', *Local Population Studies*, 2 (1969).

[2] John Patten, 'Changing Occupational Structure in the East Anglian Countryside', in H. S. A. Fox and R. A. Butlin (eds.), *Change in the Countryside* (1979).

possible to derive a valid measure of occupational diversity and of local concentrations of trades from the wills alone.

Two other types of probate records are more helpful: the probate *acta*, specifically the men who acted as sureties for the administrators of estates; and, more importantly, the probate inventories produced before the archdeaconry and consistory courts. Neither record has survived for the diocese of Rochester, but both exist in full series for the diocese of Canterbury from the 1560s. The great value of inventories has already been shown in the examination of farming practices; they are equally helpful to the study of occupations and the comparative prosperity of men who practised different trades. The inventories provide the backbone of the first half of this chapter, with some comparative evidence from the occupations of men who served as sureties for administrators of estates. The inventories cover a large population, and throw up a far greater number of people with recorded occupations than can be retrieved from wills, depositions in church courts or the sureties. An unknown, but substantial share, of adult males is unrecorded in probate records of any kind. *Most* of the wealthier inhabitants and *some* of the poor are covered by extant inventories, and it is untrue to claim that very small estates (under £5 in value) were never the subject of probate inventories. But a majority of poor adults are not covered. People who made wills are represented by inventories, but many inventories also survive for intestates. The well-known deficiencies of inventories – they record only cash, chattels and debts and ignore real property – are not particularly germane to the questions posed in this chapter, although they will have the effect of under-rating the total wealth of owner-occupier farmers more than any other occupational group.

A further deficiency of the inventories for Canterbury diocese is that they do not systematically record an occupation for each inventory. In many cases the trade or occupation followed by the deceased cannot be known, unless it can be inferred from the person's chattels. This is particularly unfortunate in the case of inventories which show no trade goods or tools and no real agricultural activity (beyond a cow or two). In such cases (and where an occupation is not stated) the person may have been a labourer, a semi-skilled artisan who owned no occupationally specific tools, a retired person or occasionally a minor. A similar doubt arises from inventories which record what appear to be extremely small farms. Should such individuals be counted as 'farmers' (which would of course lower the average value of farmers' estates in the analysis) or should they be recorded as 'labourers', 'smallholders' or 'cottagers'? The records do not speak clearly for themselves. The analysis of occupations in this chapter follows the conventions used in chapter 4: only persons with farms large enough to support a family (and who do not appear to have followed a non-farming occupation as well) have been classified as 'farmers'. Many of the smallholders may have been skilled artisans or building workers, others were no doubt agricultural labourers for part of the year. The practice followed in this chapter has been to distinguish between those who appear from their inventories to have carried on some limited husbandry (called 'smallholder plus?') from those whose inventories suggest neither a specific trade nor even a smallholding (called here 'labourer or retired').

The occupational breakdown derived from the probate inventories is not a representative sample in a scientific sense. But it does represent something of a cross-section of Wealden society, with certain notable exceptions. The 'poor' are represented in the inventory sample but not in proportion to their real share of the population, nor in their full occupational diversity. The building trades, as well as bakers and butchers, are heavily under-represented in the inventory sample because their inventories are not sufficiently distinguishable. Women are under-represented throughout, simply because the personal estates of few women ever came to the attention of the probate courts. Where a woman's inventory shows a clearly recognizable trade or a family-sized farm, they have been included here in the appropriate occupational categories. Even recognizing all the drawbacks, the inventory evidence is the best available source to study the trades and occupations of the Weald's inhabitants.

The Kent Weald inventory sample used in the present chapter includes all 1,400 identifiable inventories from thirteen parishes, proved in both the archdeaconry and consistory courts between 1565, when the series begin, and 1599.[3] The very small parish of Frittenden has been merged with neighbouring Cranbrook (which has the effect of slightly decreasing the artisan manufacturing element of the larger of the two parishes). In all, just under 1,200 inventories can be safely assigned to one of our trade or occupational groups. The remaining 230-odd inventories are mainly those of women who do not appear to have been engaged in a trade or in farming, along with forty-three miscellaneous or uncertain male inventories.

Table 5.1 offers a breakdown of occupations of male sureties whose occupations were stated when they put up bonds for the administrators of deceased persons' estates in the Canterbury archdeaconry court between 1560 and 1610, and can be compared with a breakdown by parish of occupations represented in the probate inventories.[4] There are just over 900 men with recorded trades in the sample of sureties. But, given the nature of the source, it is more likely to include a larger proportion of relatively wealthy individuals, and therefore is less representative than the inventories of the area's occupational structure.

The most striking feature of this crude sample of Wealden occupations is the diversity of trades present in rural parishes, even if the partly urbanized parishes of Cranbrook and Tenterden are ignored. In rural Rolvenden, where approximately three out of five male sureties were called yeoman or husbandman, besides the textile trades (nine weavers, one clothier) there were also three shoemakers, three carpenters, two smiths, and one tailor, glover, mason, brickmaker and labourer. Marden boasted a substantial clothmaking element, but also was the home of

---

[3] Inventories from KAO PRC 10/1–29; PRC 21/1–17; PRC 28/1–3.
[4] KAO PRC 3/15–28.

Table 5.1 *Wealden occupations from probate acta, 1560–1610*

Parish	Number	No. of non-farming trades	Farmers	Textile trades as a percentage of non-farming sureties
Benenden	74	9	40 (54%)	73%
Bethersden	55	9	39 (71%)	44%
Biddenden	106	12	39 (37%)	75%
Cranbrook/Frittenden	155	21	46 (30%)	58%
Goudhurst	68	17	17 (25%)	46%
Halden	22	4	17 (77%)	20%
Hawkhurst	83	15	36 (43%)	51%
Marden	51	12	24 (47%)	46%
Rolvenden	56	9	33 (59%)	44%
Smarden	83	13	46 (55%)	43%
Staplehurst	57	10	28 (50%)	69%
Tenterden	98	20	48 (49%)	20%

Note: 'Textile trades' means clothier, weaver, fuller and shearman only.

sureties whose recorded trades included three butchers, two tailors, two thatchers, a carpenter, a mercer, a tanner, a shoemaker, a cooper and a trugger! The sureties were admittedly not a representative sample of adult males, since the process normally excluded men who would not be considered 'honest' (i.e., financially independent) enough to serve: labourers, cottagers and the poorest artisans. But it does point to a high level of occupational heterogeneity, whether or not one includes the concentration of textile workers in a number of parishes. But, unlike the larger and more representative inventory sample, it is based on the trades and additions given by the sureties themselves, rather than on the occupations inferred by twentieth-century historians.

A more detailed set of categories – several by their very nature artificial – can be given for the 1,200-odd persons identified by occupation from a thirteen-parish probate inventory sample, and displayed in table 5.2. The procedure used here was to class persons under a single occupational group: thus an inventory which shows clearly the tools of a working weaver, but also suggests a thirty acre farm, has been classified as a weaver (within the textile trades). This method obviously over-simplifies the nature of economic activity in the Weald, since a significant share of artisans and tradesmen were also working farmers. But, since the large number of small farms has been stressed in the preceding chapter, it is the wide variety of trades and manufacturing which now demands emphasis. A glance at table 5.2 shows that, even in the Weald, farming was the most common occupation. Nevertheless, only about 40 per cent of adults whose chattels were inventoried were full-time farmers, and this is likely to have been a real maximum because

Table 5.2 *Occupations in Wealden probate inventories, 1565–1599*

Occupation	Benenden	Bethersden	Biddenden	Cranb/Frittenden
Farmers	38 (34%)	51 (50%)	28 (30%)	46 (29%)
Smallholder plus?	7 (6%)	15 (15%)	9 (10%)	15 (9%)
Labourer or retired	20 (18%)	15 (15%)	20 (21%)	33 (21%)
Textile trades	26 (23%)	11 (11%)	28 (30%)	40 (25%)
Carpenter	3 (3%)	3 (3%)	2 (2%)	3 (2%)
Building trades	–	1 (1%)	–	–
Smith	1 (1%)	2 (2%)	4 (4%)	3 (2%)
Shopkeeper	6 (5%)	1 (1%)	–	8 (5%)
Tailor	2 (2%)	2 (2%)	–	2 (1%)
Shoemaker	1 (1%)	1 (1%)	3 (3%)	1 (1%)
Leather trades	2 (2%)	–	1 (1%)	3 (2%)
Miller/brewer	1 (1%)	–	–	5 (3%)
Professional	4 (4%)	–	–	2 (1%)
Totals	*111*	*102*	*95*	*161*
Misc. and non-farming widows	19	29	23	38

Occupation	Goudhurst	Halden	Hawkhurst	Marden
Farmers	26 (26%)	29 (62%)	23 (27%)	40 (49%)
Smallholder plus?	15 (15%)	4 (9%)	14 (17%)	11 (14%)
Labourer or retired	17 (17%)	8 (17%)	22 (26%)	15 (19%)
Textile trades	15 (15%)	1 (2%)	14 (17%)	7 (9%)
Carpenter	4 (4%)	3 (6%)	3 (4%)	2 (3%)
Building trades	2 (2%)	–	–	–
Smith	10 (10%)	–	2 (2%)	–
Shopkeeper	4 (4%)	1 (2%)	1 (1%)	2 (3%)
Tailor	2 (2%)	–	–	3 (4%)
Shoemaker	–	–	2 (2%)	–
Leather trades	1 (1%)	1 (2%)	4 (5%)	1 (1%)
Miller/brewer	2 (2%)	–	–	–
Professional	–	–	–	–
Totals	*99*	*47*	*85*	*81*
Misc. and non-farming widows	17	7	15	16

Occupation	Rolvenden	Smarden	Stapleh.	Tenterden	Totals
Farmers	56 (56%)	38 (43%)	30 (44%)	62 (41%)	467 (39%)
Smallholder plus?	12 (12%)	23 (15%)	2 (3%)	16 (11%)	133 (11%)
Labourer or retired	15 (15%)	10 (11%)	17 (25%)	40 (27%)	232 (20%)
Textile trades	8 (8%)	18 (20%)	9 (13%)	8 (5%)	185 (16%)
Carpenter	3 (3%)	4 (5%)	2 (3%)	2 (1%)	34 (3%)
Building trades	4 (4%)	–	–	1 (1%)	8 (1%)
Smith	1 (1%)	1 (1%)	–	2 (1%)	26 (2%)
Shopkeeper	–	3 (3%)	3 (4%)	6 (4%)	35 (3%)
Tailor	1 (1%)	–	2 (3%)	3 (2%)	18 (2%)
Shoemaker	–	1 (1%)	1 (2%)	1 (1%)	11 (1%)
Leather trades	–	1 (1%)	2 (3%)	3 (2%)	19 (2%)
Miller/brewer	–	–	1 (2%)	4 (3%)	13 (1%)

Table 5.2 (cont.)

Occupation	Rolvenden	Smarden	Stapleh.	Tenterden	Totals
Professional	–	–	–	2 (1%)	8 (1%)
Totals	*100*	*89*	*69*	*150*	*1189*
Misc. and non-farming widows	25	12	4	35	240

Note: To nearest whole percent. 'Farmers' incl. graziers; 'textiles' incl. clothier, weaver, fuller, shearman; 'leather' incl. tanner, currier, glover.

farmers' inventories are easily identified, whether or not an occupational addition is given on the document. The predominantly agrarian parishes in the eastern Weald, Rolvenden and Halden, produced absolute majorities of farmers and graziers, who followed no other trade, and even semi-urban Tenterden shows farming as the main occupation of more than 40 per cent of the classified inventories. In Rolvenden less than 20 per cent and in Halden under 15 per cent of the inventories show an identifiable non-farming occupation (other than the artificial categories of smallholder and labourer). Marden and Bethersden, further north, also appear from the inventory sample to have been more committed to agriculture than the circle of parishes around Cranbrook, although both parishes had some clothmaking activity. By contrast, Cranbrook and its neighbours (especially Biddenden, Goudhurst and Hawkhurst) show full-time farming as the occupation of under thirty per cent of adults with classified inventories.

Throughout the region, and even if the non-manufacturing parishes are included, the Wealden inventories suggest a far more complex and diversified occupational structure than is seen in several studies of other parts of England. In the parish of Tottenham High Cross in the late sixteenth century, no less than 67 per cent of adult males were farmers or agricultural labourers, and in early sixteenth-century Rutland the great majority of adult males were engaged in farming, leavened only by a very few common rural craftsmen.[5]

The rural area which appears most comparable to Wealden Kent is early seventeenth-century Gloucestershire, as revealed in the muster survey of 1608 which the Tawneys analysed half a century ago. They found that – after excluding the three larger towns of Gloucester, Tewkesbury and Cirencester – about half the adult male population were full-time farmers or agricultural labourers, although their share rose to two-thirds in certain hundreds and dropped to under one-third in the most industrialized hundred. In Gloucestershire as a whole, what we have called the textile trades accounted for just over 15 per cent of adult male occupations, with other, more common trades and crafts accounting for the bulk of the remaining one-third of adult males (except an uncertain category of household servants and unspecified servants who made up 7 per cent of classified adult males). In certain hundreds in the heart of the Cotswolds wood-pasture region, however,

[5] Avery, 'Male Occupations'; Cornwall, 'The People of Rutland'.

Table 5.3 *Male occupations in Westerham, Kent, 1559–1569*

Agriculture (yeoman, husbandman, labourer, falconer)	33 (32%)
Makers of articles of dress (tailor, shoemaker)	12 (11.5%)
Textile trades (weaver, shearman)	11 (10.5%)
Woodworking trades (carpenter, cooper, fletcher, sawyer, millwright, ploughwright)	12 (11.5%)
Building trades (tilemaker, tileburner, mason)	4 (4%)
Smiths	3 (3%)
Food and drink (butcher, cook, butterman, rippier)	6 (5.5%)
Gentry, Professional (Gent., cleric, surgeon, surveyor)	10 (9.5%)
Shopkeeper (mercer)	1 (1%)
Leather trades (tanner)	4 (4%)
Misc. (4 colliers, 2 parish clerks, tinker, minstrel)	8 (7.5%)
Total	104

textile workers made up no less than 40 per cent of recorded male occupations; an even higher proportion than that suggested by the inventories from the Weald shown in table 5.2.[6]

The crucial significance of wage labour in the Kent Weald is also suggested by the inventory sample shown above. Persons classified as 'smallholder plus something else' and as 'labourer or retired' made up more than 30 per cent of all adults with identifiable inventories: the vast majority of them must have depended on wages for all or a substantial part of their incomes. The share of those two categories rises to over 37 per cent in partially urbanized Tenterden and to as high as 42 per cent in poor, densely populated Hawkhurst. The latter parish could with justice be described as proletarianized as early as the Elizabethan period.

The most common non-agrarian occupation among males in the Kent Weald was weaving: more than 10 per cent of inventories were those of weavers. This proportion would undoubtedly be reduced if inventories from the western Weald parishes (in Rochester diocese) had survived to be included in table 5.2. There, only two parishes, Brenchley and Horsmonden, supported an active clothmaking industry. In the present sample, only in Halden was the woollen industry unimportant. At the other extreme, a fifth of inventories in Smarden, almost a quarter of inventories in Benenden, Cranbrook and Frittenden, and about 30 per cent in Biddenden are of residents involved in the three basic textile trades. In Goudhurst and Hawkhurst those trades make up at least 15 per cent of all classified inventories. And the economic significance of clothmaking was even greater than suggested by the inventory sample. As will be shown in chapter 6, spinning yarn for Wealden looms was probably carried on in most households in the Kent Weald, except in the far west. For the moment, the great diversity of occupations in almost all Wealden parishes can be emphasized.

[6] Tawney and Tawney, 'An Occupational Census', pp. 36, 44, 45.

Table 5.4 *Cranbrook male occupations, 1653–61*

Agriculture	81 (26%)[a]
Textile trades	140 (45%)[b]
Food and drink	13 (4%)[c]
Woodworking trades	13 (4%)[d]
Building trades	12 (4%)[e]
Smiths, metal workers	7 (2%)[f]
Gentry, professional	7 (2%)[g]
Makers of articles of dress	14 (4.5%)[h]
Shopkeepers, dealers	9 (3%)[i]
Leather trades	6 (2%)[j]
Carriers, etc.	7 (2%)[k]
	Total 309

Notes: [a] Incl. 70 husbandman, 7 yeomen, 2 labourers, 2 gardeners
[b] Incl. 77 weavers, 50 clothiers, 5 clothworkers, 3 dyers, 1 millman, 2 cardmakers, 2 feltmakers
[c] Incl. 5 butchers, 5 millers, 2 alehouse keepers, 1 brewer
[d] Incl. 10 carpenters, 2 coopers, 1 wheeler
[e] Incl. 4 masons, 4 bricklayers, 2 thatchers, 1 glazier, 1 brickmaker
[f] Incl. 4 smiths, 1 brazier, 1 collier, 1 forgeman
[g] Incl. 2 gentlemen, 3 barber-surgeons, 1 cleric, 1 scrivener
[h] Incl. 9 shoemakers, 5 tailors
[i] Incl. 4 mercers, 2 barbers, 1 haberdasher, 1 chandler, 1 fellmonger
[j] Incl. 2 tanners, 2 glovers, 2 saddlers
[k] Incl. 4 rippiers, 2 carriers, 1 packer
larger numbers of men who worked in the furnaces and forges?

Another indication of the high level of occupational diversity in the region can be found in the parish of Westerham, whose southern half extends into the Weald proper, and which contained a small market centre. Its total population was only about 650 at this time. For ten years from 1559 its parish clerk entered male occupations along with names in the baptism and burial registers (see table 5.3).[7] A similar, detailed parochial sample can be collected from the marriage register of the parish of Cranbrook during the midseventeenth century. The local importance of woollen textile industry stands out clearly (see table 5.4). A similarly varied range of occupations would have been found in late sixteenth-century Cranbrook, and the town of Tenterden would have had almost as many different trades (although very few of the basic textile trades). Smaller market centres like Tonbridge and Goudhurst did not support quite the variety of trades, though they would have had as many occupations as Westerham.

In the inventory sample as a whole no other craft or trade besides clothmaking stands out from the rest. In most of the sample parishes the list of occupations

[7] Westerham parish register, in the church.

mirrors what historians have come to expect in the more populous rural areas. The notable difference in the inventory sample is that building workers, dealers in food and drink and carriers are less numerous than they are in the sources which record all male occupations. There were, no doubt, many building artisans and suppliers of food and drink among the inventories categorized here as smallholders or as labourers.

Not only was the Weald's occupational structure quite varied throughout the region, there were in addition quite distinct concentrations of specialized trades and industries, whose workers produced goods for markets which extended far beyond the boundaries of the Weald. Foremost among them was the woollen textile industry, which deserves separate treatment. Less important in terms of employment, but equally characteristic of the Weald's particular geography, are two others: the leather industry and the production of iron and metalwares, to which we now must turn.

It was only natural that there should be a heavy leather industry in the Weald during the early modern period. The raw materials needed to produce tanned leather existed here in abundance. Since, as we have seen, the rearing and fattening of cattle was the mainstay of Wealden farming regimes, hides were readily available to local tanners. To the extent that large numbers of cattle reared in the Weald were driven to London for sale, Wealden tanners obtained additional hides from butchers in the capital. In either case, the tanner's basic raw material was available locally or within thirty to fifty kilometres. The leather producer's other key ingredient was his tan, the compound made of ground oak bark. It was the soaking of shaved hides in a solution of tan and water for periods of between six months to over a year that transformed hides into leather. And there was no lack of oak bark in the Weald.[8] Many Kent Weald parishes can be shown to have had at least one resident tanner during the second half of the sixteenth century. But the inventory sample (table 5.2) makes it clear that in the central and eastern Weald the leather trades were present only in small numbers. The parish of Staplehurst, which has been examined in some detail in earlier chapters, can serve as an example. Throughout the Elizabethan period, there were two tanners operating in Staplehurst, both of them members of families long resident in the parish. Tanning as a trade seems to have run strongly in families: many fathers appeared to have passed on knowledge of their craft to their sons. This was demonstrably the case in Staplehurst, where the Hodges and the Osbornes (or Usbornes) produced tanners in at least two generations. A John Osborne of Staplehurst, 'tanner', died in 1502. In his will he left his main messuage, a tan house and all the tuns and instruments of the tan house to his son Thomas. The younger son got just one piece of land and 12 marks in cash. John Osborne probably owned under twenty acres in all. The tanning trade followed the eldest male line for the next two generations at least, and the family's economic standing rose quickly.

[8] On the industry in general see Leslie A. Clarkson, 'The English Leather Industry in the Sixteenth and Seventeenth Centuries', unpublished Ph.D thesis, Nottingham University, 1960.

The elder son Thomas died in 1534, not before passing on his special skills to his eldest son, another Thomas Osborne, who became a tanner in his turn and lived until 1591. John's eldest grandson by his younger son, called Osbert, became a shoemaker and died in 1570. The Thomas Osborne, tanner, who died in 1591, was succeeded by his son of the same name, also a tanner, who was buried in Staplehurst in 1612.

The Hodges are not so well documented, but we know that Michael Hodges (d. 1567) was a tanner who also ran a family farm. He was one of the sons of William Hodges of Staplehurst who died in 1544, leaving lands to both sons and a 40-mark portion to an unmarried daughter. Michael Hodges appears to have died quite young, leaving two young sons and lands in Staplehurst and Marden. Many years later his younger son Walter was trading successfully as a tanner. He was rated to the 1597 subsidy, married rather late, in 1602, and served as a churchwarden for Staplehurst in 1607–8. Both wills and probate inventories survive for Michael Hodges and Thomas Hodges (d. 1591). Hodges left a small landed estate and chattels valued at £74. His livestock and the planted corn suggest a farm of at least twenty-five acres, and his trade goods were worth £27, of which eighty-eight hides made up the lion's share (£20 10s.). His tuns and vats were priced at £4 10s. and he had four loads of tan worth £1 6s. 8d. The total value of his chattels, £74, was the exact median among the thirteen tanners with surviving inventories for the period 1565–79. But he was nonetheless quite a wealthy man: the median value of all the Weald inventories from the sample parishes between 1565 and 1579 was just £30. Michael Hodges's household at the time of the 1563/4 listing of Staplehurst's communicants was somewhat larger than average: besides his wife and at least one infant, there were two resident male servants and one maidservant.

Among the appraisers of Hodges's goods was the parish's other tanner, Thomas Osborne, who operated on a far larger scale than Hodges. Osborne was to live until 1591, and had at least nine children baptized at Staplehurst between 1539 and 1560. His business dealings involved him in the London leather trade, and he was fined twice – in 1563 and 1573 – for infractions of the statutes which regulated leather production. He was apparently already quite a prosperous producer when assessed at £20 in goods for the subsidy of 1543/4. His rating of £35 in goods in the subsidy book of 1572 represents a major rise in economic status, given the degree of under-assessment by then commonplace. In 1572 he was one of the half-dozen or so leading householders in the parish. His household of 1563/4 consisted of his wife, at least one unmarried daughter of communicant age and four servants, three of them male. By the time Thomas Osborne was buried, as an 'ancient householder', his tanning and farming activities had made him one of the three richest men in the parish; the others were the resident squire and a very well-off clothier. Osborne's inventory total came to about £535, and included good debts owed to him of almost £150. Like other wealthy, older men (and women), he invested some of his profits in loans to local people, though some of the debts were probably trade debts owed Osborne by local shoemakers. Osborne was a substantial farmer as well as a manufacturer: his winter wheat extended to ten acres and his livestock included a team of six oxen, thirty other cattle, seven horses and twenty sheep. His home farm would have come to around 100 acres, and must have provided a substantial cash income. Osborne's trade goods show his continuing prosperity as a tanner, even in very old age: they totalled £173, most of it in the form of leather and hides waiting to be processed. But he also had oak bark in the tan house worth £13. Osborne's inventory total was the highest of any tanner for the whole period covered by the sample; it put him in a class with the wealthiest clothiers, the top yeoman farmers and probably the lesser gentry. Unfortunately there is no evidence about the real annual income or production levels of any of the known Wealden tanners. Hodges represents the typical country tanner, while Osborne was one of a fairly small elite of major tanners with a regular trade to London.[9]

Very few tanners were poor. Of the sixteen tanners represented by an inventory between 1565 and 1610, only one had chattels worth less than £50; the median inventory value was £93, and eight of the sixteen owned goods valued at over £100.[10] Tanning was not a trade for men without capital; as Leslie Clarkson has emphasized, producing leather from hides was a slow process. Though the basic equipment for tanning hides was not costly, certainly under £10 or £15 in the 1560s and 1570s, a tanner required a substantial circulating capital. Clarkson estimates that a tanner might have at least ten times as much money tied up in hides at various stages of production as he had in tools and vats. It was unlikely that anyone became an independent tanner without £50 to £100 invested in raw materials and equipment. On the other hand, even tanners who operated on as large a scale as Thomas Osborne needed no more than two or three employees. Unlike the production of woollen cloth, all the processes involved in heavy leathermaking were carried out on the tanner's own premises, with his own servants' labour.[11]

The tanning trade was to be found throughout the Weald, but was heavily concentrated in the western Weald. Although there are no systematic sources to study occupations in the western parishes, the record of penal informations brought against tanners in the Court of Exchequer in Elizabeth's reign can be plotted on the map. Five parishes stand out for the number of tanners charged with infractions of the penal statutes regulating the preparation of leather: Brasted and Westerham,

[9] Hodges: Michael H., will (KAO PRC 17/40 fo. 174), inventory (PRC 10/4 fo. 231), household (PRC 43/13/31); Wm. H., rated £20 goods in 1543/4 (PRO E 179/125/273), will (KAO PRC 17/23 fo. 244ᵛ); Walt. H., 1597 subsidy (PRO E 179/127/516), also Staplehurst parish register; called tanner in recognizance (KAO QM/SRc/1605/143). Osbornes: John O., tanner, d. 1502, will (KAO PRC 17/8 fo. 182); Thos. O., tanner, d. 1591, will (PRC 17/48 fo. 81), inventory (PRC 10/18 fo. 367), informed against (PRO E 159/346 Rec. Trin. rot. 116d, E 159/365 Rec. Mich. rot. 529), subsidies (E 179/125/273; E 179/126/423), household (KAO PRC 43/13/31); Thos. O., tanner, d. 1612, Staplehurst parish register and inventory (PRC 10/36 fo.523).

[10] The main inventory sample of thirteen tanners plus three others who died between 1600 and 1610: KAO PRC 10/30 fo. 426; 10/32 fo. 176; 10/34 fo. 360.

[11] Clarkson, 'The English Leather Industry', esp. chapter 2 and pp. 181–4.

which lie on the Chart just to the north of the Weald, Edenbridge to the south of the first two, and Tonbridge and its smaller neighbour, Leigh. Far more tanners from the southwestern corner of Kent found themselves answering informations than from any other part of the county.[12] Certain names crop up repeatedly: the Amhersts of Tudeley, the Ashdowns of Tonbridge and Leigh, the Deanes of Brasted, Edenbridge and Sundridge, the Sones or Sownes of Brasted and Edenbridge and the Staceys of Westerham. Several families had numerous members involved in the industry, often over several generations.[13] The biggest group of tanners came from Brasted (itself a small market centre), but most of the parishes in the southwest corner of Kent had some leather manufacture. The regular appearance of the west Weald tanners in the Exchequer, usually for defects in leather being sold at the capital's leather market, shows that their production was well above local requirements.

It would be an exaggeration, however, to portray the leather industry in this part of the Weald as in any way equivalent to clothmaking in the central Weald. The

---

[12] PRO E 159/340 ff., *passim*. Some west Weald tanners can be also identified from wills proved in the Rochester Consistory court (KAO Drb/Pwr) and in the Prerogative Court of Canterbury (PRO PROB 11).

[13] Amhersts: Nic. A. of Tudeley, informed against 1560, 1561, 1563, 1566 (PRO E 159/341 Rec. Mich. rot. 61d, 342 Rec. Hil. rot. 71, 346 Rec. Trin. rot. 115, 353 Rec. Trin. rot. 269d); will of Nic. A. of Tudeley, perhaps same man, 1600 (KAO DRb/Pwr 19 fo. 130), leaving lands in Capel and Tudeley, with a tan house, tan yard and tan barn. Ashdown: John A. of Chiddingstone, tanner, d. 1488, will (PRO PROB 11/8/12) refers to his tan house; Wm. A. of Leigh, tanner, d. 1551, will (KAO DRb/Pwr 11 fo. 149), the son of John above; Thos. A. of Tonbridge, 'tanner', d. 1558, will (DRb/Pwr 12 fo. 220); Ric. A. of Leigh, 'tanner', brother of Thos. (KAO U 1290/E8, U 1823/1/T7), whose son fell accidentally into a tan vat and drowned, 1583 (PRO KB 9/661 no. 254); John A. of Leigh, 'tanner', son of Ric., in the 1590s (KAO QM/SRc/1598/93). Deane: Thos. D. of Brasted, informed against 1561, 1569, 1575 (PRO E 159/344 Rec. East. rot. 45, 358 Rec. Hil. rot. 119, 369 Rec. Mich. rot. 194); Wm. D. of Sundridge, informed against 1566, 1569 (E 159/353 Rec. Trin. rot. 109, 358 Rec. East. rot. 122d); John D. of Edenbridge, informed against 1570, 1573 (E 159/359 Rec. Hil. rots. 324, 330d; 365 Rec. Mich. rot. 352). Sone: Steph. S. of Brasted, 'tanner', 1539 will (PRO PROB 11/27/31) w/son John and two male servants; Martin S. of Brasted, informed against 1535, 1553, 1566 (E 159/313 Rec. Trin. rot. 21, 332 *sub* Recognizances, 353 Rec. Trin. rot. 264); John S. of Brasted, son of Steph., 1565 will (PROB 11/48a/32–3) w/sons John and Wm, informed against 1560, 1563 (E 159/341 Rec. Mich. rot. 202d, 346 Rec. Hil. rot. 125); Geo. S. of Edenbridge, brother of John and Martin, 1571 will (PROB 11/53/11) leaves land in Cowden, Edenbridge and Westerham, informed against 1566, 1567 (E 159/353 Rec. Trin. rot. 107, 356 Rec. East. rot. 231); John S. of Edenbridge, son of John above, informed against 1561, 1563, 1566, 1569 (E 159/342 Rec. East. rot. 58, 346 Rec. Trin. rot. 117d, 353 Rec. Trin. rot. 100, 358 Rec. Hil. rot. 116d); Wm. S. of Leigh and Brasted, informed against 1570, 1573, 1578 (E 159/359 Rec. Hil. rot. 333d, 365 Rec. Mich. rot. 358, 375 Rec. Mich. rot. 114) and a deed shows that he owned a messuage and 32 acres in Brasted, 45 acres in Sundridge and a shop in Sevenoaks shambles (KAO U 1024/T1). Stacey: John S., sen. of Westerham, 1486 will (KAO DRb/Pwr 6 fos. 131, 133) left main messuage to son John; John S., tanner, son of above, as executor of will of a Thos. S. in 1504 (DRb/Pwr 6 fo. 106); Wm. S. of Westerham, tanner, 1566 will (PRO PROB 11/48b/32) w/sons Wm. and Thos., held lease of manor of Squerries of the Isleys; informed against 1553 (E159/332 *sub* Recognizances); Reg. S. of Westerham, a poor relation of Wm. S. above. In 1566 he owed Wm. £100 and was leasing his tan house (PROB 11/48b/32), informed against 1566 (E 159/353 Rec. Trin. rot. 99); Thos. S. of Westerham, ?son of Wm. above, as tanner in 1595 recognizance (KAO QM/SRc/1595/83); his 1615 will (PRO PROB 11/126/82) left lands to 1 son and £80 and £90 portions to two others.

latter was a major industry involving thousands of workers on a part- and full-time basis; the leather manufacture of the western Weald was a local concentration of what was a widespread trade in parts of Kent and in other shires. From the scrappy evidence that can be mustered, the western Weald seems to have been occupationally less diversified than the central and eastern Weald. But even here, the market centres, ranging from Edenbridge to Tonbridge Town, introduced an element of greater variety in the trades and occupations carried on within what was after all a comparatively thinly populated region. And in several of the High Weald parishes of this district an altogether less commonplace industry was taking root in the early sixteenth century: iron.

The iron industry – more than any other aspect of Wealden history – has received enormous, some might say exaggerated, attention from historians and archaeologists. With perhaps understandable – if not justifiable – enthusiasm, historians since the end of the nineteenth century and the 'discovery' of the Industrial Revolution have researched the origins of the early iron industry in the Weald of Kent and Sussex. The story has been told frequently, and in great detail.[14] In terms of numbers of furnaces and forges, the Wealden parishes of Sussex were the heartland of sixteenth- and seventeenth-century iron production, and therefore this study will not need to concentrate on the iron industry. It was not of first importance to the local economy of the Kentish Weald. Probably the most important impact of ironmaking in the Kent Weald was its allegedly voracious appetite for wood, especially in parishes where it competed with local clothiers who needed large quantities of firewood to heat their vats for washing and dyeing wool. By the 1570s alarmists were predicting the imminent disappearance of the Wealden forests. In 1578 an Admiralty official wrote that 'there are not so few as an hundred furnaces and iron mills in Sussex, Surrey and Kent, which is greatly to the decay, spoil and overthrow of woods and principal timber, with a great decay also of tillage'.[15] Agitation against the ironworks was eagerly supported by the clothiers of the Kent Weald, who later promoted a bill presented to the House of Commons in 1593, 'for the maintenance of clothing in the parish of Cranbrook and within eight miles of the same'. They claimed that clothmaking had fallen into decay because of the great quantities of timber consumed by nearby ironworks. Their bill would have prohibited the construction of any new ironworks, and required that local ironmasters use only wood from their own lands. The bill did not become an act.[16]

The legislation that was enacted was prompted more by the needs of the

[14] On the iron industry see Ernest Straker, *Wealden Iron* (1931); H. R. Schubert, *History of the British Iron and Steel Industry* (1957); G. F. Hammersley, 'The Charcoal Iron Industry and its Fuel', *EcHR*, 2nd series, 26 (1973); D. W. Crossley (ed.), *Sidney Ironworks Accounts, 1541–1573* (Camden Soc. 4th series, 15, 1975); J. J. Goring, 'Wealden Ironmasters in the Age of Elizabeth', in E. W. Ives *et al.* (eds.), *Wealth and Power in Tudor England* (1978); and now Henry Cleere and David Crossley, *The Iron Industry of the Weald* (Leicester, 1985).   [15] PRO SP 12/117 no. 39.
[16] HMC, *Third Report*, App. p. 7.

Admiralty and the shipbuilders of the Thames, than by the competing local interests. An act of 1585 prohibited the burning of full-grown 'timber trees' by ironmasters, something which was not the normal practice of the ironworks in any case.[17] The armaments demand of the war against Spain encouraged an expansion of Wealden ironmaking, but there is evidence of only two additional ironwork sites in the Kent Weald between 1574 and 1588.[18] More than a generation later, in 1637, the Cranbrook clothiers – now almost certainly correct in their jeremiads on the state of the Wealden textile industry, although incorrect in their explanation for its decay – were once again protesting to the government about the timber demands of the King's own gunfounder in the Weald, John Brown. They asserted that ironmaking threatened the ancient trade of clothmaking.[19] Within a generation both Wealden clothmaking and ironmaking would be in full retreat.

The Wealden iron industry witnessed its first boom during the reign of Henry VIII when the imported technology of water-driven blast furnaces was put to work in dozens of new ironworks, almost entirely in Sussex. At this first stage of industrial expansion, ironmasters depended heavily on French ironworkers. The 1550s and 1560s saw the migration of the new technology to High Weald parishes in Kent; the first modern blast furnace in the Kent Weald was built in Tonbridge parish by Davy Willard in 1552/3. The doubling of the number of furnaces and forges between the 1550s and 1570s produced alarums from both Kentish clothiers and the shipbuilding interest. Nevertheless, the great bulk of the hundred-odd ironworks lay in Sussex. In 1574 there were ironworks in just eight Kent Weald parishes (counting Lamberhurst, with its three forges as part of Kent): Cowden, Ashurst and Tonbridge in the west, and Horsmonden, Goudhurst, Lamberhurst, Cranbrook and Hawkhurst in the central Weald. There were just eight blast furnaces at work in the Kentish Weald (one each in Cowden, Ashurst, Goudhurst, Cranbrook and Hawkhurst, and two in Tonbridge), along with nine or ten forges. The biggest concentration of ironworks was in the extensive parish of Tonbridge: two furnaces and at least two forges.[20] The furore over timber supplies centred on that part of the High Weald where clothiers and ironmasters were in direct competition for firewood: the four neighbouring parishes of Horsmonden, Goudhurst, Cranbrook and Hawkhurst. A survey of 'woods felled within these twenty years last past in diverse clothing parishes, which have been best wooded in the Weald of Kent', compiled about 1574, probably originated among the clothiers and can hardly be taken at face value. It alleges that some 6,542 acres of woods in eight parishes had been felled during the previous twenty years, and that only 607 acres of woods remain unfelled. The authors of the survey were apparently able to distinguish between woods felled for

[17] 27 Eliz. I, c. 19. [18] Cleere and Crossley, *Iron Industry of the Weald*, p. 166.
[19] PRO SP 16/363 nos. 55–6.
[20] See map in Goring, 'Wealden Ironmasters' and gazetteer in Cleere and Crossley, *Iron Industry*. Derondale (or Dundle) forge appears more likely to have been in Lamberhurst than in Pembury: see J. K. Wallenberg, *The Place Names of Kent* (Uppsala, 1934), p. 201, and Ordnance Survey map, sheet 188, 'Maidstone and the Weald of Kent'.

'fuel and clothing' and woodland acreage felled 'for ironmaking'. How they were able to calculate with such exactness the eventual destination of all the timber cut in the previous two decades is not explained. Their figures should probably be read as estimates only, if not worse. Of the total acreage felled, the survey calculates that 4,782 acres (or over 70 per cent) lay in the parishes with ironworks: Cranbrook, Goudhurst, Hawkhurst and Horsmonden. Again, of the total acreage felled, the paper claims that 2,924 acres (45 per cent) were intended as fuel for the iron industry, the remainder for domestic fuel and the clothiers. Yet the paper shows that Wealden woodland owners were not simply clearfelling with no thought for the future. The survey admits that of the 6,542 acres felled, over 4,300 acres had been coppiced. The most suspicious 'finding' of the anonymous survey is the contention that just 600 acres of woodland remained in the whole of the eight parishes (which covered 55,000 acres)! It is, of course, possible – although not likely – that there had been a sudden expansion of both iron and cloth production between the mid 1550s and mid 1570s, which consumed the bulk of standing timber in all these parishes. But if that was the case, the expanded demand for iron ordnance from the middle of the next decade could not have been met. Perhaps ironmasters obtained wood from further afield, and possibly a greater proportion of the iron produced came from furnaces in other parts of the Weald. Unfortunately there are no surveys of the acreage of woodland felled to fuel the furnaces of Cowden, Ashurst and Tonbridge. But, as was shown earlier, there was far more extensive woodland and waste in the western parishes of the Weald, especially in the enormous Lowy of Tonbridge.[21]

The men who owned and managed the Wealden ironworks in Kent and Sussex have in most cases been identified by earlier historians. Many of the furnaces and forges were first erected by local landowners, of whom the Sidneys are only the most well-known and well-documented (especially for their ironworks at Roberts-bridge, Sussex) example. But a number of Kent gentry families were also involved, even if not usually as direct managers: the Willoughbys at Bough Beech furnace and forge in Hever (from about 1588), the Wallers for a furnace and forge in Ashurst, George Harper and Thomas Culpeper (and later Thomas Fane) at Vauxhall furnace in Tonbridge, the Darrells at Chingley forge and furnace in Goudhurst, Sir Alexander Culpeper at Bedgebury furnace in Cranbrook and, not least, Sir Richard Baker, who owned a forge near his mansion at Sissinghurst and Frith furnace in Hawkhurst. Not all of these gentlemen-investors may have taken a day-to-day interest in their industrial enterprises, but they knew a potential money-spinner when they saw it, especially after the middle of the sixteenth century. With the growing demand for iron in the second half of the century – not least from the Crown for naval ordnance – and a plentiful supply of iron ore (in the form of clay ironstone) in the High Weald, as well as wood aplenty on their own lands,

---

[21] The 1574 'survey': PRO SP 12/93 fo. 148.

ironmaking was an excellent investment. If nothing else, it promised a return more tangible than the pleasures of hunting and shooting game from their extensive woodland acreage. None of these gentry entrepreneurs were 'new men' from commercial backgrounds.

The working ironmasters, who in most cases built and managed the ironworks, are an even more intriguing set of individuals. Only a few of them had access to sufficient capital to develop furnaces and forges from their own resources, but without their specialized knowledge there would have been no Wealden iron industry. Jeremy Goring has provided a lively account of their activities and of their ties with local landowners. Some were able to use their industrial and business skills to great advantage; others were financial failures or merely survived. The career of Thomas Browne of Ashurst, Chiddingstone and Brenchley – known both as ironmaster and gun founder – exemplifies the efforts of working ironmasters to obtain control of the ironworks, which in many cases had been financed by gentry landowners. Browne may already have been the tenant of Thomas Willoughby's works in Hever, when in 1589 he paid £1,074 for the iron furnace and 191 acres of land in Chiddingstone and Hever. Whether or not Browne had to borrow to finance the purchase in the first instance, or ran into financial difficulties soon afterwards, by the following year he was mortgaging his new property for £300 to a minor local gentleman. Browne seems to have had further money problems during the 1590s, and became indebted to Thomas Hadilow, citizen and salter of London, to the tune of £1,800. Hadilow recruited several other Londoners as joint backers of Browne's enterprise, and when the investment proved unsuccessful (about 1600) one of these men sued Hadilow in the Court of Requests. By that date, according to the plaintiff, Browne was 'utterly decayed and in prison' and was 'no ways able to pay his debts'. In 1596, the same year Browne was appointed Queen's Founder of Iron Ordnance, he had entered into a contract with Thomas Sackville, to provide 400 tons of iron ordnance, at the price of £7 6s. 8d. per ton. This was a large order, and Browne could not finance the operation himself. He borrowed from the Londoners, but for one reason or another the contract was not completed, and Browne ended up more deeply in debt – and in debtors' prison. Browne's story shows just how different ironmaking was from most other forms of manufacture in this era: its high capital requirements made it unlikely that working ironfounders could build and operate a furnace on their own account. Outside capital seems to have been commonplace, either in the form of initial investment in plant by gentry landowners, or in loans from wealthy merchants of London. Nevertheless, Thomas Browne survived, and was succeeded as royal gunfounder by his more famous son John, who was granted Thomas's patents in 1615.[22]

---

[22] Goring, 'Wealden Ironmasters'. Browne: KAO U 1000/7/T8; PRO Req 2/191/37. Browne was involved in another suit over the delivery of iron in 1596. In his bill Browne claimed that he 'keepith always at the least 150 men at work', possibly an exaggeration of the labour force of one furnace and one forge: PRO Req 2/32/67; KAO TR 1295: Browne MSS.

Not all Wealden ironmasters, however, ended up in gaol. The multifarious activities of Davy Willard of Hadlow included the management as a tenant of at least one furnace and two forges in Tonbridge, as well as his extensive leasing of farmland in the same area, noticed in chapter 2. Thomas Dyke of Horsmonden, 'yeoman', owned Derondale forge in Lamberhurst and was the tenant of Chingley furnace in Goudhurst during the 1570s. He was born and educated in Suffolk, had arrived in Kent by 1560 and by 1572 was assessed at the respectably well-off level of £13 in goods (in Horsmonden). By the mid 1570s he was a prominent ironmaster, as a tenant and on his own account. In 1573 he purchased Derondale forge, along with fourteen acres in Pembury and Frant (Sussex) and Derondale Woods (130 acres) in Lamberhurst and Brenchley, from the Darrells for over £1,400. By 1574 he was also the tenant of Chingley furnace in Goudhurst (also owned by the Darrells). In 1576 he was informed against for making a usurious bargain in which he sold £270 worth of iron to a London merchant. He added yet another blast furnace to his operation in 1579, this time as the Darrells's tenant of a furnace in Horsmonden. The lease of Chingley furnace included 100 acres of woodland in Scotney Park (which surrounded the Darrell seat) and 360 acres of woodland at Chingley. When Dyke came to assign his lease to another ironmaster in 1597, the rent was to be £100 per annum. There are also scattered references to Dyke's extensive wood purchases during the 1580s and 1590s: he paid £600 for all the woods of the late Sir Walter Waller in Frant, Sussex in 1582. Dyke also bought land for investment: fifty-four acres in Lamberhurst in 1583, forty-five acres in Pembury and Brenchley in 1587, and – as Thomas Dyke, sen., 'gent' of Pembury – over 300 acres in Brenchley and Lamberhurst in 1606. In the subsidy of 1598 he had the very high assessment of £50 in goods. According to his 1614 will, Dyke also owned ironworks in Yorkshire and had invested heavily in the East India, Virginia and Bermuda companies. By that time he was wealthy enough to leave £400 to endow four preachers in Kent, Sussex, Suffolk and Yorkshire.[23]

Dyke, of course, was not typical of Wealden ironmasters. Few operated on such a scale, and very few were as successful. Richard Streatfield of Chiddingstone was a lesser contemporary of Dyke's, whose ironmaking business was based on one furnace (which he owned) and the associated forge (which he leased at £20 per annum). When he died in 1601 his trade goods were valued at about £1,200, over half of which was in the form of charcoal for his furnace. His will makes no mention of the ironworks, but reveals a successful businessman, with six named servants, and a growing landed estate large enough to be sensibly divided between three sons. He was wealthy enough to leave a few acres to endow local poor relief, disperse £14

[23] Goring, 'Wealden Ironmasters', pp. 218, 220; subsidy: PRO E 179/126/424; usury: E 159/370 Rec. Hil. rot. 58; wood purchases: E 159/370 Rec. Trin. rot. 136 and PROB 11/90/60 (will of Edward Cayley); as feoffee for Alexander Culpeper in 1560: PRO CP 25(2) File 2399 no. 246; Derondale forge purchase, leases of furnaces and other land purchases: E. Sussex R.O. Dyke(Hutton) MSS. nos. 602–7, 297–9, 302–3, 319–21, 353–6.

in cash doles to the poor of five adjoining parishes and set aside £300 for his daughter's portion.[24] There were, however, only a handful of such men in the Kent Weald in the late sixteenth century. What of the larger numbers of men who worked in the furnaces and forges?

The men who operated the blast furnaces and forges have left only shadowy traces in the records. They can rarely be identified from probate inventories (even if their goods were ever inventoried) because, like modern wage workers, they laboured at the industrialists' works and used his tools. And, since ironmaking itself was a seasonal trade, they may have had other occupations or farms to support themselves when not employed by the ironmasters. Very few identified their trade in wills, and probably very few – if any – made wills. There is a reference to a Robert Austen as the 'filler' of Mr Culpeper's furnace, in the will of another man in 1587, but no furnacemen's wills. Iron craftsmen only found their way into the records in exceptional circumstances. The three-year old son of Nicholas Jerrat, 'founder', was accidentally drowned in Horsmonden furnace pond in 1592. Nicholas was one of the few foreign craftsmen still working in the Wealden iron industry by that era: the Horsmonden parish register refers to him as a 'Frenchman'. But just two decades earlier, in 1571/2, five of Davy Willard's workmen were aliens, charged a flat poll tax of 4d. each in the subsidy. We also hear of John Williams, 'servant' of David Willard, who died in an accident at a furnace in Tonbridge in March 1565. And there was Michael Collin of Horsmonden, 'founder', identified because he was indicted at the assizes in 1564 for burglary and the theft of branding irons and other tools from the furnace at Horsmonden.[25]

The primary iron workers, however, were a small and historically elusive group of men. There are no identified ironworkers among all the Wealden deponents in Canterbury diocese church court cases between the 1560s and 1609, for example. And only three can be identified in the Kent quarter session records of the 1590s, although there are hundreds of people with occupations recorded in quarter session recognizances.[26] A case in Chancery involving the early Vauxhall furnace at South Frith in Tonbridge gives some idea of employment practices in the early iron industry. Richard True of Tonbridge, 'ironfounder', sued one Andrew Firminger over unpaid wages, claiming that he had been hired by Firminger (the duke of Northumberland's agent or manager at the furnace) 'to blow certain foundays of iron' at the furnace , at 15s. per founday. True asserted that indeed he had blown

---

[24] PRO PROB 11/98/70; KAO U 908, quoted in C. W. Chalklin, *Seventeenth Century Kent* (1965), p. 134.

[25] Austen: PRO PROB 11/72/11; PRO KB 9/681 no. 154; KB 9/610 no. 250. Aliens polled in 1571/2 at PRO E 179/126/424, in Southborough, Tonbridge. There is also an inquest in 1566 on the death of John Huswiffe of Ashurst, 'finer', at the hands of Robert Templer of Hartfield, Sussex, 'hammerman': PRO KB 9/621 no. 86; Collin: PRO Ass 35/6/4 mm. 32–3; also a Thomas Brooker of Biddenden, 'forgeman' as a surety in 1596: KAO PRC 3/25 fo. 10.

[26] They are Thomas Leigh of Ashurst and Morgan Standen of Goudhurst, both hammermen, and John Turner of Speldhurst, gunfounder: KAO QM/SRc/1594/45 and 77; QM/SRc/1598/56.

'13 foundays and 2 days', as well as hiring two additional men to help, at his own cost. Firminger replied that while he was in charge True had blown nine foundays, for which he had been paid; but that the duke then farmed the furnace to George Harper and Thomas Culpeper, thus discharging Firminger from his job and any responsibility to pay the founder for any further work.[27] It seems that sixteenth-century ironmasters employed very few full-time skilled workers directly. What skilled ironfounders earned remains unclear, since it is not known how long it took to 'blow' a founday, or how regularly they were employed. It may also be that when a furnace was in operation, the great majority of the men at work were unskilled labourers, working under the direction of a handful of skilled ironworkers. It also appears that many of the craftsmen in the industry worked as self-employed artisans. This also seems to have been the situation of colliers (i.e. charcoal burners) who prepared the fuel for the blast furnaces, for a number of whom there are scattered references in contemporary records.[28]

If much has been written about Wealden ironmaking, very little attention has been paid to the secondary metalware industry. But the two were intimately linked. Producers of iron tools could be found in some profusion in the Weald. However, the secondary metalworkers were concentrated in a very small part of the wider High Weald ironmaking zone. Leaving aside blacksmiths, who could be found in most Wealden parishes throughout the century, metalworkers were likely to live in just two, neighbouring parishes: Goudhurst and Horsmonden (with some spillover into Brenchley). Unfortunately for historians, there is far less surviving probate material for Horsmonden, and, crucially, no probate inventories. Horsmonden, too, was a smaller parish than Goudhurst, with no more than 600 inhabitants in the 1560s, in comparison to Goudhurst's 1,500. By the 1580s there were two iron forges and a furnace in Goudhurst, one furnace in Horsmonden and several ironworks in Lamberhurst which adjoins both parishes. Metalsmiths can be identified in both parishes, and, because many were independent master craftsmen who owned their own tools, they can be identified from probate inventories.

There was a noticeable tendency towards family dynasties in the several toolmaking trades. Two families can be offered as examples. The Brattles were a widely ramified clan, with members living in Goudhurst, Horsmonden and Brenchley throughout the century. Many of them were scythesmiths and at least one called himself a cutler. One of the numerous Thomas Brattles, a scythesmith, had an interest in the blast furnace in Horsmonden in the 1570s. Not all of this numerous family can be assigned to a trade, but their involvement in metalwares

[27] PRO C1/1387/53–4, dated about 1553.
[28] Colliers include Wm. Dunstan of Horsmonden (see will of his landlord Thos. Bishop: PRO PROB 11/82/55); Ric. Vynton of Tonbridge and Nic. Johnson of Biddenden (recognizances at KAO QM/SRc/1594/77 and 1598/111); And. Goodhew of Brenchley (KAO PRC 3/21 fo. 192 in 1585); Phil. Ruberbe of Goudhurst (PRC 3/19 fo. 154 in 1575); Dennis Ruberbe of Goudhurst, 'collier', owned chattels worth £25 in 1575, but Jas. Bassett, also a Goudhurst collier, had goods worth just £3 3s. (PRC 10/8 fo. 94, 10/13 fo. 8).

goes back to Henry VIII's reign if not earlier. Thomas Brattle, sen. of Goudhurst (d. 1551) was a scythesmith, who was succeeded by five sons, at least one of whom lived in Horsmonden. Before this, a Richard Brattle, 'cutler' of Brenchley (d. 1535), owned lands in both Brenchley and Horsmonden and mentioned four male servants in his will. At the end of the century another Thomas Brattle of Goudhurst (d. 1591) left chattels worth over £190, and his inventory shows that he ran a farm as well as manufactured scythes.[29]

The Rode family of Goudhurst provides an equally telling example of family continuity in toolmaking. There are wills from male members of the family dating back to 1497, when a John Rode of Goudhurst – trade unknown – died, leaving a messuage to his son Edward. That Edward died in 1527, to be succeeded by at least three sons, and was wealthy enough to ask for burial in the church. Two of his sons, Richard (d. 1548) and Thomas (d. 1535), called themselves scythesmiths, left wills and passed lands to their own sons. Richard Rode, sen. (d. 1548) left cash legacies totalling over £50 in addition to gifts of livestock from his farm, and divided his lands among four sons. Much of his estate had been purchased in his lifetime. He also had a lease of a grinding stone at nearby Bradford Mill. In the next generation at least one son, Edward, also worked as a scythesmith. When he died in 1573, his inventory was valued at £131, including trade goods worth about £30 (forty-two dozen scythes were priced at £18). He too ran a family sized farm. In 1580 there was yet another Richard Rode in Goudhurst, practising as a 'scythemaker'.[30]

Numerous other metalsmiths lived in these two parishes during the sixteenth century. None who left inventories was poor; most were among the better-off tradesmen of their parishes, and a few were quite rich. Many of them followed a dual family economy, combining farming with the production of metalwares, similar to the metalworkers of South Staffordshire studied by Pauline Frost. But these two regions of rural industry were not identical. In Staffordshire, the majority of metalsmiths were nailers, not usually a lucrative trade, whereas in the Kent Weald most metalworkers made farming tools. Not a single nailer has been identified in the records of the sixteenth-century Weald. What appears to be common to several regions with a metalware industry is the combination of craft with farming. Some metalsmiths in the Kent Weald were just smallholders, but a significant number were 'full-time' farmers as well as 'full-time' metalworkers. Hugh Morley of Goudhurst, 'scythesmith' (d. 1591), left chattels valued at £166. What might be called his trade goods – the tools, fuel, iron and his stock of ready-made scythes – came to about

---

[29] For comparable local examples see David Hey, 'A Dual Economy in South Yorkshire', *AgHR*, 17 (1969); Pauline Frost, 'Yeomen and Metalsmiths: Livestock in the Dual Economy of South Staffordshire', *AgHR*, 29 (1981); Thos. Brattle with furnace: Cleere and Crossley, *Iron Industry of the Weald*, App. C, no. 120; Thos. Brattle, scythesmith: KAO PRC 17/27 fo. 121; Ric. Brattle, cutler: KAO DRb/Pwr 9 fo. 196.

[30] John Rode: KAO PRC 17/6 fo. 305; Edw. Rode: PRC 17/17 fo. 166; Ric. Rode: PRC 17/26 fo. 258v; Thos. Rode: PRC 17/20 fo. 212; Edw. Rode: PRC 10/6 fo. 299; Ric. Rode: will of a servant, PRC 17/44 fo. 167.

£40. But his inventory also shows that he worked a farm of about fifty acres. An even wealthier metalsmith, Robert Lake of Goudhurst (d.1595), held a stock of '22 hundred of scythes', priced at over £180, out of a total inventory worth £390. He too occupied a farm, of thirty to forty acres.[31]

Blacksmiths practised their trade in a majority of Wealden parishes. Working from the probate inventories alone, there were sixteen blacksmiths resident in eight out of fourteen Wealden parishes in Canterbury diocese between 1565 and 1600. Blacksmiths were not as wealthy as their counterparts in the more specialized metalware trades, the whitesmiths (usually called scythesmiths in contemporary documents): the median inventory of blacksmiths was about £60 (mean = £63). The wealthiest blacksmith owned personal property worth £137, considerably below the level of the richer toolmakers. But the wealthier blacksmiths, like the scythesmiths, ran farms in addition to their craft businesses.[32] The most striking difference between the two categories of smiths was in the value of raw materials and finished tools owned by the scythesmiths. The trade goods of blacksmiths were usually limited to a pair of bellows, an anvil or two and a dozen or so iron tools such as hammers and tongs. Very few owned more than a tiny stock of iron and small amounts of fuel. Rarely were such trade goods valued at more than £5 or £10. The scythesmiths – like the tanners – usually held trade goods worth five or ten times that amount. The toolmakers could be called capitalists or manufacturers, whereas blacksmiths tended to possess little capital (except for a farm) and serviced only their immediate local area. Scythesmiths produced tools for sale in more distant as well as in local markets. What is not known is whether the wealthier scythesmiths acted as middlemen suppliers of iron to local blacksmiths, or if the latter obtained their iron directly from Wealden ironmasters. There was enough iron and steel in some scythesmiths' inventories to have satisfied their own as well as the needs of several blacksmiths. Since toolmakers bought iron in much greater quantities than blacksmiths, the former should have obtained their raw material more cheaply. Thus they were in a position to act as wholesale iron dealers, as well as manufacturers of tools. This is exactly the role played by the wealthier clothiers of the Weald, who supplied petty clothmakers with wool and dyestuffs, as we shall see in chapter 6.

As there was a clear-cut hierarchy of wealth within the metal trades, so there were also wide variations in wealth among the practitioners of most occupations. In

[31] Hugh Morley: KAO PRC 10/20 fo. 478; Robt. Lake: PRC 10/25 fo. 569 and will as 'yeoman': PRC 17/50 fo. 151. Known Horsmonden metalsmiths include: Wm. Allen of Brenchley or Horsmonden, scythesmith and Ric. Harding, cutler, witnesses to will of Wm. Dyrkin of Horsmonden, scythesmith: KAO DRb/Pwr 13 fo. 247v; Wm. Hall of the same, scythemaker: DRb/Pwr 13 fo. 461 (Thos. Dyke was a witness); Steph. Cogger, scythesmith: KAO QM/SRc/1599/149; Renny Durant, 'ironpot founder' (d. 1591): PRO PROB 11/79/34; Thos. Humfrey, scythesmith: PROB 11/98/71; John Hope, 'sicklemaker': KAO DRb/Pwr 20 fo. 71.

[32] Blacksmiths identified from probate inventories written between 1565 and 1600 in Benenden, Bethersden, Biddenden, Cranbrook, Goudhurst, Hawkhurst, Marden, Tenterden; no blacksmiths' inventories for Frittenden, Halden, Sandhurst, Smarden or Staplehurst.

Table 5.5 *Values of estates of tradesmen and craftsmen, 1565–99*

Occupation	Under £10	£10–20	£20–30	£30–40	£40–60	£60–100	£100+
Weavers (123)	6.5%	19.5%	25.2%	15.5%	16.3%	10.6%	6.5%
Clothiers (47)	–	6.4%	4.3%	4.3%	4.3%	27.7%	53.2%
Shopkeepers (30)	–	6.7%	3.3%	23.3%	23.3%	30%	13.3%
Smiths (25)	–	8%	24%	–	20%	16%	32%
Carpenters (32)	–	9.4%	34.4%	15.6%	15.6%	12.5%	12.5%
Tailors (22)	13.6%	18.2%	13.6%	13.6%	13.6%	4.6%	22.7%
Shoemakers (12)	16.7%	25%	8.3%	16.7%	–	25%	8.3%
Tanners (13)	–	–	7.7%	7.7%	15.4%	38.5%	30.8%
Millers and brewers (14)	–	–	–	21.4%	28.6%	28.6%	21.4%

	Average Values of Estates						
	1565–79		1580–9		1590–9		1565–99
Occupation	Median	Mean	Median	Mean	Median	Mean	Mean
Weavers (123)	£34	£40	£24	£40	£29	£39	£40
Clothiers(47)	£116	£301	£112	£125	£74	£108	£116
Clothworkers (12)	£30	£54	£43	£40	£48	£50	
Shopkeepers (30)	£45	£51	£65	£67	£54	£88	£66
Smiths (25)	£58	£88	£30	£43	£148	£148	£91
Carpenters (32)	£32	£42	£33	£42	£38	£62	£52
Tailors (22)	£22	£35	£104	£112	£28	£37	£69
Shoemakers(12)	£28	£26	£16	£46	£40	£63	£38
Tanners (13)	£74	£83	£57	£141	£460	£355	£159
Glovers (6)	£132	£113	£40 (1only)		£31 (2only)		£73
Millers and brewers (14)	£95	£109	£45	£50	£53	£54	£76

Note: smiths includes blacksmiths and whitesmiths.

addition, there were clear status and wealth differences *between* different trades. Table 5.5 displays the average values of tradesmen's inventories in the late sixteenth century, as well as the distribution of values of the personal estates of certain common occupations. In most trades there were individuals whose goods were worth less than £20 or £30. But with some occupations they account for a very large share of all who followed that trade; in other occupations the 'poor' are a tiny minority, in many cases probably retired men. In some occupations, most notably tanners and clothiers, those with goods worth over £50 or £60 are the typical representatives of that trade. By comparison, the average inventory of men who appear to have been full-time farmers in the Elizabethan Weald was worth between £50 and £55, a large share of which represented the value of their livestock. The personal estates of tradesmen therefore span the whole range of values of farmers' inventories – and dip well below that range as well.

Among the most interesting findings that emerges from an analysis of tradesmen's inventories is the wide spread of values in most trades. In part, no doubt, the variation is an illusion, because inventories were made at different stages in individuals' life cycles. The very small estates of a few individuals in several of the more prestigious trades may have been those either of young men just beginning their careers, or of retired tradesmen. Nevertheless, the distributions of values of personal estates do demonstrate the wide differentials possible in the same trade. Taken as a group, the sample has some validity as a picture of the relative wealth of the different occupations represented. But there are notable gaps in the occupational structure, caused not only by the relative poverty of individuals in some trades, but also by the difficulty of inferring occupations from the chattels listed on an inventory. Both factors are probably at work in the near absence of building workers (other than carpenters) from the inventory sample. There is plenty of evidence to show that the region supported specialized construction workers – masons, glaziers, bricklayers and thatchers – but they do not surface in the inventories. They used common tools, worked with the customers' own materials and many were probably too poor to attract the notice of the probate courts in any case. Similar obstacles prevent the inclusion of butchers, bakers and barbers. For a few trades there were too few identified inventories to be of any statistical significance. There was a single tinker's inventory, of the 1580s, that could be identified (£26), just two chandlers (£16 and £25) and only two colliers (£25 and £3). There were just seven inventories of occupations normally grouped together as 'professionals' (the mean of their estates was £92).

Comments must therefore be limited to the occupational groups for which there is enough data. That a quarter of all weavers (with inventories), for example, had personal estates worth less than £20 is hardly surprising. More remarkable is the quarter of weavers' inventories whose chattels were valued at £50 or more. Most shoemakers' estates fall within the poorest categories, and yet four of that trade owned chattels worth at least £60. Both carpenters (which include joiners and sawyers here) and smiths (including blacksmiths as well as toolmakers) also showed enormous differences in personal wealth. A few examples will illustrate the prosperity of some and the relative poverty of others more readily than the statistics. John White, a carpenter from Smarden, died in early 1572 leaving goods worth under £25. He was a part-time farmer as well as a craftsman. He had wheat in the ground worth £4 (about two or three acres), two cows, some swine and poultry valued at £4 13s. 4d. and 13s. 4d. in stored corn. His carpenter's tools were rated at just 8s., and the rest of his goods, about £14 worth, was household stuff. White is as good an example as any of the artisan-smallholder. Between his craft earnings and his own small-scale husbandry, he and his family probably managed to maintain a comparatively reasonable standard of living in most years, a conclusion underlined by his £14 worth of housewares. Many inventories of cottagers like White survive, although the craft of many of them is unknown. But as the manorial rentals discussed in chapter 2 suggest, there were hundreds of freeholders in the Weald with less than ten acres; many of them would have been craftsmen like John White. About four years after White's death John Sharpe of the same parish died. He too was a carpenter – in this case a joiner – but his chattels were worth four times as much as White's. His joinery tools ('with planes and chisels') and planks of timber were worth almost £7 alone. He had a plough and a wagon and farmed on a substantial scale by Wealden standards. His corn in the ground consisted of seven acres of wheat and four acres of oats and peas (suggesting total arable acreage of fifteen or sixteen acres). He also owned six kine, two oxen, two steers, three two-year heifers, a one-year bud and two calves, as well as two mares, all valued at over £30. There are no debts listed, and therefore Sharpe's clothes and household goods were worth more than £50, or twice the value of John White's whole estate.[33] Sharpe's prosperity appears to have been due as much to his farming as to his joinery business. Craftsmen at both ends of the spectrum of wealth (and in the middle) in Smarden and elsewhere in the Weald were often active farmers. John White, the carpenter, was a smallholder of six or eight acres, while John Sharpe, the joiner, was farming for the market on forty acres or more.

Many craftsmen appear 'poor' from their inventories because they were not also farmers. In terms of *money income* they might not have been much worse off than some of their colleagues in the same trade who did some farming – if both were employed as regularly in the same craft. But such is the weakness of using the ownership of goods as a measure of economic position. Edward Waghorne of Hawkhurst, a blacksmith who died in 1591, might be a case in point. His total estate was worth just over £20, making him one of the 'poorest' smiths in the whole sample. He had no farm or smallholding. In his workshop were two anvils, three sledgehammers, one rickhorn, four hammers, fifteen pairs of tongs, a pair of bellows and some coal and iron. In all, his trade goods came to £3. Besides a pound and a half in cash and 5s. in wood, the rest was household stuff.[34] One would like to know his income; clearly he was not a wealthy man, but was he 'poor'? Having a sideline in farming was commonplace, but not necessary for an artisan's survival. Nevertheless, in most cases 'wealthy' craftsmen and manufacturers in the Weald also actively farmed. In many instances the value of their livestock and corn was considerably higher than that of their 'trade goods'. The inventories of such men do not inform us about how much labour such mixed enterprises employed, but in cases like John Sharpe and the well-off scythesmiths mentioned above, hired labour would have been essential, even assuming that prosperous craftsmen had apprentices at the same time.

---

[33] KAO PRC 10/5 fo. 299; 10/8 fo. 263.   [34] KAO PRC 10/22 fo. 30.

Comparing trade with trade, the Wealden clothiers were undoubtedly the wealthiest occupational group. More than three-quarters of clothiers' inventories were valued at £60 or more. The handful of what look like 'poor' clothiers' inventories are of men no longer in business plus one or two apprentices. And the greater wealth of clothiers is, to an extent, artificially understated by the absence of inventories of the most successful clothiers with wills proved in the Prerogative Court of Canterbury. Standing behind the textile manufacturers were the leather manufacturers. Almost 70 per cent of tanners' inventories were valued at £60 or over, although very few were worth in excess of £250, a commonplace total for the elite of Cranbrook clothiers, as we shall see in chapter 7. Next in order of wealth were the smiths of all kinds, of whom almost a half had personal estates of £60 or more. And, if the blacksmiths are excluded, the smiths who manufactured metal tools are also to be numbered among the region's wealthiest occupational groups.

One of the most remarkable features of the Wealden economy is that manufacturers – of cloth, leather and metalwares – were at the top of the hierarchy of wealth. The economic leadership of this rural area was no longer firmly in the hands of its wealthier farmers and landowners. The Weald was dominated by a mixed elite of commercial farmers (including gentry) and prosperous manufacturers. Big yeoman farmers remained a numerous and powerful group, as demonstrated in chapter 4. But in the parishes of the central and eastern Weald covered by the inventory sample they formed just one part of a local upper class. As a group, the full-time farmers and graziers were not as wealthy as the manufacturers: only about 46 per cent of farmers' inventories were worth £60 or more. Only about a quarter were rated at £100 or above, as compared to over 30 per cent of tanners' and smiths' inventories, and well over half of clothiers' inventories (table 5.5 above). In certain parishes – such as Halden, Rolvenden or Sandhurst – the wealthy elite would be almost entirely made up of gentry and yeoman farmers. The same is probably true for some parishes in the western Weald, which do not figure in the inventory sample. But even in the west, the wealthier tanners and a handful of ironmasters diluted the domination of farming wealth.

In all parts of the Weald, however, there were poor tradesmen and artisans aplenty. The trades that stand out in the inventory sample as the least wealthy are the weavers and the shoemakers: over the whole period 1565–99 two-thirds of both groups owned personal estates worth less than £40. Tailors, too, should probably be added to the list of 'poor' trades: about 60 per cent of tailors with inventories were worth under £40. The other trades which undoubtedly shared the bottom rungs of the economic ladder are those most difficult to identify from inventories: building workers, bakers and alehouse keepers. In reality they were certainly more numerous than tailors and shoemakers, but the surviving sources prevent us from making any kind of meaningful comparison among all the 'poor' trades. A large, but unknown, share of people who followed familiar trades like these are not included in the occupational analysis of table 5.5, either because their trade has not been identified and they are included among the catch-all categories of smallholder or labourer, or because no inventory was made of their goods in the first place. But it is worth bearing in mind that if something of the order of a third to a half of adult males are not represented by inventories, then the real proportion of the adult population that worked for wages – who neither ran a family-sized farm nor were independent master craftsmen – may have been a good deal higher than the 30 per cent or so suggested in table 5.2 above. Undoubtedly many independent but poor petty tradesmen were among those with no inventories, but it is unlikely that many full-time farmers were ignored by the probate courts. Thus the bulk of the adult males (and of course many women who worked for money wages) whose chattels were not appraised must have been wage earners.

The Kent Weald as a whole was therefore well on the road to what may be called 'modern' social relations of production. But was it a homogeneous region? What can be discovered about the geographical distribution of wealth in the Weald? It has already been shown (chapter 3) that there were significant variations in population density in different parts of the Kent Weald, that in some areas within the Weald landholdings were more fragmented and there were very large numbers of petty freeholders compared to other areas (chapter 2), and that rural manufacturing was concentrated in parts of the Weald.

Were there also substantial differences in wealth or income between different parts of the Weald, and can such variation be related to any of the other specific characteristics of these small sub-regions of the Weald? The evidence which survives to answer these questions is inevitably flawed, but good enough to justify the attempt. For the early sixteenth century there are the records of parliamentary taxation, the subsidy rolls. For the most inclusive general taxation of the sixteenth century – the 1524/5 subsidies – however, parts of the Weald are not covered. Equally unhelpful, in the subsidy rolls for Kent, taxpayers are usually listed within the ancient administrative divisions known as hundreds, rather than assigned to a parish. Since the boundaries of Wealden hundreds do not coincide with parish boundaries, it is not possible to relate the reasonably accurate early sixteenth-century tax records to the best late sixteenth-century sources – probate records and registers of baptisms and burials. The best that can be done is to use both types of evidence, relating the figures to approximate sub-regional divisions within the Weald. The absence of probate inventories for the western Weald remains a serious gap.

The Tudor subsidy rolls have been widely used by historians, and need little formal introduction.[35] Taxpayers could be assessed in a number of different ways:

[35] An introduction is M. W. Beresford, *Lay Subsidies and Poll Taxes* (1963). R. S. Schofield, 'Parliamentary Lay Taxation, 1485–1547', unpublished Ph.D. thesis, University of Cambridge, 1963 is basic. See also John Sheail, 'The Regional Distribution of Wealth in England as indicated in the Lay Subsidy Returns of 1524/5', unpublished Ph.D. thesis, University of London, 1968; J. Sheail, 'The Distribution of

on wages (only in 1524/5), on the value of their goods or on their annual income from lands and fees. The subsidy assessors were supposed to rate taxpayers on that method which produced the greatest tax liability; thus a person taxed on his or her goods was not necessarily landless. The rating on goods was supposed to ignore a worker's basic tools, but even this exemption does not explain why so many taxpayers were assessed as having chattels worth only £1 or £2. The very low ratings on goods – and the assessments at £1 or £2 in wages – are more likely notional levels which indicate relatively poor but taxable persons, rather than accurate valuations of those taxpayers' goods or total annual incomes. There has also been debate about what proportion of the adult population (or adult male population) was considered too poor even for inclusion in the taxes levied in 1524/5, a subsidy which drew in more taxpayers than any other during the sixteenth century. The lay subsidy of 1543/4 affected almost as many persons as that of the 1520s, and – unlike 1524/5 – there is at least one complete return for almost every area within the Kent Weald. From 1547 the value of lay subsidy returns as evidence of wealth or income declines. The numbers of persons rated to the subsidy in the late sixteenth century drops precipitously, at the same time as the English population was rapidly growing. Equally damaging, the recorded assessments of those who were rated became ludicrously unrealistic, with the greatest under-assessment reserved for the very rich: the wide differentials between people of middling wealth and the elite of gentry and merchants become enormously squeezed.[36]

The declining reliability of subsidy rolls is suggested by the tax lists for the Wealden hundred of Cranbrook. In 1524/5 608 persons were rated to the subsidy, which was expected to produce about £173. By 1543/4 only 503 taxpayers were included, but the total tax payable had risen to £238. By 1571/2 the number of taxpayers was just 38 per cent of those rated in 1524/5, and the tax take was just £107, less than two-thirds of what had been collected from the hundred half a century earlier, and following more than thirty years of accelerating inflation.[37] In the face of such a fiscal charade, it is sensible to use only the early Tudor tax rolls for studying economic differences between areas.

One further issue must be mentioned: to analyse variations in wealth between different parts of the Weald, it is important to know not just how many taxpayers there were in each hundred, but the surface area as well. While there are relatively

Taxable Population and Wealth in England during the Early Sixteenth Century', *Trans. Instit. Brit. Geographers*, 55 (1972); R. S. Schofield, 'The Geographical Distribution of Wealth in England, 1334–1649', *EcHR*, 2nd ser., 18 (1965); R. B. Smith, *Land and Politics in the England of Henry VIII* (1970), chapter 3; and now J. C. K. Cornwall, *Wealth and Society in Early Sixteenth Century England* (1988). R. Fieldhouse attempted to relate the tax rolls of the 1540s to probate inventories in 'Social Structure from Tudor Lay Subsidies and Probate Inventories', *Local Population Studies*, 12 (1974).

[36] See Roger Schofield, 'Taxation and the Political Limits of the Tudor State', in Claire Cross *et al.* (eds.), *Law and Government under the Tudors* (1988).

[37] PRO E 179/125/324; E 179/124/259; E 179/126/423.

Table 5.6 *Tax payable by Wealden hundreds*[38]

Hundred	1524/5	1543/4 (%)	1545/6 (%)
Westerham		£29 (3.7%)	£67 (4.6%)
Somerden		£45 (5.8%)	£63 (4.3%)
Tonbridge		£30 (3.8%)	£109 (7.5%)
Wachlingstone	£16	c.£22 (2.8%)	£29 (2%)
Brenchley		c.£67 (8.6%)	£79 (5.4%)
W. Barnfield		c.£10 (1.3%)	£38 (2.6%)
Marden		£44 (5.6%)	£110 (7.5%)
E. Barnfield	£17	£17 (2.2%)	£43 (2.9%)
Cranbrook	£173	£238 (30%)	£447 (30.6%)
Barclay	£56	£89 (11.4%)	£172 (11.8%)
Selbrittenden	£41	£35 (4.5%)	£78 (5.3%)
Rolvenden	£33	£53 (6.8%)	£68 (4.7%)
Blackborne	£86	£103 (13.2%)	£159 (10.9%)
Totals		£782	£1,462

Sources: 1524/5 (PRO E 179/124/186; E 179/125/324); 1543/4 (PRO E 179/124/256; E 179/124/259; E 179/124/262; E 179/125/268;E 179/125/275); 1545/6 (E 179/125/300–301, 307.

accurate figures for the areas covered by all the early nineteenth-century parishes, the size of the Wealden hundreds is not so certain. In the tables below, the acreage of hundreds is drawn from the national gazetteers of the 1860s, but with limited confidence about what relation they bear to the sixteenth-century boundaries.[39] Before proceeding to a more detailed analysis of wealth (as measured by taxation) in different parts of the Weald, a number of tables set out the position of all the Wealden hundreds in terms of tax paid, tax paid per thousand acres and taxpayers per thousand acres.

A number of major contrasts between the different parts of the Weald become apparent if tables 5.6–8 are studied together. The hundreds are listed roughly in geographical order, moving from west to east, and the figures reveal quite outstanding disparities in taxable wealth between the west Weald hundreds and those of the central Weald. The four large central hundreds of Cranbrook, Marden,

[38] Figures for Westerham hundred include Brasted vill; entry for Tonbridge Lowy for 1543/4 comes from the 2nd payment, of 36 Henry VIII, unlike other hundreds which are from the first payment. Amounts for 1543/4 for Wachlingstone, Brenchley and W. Barnfield are based on a defective MS. Wachlingstone's total includes amounts for missing burghs, according to the proportions paid by those burghs in 1524–5 and 1545–6. Westerham and Blackborne hundreds are only partially in the Weald.

[39] *The National Gazetteer; The Imperial Gazetteer.* An additional limitation of the subsidy roll evidence is that Tenterden, being a limb of the Cinque Ports, was not liable to parliamentary lay taxation: Tenterden hundred is not to be found on the Kent subsidy rolls, and thus a relatively wealthy part of the Kent Weald is missing from this analysis.

Table 5.7 *Weald hundreds: taxpayers per 1000 acres*

Hundred	1524/5	1543/4	1545/6
Westerham (13,000a.)		14.2	7.3
Somerden (15,000a.)		14.8	7.2
Tonbridge (21,000a.)		12.3	7.0
Wachlingstone (12,000a.)	13.1	12.5	
Brenchley (15,000a.)		20	9.5
W. Barnfield (4,000a.)		18.7	6.0
Marden (16,000a.)		16.6	9.8
E. Barnfield (6,500a.)	23.5	18.3	11.5
Cranbrook (14,000a.)	43.4	35.9	19.3
Barclay (7,200a.)	35.4	36.0	19.2
Selbrittenden (6,000a.)	32.2	22.3	15.5
Rolvenden (12,000a.)	16.2	14.3	9.1
Blackborne (18,000a.)	19.8	15.3	8.7

Table 5.8 *Weald hundreds: tax due per 1,000 acres (in shillings)*

Hundred	1524/5	1543/4	1545/6
Westerham		30.8	75.4
Somerden		58.7	65.3
Tonbridge		28.6	103.8
Wachlingstone	26.7	c.37	48.3
Brenchley		c.89	105.3
W. Barnfield		50	188
Marden		55	137.5
E. Barnfield	52	52	132
Cranbrook	247	340	639
Barclay	155	247	478
Selbrittenden	137	117	260
Rolvenden	55	88	113
Blackborne	95	114	177

Barclay and Selbrittenden – which cover much of the Wealden broadcloth region – yielded one half of the total tax raised in the Weald in 1543/4 and 55 per cent of the total in the subsidy of 1545/6 which excluded many of the less well-off rated in the previous subsidy and taxed the better-off more severely. The four 'wealthy' hundreds included just slightly over a quarter of the surface area of the thirteen hundreds included in the tables. Taxpayers were thick on the ground in the four central hundreds: about twenty-seven per thousand acres in 1543/4, whereas the average for all the Weald hundreds was around eighteen per thousand acres. Even more impressive was the level of tax raised in the central hundreds, at over 188s. per thousand acres in 1543/4, as compared to the Weald average of 106s. In 1545/6 the central hundreds paid at the rate of 374s. per thousand acres, just about twice the average for the Weald as a whole, 190s. per thousand acres.

The western Weald was comparatively poor – if the amount of tax is anything to go by. The four westernmost hundreds of Westerham, Somerden, Tonbridge and Wachlingstone cover 38 per cent of the land area of the hundreds under study, but they produced just 16 per cent and 18 per cent of the tax collected in 1543/4 and 1545/6 respectively. In 1543/4 there were relatively few taxpayers in these western hundreds: just about fourteen per thousand acres, or well under the average for the Weald. This tallies well with what is known about the overall density of population in the west Weald parishes, discussed in chapter 3. And the gap between the western hundreds and the rest was even greater if measured in terms of the tax yield: in 1543/4 the western hundreds paid about 41s. per thousand acres, less than half the average for the Weald, and in 1545/6 they yielded 88s. per thousand acres, again under half the Weald average. The west Weald hundreds produced only about a quarter of the revenue collected in the clothing hundreds, if measured in terms of yield per thousand acres.

A third group of hundreds in the east of the Weald – Rolvenden and Blackborne hundreds – resembled the four western hundreds in producing a comparatively low number of taxpayers: about fifteen per thousand acres in 1543/4. But they had more well-off taxpayers than in the west. The eastern sub-region yielded 104s. per thousand acres in 1543/4, almost exactly the average for the Weald as a whole, and 151s. per thousand acres in 1545/6, somewhat lower than the average in that year but nevertheless considerably above the level of tax taken in the western hundreds.

In terms of taxable wealth, then, the Weald was not a homogeneous region. The disparities between the sub-regions can be understood more clearly if the distribution of taxation in representative hundreds is examined in detail. Starting in the west, Somerden hundred covered about 15,000 acres, mainly in the parishes of Chiddingstone, Cowden, Hever and Penshurst. Cranbrook hundred, of about 14,000 acres, included most of the parishes of Cranbrook and Frittenden and parts of Benenden, Goudhurst and Staplehurst. Rolvenden hundred in the east included most of the parish of Rolvenden and part of Benenden, covering 12,000 acres in all.

Tables 5.9 and 5.10 show the distribution of tax payments in the three hundreds. The contrast between Cranbrook hundred and the other two is apparent among taxpayers both at the bottom and top of the tax bands. Only Cranbrook had a substantial minority of higher rate taxpayers, and only there did less than half of all taxpayers pay under 10s. in tax. Rolvenden hundred appears somewhat less 'poor' than Somerden: it had a slightly larger number of higher rate taxpayers, a slightly smaller number in the lowest band. But Cranbrook's wealth stands out clearly. However, this comparison between the three hundreds gives the impression that Cranbrook hundred had a smaller proportion of relatively poor inhabitants than either of the other two; a false impression, as it turns out.

Table 5.9 *Taxation in three Wealden hundreds, 1545/6*

Tax Paid	Somerden	Cranbrook	Rolvenden
Under 10s.	73 (68%)	108 (40%)	65 (60%)
10s.–19s.	25 (23%)	61 (23%)	28 (26%)
20s.–39s.	7 (6.5%)	47 (17%)	7 (6%)
40s.–79s.	1 (1%)	28 (10%)	7 (6%)
80s. or over	2 (1.5%)	26 (10%)	2 (2%)

Sources: as in Table 5.6.

Table 5.10 *Taxation in three Wealden hundreds, 1524/5*

Assessment	Wachlings.	Cranb.	Rolv.
£1 goods/wages; under £1 p.a. lands	40%	30%	35.5%
£2 goods/wages; £1 p.a. lands	16.5%	31%	13%
£3 goods/wages; to £1 19s. p.a. lands	9%	7%	10%
£4–5 goods; £2 p.a. lands	11%	6.5%	14.5%
£6–10 goods; £3–£6 p.a. lands	16.5%	12%	15.5%
£11–19 goods; £7–£19 19s. p.a. lands	6%	6%	8%
£20 or over, goods or lands	1%	7.5%	3.5%

If the distribution of tax assessment for a different subsidy – one that included a higher proportion of the adult population – is analysed, a different picture emerges. The subsidy voted in 1523 attempted to do just that. Because the returns for Somerden hundred are lost, another west Weald hundred, Wachlingstone, will have to serve in its place (Table 5.10).

The 1524/5 subsidies affected far more people than any other in the sixteenth century, and provide a more reliable picture of the distribution of wealth in different parts of the Weald than any other. In the returns tabulated here, for the first payment of the subsidy, there were 157 taxpayers in Wachlingstone hundred, 608 in Cranbrook and 194 in Rolvenden. Cranbrook's overall wealth in 1524/5 can clearly be seen: the mean tax paid there was 5.7s., as compared to 2s. per taxpayer in Wachlingstone and 3.4s. in Rolvenden. Cranbrook also had an elite of 5 per cent of taxpayers assessed at £30 or more in lands or goods. In Wachlingstone there were no such assessments, and in Rolvenden just three men were rated at £30 or over. The superior wealth of Cranbrook hundred is also shown by comparing the amount of tax paid per acre in the sample hundreds. Wachlingstone yielded about 27s. per 1,000 acres in 1524/5, Rolvenden double that at 55s. per 1,000 acres, but Cranbrook paid at the rate of 247s. per 1,000 acres.

But the structure of wealth in these hundreds is quite complex, as the distribution of assessments in table 5.9 shows. Cranbrook's wealthy elite was dwarfed by its enormous class of quite poor inhabitants. Wealth was distributed most unevenly in Cranbrook hundred, and most evenly in Rolvenden. The lowest two bands of assessments accounted for under half the taxpayers in Rolvenden hundred but over 60 per cent of them in Cranbrook. In fact, Cranbrook was the only hundred with surviving returns to have 60 per cent or more in the two poorest bands in 1524/5. By contrast, the two other hundreds had many more of their taxpayers assessed in the three middle bands than Cranbrook. In Wachlingstone more than a third of taxpayers were rated in the middle bands, in Rolvenden it was as much as 40 per cent, but in 'wealthy' Cranbrook only about a quarter were rated in the three middle bands. The distribution of wealth shown in the table hints at what might be called the underside of Cranbrook hundred's 'prosperity': wealth was already in the 1520s quite polarized, with a large proportion of the area's families living on incomes which sixteenth-century governments and subsidy commissioners did not normally consider worth taxing. In 1524/5 the assessors rated almost a third of Cranbrook's taxpayers on their wages; in no other hundred were more than a quarter assessed on wages. A major share of those relatively poor adults taxed in 1524/5 must have worked in the Cranbrook textile industry, whose workers figured so prominently in the occupational data examined earlier.

As we shall see in chapter 6, thousands of households depended on the outwork offered by the wealthy clothiers of Cranbrook and the neighbouring parishes. In Cranbrook hundred the elite of clothiers and other wealthy tradesmen lived cheek by jowl – almost – with the workers on whom their prosperity depended. And the Cranbrook clothiers' influence reached beyond Cranbrook hundred. It is most visible in the smaller hundred to the south, East Barnfield, which covered most of Hawkhurst parish. Hawkhurst had few wealthy clothiers among its residents, but plenty of outworkers in the cloth industry. Whereas Cranbrook hundred yielded 5.7s. per taxpayer in 1524/5, East Barnfield produced just 2.2s. per taxpayer, the lowest average for any hundred in the central Weald covered by extant returns. It would seem that much of the 'wealth' produced by the inhabitants of East Barnfield hundred migrated to Cranbrook.

To sum up, the evidence of taxation from the first half of the sixteenth century shows that the economy of the Kent Weald was already extremely varied, with large disparities in overall wealth – and in the distribution of wealth – between different areas. The more sparsely populated western hundreds were also – in terms of total taxable wealth – the poorest, the populous central Wealden sub-region the 'wealthiest', and the less 'industrialized' eastern hundreds occupied a middle position. But the subsidy rolls of the 1520s also demonstrate that there were often many more poor individuals in the 'wealthy' areas than in the 'poor' hundreds. It would be interesting to know if such local variations in the distribution of wealth became more extreme in the later sixteenth century. But the subsidy rolls of the second half of the century are of little value as a guide to the distribution of wealth among the population as a whole: the majority even of adult males were not rated to the subsidy. The Elizabethan tax returns can only offer a few hints about the relative positions of the different sub-regions of the Weald.

The broad sub-regional differences in taxable wealth, already noticeable in the 1520s, persisted in the 1570s. But they have become less extreme. The four central hundreds (Marden, Cranbrook, Barclay and Selbrittenden) were responsible for 42 per cent of the total Weald tax, compared to 55 per cent in 1545/6. And the contribution of the four hundreds of the west Weald had grown from 18 per cent to 28 per cent in the same period. The four central hundreds yielded far more in revenue per acre than the other parts of the Weald, but at 98s. per 1,000 acres in 1571/2, it was now just double the rate per acre of the western hundreds (at 46s. per 1,000 acres). The two eastern hundreds paid at about the average rate for the Weald as a whole, similar to their contribution in the 1540s. It would appear that two things were happening: the greater wealth of the central Weald textile district remained but was no longer growing at the pace of the early sixteenth century, or was not growing at all. This tallies with the known stagnation in demand for the high quality broadcloth which the area produced. At the same time, the population and probably the taxable wealth of the western Weald was still growing. The demonstrable expansion of the west Weald iron industry after 1550 is just one explanation why the area was beginning to catch up economically with the traditionally 'wealthy' districts of the Weald.

A more detailed analysis of the changing distribution of wealth within the Weald in the *later* sixteenth century can be assembled from probate inventories. Even with all their deficiencies,[40] as a source they remain superior to the Elizabethan tax returns. However, our analysis of local and chronological variations in inventoried wealth is limited to the central and eastern Weald, within the diocese of Canterbury. Table 5.12 sets out the distribution of personal wealth in the Elizabethan inventories for fourteen sample parishes. Although the inventory sample covers a less extensive area than the tax returns, there is nevertheless considerable local variation. At first glance, there appears to be quite an even spread of inventoried wealth across the range of values. But the differences between parishes need to be explained, and – with any luck – related to differences in occupational structure and in wealth as measured by the tax returns.

To begin with, did all parishes generate a similar number of inventories relative to their populations? The fourteen parishes in table 5.12 had about 12,000 inhabitants at the beginning of the Elizabethan period (table 3.12). But not all produced their 'expected' numbers of inventories, while several had more than might be predicted. Bethersden, Rolvenden, Sandhurst and Tenterden generated

[40] Margaret Spufford, 'The Limitations of the Probate Inventory', in John Chartres and David Hey (eds.), *English Rural Society, 1500–1800* (1990)

Table 5.11 *Taxation in Wealden hundreds, 1571/2*

Hundred	Tax payable	(%)	Tax/1,000 acres (shillings)
Westerham (13,000a.)	£23	(4.6%)	35.4s.
Somerden (15,000a.)	£53	(10.6%)	70.7s.
Tonbridge (21,000a.)	£46	(9.2%)	43.8s.
Wachlingstone (12,000a.)	£18	(3.6%)	30s.
Brenchley (15,000a.)	£42	(8.4%)	56s.
W. Barnfield (4,000a.)	£5	(1%)	25s.
Marden (16,000a.)	£36	(7.2%)	45s.
E. Barnfield (6,500a.)	£17	(3.4%)	52s.
Cranbrook (14,000a.)	£107	(21.4%)	153s.
Barclay (7,200a.)	£41	(8.2%)	114s.
Selbrittenden (6,000a.)	£28	(5.6%)	93s.
Rolvenden (12,000a.)	£32	(6.4%)	53s.
Blackborne (18,000a.)	£52	(10.4%)	58s.

Sources: PRO E 179/126/422–4. Somerden 100 is exceptionally high because of Sir Henry Sidney's tax of £17, on £160 p.a. in lands, most of which were not in Somerden 100.

Table 5.12 *Inventoried wealth by parish, 1565–99*

Parish (No.)	Up to £20	£20–30	£30–60	£60–100	£100+
Benenden (112)	18(22%)	16(14%)	31(28%)	18(16%)	22(20%)
Bethersden (107)	41(38%)	16(15%)	28(26%)	15(14%)	7(7%)
Biddenden (97)	33(34%)	12(14%)	23(24%)	19(18%)	10(10%)
Cranb./Fritt (169)	40(24%)	21(12%)	49(29%)	31(18%)	28(17%)
Goudhurst (102)	23(23%)	21(20%)	26(25%)	18(18%)	14(14%)
Halden (48)	11(23%)	7(15%)	19(39%)	3 (6%)	8(17%)
Hawkhurst (91)	33(36%)	17(19%)	22(24%)	7 (8%)	12(13%)
Marden (83)	29(35%)	12(14%)	18(22%)	10(12%)	14(17%)
Rolvenden (107)	27(25%)	20(19%)	25(23%)	16(15%)	19(18%)
Sandhurst (55)	12(22%)	10(18%)	15(27%)	5 (9%)	13(24%)
Smarden (90)	33(37%)	12(13%)	22(24%)	10(11%)	13(15%)
Staplehurst (69)	20(29%)	17(25%)	11(16%)	11(16%)	10(14%)
Tenterden (157)	42(27%)	17(11%)	31(20%)	27(17%)	40(25%)
Totals (1,287)	*369(29%)*	*198(15%)*	*320(25%)*	*190(15%)*	*210(16%)*

more inventories than expected, while Cranbrook and Frittenden, Goudhurst and Hawkhurst all produced less.[41] It is not easy to explain why Bethersden (a parish

[41] Beths. (5.6% of population, with 8.3% of inventories); Rolv. (5.8% of population but 8.3% of inventories); Sandh. (3.2% of population but 4.3% of inventories; Tent. (9.6% of population but 12.2% of inventories). Cranb./Fritt. (19.2% of population but only 13.1% of inventories);

with some clothmaking but not densely populated) should have had a higher than average number of male inventories. Sandhurst was almost wholly agricultural and among the least densely populated parishes in the High Weald, while Rolvenden was mainly agricultural, close to the Weald average of population density and, as noted earlier, part of a hundred with relatively evenly distributed taxable wealth. Tenterden was a large parish, with a significant urban core, but with only very limited involvement in clothmaking. If literacy levels were slightly higher in Tenterden than in some of the surrounding parishes, there may have been a greater chance of written inventories being drawn up here than elsewhere. The parishes with fewer than expected inventories form a definite group. Cranbrook and Frittenden, Goudhurst and Hawkhurst all had substantial numbers of artisans and outworkers, who made up at least a large minority of the parishes' inhabitants. Many of such men would have owned too few chattels at their death to be worth appraising. These parishes were also among the most densely populated in the Kent Weald.

The most straightforward way of highlighting the local differences in inventoried wealth is to compare each parish's distribution to the distribution of inventory values across the sample, shown in the last line of table 5.12. To begin with, five parishes stand out for the relatively large number of inventories worth less than £20. Bethersden (38 per cent), Biddenden (34 per cent), Hawkhurst (36 per cent), Marden (35 per cent) and Smarden (37 per cent) each showed a considerably higher share of 'poor' inventories than the Weald sample (at 29 per cent). And three of those also produced well under the average numbers of wealthier inventories (valued at £60 or over): Bethersden (21 per cent), Hawkhurst (21 per cent) and Smarden (26 per cent), where the Weald average was over 30 per cent. At the other extreme, several parishes had rather more than the average number of wealthy inventories: Benenden (36 per cent), Cranbrook and Frittenden (35 per cent) and especially striking, Tenterden (43 per cent). And several of those also produced lower than average numbers of 'poor' inventories: Benenden (just 22 per cent) and Cranbrook and Frittenden (24 per cent), although Tenterden had just slightly below the average share of 'poor' inventories. Two other parishes, Halden and Sandhurst, had well below the average proportion of 'poor' inventories; but the first of these generated very few wealthy inventories while Sandhurst had slightly over the average share of inventories worth £60 or over. Both Halden and Sandhurst were fundamentally agricultural parishes, and yet it was Sandhurst (on the High Weald) which seemed to have a significant elite of wealthy farmers that was absent from Halden. Among the 'poorer' parishes two have much in common. Both Bethersden and Smarden had many 'poor' inventories and few wealthy ones. Both lie in the Low Weald, and both supported some clothmaking, in this case the manufacture of cheap, narrow woollens rather than the more valuable broadcloths. One additional

Goudh. (12% of population but 7.9 per cent of inventories); Hawkh. (9.4% of population but 7.1% of inventories).

parish seems to fit neatly with Bethersden and Smarden: Hawkhurst in the High Weald, a parish dependent on outworking in the cloth industry, which produced very many 'poor' inventories and very few high value ones. The only significant differences between Hawkhurst and the other two were that Hawkhurst was much more densely populated, and its inhabitants were more heavily involved in clothmaking than the people of Bethersden and Smarden.

The 'wealthy' parishes turn out to be a very mixed group. Benenden and Cranbrook and Frittenden were clothing parishes, mainly in the High Weald and also quite densely populated. There were somewhat more inventories than expected from Benenden, but considerably fewer than expected from Cranbrook and Frittenden; the inventories from the last two, therefore, do not represent as large a share of the parish's population as they do for Benenden. If they had done, it is likely that Cranbrook and Frittenden would have produced both a higher than average number of 'poor' inventories as well as a large number of high value inventories. Rolvenden, Sandhurst and, most clearly, Tenterden also rank as well-off parishes by the same combination of criteria. The first two were not densely populated and both they and Tenterden were predominantly farming parishes.

Since the inventories are among the very few sources that shed any light on Tenterden's economic position, it will be valuable to pause for a more detailed look. The inventories show that there was considerable diversity of occupations in Tenterden parish (table 5.2), which suggests an urban core which offered a moderately large variety of goods and services. When the same inventories are analysed by value, the parish appears to have been more prosperous than several neighbouring parishes (e.g. Halden). There were forty inventories valued at £100 or above, more than from any other parish. Goudhurst, with a population of about 1,500 in the 1560s – some 300 more than Tenterden's – yielded just fourteen inventories at that level, and Hawkhurst, whose total population was roughly similar to Tenterden's, produced only a dozen inventories at £100 or more. Tenterden parish contained an incorporated borough, which was a limb of the Cinque Ports, and a number of outlying hamlets. The size of Tenterden Town is uncertain, and the inventories suggest that we should not think of Tenterden as a strictly 'urban' parish.

A glance at the twenty-five inventories valued at £150 or above shows that livestock rearing and fattening was the foundation of Tenterden's wealth. At least eighteen of the twenty-five very wealthy inventories were of large-scale graziers and farmers; four more were of wealthy shopkeepers (mainly woollen drapers) and there was one clothier and one tanner (both of whom also farmed).[42] The more informative inventories of Tenterden graziers show that they both reared their own

---

[42] Tenterden male inventories at £150 or more: KAO PRC 10/1 fo. 48v; 10/3 fo. 146; 10/4 fos. 17, 85; 10/5 fo. 26v; 10/6 fo. 151v; 10/7 fo. 196; 10/10 fo. 251v; 10/12 fo. 250; 10/13 fos. 17, 54; 10/14 fos. 58, 71v, 83, 103; 10/15 fo. 184; 10/17 fo. 365; 10/19 fos. 36, 134, 146; 10/22 fo. 68v; 10/23 fo. 364; 10/25 fo. 47; PRC 21/6 fo. 244; 21/17 fo. 105.

stock as well as fattened cattle bought in from other parts of the country. Tenterden
Town was not only a varied commercial marketplace, with formal links to the
channel ports, but also a busy agricultural marketing centre. Its ruling elite was tied
as firmly to the rural hinterland (via their own large farms) as it was to the business
life of the town. Tenterden was the most important centre of wealth in the Kent
Weald after Cranbrook, and one whose prosperity continued unabated at the end
of the sixteenth century. Its wealth was that of a traditional market town, not unlike
many others in all parts of lowland England. Cranbrook's was based more on the
manufactures than the agriculture of its hinterland, which produced much wider
extremes of affluence and poverty among its densely packed population.

The inventory sample as a whole appears to show quite marked economic
differences at the most local level. 'Poor' and 'wealthy' parishes sit cheek by jowl
with one another, irrespective of the geographical similarities which might be
expected to influence areas larger than one or two parishes. Both wealthy and poor
parishes existed in the High and the Low Weald. In fact, the complex patchwork of
occupational structure and wealth on the ground seems to have been the product
of human industry: the evolution of landholding during the preceding two or three
centuries and the location of different kinds of employment were more important
than sub-regional differences in topography or soil fertility in determining the social
and economic geography of the Elizabethan Weald.

Finally, how did the Weald's inhabitants cope with the economic pressures of the
late sixteenth century? In the absence of Elizabethan tax records comparable to
those of the early sixteenth century, it is the probate inventories that have to be
drafted into service yet again. Against a background of a rising rural population, did
the wealth catalogued in inventories keep pace with inflation between the 1560s
and the end of the century? Table 5.13 sets out the distribution of inventory values
by five-year periods from the sample Wealden parishes.

Between the 1560s and the 1580s the economic position of those represented by
probate inventories appears to have improved. The median value of personal estates
rose by almost a fifth, measured in absolute values. In addition the proportion of
'poor' inventories, those under £30, fell from about half to just under 40 per cent,
and there was a jump in the share of inventories valued at £100 or over from a tenth
to about a fifth of all inventories. But this rise in the values of chattels came to an
abrupt end in the last decade of the century, involving an apparent fall in the early
1590s followed by a recovery in the last quinquennium – but only to the level of
the preceding decade. It could be argued that the 'decline' of the early 1590s may
have been no more than the result of additional not so well-off people being
included in the sample during that particular five-year period. But it is more likely
that the larger numbers of inventories in the 1590s is a reflection of the higher levels
of mortality prevailing in that decade, rather than a change in the coverage of the
source. The lower numbers of inventories in the 1570s seems to be perfectly in line
with the known decline in crude mortality rates for that decade. In fact, given what

Table 5.13 *Wealth in male inventories by quinquennia, 1565–99*

Total value	1565–9	1570–4	1575–9	1580–4	1585–9	1590–4	1595–9
Under £20	33%	30%	24%	28%	26%	32%	26%
Under £30	50%	51%	41%	38%	39%	48%	39%
£30–£60	25%	25%	28%	23%	27%	19%	29%
£60–£100	15%	10%	14%	16%	15%	16%	17%
£100+	10%	14%	17%	22%	19%	17%	15%
Median	£30	£30	£35	£38	£40	£31	£41
Mean	£56	£57	£67	£70	£67	£63	£62
No.	209	158	137	193	172	237	198

has been said about rising Wealden populations in the decades after 1520 or 1530, the numbers of inventories in the last twenty or thirty years of the century are surprisingly low. It may well be that rather than becoming more inclusive, this source covers a decreasing share of the Wealden population, and therefore the apparent rise in personal wealth was to a degree illusory.

If, nevertheless, the rise in the money values of inventories between the 1560s and 1580s is taken at face value, did that increase in wealth keep up with contemporary changes in price levels? The answer would appear to be negative. The Phelps Brown and Hopkins price index of a basket of common consumables (where the mean for 1451–75 = 100) rose from 283 in the years 1565–9 to an average of 472 during the 1590s. Another, perhaps more appropriate, price series is that for cattle sold in England assembled by Peter Bowden. The rise between the 1560s (average 290) and the 1590s (average 465) is slightly less steep than the former series.[43] Whichever measure of inflation is chosen, it is clear that prices were rising more sharply than the values of Wealden inventories. Between the 1560s and the early 1580s, some families in the Weald were managing to improve their material circumstances; it is they who figure largely in the probate inventory evidence. Many others were barely maintaining their economic position – if not falling behind – in the face of rising commodity and land prices. In the last decade of the century it is doubtful if any – other than the small number of wealthy farmers and tradesmen whose expenditure on foodstuffs made up only a small part of their total spending – were improving their economic position. The middling people, whose inventories always made up a large majority of the sample, were not keeping pace with inflation in the 1590s. If we take into account both the declining values, in real terms, of personal wealth shown in probate inventories, and of the growing share of the Wealden population whose chattels were not inventoried, it must be concluded that the material circumstances of most of the region's population were

---

[43] E. H. Phelps Brown and Sheila V. Hopkins, 'Seven Centuries of the Prices of Consumables, Compared with Builders' Wage Rates', *Economica*, new. series, 23 (1956); Joan Thirsk (ed.), *The Agrarian History of England and Wales, iv, 1500–1640* (Cambridge, 1967), p. 860.

declining. In the face of inflation, rising population and falling living standards for many families, the question of rural employment must take centre stage. And it was to the manufacture of woollen textiles that the greatest number of the region's poor and middling families turned: either to supplement their agricultural earnings or just to survive. It is this crucial industry that is the subject of the next two chapters.

6

The textile industry in the Weald

The manufacture of woollen textiles was a flourishing industry in the Kentish Weald long before the sixteenth century. Local tradition has it that one of Edward III's imported Flemish weavers set up shop in Cranbrook in the 1330s, thus founding the Wealden broadcloth industry. The story is probably apocryphal.[1] By the middle of the fifteenth century, however, clothmaking in the central Wealden district was well established and was probably responsible for the bulk of cloth production within the county, although clothmaking was still a significant industry in Canterbury. The second half of the fifteenth century ushered in a period of sustained expansion in Wealden clothmaking, in line with the growth of textile production in England as a whole. The somewhat sketchy accounts made in the 1470s by the farmers of the tax on woollen textiles, the ulnage, show that the residences of men who paid were predominantly in the Weald. The number of cloths 'produced' and taxed had by this time become conventionalized, fictional totals.[2] By Henry VIII's reign the scale of Wealden woollen production – although not precisely quantifiable – was large and growing. The subsidy rolls of the 1520s imply that the industry was already dominated by the larger clothiers: the tax assessments of the major Cranbrook clothiers placed them on a level with the local gentry.[3] The social and economic structure of the industry was by this time established in the pattern which would continue for another century before its long, slow demise in the seventeenth century. That framework was the domestic form of production organized by men with capital. The clothiers 'put out' their raw materials to independent craftsmen and women who processed them in their own homes. Most of the processes of

---

[1] See, e.g., C. C. R. Pile, *Cranbrook: A Wealden Town* (Cranbrook and Sissinghurst Local Hist. Soc., 1955), p. 24; Robert Furley, *A History of the Weald of Kent* (1874), ii, chapter 19.

[2] PRO E 101/339/20.

[3] PRO E 179/125/324: in Cranbrook hundred in the 1524/5 subsidy, Thos. Wilford, gent. was rated at £50 per annum in lands, Thos. Roberts, gent. at £30 per annum and Anne Culpeper, gentlewoman at £57 in goods. The leading clothiers included Steph. Draner, rated at £300 in goods, Richard Courthop at £200, Alex. Courthop at 200 marks, Wm. Lynch at £160, John & Laur. Sharpe at £100 each and Ric. Barre at £60.

manufacture took place away from the workshops of the clothiers, and were carried out by spinners, weavers, fullers and shearmen on their own equipment. Besides the relatively small number of major clothiers – who may each have normally kept several hundred outworkers in employment – there were both in the early and the late sixteenth century dozens of small-scale clothiers, many of whom produced no more than a dozen or two broadcloths per year and had no more than a handful of cloths in production at any given moment. Also by the early sixteenth century the Wealden woollen industry was divided into two branches according to the different types of cloth being produced. The manufacture of heavy broadcloths, weighing at least eighty-six pounds and a minimum of twenty-eight yards in length, was concentrated in the central Weald. A region in the north of the Weald and in half a dozen parishes in the Chartland to the north specialized in kerseys, cloths weighing nineteen or twenty pounds and only sixteen or seventeen yards in length. Both were manufactured by putting out methods, although many kerseymakers wove their own cloths.[4]

When Kentish weavers combined to produce a list of complaints and demands in the late 1530s, they were described as being from 'the Seven Hundreds', i.e., the seven Wealden hundreds of the county. Their concerns betoken the existence of a highly elaborate and differentiated industry. They asked that no clothier keep and use more than one loom for weaving in his own house, that clothiers pay for work done by spinners and weavers in ready money and not in goods, and that a regular procedure be established for the arbitration of disputes between clothiers and weavers.[5] By the 1530s, when textile manufacturing was in the midst of what appeared to be another era of expansion, clothmaking was carried on within a defined and limited district of the Weald and a few adjacent villages. Only after the mid Elizabethan period was there any cloth manufacture outside of those districts, when the making of 'New Draperies' was established in Sandwich and in a few other parishes in northeast Kent. During the century covered by this study the Wealden broadcloth trade remained the basic core of cloth production in the county, and its location can be mapped fairly precisely by the use of probate and other records.

The wills made by clothiers give one picture of the location of the Wealden woollen industry. Of just under 200 wills proved either in the Prerogative Court of Canterbury or in local diocesan courts, over three-quarters of the clothiers resided in just nine parishes: Cranbrook (47), Biddenden (26), Benenden (18), Goudhurst (14), Staplehurst (10), Rolvenden (8), Brenchley (7), Smarden (7), and Yalding (6). There were four to six clothiers' wills from six other parishes: Tenterden, Hawkhurst, Marden, Pluckley, Hothfield and Tonbridge.[6] A more inclusive measure of the

[4] Weights and dimensions of cloths drawn from statutes 5 & 6 Edward VI, c.6 and 4 & 5 Ph & M, c.5.
[5] BL Cotton MS. Titus B.1 fo. 193. Not dated but c.1536.
[6] Source: all wills from Rochester and Canterbury dioceses, as well as Prerogative Court of Canterbury wills, dated 1480s to 1600, in KAO and PRO.

Table 6.1 Residences of clothiers (from all sources)[7]

Parish	1480s–1540s	1550s–70s	1580s–90s	Totals
Cranbrook	54	82	30	166
Biddenden	20	49	31	100
Benenden	19	24	15	58
Goudhurst	19	14	8	41
Hawkhurst	2	24	9	35
Smarden	5	14	7	26
Staplehurst	8	12	4	24
Horsmonden	5	13	4	22
Tenterden	8	7	5	20
Hothfield	2	10	6	18
Brenchley	2	13	1	16
Tonbridge	1	11	3	15
Egerton	2	5	7	14
Rolvenden	8	3	2	13
Lenham	2	7	3	12
Marden	2	2	8	12
Pluckley	4	4	2	10
Yalding	2	3	4	9
Lynton	2	2	4	8
Bethersden	0	5	2	7
Totals	167	304	155	626

importance of clothmaking in different parishes can be obtained by a survey of probate inventories. This is possible, however, only for the period after 1565, and for Canterbury diocese. The large numbers of persons involved in clothmaking (clothiers, weavers, fullers and shearmen) in a few parishes is striking: the highest, for the years 1565 to 1599, is from Biddenden. There 29.5 per cent of all inventories where occupations could be identified showed an involvement in clothmaking. Other parishes with high concentrations were Cranbrook (25 per cent), Benenden (23.4 per cent), Smarden (20.2 per cent), Hawkhurst (16.5 per cent), Goudhurst (15.1 per cent), Staplehurst (13.2 per cent), Bethersden (10.8 per cent), Marden (8.6 per cent) and Rolvenden (8 per cent).[8] These figures demonstrate the geographical concentration of Kentish clothmaking in the middle of the century. Only two parishes from outside Canterbury diocese should be added: Brenchley and Horsmonden, which adjoined Goudhurst in the central High Weald. A final guide

---

[7] There were also identified six clothiers each from Tudeley and Hunton, five from Headcorn and one to three each from Frittenden, Ashford, Leeds, Ulcombe, Capel and Chiddingstone.

[8] From sample of 1,189 probate inventories from Canterbury diocese, 1565–99 in KAO classes PRC 10, 21 and 28. Cranbrook's share of textile workers' inventories would have been higher if the sample included PCC inventories which have been lost: we know that many wealthy Cranbrook clothiers' estates were proved in the PCC.

to the location of the cloth industry is the pattern of residence of clothiers, as recovered from all types of sources. The numbers are large enough to be divided into chronological periods.

The numbers of clothiers living in a given parish is not, of course, a foolproof indication of how many people were employed in clothmaking, nor of the volume of production in each parish. Parishes were of widely differing sizes. But in table 6.1 the importance of the textile industry in a few key parishes is demonstrated yet again. The five parishes with the greatest concentration of clothiers – accounting for 64 per cent of the total – were all located in the main broadcloth region within the Weald proper. The narrow cloth district, which included Smarden, Hothfield, Egerton, Lenham, Pluckley and Bethersden, was responsible for a much smaller volume of production, its clothiers were generally less wealthy men, and a good part of its output was in the hands of independent weaver-clothiers, known as 'kerseymakers'. Some, therefore, were not given the title 'clothier' and hence do not figure in the table above. The numbers in the above table must not be taken too literally. The table fairly represents the geographical distribution of clothiers' residences within the two clothing districts, but is not an accurate guide to the economic fortunes of Wealden clothmaking in different parishes. The high number of clothiers identified during the middle decades of the century is no tribute to the industry's prosperity, but merely the result of additional sources which are available during those decades, more especially the lists of clothiers fined for infractions of the clothmaking statutes at Blackwell Hall in London.[9]

Having established that clothmaking was geographically concentrated *within* the Weald, it is time to consider the volume of production as well as the varieties of cloth being produced. The output of the Kentish textile industry, either in the early or the later part of the century, cannot be calculated with any certainty. There are no records which enumerate all cloths produced, merely records of cloths exported. In principle, every cloth manufactured for sale should have been taxed and sealed by the ulnagers, but since the Crown had been farming out the ulnage since before the sixteenth century, there were no Crown records of the numbers of cloths sealed by the farmers of the ulnages. It is possible to compare the rents paid by farmers of the ulnage in different counties, but they may not have been very sensitive to changing levels of output in each region over the sixteenth century.[10] All that remains to work from are a variety of private, contemporary estimates of

---

[9] See M. Zell, 'The Exchequer Lists of Provincial Clothmakers Fined in London during the Sixteenth Century', *BIHR*, 54 (1981).

[10] The farm of the ulnage for Kent was granted to John Baker, jun., Esq. in 1554 for just £27 1s per annum (PRO E 159/33 Rec. Hil. rot. 81). By contrast the farm for Yorkshire and Hull was let at £95 per annum in 1547 (*Cal. Pat.*, 1553, 308) and that for Gloucestershire, the city of Gloucester and Bristol was farmed at £65 per annum in 1552 (*Cal. Pat.*, *1550–53*, 304). There is no way of knowing to what extent the farm of the ulnage represented the real value of the ulnage fees likely to be collected in each area.

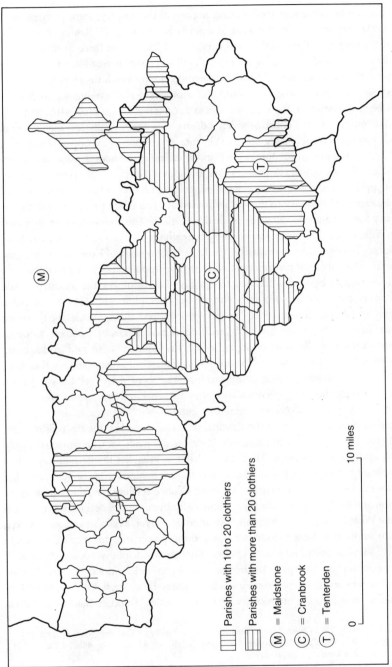

Parishes with 10 to 20 clothiers

Parishes with more than 20 clothiers

Ⓜ = Maidstone

Ⓒ = Cranbrook

Ⓣ = Tenterden

0   10 miles

Figure 6.1 Weald parishes with ten or more clothiers

production in the various clothmaking regions of the country, some perhaps more accurate than others. On the basis of sources like these G. D. Ramsay has shown that the output of the Wiltshire industry, one of the two or three most important in England, varied from as low as 15,000 cloths in a slump year like 1565 to about 45,000 at its peak in 1606.[11] Most of the white, undressed cloths of Wiltshire were destined for export markets. The output of another key clothmaking region, Suffolk, has been estimated at about 20,000 cloths per annum during Elizabeth's reign.[12]

The output of the Kentish woollen industry was undoubtedly less than those of such major clothmaking regions as Wiltshire or Suffolk. Only one contemporary estimate has surfaced for this period, and it claims that 'there is made within the Weald of Kent yearly by estimation xi or xii thousand cloths '. The assertion appears in a paper giving reasons why unfinished, coloured Kent cloths should be allowed to be exported, contrary to the statute passed in 1566 which prohibited the export of any Kent or Suffolk cloths not finished in England. The arguments were prepared for William, Lord Cobham, who in the aftermath of the 1566 Act sought to obtain a licence to ship 2,000 'unwrought' cloths out of the shire of Kent, contrary to the statute. The burden of his argument was that if a proportion of Kentish cloths were not allowed to be sold unfinished to Continental customers, the industry would decay and many workers would be thrown out of employment. Already, the paper claims, in the several years since the 1566 prohibition, 'there is made one thousand cloths less yearly' in the town of Cranbrook alone. If, claims Cobham, 2,000 or 3,000 cloths were allowed out under licence, the 'residue of our said cloths, being eleven or twelve thousand, shall be dressed in England '. He was claiming, therefore, that the Kent industry could easily produce 13,000 or 14,000 cloths per year.[13] Unfortunately, neither Cobham's letter nor the enclosed arguments give details about what types of cloth are referred to: presumably they were converting Kent broadcloths and kerseys into the notional shortcloths used by the customs officials.

Given the absence of official figures, the estimates made for Cobham are the only basis upon which to work. They show that the Wealden textile industry was a significant producer of woollens, but of second rank behind the major manufacturing regions of England: the Wiltshire–Somerset–Gloucestershire area, the Suffolk-Essex region and the Yorkshire industry. Cobham's figures do not reveal what proportion of the Weald's output was normally exported. However, a number of pointers exist which imply that Kent broadcloth was produced primarily for export. To begin with, as will be described in detail below, Kentish broadcloth was a luxury fabric. It only occasionally appears in the inventories of provincial woollendrapers or other shopkeepers, and then only in very small quantities. By contrast, Kentish broadcloth appears conspicuously in records of cloths passing through Blackwell Hall in

[11] G. D. Ramsay, *The Wiltshire Woollen Industry in the 16th and 17th Centuries* (1943) pp. 66n, 71.

[12] J. E. Pilgrim, 'The Cloth Industry in Essex and Suffolk, 1558–1640', unpublished M. A. thesis, University of London, 1938, p. 147.

[13] BL Cotton MS. Vesp. F.xii fo. 168. Cobham's licence *Cal. Pat.*, 1566–9, no. 1139.

London, where the capital's export merchants commonly purchased cloth for sale abroad. Total cloth exports from England (the vast majority being traditional woollens) were averaging about 110,000 to 120,000 cloths per year in the 1560s, and if it is true that most Wealden broadcloth formed part of that flow, then the Weald was supplying slightly under 10 per cent of the country's woollen exports. Certainly Kent broadcloths feature prominently in the various Blackwell Hall lists. Among cloths fined for various infractions during three sample periods (September 1550–March 1551, August–November 1551 and October 1554–October 1555) fifty-six out of 256 broadcloths (22 per cent) were of Kentish (i.e., Wealden) origin. During the same twenty-five months there were also about 300 narrow cloths seized by the Blackwell Hall searchers – none were from Kent. It appears that the share of Kent cloths among the more valuable, full-size broadcloths exported from London was well in excess of 10 per cent of the total.[14] As late as 1622 – at the height of the trade depression – Kentish broadcloths made up a substantial proportion of the cloths in store at Blackwell Hall. In the Main Storehouse there were 1,163 cloths unsold, of which 899 (or 77 per cent) were of Kentish origin. In addition there were 323 cloths in the Wiltshire Hall and a total of 433 cloths in the Gloucester, Worcester, Reading and Somerset Halls. Among the cheaper cloths lying unsold, there were 5,000 'pieces' (?Northern kerseys) in the Northern Hall and 853 Northern 'cottons'. Thus among the 1,900 odd broadcloths, some 47 per cent were Kentish cloths, produced by 221 different Kentish clothmakers.[15] A variety of evidence suggests that the Wealden textile industry contributed significantly to the national output of high quality woollens, although in terms of the volume of production it remained one of a number of second-ranking clothmaking regions.

The Kentish woollen industry produced two basic varieties of cloth: low value, narrow-width kerseys, woven in several north Weald and adjacent parishes, and heavy, high-quality broadcloth whose manufacture was carried on primarily in about half a dozen parishes in the vicinity of Cranbrook. This chapter will devote most attention to broadcloth production, both because of its more elaborate, 'capitalist' organization and because of its greater importance in terms of volume and value of output, as well as the larger numbers employed by this branch of the trade. Already, by the late fifteenth century, various types of cloth were distinguished by their county or town of manufacture. The wide-ranging qualities, weights and lengths associated with the different clothmaking regions in fact preceded the mid Tudor statutes which sought to define legally the different varieties of English woollens. The first act to define the sizes and weights of regional cloth types – 5 & 6 Edward VI, c.6 – was drafted after the examination by the House of Commons committee of knowledgeable clothiers and merchants in 1551. They,

---

[14] Sample periods drawn from PRO E 159/330 Rec. Mich. rots. 173, 145 and E 159/335 Rec. Mich. rot. 233.   [15] PRO SP 14/128 fo. 100 sqq.

in effect, told the MPs what each variety of cloth should be like after 'scouring, thicking and drying'. Kent broadcloths (like Reading broadcloths) were to be at least twenty-eight yards long, a yard and three-quarters in width and weigh at least ninety pounds each. The next heaviest cloths – the coloured long cloths of Norfolk, Suffolk and Essex – were to have the same dimensions as the Kents, but a minimum weight of only eighty pounds. The same act commanded that ordinary kerseys should be seventeen to eighteen yards in length and weigh at least twenty pounds. Cloths of this latter type were produced in Kent on a relatively small scale, but were extremely important to a number of northern clothmaking regions. The 1551 Act was modified by another statute in 1557 (4 & 5 Philip & Mary, c.5), as it stated, at the request of the clothiers. Henceforth the coloured broadcloths of Kent had only to weigh eighty-six pounds, while kerseys were to be at least sixteen yards long and weigh at least nineteen pounds. The minimum weight for the single most important variety of English export cloth, the white West Country broadcloths, was reduced from sixty-four to sixty-one pounds. They were also permitted to be two yards shorter than the coloured cloths of Kent, Reading, Suffolk and Essex.

Not only were Wealden broadcloths the longest and heaviest type recognized by statute; in practice the export quality broadcloths from Kent were often significantly longer (and therefore heavier) than the statutory minimum. The ledger of Thomas Howell, a Draper of London, covering the period from about 1519 to 1528, records his purchases and sales (in Spain) of many 'long Kentyshe cloths'.[16] Many of the Kentish cloths seized for minor infractions at Blackwell Hall were likewise described as 'long' cloths. In October 1532 seven 'Kentish longs', twenty-three 'long russets' and four 'long azures' were among the Kent cloths seized.[17] The early Elizabethan port books for London tell the same story: between May and August 1565 (when the county of origin of broadcloths was recorded) customers reported about 450 'long Kents' exported to the Low Countries, but less than a score of 'short Kents'.[18] About forty years later, Lionel Cranfield, in responding to a request from a Flemish buyer for 6,500 cloths per year, pointed out that the Fleming's specific order for 3,250 cloths of 'mingled colours' didn't take into account the huge variety of cloth qualities and lengths. As an example, Cranfield informed him that 'there be mingled coloured Kentish cloths that contain from 32 to 40 yards. Of them, there be to be had of all prices from £9 to £40 sterling.'[19] Finally there is the description by a deputy ulnager of the cloths produced by the Cranbrook clothier Richard Sharpe between 1607 and 1610: they 'did contain one with another' thirty-two yards in length.[20]

As Cranfield emphasized, not only did Kent broadcloths vary in length, they varied even more in quality and price. The most commonly found distinction made by sixteenth-century merchants and clothiers was between ordinary quality and

---

[16] Drapers' Company, London, MS. C/AL 1 fos. 14, 22, 23, 39v.
[17] PRO E 159/311 Rec. Mich. rot. 50.   [18] PRO E 190/2/1.
[19] HMC, *Sackville (Knole) MSS.*, 2 (1966), p. 146.   [20] PRO E 134/10 Jas. I/Mich. 18.

'fine' cloths. The Kent cloths recorded in the 1565 port books, for example, were described as 'long Kents' or as 'long fine Kents'.[21] The extremely wide range of prices given for Kentish cloth is a further sign of well-understood differences in quality. In the mid 1520s Thomas Howell was paying as little as £3 apiece for certain ordinary quality (and length) Kentish tawneys and russets, but substantially more for either 'fine' cloths or 'long' cloths: between £5 16s. and £8 each for 'fine Kentish russets' or 'long Kentish russets'.[22] Probate inventories of Wealden clothiers and merchants who owned broadcloths confirm the records of London merchants. The finished cloths on hand at the death of one of Cranbrook's most prosperous clothiers, Peter Courthop, in 1567, were appraised at £186 in all. They ranged from £9 10s. each to a 'fine blue' valued at £24. Most were valued at between £10 and £15 each. But even a 'cloth's yarn of fine blue' was appraised at £20. In contrast, the yarn for a 'white-grey' cloth was rated at just £8 10s.[23] The wealthy Cranbrook merchant Thomas Ruck (d. 1583) had in his warehouse a modest selection of finished, local broadcloths: one 'sky colour' at £11, two 'fine plunkets' at £12 each, a 'fine medley' at £13 and two 'fine blues' valued at £18 each.[24]

Earlier in the century there is plenty of evidence of price differentials of over 100 per cent for different qualities and colours of Kent broadcloth. The London Mercer and Merchant Adventurer, Thomas Kitson, paid as little as £4 2s. for a grey Kent cloth in 1530, but £7 for a Kentish russet (obviously of higher quality) in 1531 and £7 6s. 8d. each for certain russets in 1536.[25] The different quality criteria which governed price differentials are shown by the appraisal of cloths owned by Stephen Draner, a major Cranbrook clothier and businessman, at his death in 1540.[26]

8 'coarse russet cloths' @ £5 each	£40
8 russets, a marble cloth and 3 others @ £6 each	£72
3 azure coloured cloths @ £7 each	£21
2 'brown blue' cloths @ £10 each	£20
2 'fine brown blues' @ £15 each	£30

The Merchant Adventurer John Quarles, in the 1590s, was made aware of the crucial difference that the quality of his cloths could make in the minds of his Dutch buyers. He was advised by his factor in Stade 'not to buy any Kentish cloth under £10' in 1593. In 1594 the factor asked Quarles to buy seventy Kentish cloths at £12 'rough' (i.e. unfinished) and twenty-two at £15 each. Again he recommends that Quarles, 'buy none under £11' for they will not sell. At this point Quarles's agent was selling the Kent cloths at between £18 and £22 each, but this was, of course, after the rough cloths had been dressed by London clothworkers.[27] The wide range in value of different varieties of Wealden broadcloth, as well as the relatively high

[21] PRO E 190/2/1 and E 190/1/3.   [22] Drapers' Co. MS. C/AL 1 fos. 18v, 39v, 52v.
[23] KAO PRC 28/1 fo. 117.   [24] KAO PRC 21/6 fo. 460.
[25] CUL, Hengrave Hall Dep. MS. 78(2) fos. 25v, 30, 152.   [26] PRO PROB 2/525.
[27] PRO SP 46/176 fos. 15v, 21, 23, 36v.

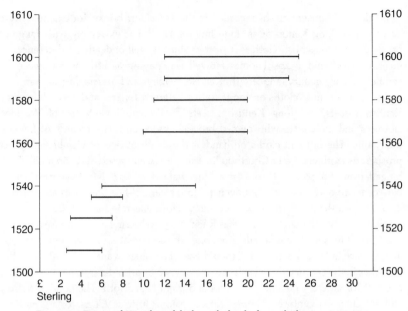

Figure 6.2 Prices of Kent broadcloths: wholesale from clothiers, 1500–1600
Sources: PRO C1/668/56; C1/746/23; C1/427/40; C1/1341/71; Drapers' Co. MS.
C/AL 1; Cambridge University Library, Hengrave Hall Deposit 78(1,2); PRO SP
46/176; PROB 2/525; KAO PRC 28/1 fo. 117, 21/6 fo. 460, 28/5 fo. 184, 21/17 fo.
255, 28/4 o. 33.

value of all Kent broadcloth can be seen in the inventories of major urban
woollendrapers. The stock of Alderman Christopher Scott of Canterbury in 1568
included several types of broadcloth alongside a range of cheaper fabrics. His
broadcloth (including brown blue, red, sheeps colour, ash colour and new colour)
was appraised at 6s. per yard or above. The 'fine red' was valued at 9s. 4d. a yard.
By contrast, frisados and bays were valued at between 2s. 2d. and 3s. per yard,
various kerseys at 1s. 8d. to 3s. 4d. a yard and 'Sandwich say' at 4s. per yard.
Cheaper still were cottons, friezes and fustians, at 6d. to 1s. 3d. per yard.[28] Of course
the price differential between broadcloth and cheaper fabrics was not as extreme as
it first appears: almost all the cheaper textiles were significantly narrower than
broadcloth. Nevertheless, Kent broadcloth was also much finer and heavier. Fabric
of this quality was clearly not used by most English people for ordinary garments.

The wide differences in prices paid for Wealden broadcloths of different qualities
– although rarely as extreme as the range mentioned by Lionel Cranfield (400 per
cent) – can be found from early in Henry VIII's reign to the early seventeenth
century. As far as export quality cloths were concerned, the more expensive cloths
were priced at anything up to two and a half times that of the standard broadcloths

[28] KAO PRC 21/1 fo. 25.

(see figure 6.2). Two factors appear to govern these price differencess – length and quality. And 'quality' itself was an amalgam of different criteria: the quality and fineness of the original wool; the colour of the cloth, itself a reflection of the costs of different dyestuffs and dyeing procedures; and the fineness of the weave, hence the weight and wearing quality of the fabric. Throughout the century Kentish clothmakers were producing cloths in both ordinary and fine quality, as well as in different lengths. Where Kent textiles appear to have been changing, however, was in the range of colours (and probably designs) available to buyers.

The records of Kent broadcloths purchased or exported by London merchants in Henry VIII's reign show the relatively narrow range of colours on offer before mid century. In the 1520s Thomas Howell shipped Kent cloths described as russets, tawneys, marble colour and brown blues. In the next decade the Mercer Thomas Kitson bought cloths of the following colours: russets, tawneys, tawney medley, grey, azure and camlet colour.[29] In the accounts of both men, however, the majority of Kent cloths described in any detail were made up of russets and tawneys. It would appear that in those decades of expanding woollen production and export, Kentish clothiers were not forced to experiment in order to secure orders for their cloths. The Act of 1551, referred to earlier, also regulated the colours permitted in English broadcloths. Only the following colours were to be allowed: scarlet, red, crimson, murray, violet, puke, brown blue, black, green, yellow, blue, azure, orange, tawney, russet, marble grey, sad new colour, sheeps colour, watchet, lion colour, motley and iron grey.

Even the shades permitted by the 1551 statute implied that broadcloths were already being manufactured in a wider range of colours than a generation earlier. By the early 1560s Kentish broadcloths appeared in a much wider variety of shades and mixtures than two decades earlier. Among cloths seized for various faults at Blackwell Hall in the year beginning Michaelmas 1561 were fabrics dyed in thirteen different colours.[30] Peter Courthop's 1567 stock of cloths included eleven different hues: the traditional russets and tawneys plus azures, brown blues, new colour, sheeps colour, medleys, green, red, yellow and white grey. The cloth seizures at Blackwell Hall in the 1560s and 1570s revealed Kentish broadcloth manufactured in 'rats colour', grey, iron grey, grey marble, turquoise (or 'Turkey'), sad new colour, sky colour and vesse.[31] By 1603 more new mixtures and colours had appeared in clothiers' inventories: pepper colour, red and green, mallard colour, plunket, silk colour, Dutch marbles, black, red and green, and pheasant colour along with many of the old standbys. In 1606 a clothier's inventory from Smarden added several new shades to the list: damson colour and 'endygreen'.[32] Clothiers in the Weald were quite obviously responding to the changing market conditions brought about by

[29] Drapers' Co. MS. C/AL 1 *passim* and CUL Hengrave Hall Dep. MS 78(1), (2), *passim*.
[30] G. D. Ramsay, 'The Distribution of the Cloth Industry in 1561–2', *EHR*, 57 (1942), p. 362.
[31] KAO PRC 28/1 fo. 117; PRO E 159/342 ff.
[32] KAO PRC 21/6 fo. 460; 21/17 fos. 167, 255; 28/4 fo. 33; 28/5 fo. 184.

two related developments: the general stagnation in demand for heavy broadcloths in traditional European markets, and the rise of the colourful new draperies. The production of traditional woollens in an increasing variety of colours and designs suggest that even before the beginning of the seventeenth century the 'folly of fashion' had begun to play a part in English clothmaking. The clothiers of the Weald no doubt felt that they were responding adequately to the challenge of competition from both foreign and English producers. Only the experience of the depression in the cloth trade in the decades following the Cockayne experiment would show that their innovations were not far-reaching enough to save the Kentish broadcloth industry from what now appears its inevitable decline.

The production of Kentish woollen cloth and the people involved in the manufacturing processes are the subjects of the remainder of this chapter. After a brief look at the supply of raw materials which went into the making of broadcloths and kerseys, the several stages of production, each involving different skills and – usually – different personnel will be examined in turn: dyeing, spinning, weaving, fulling and finally the finishing processes carried out by the shearmen – when the last stages were carried out in Kent, which as has been noticed was not uniformly the case. The clothiers – as manufacturers, entrepreneurs and rentiers – will be examined in chapter 7 which will look at the wider implications of their multifarious roles and economic relationships.

The initial stages of cloth production were carried out by the clothier and his resident servants. The raw wool was washed and oiled: tuns and vats invariably appear among clothiers' shop goods in inventories. The next step was to sort the wool into various lengths and qualities. William Colliar, a Marden clothier, had a 'culling chamber' in his house, and George Ramsden of Biddenden referred to his 'culling shop' in his will. Culling baskets or wool baskets feature in many clothiers' inventories. Another clothier, Robert Gibbon of Hawkhurst, had a 'culling board'.[33] Once sorted, the wool was ready for carding, but to what extent this process was carried out by the clothier's servants or in the homes of his outworkers is by no means certain. Most of the wool used by Wealden clothmakers was of short-staple varieties, and 'woolcards' (or 'stockcards') figure in a majority of the inventories of adult householders in the Weald, be they weavers or farmers. The region supported specialized cardmakers.[34]

Once washed, sorted (and possibly carded), the different batches of wool were weighed and dyed. Clothiers normally prepared and dyed wool for individual

---

[33] KAO PRC 10/2 fo. 106v; PRC 17/49 fo. 326; PRC 10/20 fo. 82.
[34] See, e.g., inventories of Nic. Walter of Goudhurst, broadweaver and Geo. Black of Sandhurst, a small farmer: KAO PRC 10/19 fo. 180; 10/20 fo. 107. Cardmakers: CCL PRC 39/10 fo. 15v; 39/24 fo. 136; KAO: Biddenden parish register, bur. of Robt. Webbe, 'a cardmaker', Oct. 1587; see also apprenticeship indenture of Sept. 1611, in which a poor weaver's son was apprenticed for eight years to a local cardmaker, the premium of £4 being paid by the parish: KAO U1823/37/Q5.

cloths. Hence we find in inventories entries like 'one cloth's wool, a fine blue', or 'a fine marble and two russets of 20 and 18 yards in wool'.[35] Having selected the wool, the clothier prepared a known weight of wool for a particular cloth, which would be dyed separately. The colouring of the basic raw material was the most important and skilled operation carried out in the clothier's workshop (hence its common designation as the 'dyehouse'). Depending upon the dyes used, it represented a significant proportion of the value added to the wool. In the 1580s, for example, raw fleece wool in clothiers' stocks was valued at about 2s. 10d. per quarter, 'white wool' (i.e. culled and cleaned) at about 3s. 6d. per quarter, but dyed wool ranged in value from 4s. 4d. to 9s. per quarter.[36] A clothier's apprenticeship included some training in weaving,[37] but instructions in the mysteries of dyeing wool must have formed the core of a clothmaker's special technical knowledge. So much so that specialized, independent dyers were not generally found in the Weald. Men who had dyeing skills, often referred to as 'woadsetters' in Kent, rarely seem to have worked as independent craftsmen, but are usually found as full-time employees of clothiers. With the addition of a little capital, they could easily have become clothiers.[38]

'Dyed in the wool' Kent broadcloths were manufactured in a wide variety of colours and mixed shades by the second half of the century, and much of the price variation reflected the costs of different dyes and the length of the dyeing process for different colours and mixtures. From the dyestuffs in clothiers' inventories it seems that they used − in varying combinations − dyes of two basic colours: reds (madder, brazil and later cochineal) and blues (woad, copperas and later indigo). Woad was by far the most important of the dyes, both because the blue shades were among the most common (and valuable) colours for Kent broadcloths, but also because woad was used to set other colours. There is no evidence of the time required to dye known quantities of wool, or, for that matter, how time-consuming were all these initial stages in clothmaking. Commonsense suggests that the wealthier clothiers, each with three or more resident servants, could process wool more rapidly than their less-well-off competitors using only family labour and perhaps a single apprentice.

Once dyed, the wool was ready to be divided into consignments and distributed by the clothier to 'his' spinners. Surviving evidence suggests that relatively small

---

[35] KAO PRC 28/1 fo. 117; PRC 10/7 fo. 123v.

[36] KAO PRC 10/16 fos. 406, 429; 10/18 fo. 209; 10/19 fo. 174. In Peter Courthop's 1567 inventory red dyed wool was priced at 1s. per pound, blue wool as much as 1s. 10d. per pound, whereas fleece wool was worth under 10d. a pound: PRC 28/1 fo. 113.

[37] Steph. Pattenden expected his son's apprenticeship to a clothier to include weaving: KAO PRC 32/15 fo. 31v (of 1527).

[38] E.g., John Johnson of Cranbrook, 'woadsetter', bur. April 1603: KAO: parish register; Steph. Fissenden of Goudhurst, 'woadsetter', in 1596 recognizance (KAO QM/SRc/ 1596/57); John Post of Biddenden, 'woadsetter', 1574 will (KAO PRC 17/42 fo. 73); and Wm. Lellisden of Benenden, 'woadsetter', who, exceptionally, seems to have been an independent dyer; 1534 will (KAO PRC 17/20 fo. 213).

quantities of wool were placed with individual spinners, and the yarn collected within the space of a few weeks at most. Most contemporary estimates claim that the 'average' spinner – usually a woman – could convert about one pound of wool per working day into yarn.[39] Working a six-day week, it would have taken a single spinner eighty-five to ninety days (or fourteen weeks) to produce the yarn for a single Kent broadcloth of the statutory minimum weight. Clearly, no clothier operated on that basis, but even if the clothier divided his eighty-six pounds of wool between fourteen spinners, he would still have no more than the yarn for one broadcloth per week. The organization of yarn production, therefore, was crucial to the speed of clothmaking – and equally crucial to the population of a textile region as a major source of employment. No clothier, however great his wealth, could translate his superior capital resources into profitable clothmaking unless he could recruit a large corps of spinners. As Lord Cobham pointed out in the late 1560s, with only slight exaggeration, 'the making of a broadcloth consisteth not in the travail of one or two persons, but in a number as of xxx or xl persons at the least, of men, women and children.'[40]

Simply to spin the yarn required for Kent's cloth output in the 1560s – say 12,000 cloths per year – would have required over 3,000 spinners working 300 days per year full-time. As is well known, spinning was frequently a by-employment, and it might be unwise even to assume that spinners were employed producing yarn on as many as 150 or 200 days each year. But if 150 days is taken as a notional commitment (and to include some help by children), then Wealden clothiers would have needed to employ around 6,000 spinners to make up their wool. If 12,000 cloths proves to be an over-estimate, and in fact represents 12,000 'shortcloths' each of about sixty-four pounds, the industry would still have needed almost 5,000 spinners, each at work for at least 150 days per year. Recalling the estimate made in chapter 3 of the population of the Kent Weald – about 25,000 at the time of Lord Cobham's estimate of cloth output – it would appear that about one person out of five among the entire Wealden population worked as a spinner for local textile makers. If, in fact, spinning was concentrated in the Wealden parishes known to have supported clothiers, then the proportion of the population in those twenty or twenty-five parishes who spun wool would have been significantly greater than 20 per cent. In practice, the proportion was not that high because spinners were drawn from Wealden parishes in Sussex as well as Kent. The magistrates of the 'Wealdish part' of Pevensey rape reported to the Privy Council in 1632:

As for work for the poor, our part of the country affordeth great plenty by reason of our vicinity to the clothiers of Kent, who set work for women and children, and by reason of our ironworks, which yield employment for stronger bodies.

[39] See M. F. Roberts, 'Wages and Wage-earners in England', unpublished D.Phil. thesis, University of Oxford, 1981, p. 281 and sources cited there; HMC, *Fourteenth Report*, App. 8 (Bury St Edmunds), p. 159.   [40] BL Cotton. MS. Vesp. F.xii fo.168.

Finding enough spinners at the peak periods of clothmaking must have been no easy task, given the prevailing wage levels for spinning yarn. Even in the late sixteenth century the estimated piece rate for spinning was only 2d. to 3d. per pound of wool (which was, in effect, the per diem wage).[41] The spinners may have earned slightly more if they were paid to card the wool as well as spin it, but there were certainly few other adult occupations which were paid as little as this in the 1580s or 1590s.

Is it in the least surprising, therefore, that spinning was seen as work for women (or children)? The wage differential between the sexes was seen at its starkest in the textile industry; it was of enormous significance because of the large number of women employed. The result was that the average cost of spinning the yarn for a standard length Kent broadcloth was under £1. By contrast, the value added to the plain white wool for one cloth in the dyeing process was two to three times that figure.[42] Against the backdrop of a rapidly increasing population spinners could be found even at 2d. or 3d. per day. The women who spun wool for Kentish clothiers are among the most poorly documented of all occupational groups. As for most women, when they do make an appearance in the records, they are identified by reference to their marital (or widowed) state, rather than by their work. Even in a region like the Kent Weald – where female spinners were ubiquitous – the normal sources prove to be of little value. An idea of the number of women who worked as spinners can only be arrived at by inference, from the estimates of the output of the local textile industry. Only anecdotal information can be found about individual spinners, from a limited number of sources. The wills of clothiers occasionally record debts owing to spinners, or record legacies to women identified as spinners: both appear infrequently. Scattered, unsystematic evidence can also be found in probate inventories and the accounts of administrators of deceased clothiers' estates.

They all point to the conclusion that clothiers paid their spinners in arrears, and that frequently the wages owed covered work done over considerable periods. The widow of Alexander Sheffe, a major Cranbrook clothier, claimed allowance for paying off a large number of her late husband's debts. Among them were sums of 11s. 1d. each for spinning, owed to 'Sowton's wife', 'Smith's wife' and 'the wife of Alexander Sheffe, weaver'. At an average rate of 2d. per diem, her husband owed each of these women payment for over fifty days' work! John Bawden, a clothier of Horsmonden, noted in his will that he owed 'Mother Richards' £2 10s. for spinning: even at 3d. per day, she had not yet received her wages for 200 days' work.[43] Peter Courthop (d. 1580), a leading Cranbrook clothier, left 5s. each to '20 of my poorest spinners', and Alexander Lake of Goudhurst (d. 1580) willed 1s. each to '8 of my poor spinners'; seven were wives of named men, the eighth was a widow. Finally, Edmund Colvill, one of Cranbrook's wealthier clothiers of the 1590s, left 5s. each to seven named spinners, and another 5s. to be divided between

[41] See Roberts thesis 'Wages' (n. 39 above) pp. 281–3 and PRO SP 12/244 nos. 126–30; SP 16/192 no. 99 (fo. 147).   [42] See n. 36 above.

[43] KAO PRC 21/16 fo. 150 sqq; PRO PROB 11/47/15: Bawden also owed sums to two other spinners.

the rest of his spinners.[44] Clothiers of the rank of Courthop put out wool to far more families than the twenty 'poorest' to whom he directed his charity. Other clothiers' wills include small doles to named individuals, but without identifying them as their spinners, as distinct from other deserving cases. Legally, of course, the debts due to spinners should have been paid by clothiers' executors without specific instructions in a will. Nevertheless, out of almost 200 Wealden clothiers' wills from the 1480s to the first decade of the seventeenth century, the roll call of charity towards 'poor spinners' is hardly impressive.

Both wives and widows spun, but there is no hard evidence on the extent to which children were drafted in to help. Spindles (known as 'trendles' in most Wealden inventories), and, less frequently, spinning wheels, are found in at least half of all Wealden probate inventories between 1565 and the end of the century, alongside woolcards and stockcards. All manner of households possessed them. The goods of James Basset of Goudhurst, collier (d. 1580), totalled just £3 3s., according to local appraisers. He owned no livestock or farm goods, his professional tools (including two wheelbarrows) were valued at just 3s., but in his house were the requisites for spinning: three spinning 'trendles', a pair of stockcards and a pair of handcards. Robert Spencer, the parson of Frittenden in 1582, had goods valued at £77 in all, including livestock, corn on the ground and books worth £5. But also in his house were two linen wheels and a woollen wheel. Finally, a small farmer, William Taylor of Biddenden (d. 1584), who apparently engaged in no other trade but agriculture, had a pair of stockcards and a trendle in his house.[45] It is needless to add that the basic tools for spinning wool were also normally to be found among the goods of specialized textile workers. They also appear very frequently in widows' inventories.[46] In the central Weald at least – and to a lesser extent in the villages and hamlets on its northern fringes – some spinning was carried out in most households. For poorer families the earnings of wives and widows, and probably children, may have bridged the gap between going hungry and a lean subsistence. In somewhat better-off households the income from spinning was a useful supplement, even if not the critical means of survival which it was for the poor. And in wealthier households spinning wool was most likely one of the multifarious tasks of resident female servants, which added slightly to the income of the householder. It was in the interests of the clothiers that as many people as possible, within a day's ride of their residences, be able and willing to spin, even if for many it was not a full-time occupation. By the end of the century spinning also no doubt figured in the calculations of local poor law officials and their rate-paying neighbours.

The output of thousands of spinners was regularly collected by clothiers, who would gather together the yarn intended for specific cloths and put it out again to local weavers to make up into cloth. Weavers, in comparison to spinners, are a well-

---

[44] KAO PRC 32/34 fo. 64; PRC 17/43 fo. 431; PRO PROB 11/87/23.
[45] KAO PRC 10/14 fos. 8v, 64v, 117v.
[46] E.g. KAO PRC 10/14 fos. 13, 159, 191v, 207, 213.

documented group. As was noticed in chapter 5 they included men (and widows) of widely differing degrees of wealth, which, it can be argued, was a function of two different factors. Some weavers were quite well off because of the scale of their weaving business and the number of servants they employed. Others were relatively wealthy as a result of their dual employment as farmers and weavers. And of course, some combined weaving on a large scale with a substantial farm and profited from both occupations.

In contrast to spinning, which was a relatively unskilled job (or at least a skill which was widely distributed) and a spare-time occupation for many in the Weald, weaving in this region was overwhelmingly a specialist occupation. While most Wealden households owned the basic tools for spinning wool, only a small but significant minority contained looms. Weaving also was a gender-specific trade. Even though no weavers' guild existed in the Weald, weaving was nonetheless a craft normally acquired through a formal apprenticeship by young men. The great bulk of cloth was woven by full-time specialist weavers – although many professional weavers had farms as well. With or without farms, weavers were independent master craftsmen not directly employed by the clothiers whose yarn they wove. At the same time, they remained dependent upon clothiers for work: few weavers wove their own yarn for sale as cloth, and weavers' probate inventories rarely show more than tiny quantities of wool or yarn owned by the deceased. The only exception to this rule were a relatively small number of men whose businesses occupied the borderland between clothier and weaver. In the kerseymaking district a number of probate inventories show men who operated as clothiers (as shown by the presence of raw materials and very basic dyeing equipment) and as weavers (suggested by their looms). Robert Packnam of Lenham, 'kerseymaker' (d. 1608), was a prosperous example of the clothier-weaver. His goods included kersey cloth valued at £45, wool and yarn rated at £50 and he owned two kersey looms. He was performing the roles of both weaver and clothier.[47]

In the dominant broadcloth sector, by contrast, the distinction between clothiers and weavers was maintained, even though a minority of clothiers owned a loom. Normally the clothier delivered the coloured yarn intended for particular cloths to one of his regular weavers. Broadcloth weavers usually owned one or two broadlooms (occasionally three), each of which required two people to operate. Payment for weaving was by piece rate, so much per yard of broadcloth woven, and was also paid in arrears. Contemporary estimates agree that weavers produced broadcloth at the rate of about two yards per day, working on a single broadloom.[48] Hence the weaving of a typical thirty-yard Kent broadcloth would occupy a weaver and his assistant for just over two weeks. By the same token a prosperous broadweaver with two looms and a total workforce of four could turn out four full-

---

[47] KAO PRC 10/34 fo. 227.   [48] See Roberts thesis 'Wages' (n. 39 above), p. 274.

Table 6.2 *Inventoried wealth of weavers, 1565–99*

Value	All weavers	Excluding kersey and linenweavers
Under £20	32 (26%)	23 (22%)
£20–30	30 (24%)	25 (23.5%)
£30–40	21 (17%)	19 (18%)
£40–50	7 (6%)	7 (7%)
£50–60	10 (8%)	8 7.5%)
£60–80	11 (9%)	11 (10%)
£80–100	5 (4%)	5 (4.5%)
£100 or over	8 (6%)	8 (7.5%)
Totals	124	108

sized broadcloths per month. What is difficult to ascertain from existing sources is what proportion of broadweavers operated more than one loom on a regular basis.

A portrait of Wealden weavers and of their relationships with clothiers can be drawn from a number of sources but especially useful are the wills and inventories of clothiers and of the weavers themselves. The ideal source – the business records of clothiers – may have once existed but none have been found. Most of the analysis that follows is based on a sample of all the weavers, identified through probate inventories, who died between 1565 and 1599 in twelve Wealden parishes of Canterbury diocese: Benenden, Bethersden, Biddenden, Cranbrook, Frittenden, Goudhurst, Hawkhurst, Marden, Rolvenden, Smarden, Staplehurst and Tenterden.[49] The sample lacks only Brenchley and Horsmonden, the two clothmaking parishes in Rochester diocese, and is composed of 124 persons, of whom four were identified as linen weavers, fourteen as kerseyweavers and the rest broadweavers. The narrow weavers came mainly from Bethersden and Smarden, both parishes on the fringes of the main broadcloth region. Had the sample included more parishes to the north of the Weald, the proportion of kerseyweavers would have been higher. Table 6.2 shows the distribution of inventoried wealth in weavers' inventories – including household goods, farm goods, trade goods and debts when included.

Half of all weavers owned chattels worth under £30 at the time of their death, but a tenth had goods valued at £80 or more, and more than a quarter were worth £50 or more in movables. If the kersey and linen weavers are excluded, the share of poor weavers drops somewhat, while the proportion owning goods worth £80 or more rises to 12 per cent, those with chattels of £50 or over rises to about 30 per cent. In either case the typical or median weaver's wealth at death was in the

---

[49] Parish totals were: Benenden (15), Bethersden (10), Biddenden (13), Cranbrook (26), Frittenden (2), Goudhurst (13), Hawkhurst (11), Marden (5), Rolvenden (8), Smarden (10), Staplehurst (5), Tenterden (6).

range £30 to £40. However, there are no probate inventories for most weavers, and it seems likely, therefore, that the actual proportion of poor weavers was probably considerably larger than suggested by the sample. For the majority, weaving was not a lucrative occupation.

Be they prosperous or poor, however, almost all weavers in the Weald owned their own looms. In the 1560s broadlooms, with varying quantities of accompanying, detachable pieces, were worth between £1 10s. and £2 10s.; kersey looms about £1. In the 1580s and 1590s broadlooms were generally valued in the range £2 to £3, while kersey looms were worth between £1 and £1 10s. each. Most 'poor' weavers owned their own looms, but the few who did not were poor. Of the 124 sample weavers, only eight were without looms. All eight owned goods valued at under £30, but six of the eight had chattels worth between £20 and £30; only two were among the poorest weavers in the sample (inventory total under £20). The conventional explanation would be that the eight must have rented looms from clothiers. But there is no evidence that clothiers in the Weald owned looms which they hired out to weavers. None of the dozens of clothiers' inventories show a loom owned by a clothier but in another person's house. The cost of an old broadloom was low enough to be purchased by quite poor men who had completed a weaver's apprenticeship. Or, put another way, the very poor were unlikely to obtain a full-time apprenticeship with a master broadweaver; the family that could afford an apprenticeship premium of £3 to £5 could probably also afford to purchase a broadloom at 40s. or 50s. The most likely explanations for the absence of looms in a few of the sample inventories are either that the weaver was retired and his loom had been sold or passed on to a kinsman, or that they had the use of a loom owned by a friend or relation. In one case where a man described in his will as a weaver had no loom listed among his chattels, the will explains the apparent anomaly: Christopher Obens of Rolvenden had a 'loom and tackling which is in the keeping of Richard King'.[50] Like Obens, most of the sample's 'poor weavers' owned their own looms. In fact all fourteen of the inventories worth under £15 included looms.

Many Wealden weavers owned more than one loom, if the inventory sample is in any sense representative. At least forty-two out of 106 broadweavers owned two or more looms. The appraisers did not invariably specify what type of looms were present in cases where there were two or more. In about half a dozen inventories, however, they did record that the deceased owned both a broad and a narrow loom.[51] In many more cases, the inventories specify two or three 'broadlooms', but in an equal number of cases the valuers just recorded 'two looms'. From the prices noted for the looms, it appears that the great majority of the forty-two cases involved two broadlooms. Only one of the sample weavers was credited with four looms, and just five others owned three. It may be recalled that the 1555 'Weavers Act' prohibited rural weavers from operating more than two looms, but there is no

[50] KAO PRC 17/48 fo. 356; PRC 10/19 fo. 501.
[51] E.g., Andrew Freeland of Hawkhurst (1591): KAO PRC 10/22 fo. 52.

evidence of any effort to penalize Wealden weavers who used three or more looms.[52] Five of the six weavers with three or four looms were from Cranbrook or Goudhurst, in the heart of the broadcloth region; the other came from Tenterden. There is a loose correlation between a weaver's total inventoried wealth and the ownership of two or more looms. Many of the wealthier weavers owned more than one, but a number of weavers with only average total wealth owned two looms, and at least ten of the wealthier weavers had only one at the time of their death. It would appear that the ownership of two or three looms did not lead automatically to greater than average wealth. A further requirement was to keep his looms busy, which in turn depended upon the weaver's ability to attract work from local clothiers and to retain apprentices and journeymen to operate the looms. It must have been the ambition of most weavers to develop a permanent business relationship with one or more of the district's major clothiers, from whom they were most likely to obtain regular work.

Looms aside, weavers owned hardly any trade goods associated with the textile industry. To be a weaver the requirements in terms of plant and capital were minimal – in contrast to the capital needed to function as a clothier. Once in possession of a loom, the skilled weaver's main financial problem would have been how to pay for the maintenance of his household during what may have been the long intervals between one payment for work completed and the next from the clothiers. The income earned by women in the household who spun wool may have been necessary during such intervals. Clothiers only paid their weavers after one or more cloths had been completed, and scattered evidence suggests that clothiers could be very slow in paying at all. A Cranbrook broadweaver, Henry Whitmore, was at his death in 1584 owed payment for weaving five broadcloths for Thomas Sheffe and four others for Richard Sheffe. In August 1599 a well-off Hawkhurst weaver with two looms, Edmund Chittenden, was owed almost £20 for his weaving work by three different local clothiers. His neighbour John Hamon, also among the wealthier weavers in the sample, was owed £28 by two Hawkhurst clothiers at his death in 1585. The prosperous Cranbrook clothier Alexander Dence owed money to three different weavers when he died in 1601, although in each case the amounts due were £4 or less. A somewhat later example shows the degree to which weavers might be, in effect, extending credit to clothiers who gave them work. William Burr of Marden (d. 1612) was owed 'for weaving of 33 cloths' by Samuel Sharpe of Cranbrook, one of the area's leading clothiers.[53] Burr owned two looms, so thirty-three cloths represented about 230 working days (or thirty-eight weeks) of his workshop's output without payment! Undoubtedly this is an extreme case, and it may be that Burr farmed out some of Samuel Sharpe's yarn to poorer

---

[52] Four looms: KAO PRC 10/8 fo. 209; three looms: PRC 10/8 fo. 241; 10/10 fo. 78; 10/12 fo. 94v; 10/13 fo. 14; 10/15 fo. 169; 10/25 fo. 322. Weavers' Act: 2 & 3 Ph & M, c.11.

[53] KAO PRC 10/16 fo. 55 (total inventory £38); 10/29 fo. 112 (total £140); PRC 21/7 fo. 274 (total £254); Dence: PRC 21/16 fo. 150; PRC 10/37 fo. 285 (total £68).

weavers to work for him. There is, however, no evidence of master weaver's putting out work given them by clothiers to other weavers.

Most weavers' inventories show that they had debts due at the time of their deaths, although in the majority of cases the crucial details are missing. In some cases where a weaver can be shown to have been a significant creditor, it is impossible to distinguish money owed for weaving from simple loans or other debts not associated with their trade. The prosperous Benenden weaver William Bence (d. 1595) had debts due totalling £78 – double the total inventories of most weavers. John Bathurst of Staplehurst, clothier, owed Bence £40, while John Basden of Benenden, clothier, owed £4 11s. From the inventory it is impossible to know if the £40 debt was for weaving cloth. If that was the case, it would represent an enormous amount of work done but not paid for yet. In this case a will survives which shows that Bence had in effect deposited £40 with Bathurst, which was to be repaid with interest to Bence's daughter as part of her portion when she married. The other debt owed by a clothier, for £4 11s., is much more likely to be arrears of pay for Bence's weaving work; it is about the amount paid for producing three or four broadcloths. Yet another Benenden weaver, William Tolhurst (d. 1593), was owed over £35 by four different clothiers of Benenden and Hawkhurst.[54]

From such examples it is reasonable to suppose that master weavers like Bence and Tolhurst attracted work from local clothiers, in part at least, because they were able and willing to help finance the clothier's business. In effect, the most prosperous weavers were wealthy because they could obtain more work from clothiers than could poor weavers. The latter could not sustain their households without payment for as long as men like Bence and Tolhurst, while clothiers must have been inclined to give more work to master weavers who could afford to demand payment less frequently. It was a vicious circle, and it may help to explain the huge disparities in personal wealth of different broadweavers. The first variable was the volume of their operation: the weavers with more looms could produce more cloth in a given time, and therefore attract work from clothiers anxious to turn their investment in raw materials into finished products as soon as possible. The large-scale weaver with two or more looms obviously also hoped to profit from the value of his apprentices' and journeymen's labour, above and beyond their costs in maintenance and wages. The master weaver with two or more looms was both an independent artisan and an employer of labour. Yet he was also to an extent dependent upon the clothiers. The anomalous economic position of such men puzzled (or dismayed) Friedrich Engels three centuries later: 'These small employers are neither genuine proletarians ... nor genuine bourgeois.'[55]

The chains of cause and effect operated in both directions. Weavers able to extend credit to clothiers may have acquired the financial resources to do so by increasing their weaving capacity – by buying an additional loom and employing a

[54] KAO PRC 10/26 fo. 205v; PRC 17/48 fo. 308; PRC 10/23 fo. 372.
[55] *The Conditions of the Working Class in England in 1844* (1969 edn), p. 226.

journeyman and/or maintaining an extra apprentice. By the same token wealthier weavers were more likely to hire additional labour and buy extra looms if they could obtain regular work from one or more of the bigger clothiers – even if it meant accepting payment weeks, or even months, after the work had been completed. Undoubtedly the quality of a weaver's work mattered as well: it was hardly in the clothier's interest to produce badly woven fabric, even if he didn't have to pay for the work for several months. Poor quality cloth should, all things being equal, have been more difficult to sell in London, and if it did find a buyer it might be expected to fetch less than good quality cloth. But just how important was the quality factor in determining the business relations between clothiers and their weavers is impossible to judge. The only sixteenth-century interest which raised the issue of quality were the export merchants of London – who had no doubt that clothiers were to blame for all defects in cloth.

But there is another variable which operated with the two discussed above, and which together help to explain the comparative economic success of a minority of weavers. Many weavers were also farmers. The probate inventories of the sample weavers reveal a wide continuum of weavers' involvement with agriculture. The very poorest weavers had little or no farm goods. Most of the weavers with average to slightly higher than average inventoried wealth had at least some livestock and frequently a small farm. And finally, the twenty-five wealthiest weavers – with goods valued at £60 or more – were all farmers as well as craftsmen. William Pope of Hawkhurst (d. 1595) is a good example of the most prosperous stratum of weavers. Although he owned only a single loom, his movables amounted to over £83. The debts owed him were small, and included almost £4 due 'for weaving' from two named clothiers. The majority of his wealth was in his farm goods: he owned livestock valued at £40 alone. He had over £2 worth of corn in store, as well as twelve acres of cereals planted, valued at over £14. Including his fallow grounds, he probably farmed between fifteen and twenty acres of arable as well as at least thirty acres of pasture.[56] This was the holding of a middling yeoman farmer by Wealden standards, and was undoubtedly capable of generating a surplus above household requirements. Farms of this size could not only support a weaver's family and servants in the intervals between payments for craft work; they might also produce the cash surpluses to underwrite a weaver's financial dealings with clothiers and to invest in extra equipment and/or labour. The agricultural holding enabled a weaver to survive during periods of slack demand for his craft skills, and to cope with the onerous terms of his business relations with clothiers.

In the case of William Pope, farming represented far more than a helpful sideline. But the returns even from small-scale farming meant a great deal to the less well-off weavers of the Weald. A typical example could be James Everenden of Benenden (d. 1577), whose total movable wealth amounted to under £37. He owned two

[56] KAO PRC 10/23 fo. 486.

looms, which were valued at just £3, and three local clothiers owed him almost £8. But he also ran a small farm: just three acres in crop in the summer, and four cows, three calves and a mare. His farm goods were valued at just over £9, yet his husbandry may have made all the difference between a satisfactory if meagre well-being and bare subsistence. The farm was all the more valuable to him and his large family because the land – only about twelve to fifteen acres – was his own. In his will he left 'a messuage and lands' to his wife for her life and then to all five sons.[57] Many other weavers who left similar amounts of chattels were small farmers like Everenden – but without the advantage of a freeholding. One such was William Mount of Bethersden (d. 1578), whose goods (including one broadloom) were appraised at £34. Mount's will discloses no freehold land to leave, but his inventory reveals a small farm similar in scale to Everenden's. His arable crop was no more than three acres, while the livestock consisted of four cows, two calves and a mare. Together with a reserve of corn, his agricultural goods were valued at just over £14. He was owed £1 15s. but by whom is not recorded. Mount's holding would have been similar to Everenden's – perhaps twelve to fourteen acres – but Mount would have been paying several pounds per year in rent to a landlord, a small but possibly significant difference in their day-to-day financial situations.[58]

Even taking rent into account, a significant dividing line between well-off and poor weavers in the Weald must have been between those with farms and those without. Admittedly, the amount of a person's chattels and debts due at death is an imperfect measure of relative economic standing: it would be far better to have evidence of actual income. In addition, probate inventories describe movable wealth and ignore wealth in land. On the other hand, inventories by their very nature tend to make farmers appear more prosperous than craftsmen without farms, even though a farmer with movables worth £75 may be no better off in terms of disposable income than a successful craftsman with chattels worth half that sum. There is no way of knowing if appraisers always included cash in hand, or even if they were informed about it by the deceased's immediate family. Nor is it certain that debts were always reported. Nevertheless, it is unlikely that either small farmers or weavers kept much cash lying about. They were more likely to dispose of it in the form of purchases or by making loans. Thus, even in the case of weavers who owned land but did not farm it, their gains from rent would mostly be converted into goods or debts which *should* appear in probate inventories.

In the case of weavers, the wide range of personal wealth at death should be emphasized. Was there any correlation between farming and overall wealth among the sample weavers? The key finding is that a large majority of broadweavers – eighty-four out of 104 who were householders – engaged in some agricultural activity at the time of their death. Twenty-eight just kept livestock, sometimes on a quite minuscule scale, but fifty-six out of 104 (54 per cent) were farmers in the

---

[57] KAO PRC 10/9 fo. 61v; PRC 17/43 fo. 145.
[58] KAO PRC 10/9 fo. 274; PRC 17/43 fo. 7.

conventional sense, with evidence of arable as well as pastoral husbandry. Again, the mere combination of farming and weaving provided no certain route to prosperity: many quite poor weavers were also farmers. Among the weavers with inventory totals below £40 – who made up a majority – most were involved in husbandry, although half of those only kept livestock. Among the poorest weavers – those worth less than £20 – a majority had no farming activity at all. At the other extreme, all the wealthier weavers – as measured by the value of their chattels at least – were also farmers. A large majority of weavers worth £50 and above were farmers in the full sense, with crops on the ground as well as livestock. Of course these figures cannot be taken at face value: the small minority of 'poor weavers' (with no farms) of the inventory sample represent a larger number of near-propertyless artisans for whom inventories were never made. There must have been many poor weavers, mere cottagers, who sustained their families by a combination of weaving and day labour in agriculture – in addition to wives' earnings from spinning. Their weaving skills may only have been sought by clothiers during the peak period of clothmaking, in the winter. During the remainder of the year – and during periodic trade crises when unsold cloths piled up – they survived in the same way as 'unskilled' day labourers: on wages for common agricultural, building and miscellaneous labouring jobs. How large this invisible corps of poor weavers was at different times in the century is unknowable. Some, probably, were hired for short periods by established master weavers. Others may have soldiered on as independent craftsmen/labourers, while leaving little imprint on the historical record. At least one, William Benson of Staplehurst, doubled as an alehouse keeper.[59]

What little that is known about how much independent weavers were paid would suggest that very few of them were likely to wax wealthy from their craft activities alone. The wages of fully qualified weavers who worked for someone else were regulated by the county magistrates during the Elizabethan period. They compare favourably with the annual stipends supposed to be paid to resident servants in husbandry, but were slightly lower than the amounts set for the skilled employees of either fullers or clothiers. In the 1563 wages proclamation the highest annual salary of any farm servant, that for a 'bailiff of husbandry', was £2 16s. 8d. The farmer's 'best servant' was to receive £2 6s. 8d. By contrast, the weaver's 'foreman' should be paid £3 per annum, and the ordinary journeyman was to be paid £2 10s. per year, above his keep. Clothiers' servants had their wages fixed slightly higher, at £3 6s. 8d. for the foreman and £2 13s. 4d. for ordinary journeymen. At the top of the textile workers' wages league was the fuller's 'millman' with an annual wage of £4 on top of his maintenance.[60] These maximum wages are hardly sound evidence about what journeymen textile workers actually earned, but they do hint at a conventional status-economic hierarchy among the textile trades which must

[59] CCL. X.2.9 fo. 78 (I owe this reference to Anita Thompson).
[60] Paul L. Hughes and James F. Larkin (eds.), *Tudor Royal Proclamations* (1969), ii, pp. 217; iii, p. 36–8.

Table 6.3 *Weavers and farming, 1565–99*

Inventory total	No farming	Livestock	Full farmers	Totals
Under £20	13 (57%)	6 (26%)	4 (17%)	23
£20–30	5 (20%)	9 (36%)	11 (44%)	25
£30–40	2 (11%)	7 (37%)	10 (52%)	19
£40–50	1 (16.5%)	1 (16.5%)	4 (67%)	6
£50–60	–	1 (12%)	7 (88%)	8
£60–80	–	3 (27%)	8 (73%)	11
£80–100	–	1 (25%)	3 (75%)	4
£100 or over	–	–	8 (100%)	8
Totals	21	28	56	*104*

long pre-date the 1560s. The slightly higher wages for the full-time servant of a fuller reflects not any greater skill than that of the weaver's or clothier's journeymen but the small number of men qualified to operate fulling mills. The differential between all the 'skilled' textile trades and the servants in husbandry is a reflection both of the former's formal apprenticeships and of the size of the potential labour supply in agriculture in an era of demographic growth. It is also likely that journeymen in the textile trades were older than farm servants.

But were many skilled weavers living as resident servants on annual contracts of employment? The answer must be negative. The sample of Elizabethan weavers revealed just forty-two weavers with two looms or more, over a period of thirty-five years. And it is by no means proven that all of them had two looms in operation on a regular basis. Some had a second loom for periods of peak demand, and thus were less likely to require extra, full-time servants beyond their normal household complement. After all, a weaver with two teenage children and one apprentice could operate two looms on their own when necessary. Of the forty-two weavers in the sample with two or more looms, it is likely that only those who appear from their inventories to have been wealthy employed paid, full-time journeymen, i.e., about half that number. It is most likely that the great majority of independent weavers operated with unwaged household labour – their own wives, children and apprentices. The statutory wages of weavers, therefore, are interesting but not relevant to the situation of most weavers.

Independent master weavers were paid by clothiers strictly on the basis of the amount of cloth of specific qualities they produced. There was no effort by the magistrates to fix the piece rates and thus we must rely on contemporary estimates of the costs of weaving broadcloth, and on a few figures extracted from probate records of monies owed to weavers for known amounts of work. The only other evidence of what was thought weavers should be paid is found in draft bills discussed in the 1593 Parliament, at the end of two or three generations of price inflation. The bills proposed an extended scale of payments with the highest amount to be given for weaving 'broadlisted cloth as it shall be laid upon the bar and which shall be woven in a fourteen hundred slay', and in which every ell of cloth must contain three and three-quarter pounds of yarn: 16d. per ell. The rates descended from there to 6d. per ell for cloth woven in a 'ten-hundred slay'. The highest rate, 16d. per ell, converts to 20d. per yard, and is far higher than any examples of rates actually paid for weaving in sixteenth-century Kent. The discrepancy is less surprising when it is realized that the explicit purpose of the bills was to raise the wages of spinners and weavers in the hope that there would be an improvement in the quality of English cloth. They never became law.[61]

Weavers in the Weald – in real life – were paid a variety of rates for their work, but rarely above 12d. per yard woven. The weaving of different quality cloths was remunerated at different rates. This is shown in the 1566 inventory of Isabel Castlyn, the widow of a broadweaver who continued her late husband's trade in Cranbrook. She was owed 'for weaving of three cloths, whereof one is ten pence work and two (are) eight pence work'. At the higher of the two rates, the clothier's cost for the weaving of a twenty-eight-yard broadcloth would be just 23s. 4d.[62] Another Cranbrook weaver, Henry Whitmore, was owed £5 13s. 4d. for weaving four cloths for the clothier Richard Sheffe in 1584. If the cloths averaged about thirty yards each – and many export quality cloths were longer than that – then Whitmore was being paid at the rate of 11d. per yard.[63] But weavers' wages could be considerably less than 10d. or 11d. per yard. As late as 1612 William Burr, the Marden weaver, was owed just £26 for weaving thirty-three cloths for Samuel Sharpe of Cranbrook; that converts to a rate below 8d. per yard, or less than 19s. per cloth.[64] From these slender data, it appears that weavers' rates varied widely, that rates reflected – to a degree – variations in the quality and fineness of the weaving, but that throughout the period – and especially in the late sixteenth and early seventeenth centuries – clothiers were able to keep wages down.

The natural desire of the independent, and unorganized, master weavers to obtain regular work from clothiers led them to accept low piece-rates and payment long in arrears – rather than leave their looms idle for long periods. The whip was firmly in the clothier's hand. Wages were low in part because of the expanding size of the local labour supply, but also in part because so many weavers practised dual employments. A small farm, or even a smallholding with a few animals, enabled many weavers' families to survive the lean periods with little or no income from weaving. In a wider sense, the access to land on the part of many weavers enabled the clothiers to offer piece-rates for weaving which in real terms may have been falling throughout the later sixteenth century. Making a living from weaving must have been a precarious business indeed for the many weavers who had no land to work. A fully employed weaver – using household labour – might earn £20 per annum from his craft occupation, assuming that he and his assistant worked 250

[61] PRO SP 12/244 nos. 128, 130.

[62] KAO PRC 10/2 fo. 144.

[63] KAO PRC 10/16 fo. 55.

[64] KAO PRC 10/37 fo. 285.

days per year, producing two yards of broadcloth per day at the rate of 10d. per yard. But how many weavers worked 250 days a year at the loom? That may be an over-estimate for many marginal weaver-farmers or weaver-labourers. Nevertheless, given the levels of productivity achieved by sixteenth-century broadweavers, many craftsmen (and their widows) were needed.[65]

A rough estimate of the *maximum* number of master weavers at work in the Wealden textile industry in the 1560s (or at any time in the preceding two or three decades) can be made on the basis of Lord Cobham's estimate of annual output at around 12,000 cloths. If we allow about fourteen working days per cloth, 250 working days per year per loom and a weaving rate of two yards per day, there must have been at least 650 looms in operation, requiring a labour force of around 1,300 people. If it is also estimated that up to a fifth of master weavers operated two looms, the rest just one, there may have been 500–550 independent weavers at work at any point during the 1540s or 1560s. Each loom could process about six pounds of yarn per day, the work of six full-time spinners. And, since spinning was less likely to have been a full-time occupation than weaving, there must have been at least ten to twelve spinners per loom. Weavers, however, remained the most numerous full-time, specialized workers in the local textile industry.

Clothiers collected their cloths from weavers regularly and, as we have seen, much more promptly than they paid weavers for their handiwork. The next two stages of the manufacturing process, fulling and shearing, were also the work of independent craftsmen who were similarly paid piece rates by clothiers. The fulling process invariably occurred at a fulling mill, not in the clothier's workhouse. G. D. Ramsay describes the operation:

The newly-woven fabric, scoured by fuller's earth, was thickened by the fuller or tucker, who steeped and battered it in a vat of urine.[66]

The hammers which battered the cloth were operated by a water-powered fulling mill, hence fulling had to be carried out in locations where fast-running streams were able to drive the millwheels. Many fulling mills, not surprisingly, were located to the north of the central, clothing districts of the Weald – on the southern slopes of the North Downs – while others could be found in the steep, narrow valleys of the High Weald. In contrast to spinners, weavers, shearmen and clothiers, the physical requirements of fulling mills dictated the residences of fullers, and many were some miles distant from the heart of the textile district. There are no systematic records of the ownership of fulling mills. Knowledge of their location derives from a variety of sources, including deeds, wills and the occasional court case. There were never

---

[65] Six of 105 broadweavers in the sample were widows. The highest inventory total among them was Joan Monde of Cranbrook's (1566) £50 (KAO PRC 10/2 fo. 110v). Others: PRC 10/2 fo. 144; 10/5 fo. 45v; 10/7 fo. 252v; 10/17 fo. 436; 10/19 fo. 88.
[66] Ramsay, *English Woollen Industry*, p. 10. See also Edward Baines, *Account of the Woollen Manufacture of England* (1858), ch. 1.

more than ten to fifteen fulling mills in operation at the same time, both within the Weald and within a ten to fifteen kilometres radius of the major clothing parishes. Those that can be pinpointed are shown in figure 6.3 and detailed in the appendix to this chapter. The locations of the mills highlight the two clothmaking districts: the main broadcloth region in and around Cranbrook, and the kerseymaking district to the north of the Weald. In addition there were a number of fulling mills in the Medway valley: in and around Maidstone, the major market centre within Kent which serviced the central Weald, and which was probably an important market for a portion of the local industry's output, especially the cheaper, narrow-list woollens. Nearby, at Boxley, were deposits of fuller's earth.

Only a small number of mills were needed to process the extensive cloth production of the Weald. In all the sources which list occupations only a handful of fullers can be identified for any given decade or generation. Those involved fall into three categories. First, the owners of mills – frequently gentry landowners, sometimes independent fullers who owned their own mills and occasionally rich Wealden clothiers.[67] Second, master fullers who took leases of mills from rentier owners. Third, the journeymen fullers employed by owners or lessees of mills. The total of the last two classes seems to have been no more than a few score craftsmen at any time. The mill itself represented a major investment, well beyond the resources of the typical fuller, and much greater than the clothier's typical investment in fixed plant (although not necessarily greater than his circulating capital). When Thomas Hendley, gentleman of Cranbrook, built his new fulling mill at Otham, near Maidstone, he hired a Cranbrook millwright to construct 'an overshot fulling mill with two wheels, every wheel to be 7 foot over 3 stocks with 3 floodgates well grated before the gates for saving of fish'. At the same time he had contracted with a local carpenter to put up the house surrounding the mill and a barn as well. According to one of Hendley's own memoranda the works cost him over £80.[68] And that was in 1545.

The limited number of conveniently sited fulling mills undoubtedly conditioned the economic relations between fullers and their customers, the clothiers. It probably gave the former more bargaining power than was exercised by the other craftsmen who depended upon the customs of the clothmakers. There were times when clothiers' unfinished cloths piled up at the fulling mills awaiting attention. At his death in 1567 the clothier Peter Courthop of Cranbrook owned five broadcloths described as being 'unthicked, at the mill '.[69] But it must be recalled that the profits of fulling were in many cases shared between the owner of the mill and his tenant, the master fuller. Clothiers – unless they owned their own mill – dealt entirely with the working fuller, and unfortunately there is no systematic evidence of either the charges made for processing each cloth at different points in the century, or about

---

[67] By the late sixteenth century fulling mills in Wiltshire were increasingly under the control of local clothiers, much more so than in the Kent Weald: Ramsay, *Wiltshire Woollen Industry*, pp. 18–20.

[68] KAO U 1044/F1, pp. 55–61.   [69] KAO PRC 28/1 fo. 117.

the turnover or profits of a 'typical' fulling mill. It is likely that the charges per broadcloth were well under 10s. in the sixteenth century.[70] The appearance of new fulling mills in the second half of the century – when cloth output was barely growing – suggests that the profits of a mill were large enough to justify the investment of at least £50 to build from scratch, or somewhat less to convert a corn mill into a cloth mill. In the 1540s the rental value of a fulling mill was given as £6 per annum in a Crown particular for sale, while in 1558 £9 6s. 8d. per annum. was the rent received by the Crown for two adjoining mills in Horsmonden.[71] But Crown rents were notoriously under-valued. A better guide to the value of a fulling mill is the rent received by Thomas Hendley for his new mill in the late 1540s: £13 6s. 8d. per annum.[72] The income from a mill at mid-century must have been at least double the rent paid to Hendley – if one allows for the income of the tenant – and was probably a good deal higher. The substantial costs of having others full their cloths, and the possibility of profits to be made by processing the cloth of lesser clothiers, explains why several wealthy clothiers either purchased or leased mills. Peter Short, Tenterden's leading clothier in the mid sixteenth century, owned a mill at Loose, and members of the Courthop clan of Cranbrook owned at least two mills at different times.[73]

Little is known about the economic standing of master fullers who leased mills. Roger Smith, the lessee of a fulling mill at Rolvenden owned by the Guildfords in the early 1530s, left a will which suggests a moderate prosperity. He left land to his son which could provide his widow with a £2 annuity, had at least one male servant and asked his executors to provide a £20 portion for his daughter which was to be paid out over five years.[74] John Brattle, a fuller who leased mills in Horsmonden from the Crown in the early Elizabethan period, was reasonably well-off, although not in the same league as the better-off clothiers. He left no will, but was rated at £8 in goods for the 1571/2 subsidy – among the upper third of Horsmonden's taxpayers. Brattle maintained one mill as a fulling mill, operated the other as a corn mill, and it was while working with the latter that a servant of Brattle's was accidentally killed in 1565.[75] The most successful fullers owned mills. Edward Coucheman of Loose near Maidstone (d. 1588) left chattels valued at £246, on a level with many prosperous clothiers. His will shows him to have been the proprietor of two fulling mills, as well as of just under 100 acres of land in Loose and three neighbouring parishes. He was able to leave a mill each to his two sons and some land to three other sons. The two sons who were to inherit the mills were enjoined to pay £100 portions to Edward's two youngest sons. Nine years later one of Edward's younger sons, Giles, died. He had only inherited fifteen acres of land at

[70] Julia de L. Mann, *The Cloth Industry of the West of England from 1640 to 1880* (1971), p. 318.
[71] PRO E 318/23/1278; E 159/339 *sub* Recognizances, rot. 5 or LR 6/98/12 *sub* Rents & Farms.
[72] KAO U 1044/F1, pp. 92, 95, 98.
[73] PRO PROB 11/70/28; PROB 11/22/26; KAO U 106/T1. See Appendix below.
[74] KAO PRC 32/16 fo. 35v.   [75] PRO E 179/126/424; KB 9/613 no. 277.

Loose, but called himself a fuller in his will; perhaps he worked for one of his elder brothers. Even this younger son of a millowner left chattels valued at £88. An owner-occupier fuller could accumulate substantial assets and enjoy a reasonably large income. The great majority of fullers, however, could not capitalize on the economic potential of their relatively scarce skills because most were tenants or journeymen working for wages. Here was one textile trade where the ownership of the tools of production were clearly beyond the means of most of its practitioners. The near-absence of identifiable fullers in the probate records is itself a reflection of the fact that most were employees of millowners or lessees: the contents of their inventories would give little indication of their trade. So Coucheman's prosperity was far from typical among fullers. He was the scion of a family of Cranbrook clothiers. The profits of clothmaking enabled his father to own a fulling mill, and by the time of Edward's death there were two mills in the family.[76] The lot of most fullers was to work for another man, who himself paid rent to the owner of the mill.

The final stages of the clothmaking process were also carried out by independent craftsmen employed by clothmakers and paid piece rates for each job. The several operations included in the finishing or 'dressing' of a woollen cloth were done by shearmen. Again G. D. Ramsay describes the shearman's work concisely:

The nap (of the cloth) was then raised by passing teasels, mounted on a frame, across the fabric, a process known as rowing or barbing, after which a smooth surface was created by the shearman who with a large and heavy pair of shears clipped off the fluff or rough wool. To improve the surface the nap raising and shearing were several times repeated.[77]

Many shearmen who worked in the Weald can be identified from probate and other records. But it is clear that local craftsmen did not dress and finish all Kentish woollens. There is good evidence that clothiers sold at least a part of their cloths to London merchants before they were fully finished. In the 1520s, for example, the London Draper Thomas Howell recorded payments of 5s. each to a London clothworker for dressing several 'long Kentish cloths'.[78] Much later, in the 1590s, letters addressed to the London export merchant John Quarles by his factor in the Low Countries imply that at least some of the Kent cloths bought by Quarles from rural clothiers were finished in London.[79] And, not only were Kent broadcloths not necessarily finished by local shearmen, some were exported in an unfinished state, i.e., directly after fulling. The practice was of course contrary to a long string of statutes which forbade the export of undressed woollen cloths, priced above a stated value. Kentish broadcloths were always worth in excess of the price threshold set in the Acts.[80] When not exported surreptitiously, unfinished cloths were sold abroad on the basis of Crown licences granted to favoured courtiers, who in turn sold their special privilege to London merchants who actually owned cloths. In the

[76] KAO PRC 32/36 fo. 84v; PRC 32/38 fo. 136v; PRC 21/14 fo. 318; PRO C1/973/59–60.
[77] Ramsay, *English Woollen Industry*, p. 10.   [78] Drapers' Co. MS. C/AL 1 fo. 23.
[79] PRO SP 46/176 fo. 15v for example.   [80] E.g., the statute 27 Henry VIII, c. 13.

mid Elizabethan period the privilege of exporting undressed Kentish cloths was held by William Lord Cobham. His licence of October 1568 allowed him to export 2,000 cloths per year 'unrowed, unbarbed and unshorn and not ready and fully dressed'.[81] This dispensed Cobham from the provision in the most recent act of 1566, which prohibited the export of any unfinished cloths from Kent or Suffolk. That act was promoted by the London Clothworkers' Company, who were anxious to secure work for its 'handicraft' members. But it may well have also had the effect of encouraging finishing in the clothmaking districts rather than in London. The 1566 act had been opposed by the export merchants of London, whose case was identical to that of Cobham's quoted earlier: there was not sufficient demand on the Continent for fully finished cloths. In the end the Crown compromised: it retained the general prohibition but permitted about a sixth of Kentish woollen production to be exported unfinished by Cobham's nominees.[82]

It was hardly in the financial interests of the Kent clothiers to sell their cloths to London merchants in an unfinished state. The value added to their raw materials by the final few stages of the production process was comparable to – or higher than – that generated by the initial stages of manufacture. Thus Wealden clothiers must have sought outlets for fully finished cloth when they could, and sold their wares unfinished when they had no other option. London merchants, naturally, sought to purchase undressed cloths when they could, and so take advantage of the extra profit margin to be gained by putting them out to be finished themselves. Which group, the merchants or the Kent clothiers, came out ahead in this game is uncertain. There is not sufficient evidence to measure the proportion of Kentish textiles which left their county of origin unfinished. It can only be a guess that the great bulk of fabric destined for the home market – especially the kerseys – were finished locally, whereas a substantial but unknown share of broadcloth made for the export trade was finished in London, or not finished in England at all. That a strong Continental market existed for the coloured but undressed Kent broadcloths is underlined by the stiff opposition mounted by the export merchants against the Clothworkers' Company, but also by the prosecutions begun by informers against two leading 'mere merchants' of Cranbrook in the late 1570s, William Hider and Richard Lyne, for shipping unfinished cloths.[83]

Undoubtedly a large share of Wealden textiles were finished locally. Shearmen could be found in most parishes of the central Weald and in many villages of the kersey district to the north. The geographical distribution of shearmen, identified from a number of sources, who were practising their craft between 1550 and 1610 was as follows:

---

[81] *Cal. Pat.*, 1566–9, no. 1139.
[82] 8 Eliz. I, c. 6; see G. D. Ramsay, 'Industrial Discontent in Elizabethan London: Clothworkers and Merchant Adventurers in Conflict', *The London Journal*, 1 (1975). The various arguments can be followed in PRO SP 12/41 fos. 129–33; SP 12/115 fo. 128 and BL Cotton. MS. Vesp. F.xii fo. 168.
[83] E.g. PRO E 159/375 Rec. Mich. rots. 52, 58, 58d. However, like most penal informations, none of these cases ended in a conviction, and were probably settled informally by informer and accused.

Broadcloth District		Kersey district	
Beneden	4	Bethersden	1
Biddenden	6	Chart Parva	1
Brenchley	1	Egerton	1
Cranbrook	6	Hothfield	1
Goudhurst	2	Lenham	3
Hawkhurst	3	Pluckley	4
Marden	2	Smarden	5
Staplehurst	4	(N.B. both broadcloths and	
Tenterden	1	kerseys were made in Smarden)	
Total	*29*	*Total*	*16*

Cloth finishing by local shearmen was common in both broadcloth and kerseymaking regions, although it should be remembered that both the volume and the value of woollens produced in the broadcloth district far exceeded the narrow cloth manufacture of the kerseymakers. It was to be expected that more shearmen resided in the first set of parishes than in the second. The proportion of shearmen in the broadcloth region was probably somewhat greater than suggested in the table because two of its parishes, Brenchley and Horsmonden, are poorly represented in the sources used to identify shearmen.

A better idea of the position of shearmen in the Weald can be gained by looking in more detail at a few of their number. As a trade group they can be compared with weavers on the basis of samples of individuals from each craft. To begin with, consider Staplehurst in the central broadcloth region, a parish which has been highlighted in this study as in some senses representative of the central Weald. There were two independent shearmen at work in the parish in the 1550s and 1560s. Thomas Water, the older of the two, had been in business in Staplehurst since at least the early 1540s. Between 1542 and 1566 nine children of his were baptized there, the offspring of his four marriages. No more than four survived infancy, but his eldest son John provided a link with his father's younger rival in the trade, John Hopper. John Water (born 1542) was listed as a 'servant' in the household of John Hopper in the communicant listing of 1563–4. The older shearman was never very well off, but neither could he be called poor. Rated £5 in goods in the 1543/4 subsidy, he had only a small household in 1563, with just one maidservant. By that time he had no apprentices, and must have carried on his trade with family labour alone. Water was alive in Staplehurst as late as 1572 (when rated £7 in goods to the subsidy) but then disappears from the sources; no burial is recorded in Staplehurst.[84]

Staplehurst's other shearman, John Hopper, apparently practised his craft from the late 1550s to the late 1580s, if not beyond. Born in Staplehurst about 1530 (according to a deposition of 1595), he lived there all his life, 'saving for about 7 years in his youth when he went to school '. He married a local woman in 1556 (the

[84] KAO PRC 43/13/31; subsidies: PRO E 179/125/273; E 179/126/423. Also in 1572 a Thos. Water, shearman, was owed 6s. 3d. by a local clothier, Wm. Stowe: KAO PRC 10/6 fo. 303.

first of three marriages) and the register shows ten children of his baptized between 1557 and 1588. From at least the early 1560s he also served as the parish sexton, a job he appears to have inherited from a kinsman. Hopper seems to have been among the better-off householders of the parish, although not among the wealthy elite: he had two servants in 1563–4, and when he died, aged about sixty-six in 1596, he left a messuage and lands to his three surviving sons.[85] His eldest son Tobias was left all his father's shearman's tools, and had already been trained in the craft. The following year Tobias married and succeeded his father as Staplehurst's established shearman – until his rather premature death in 1609. Both Hoppers – John and Tobias – were literate. By the time John Hopper died, he was most likely retired: at his burial the register calls him 'an old man'. His chattels were worth only about £40, but most of that consisted of a comfortable variety of household goods. We have no accurate evidence of Hopper's economic standing at mid career since, unaccountably, he is not included in the 1572 tax lists. But all the circumstantial evidence, including his schooling and his possession of a Bible and two psalters in 1596, points to a respectable, middling standard of living. He was better off than Thomas Waters, who had been by no means poor. And yet when Hopper's son Tobias died, all his chattels were valued at just £13.[86]

Compared to the personal information retrievable about some shearmen, much less is known about their business dealings or their turnover. Since most of the main clothing parishes had at least one resident shearman, it may be assumed that the bulk of their work came from local clothiers. Staplehurst, for example, always had at least three or four resident clothiers, which may have been sufficient to support one or two local shearmen. From what little evidence there is, it appears that shearmen earned about 5s. to 6s. 8d. for finishing each broadcloth, but this is of little use without knowing their likely turnover or the time needed to dress each cloth. In 1570 a shearman was owed only 27s. for finishing eleven kerseys, and it can only be suggested that the rate for dressing a broadcloth would have been about double that paid for a kersey.[87] What is more certain is that the tools and equipment needed by a working shearman cost between £5 and £8 in the Elizabethan period – several times the minimum investment of a weaver – and consisted of numerous pairs of 'shearman's shears', 'handles', shearboards, a press, a tenter and hurdles.[88]

A few shearmen, like a minority of weavers, were comparatively prosperous, if the small sample of shearmen's inventories is representative. The thirteen Wealden shearmen whose inventories were enrolled between 1565 and 1609 owned chattels worth on average £33. But the range was wide, from just £10 to £83. The four 'wealthy' shearmen, with movables of £53, £54, £60 and £83, all lived in parishes with intensive clothmaking activity and numerous clothiers: Cranbrook, Hawkhurst

[85] KAO PRC 43/13/31; deposition: CCL PRC 39/17 fo. 114v; will & inventory: KAO PRC 17/49 fo. 338; PRC 10/23 fo. 473.   [86] KAO PRC 10/41 fo. 17.
[87] KAO PRC 21/1 fo. 104. In the 1650s as much as 18s. was charged for shearing a 42-yard Gloucester medley cloth: Mann, *Cloth Industry of the West of England*, p. 318.
[88] Exemplary inventories are KAO PRC 10/5 fo. 71; 10/11 fo. 160v; 10/17 fo. 399v; 10/21 fo. 53; 10/23 fo. 473.

and Smarden. John Eskrigge of Cranbrook (d. 1581) had goods totalling £60, including £20 in good debts. He appointed as overseer Laurence Weller, one of the parish's most prominent clothiers.[89] Similarly, William Styver of Brenchley, shearman (d. 1553), chose as his overseer Robert Bathurst, a clothmaker from neighbouring Horsmonden, while the Goudhurst shearman William Brayford (d. 1559) also chose a local clothier as overseer.[90] A wealthy clothier who had perhaps given him work was an ideal overseer of a shearman's will. The examples cited hint at ongoing relationships, if not friendships. The relatively small number of shearmen with probate inventories, however, suggest that not all developed such regular business ties and that many were worth well under the £30–35 average of the few noticed by the probate courts. Compared to the dozen or so with inventories, other sources – including criminal indictments, wills, depositions and the names of men acting as sureties or giving recognizances – reveal no less than thirty-two additional shearmen working in the Weald between 1550 and 1610. It seems that only a few shearmen were able to build up their business in the same way as quite a few master weavers. They remained independent but few managed to accumulate much capital or a large farm.[91]

Why this contrast between master weavers and master shearmen developed is unclear. There were certainly far fewer shearmen than weavers, but that in itself cannot explain why the proportion of wealthy among all shearmen was smaller than among weavers. One obvious difference was that weaving was only carried out in the country, while cloth finishing could be done both in the country and in London. To the extent that clothiers were often forced to sell their cloth in an unfinished state to London merchants, Wealden shearmen were the victims of economic forces far beyond their control. The shearman's work – if it was performed in the manufacturing region – was the final stage of the manufacturing process organized by clothiers. Having collected their cloths from the shearmen, the woollens were ready to be carried to the capital, either to be sold at the public market in Blackwell Hall, or to be delivered to London merchants for whom clothiers had contracted to produce cloths of specific size, quality and colour. And it is to the clothiers who we now must turn.

Appendix: Fulling mills and fullers

Mills identified in figure 6.3:

1 *Lenham*: Mill owned by Peter Wood (or Atwood), left to his son Edward in 1504: KAO PRC 17/9 fo. 75. Another reference at KAO U24/T348.

2 *Leeds*: 'Buscom Mill', formerly of Leeds Priory. Valued at £6 p.a. when sold to William Gooding, 1544: PRO E 318/23/1278. A Stephen Bassock of Leeds, 'fuller' d. 1546: KAO PRC 17/24 fo. 156.

3 *Otham*: Mill built by Thomas Hendley, Esq, 1544/5, and leased to Walter Sugar, late of Cranbrook, at 20 mks. p.a.: KAO U1044/F1.

[89] KAO PRC 10/11 fo. 160v; PRC 17/43 fo. 376; Rated £4 in goods in 1572: PRO E 179/126/423 *sub* Cranbrook hundred.   [90] KAO DRb/Pwr 11 fo. 237v; PRC 17/31 fo. 183.

[91] Two exceptions were Thos. Peende of Hawkhurst (d. 1593), who had debts in bonds and specialties worth £53; and John Botting of Cranbrook (d. 1618) who had 10 mks. in cash and debts worth £30, out of a total inventory of £135: KAO PRC 10/22 fo. 78; 10/40 fo. 55.

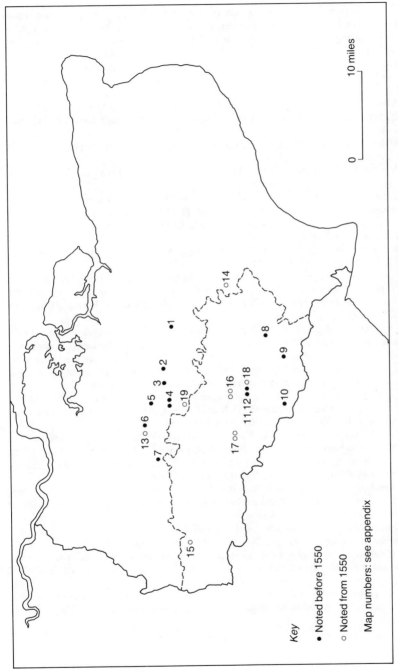

Key

• Noted before 1550

○ Noted from 1550

Map numbers: see appendix

0 _____ 10 miles

Figure 6.3 Fulling mills in operation, before and after 1550

4 *Loose*: Mill owned by Thomas Malyn in 1512 will: KAO PRC 17/12 fo. 410v. Bought from James Malyn by Peter Short, Tenterden clothier, before 1561: PRO PROB 11/70/28. Another fulling mill 'converted from an evil corn mill unto a good cloth mill' by John Coucheman, *temp.* Henry VIII; called Tylemill, *temp.* Edward VI, when tenant was Edward Coucheman: PRO C 1/973/59–60; SC12/9 no. 39, fo. 4. By 1588 Edward Coucheman owned two mills in Loose and adjoining East Farleigh: KAO PRC 32/36 fo. 84v. A Thomas May of Loose, 'fuller' as surety in 1597: KAO QM/SRC/ 1597/49.

5 *Maidstone*: Mill owned by John Courthop, Cranbrook clothier, left to his son John in 1527: PRO PROB 11/22/26. Four Maidstone fullers made recognizances in 1600: KAO Q/SR1/ m. 13.

6 *Ditton*: Mill owned by Thomas Hayman of Yalding, left to his wife in 1526: PRO PROB 11/22/30.

7 *Mereworth*: Mill owned by Thomas Moyse, leased to Thomas Seuter, 'fuller', who left lease to his son, in 1524: KAO DRb/Pwr 7 fo. 338v.

8 *Tenterden*: Fulling mill at Strikenbolds Mede owned by Sir John Guildford in 1492, leased to Richard Lucas in 1508: PRO PROB 11/9/29; KAO PRC 17/11 fo 41. Possibly a second mill by 1538: the 'fulling mill called New Mill at Eastwissel', earlier owned by Sir Edward Guildford: PRO E 328/52.

9 *Rolvenden*: Mill owned by John Guildford in 1539; lessee in 1534 was Roger Smith: PRO CP 25(2) 22/135 no. 17; KAO PRC 32/26 fo. 35v.

10 *Hawkhurst*: 'Harpynhope Mill' left by John Valence of Hawkhurst to 'brother' Hugh Ynce of London in 1490: KAO PRC 17/5 fo. 256. Fulling mill referred to in 1539 (KAO PRC 17/26 fo. 256); fulling mill sold to Edmund Roberts of Hawkhurst, merchant, in 4 Edward VI: PRO CP 25(2) 59/447 no. 38.

11, 12 *Cranbrook*: Probably two fulling mills before 1550: 'Thomas Sheffe's new fulling mill', referred to in 1516: KAO PRC 17/12 fo. 404. Another mill sold by Giles Coucheman to Walter Hendley in 1538/9: PRO CP 25(2) 22/134 no. 23. Possibly a third was 'Hockeridge Mill', owned by the Courthops until sold to Robert Hovenden, clothier, about 1550; in whose family it remained to 1630 at least: KAO U106/T1/2–6; T1/10–11.

13 *East Malling*: The 'lord's fulling mill' referred to in a 1570 coroner's inquest: PRO KB 9/628 no. 249. Information laid against Edward Beeching of E. Malling, 'weaver', for running a 'tucking mill': PRO E 159/363 Rec. Mich. rot. 206d.

14 *Great Chart*: Fulling mill owned by Edward Ellis was burgled in 1560: PRO Ass 35/4/4 m. 12. A John Pope of Little Chart, 'fuller', leased a mill in Chart, 1607: KAO U275/T26.

15 *Chevening*: A fulling mill at Chepsted was the site of the drowning of three-year old daughter of Richard Palmer 'fuller' in 1569: PRO KB 9/625 no. 173.

16 *Cranbrook area*: 'Manors' of Tolhurst and Lovehurst (owned by Thomas Wilford, Esq.) with lands in Staplehurst, Frittenden, Goudhurst and Cranbrook) included '2 fulling mills' in 1576: PRO CP 25(2) File 2456 no. 23.

17 *Horsmonden*: Two fulling mills called Bradforth Mills, leased by Crown to John Brattle of Horsmonden, in 1558 at £9 p.a.: PRO E 159/339 Recognizances rot. 5.

18 *?Cranbrook*: Messuage and fulling mill called Sprottisborne, owned by Thomas Hendley, Esq. and leased to James Cotchford in 1591. May be included in 11–12 above: PRO C 142/230 no. 61.

19 *?Boughton Monchelsea*: A fulling mill was part of Manor of Boughton Monchelsea, sold by Thomas Wyatt to Robert Rudstone in 1551; location not specified: PRO CP 25(2) 59/452 no. 4.

7

Clothiers and capitalism

The Wealden woollen industry was, as we have seen, the most important source of non-farming employment in the region. Many thousands depended wholly or partially on wages earned as textile workers. The majority of these outworkers relied on the master clothiers for their employment. Whether they were poor cottagers who eked out a bare subsistence by spinning wool on a part-time basis or quite well-off master weavers who also ran their own farms, most did not own the raw materials they processed. Admittedly, a small number of master weavers, or 'kerseymakers' manufactured their own cloths. But the lion's share of Kentish cloth production was organized by putting-out clothiers who could deploy the capital to purchase raw materials and pay the wages of the outworkers and artisans who turned wool into fine broadcloth. The clothiers, too, formed the connecting link between the regional economy and the more distant markets from where raw materials were obtained and where the finished product was sold. From the prospect of the Weald, the wealthy clothier was the dominant economic force; on his good will – and financial resources – the well-being of many thousands rested. But from the perspective of the wider English (and European) economy, how independent were the capitalist clothiers of the Weald? In the language of early-twentieth-century historians, was industrial capital – the clothiers – dominated by commercial capital, in the form of the London wholesale merchant elite? Or, on the other hand, did the major provincial clothiers operate on terms of equality with their metropolitan customers? This chapter examines the world of the clothiers, and in doing so tries to assess their role on the wider stage of early English capitalism.

The label 'clothier' was applied to a variety of men in the course of the sixteenth century. What they had in common – their training and their role as organizers of textile production by quasi-independent domestic workers – was small in comparison to the enormous differences in wealth between the small fry of the industry and the major capitalist clothiers. But who were they and where did they come from? This simple but inescapable question has proved among the most intractable to answer. The family backgrounds of clothiers in business at the beginning of the

sixteenth century are generally obscure. Some of the family names of clothiers
known to be active in about 1500 are familiar, but that is because several of their
descendants followed the same trade. Other names appear once and then vanish
from the increasingly long lists of active clothiers in the Elizabethan period. Just
twenty-five men have been identified as working clothiers in the Kent Weald
between 1470 and 1500. In almost all cases their specific family backgrounds are
unknown. In part this is simply a reflection of the lack of sources. Reconstructing the
genealogies of this early generation of clothiers is not possible because even
relatively well-off freeholders and tradesmen rarely made wills, and also because
runs of 'manorial' records which might show the passage of the small estates of free
tenants from father to son do not survive. Therefore only a few tentative
generalizations can be made about Wealden clothiers in 1500. To begin with, none
of them seem to have come from urban backgrounds. There is almost no evidence
of the migration of clothiers from towns in north Kent to the Weald. The only
exception is the tradition that the Bathursts originated in Canterbury, and
subsequently moved to Staplehurst.[1] The backgrounds of the remainder seem to
have been thoroughly rural; several bore traditional Wealden surnames like Basden,
Pattenden and Wanden.

Also apparent by 1500 is the fact that clothiers were by no means near-
propertyless artisans. Leaving aside the five men identified as clothiers solely
because their occupations were recorded when each was charged as a retainer of
Lord Abergavenny in 1503, the majority of our first cohort of clothiers were
landowners.[2] Typical was Laurence Taylor of Cranbrook, 'clothman', who died in
1490 leaving unspecified lands to two sons, 20 mark portions to his three daughters
and £40 and two cows to his wife. One of his two overseers was Stephen
Karkeregge, another of our twenty-five pre-1500 clothiers. At his death in 1500, he
left his principal messuage and a workhouse to his elder son and other lands to a
second son. One of Stephen's executors was Simon Lynch, also a clothier of
Cranbrook, who died the following year. He left land to his only son and could
afford £40 portions for his three daughters. In 1485 Simon was recorded as a free
tenant of the 'manor' of Glassenbury.[3] Most of the pre-1500 clothiers resided in one
of the dozen 'broadcloth' parishes in the central Weald. And most appear to have
held land only in their parish of residence, although the vagueness of testators'
descriptions of their landholdings leaves this uncertain.

A few clothiers were no more than minor freeholders, while others owned
moderately large estates. William Coucheman (d. 1500), the ancestor of a long line
of Cranbrook clothiers, willed lands in Cranbrook as well as a fulling mill and lands
in East Farleigh and Loose to two of his five sons. The overseer of William's will was

[1] See William Berry, *Pedigrees of the Families in the County of Kent* (1830), p. 198.
[2] PRO KB 9/430 nos. 49, 54, 58; *LP*, i, 438 (3 m. 23).
[3] Taylor: PRC 32/3 fo. 347; *Cal. Close Rolls, 1476–85*, no. 33; Karkeregge: PRO PROB 11/12/9;
Lynch: PRO PROB 11/12/14; BL Harl. Roll Y.4.

Alexander Courthop of Cranbrook, who, by the time of his death in 1525, was one of Cranbrook's wealthiest clothiers. He was probably the son of Peter Courthop of Cranbrook who owned a fulling mill and land there in Edward IV's reign and who may also have been a clothier.[4] It is certainly likely that men like Coucheman and Alexander Courthop inherited land from their fathers or uncles. Whether they were the sons of clothiers remains uncertain. Alexander Courthop left lands in Cranbrook, Biddenden and Maidstone to four sons, most of whom followed their father's occupation. Simon Lynch, mentioned earlier, flourished as a clothier at the end of the fifteenth century. He too was left at least some land by his father William (d. 1480), but whether or not the elder Lynch was a clothier by trade is unknown. The same could be said about Thomas Hendley, senior, of Cranbrook, a wealthy clothier who died by 1496. He owned lands in three Wealden parishes as well as in Romney Marsh, and chose as his executors two local gentlemen, Edward Horden and Richard Baker.[5]

The general pattern is evident by 1500: the clothiers who were long-lived and well-enough off to leave their mark on the record were at least petty landowners. They were the sons of clothiers or the sons of men whose occupation eludes us, but who almost invariably owned some land. Whether there were many 'poor' clothiers in this period – whose names are lost through lack of evidence – must remain an open question. The clothiers reported as Neville retainers could have been young men at the beginning of their careers, or representatives of a pool of unsuccessful manufacturers in an already highly stratified industry. Undoubtedly, as the century progresses, there is abundant evidence of vast disparities of wealth between clothiers of the same generation. Whether the gap between successful and petty clothmakers was as large before 1500 is not certain because the evidence is so scrappy. But clothier dynasties became commonplace in the course of the sixteenth century. It can be shown that the successful clothiers in the reign of Henry VII tended to be succeeded in the trade by a male member of the next generation; that is, if there were sons or nephews. And it goes without saying that clothiers who failed to prosper were much less likely to be followed in the trade by their offspring. Business failure in one generation ensured that the succeeding generation lacked the capital resources to operate as independent master clothiers. Even though a poor clothier's son may have acquired the basic clothmaking skills as an apprentice to his father or to another clothier, without financial resources he would be forced to seek employment as a journeyman clothier rather than attempt to set up on his own.

Two kinds of men, therefore, became clothiers in the Weald: the sons or nephews of clothiers, and the sons of relatively prosperous farmers, tradesmen or artisans whose families could afford both the apprenticeship premium demanded by master

---

[4] Coucheman (PRO PROB 11/12/12); Courthop (PRC 32/14 fo. 100; KAO U 386/T81; PRC 17/1 fo. 140).
[5] Courthop (PRC 32/14 fo. 100); Lynch (PRC 32/2 fo. 500v; PRO PROB 11/12/14); Hendley (PRO PROB 11/10/29).

clothiers and the minimum capital required to establish a clothmaking business. It would have been a substantial advantage, too, if the prospective clothier inherited at least a smallholding with a large house and outbuildings in which to carry out those stages of production which clothiers invariably did on their own premises. Documentation of this 'typical' family background of first generation clothiers is hard to obtain. But for first generation clothiers of Henry VIII's reign good examples can be found. Gervase Amyot of Benenden (d. 1537) appears to have been a master clothier of no great wealth. His family can be traced back through wills for two generations. Gervase's grandfather was Stephen Amyot of Benenden, a small farmer. Stephen left his only son Thomas a 'dwelling messuage' and lands, out of which he was to pay his mother a £1 annuity. The 1489 will was typical of many freeholding farmers of that generation. Stephen was prosperous enough to leave £1 for highway repairs in his parish and 5 marks for the hire of a chantry priest for half a year. Thomas Amyot died in 1520, leaving four sons (the eldest was Gervase) and two daughters. His will is also that of a family farmer, with no hint of involvement in textiles. His daughters were to receive portions of 5 marks each, and Thomas's house and lands were willed to Gervase, the only son who was of age. Rather than divide the family estate, Gervase was instructed to pay £10 to each of his three younger brothers, over a period of thirteen years. It was Thomas who apprenticed his eldest son Gervase to a clothier, although there is no mention of this in Thomas's will. In the course of the 1520s Gervase Amyot pursued his career as a clothier. He married Benet, the daughter of Matthew Hartrege of Cranbrook, a freeholder and farmer who died in 1517. Gervase Amyot's clothmaking business was family-based and modest in scale. Two of his younger brothers worked for him, and all three appear in the 1524/5 subsidy rolls. Gervase, the master clothier, was assessed on £3 per annum in lands, that is, among the ranks of the 'middling' taxpayers, but far below the assessments of the wealthy Cranbrook clothiers of his time. His brothers John and Richard were listed as servants, and rated at £1 and £1 10s. per annum in wages respectively. A dozen years later, at the time of his death, Gervase Amyot's business remained modest. His three under-age sons were to receive 10 marks each 'out of my stock' when they reached twenty-two; his daughter was to have a 10 mark portion also. There were small cash legacies to a number of relations, and Amyot left £1 to his sole apprentice. He still owned land, but clearly it was little more than had been left him by his father.[6]

Two generations later, it was still young men with at least a modest landed inheritance who became clothiers. Thomas Page of Goudhurst, 'clothier' died in 1597 while still in the service of a wealthy master clothier, William Austen. The unmarried journeyman clothier could nevertheless leave cash legacies totalling over £100 to various relations, as well as will his 'copyhold lands' at nearby Ticehurst (Sussex) to his brothers. The inherited customary lands were worth over £24 per

---

[6] Amyot wills: PRC 17/5 fo. 177; 17/14 fo. 110v; 17/21 fo. 69; Hartrege: PRC 17/13 fo. 256v; subsidy: PRO E 179/125/324.

annum, and Page also owned a tenement and lands at Winchelsea. He left money for funeral doles at both Goudhurst and in his native parish, Ticehurst. The general requirement – be it in the 1590s or the 1520s – seems to have been a modicum of wealth in the previous generation, rather than a clothier-father. The latter qualification helped, but was never indispensable.[7]

Being born into a clothmaking family conferred a variety of advantages on the younger generation. Education in the mysteries of clothmaking could be provided within the family, if a clothier decided not to apprentice his son(s) to another clothier. Many clothiers obtained apprenticeships for their sons with friends or relatives who practised the same trade. Given the family connections of many clothmakers, a successful mid sixteenth-century clothier was likely to have a brother or cousin in the trade. Thus relatives would send their sons to one another for their apprenticeships, and it is not uncommon to find young men working as journeymen clothiers for their uncles or cousins. In 1563 Paul Bathurst was a servant in the household of his uncle John Bathurst, a prosperous Staplehurst clothier. The Cranbrook household communicant listings of 1608–12 record a number of households of wealthy clothiers in which relatives of the head of household were resident apprentices or journeymen.[8] Whether it was the norm or the exception for working clothiers to apprentice out their sons rather than train them at home is uncertain. Numerous young men would of necessity have been apprenticed to neighbours and relations because of their father's death before their training had been completed. And, even if a young man's clothier father was quite capable of directing the boy's craft training, it was quite normal to send children to a neighbour's household. The practice of life-cycle service appears to have been as common in clothmaking as in many other trades in pre-industrial England. The Cranbrook household lists reveal a number of sons of well-off clothiers acting as apprentices or journeymen in another clothier's household. In 1612 the son of one of Cranbrook's leading clothiers, John Bennitt, was the apprentice of Richard Coucheman, senior, another well-off Cranbrook clothier. Likewise in 1608, Thomas Sheffe (a scion of one of the parish's leading clothmaking and merchant families) was living in John Sharpe's household as his apprentice. And the Staplehurst clothier Stephen Buckhurst sent his son Thomas into the household of the wealthy Cranbrook clothmaker, Richard Courthop, in 1608.[9]

Apprenticeship formed the basis of a clothier's career. There is little evidence about the nature of craft training given by fathers to their own sons. Only the formal apprenticeships of young men to masters who were not their fathers have left any record. Yet there was no gild or company of master clothiers in the Weald,

[7] PRO PROB 11/90/74; Austen: PRO PROB 11/128/79 (of 1616).

[8] Bathurst (KAO PRC 43/13/31); Cranbrook (KAO P100/28/1): e.g., John Sharpe (1608, Town) w/apprentice Alex S, jun.; Richard Sharpe (1608, Plusshingherst) w/cousins or nephews John and Thos. S. as apprentices; Peter Courthop (1610, Goddard's Green) w/younger brother Caleb C. as apprentice or journeyman; Thomas Colvill (1612, Milkhouse) w/apprentice Sam. C. and journeyman Edm C.   [9] KAO P100/28/1.

nor any local institutions to enforce a minimum apprenticeship period, or prevent men setting up as clothiers without an apprenticeship. There are no surviving apprenticeship indentures from the sixteenth-century Weald, nor any obvious cases of magistrates enforcing the terms of a clothier's apprenticeship in the surviving quarter session records. Yet without doubt a formal period of apprenticeship was the normal career route followed by Kent clothiers. And from the point of view of many master clothiers, taking on apprentices was a crucial part of their businesses.

The wills of clothiers who died leaving under-age sons provide some evidence of the nature of a clothier's education. Stephen Pattenden of Rolvenden (d. 1527) left instructions for his son's education which were more explicit than most:

I will that John my son go to school unto he be 15 years of age, and then he to be prentice to John Sharpe of Cranbrook or to some other honest man to learn weaving and clothmaking.

John Spice, a petty clothier of Pluckley, was more vague in his 1545 will. He left his son John in the custody of George Wolton, a substantial local clothier – 'and he to teach him his occupation' – rather than in his wife's custody. Wolton and Spice's widow were appointed joint executors, and Wolton was to have the use of the boy's goods in return for his upkeep and education. The wealthy Tenterden miller and merchant George Phillip died in 1551, leaving three sons (the eldest was almost seventeen). He instructed his wife and executors to set his younger sons to school 'until they can write and read English perfectly'. Then the executors were to provide one son an 'honest master in the occupation of clothmaking' at age fifteen. The boy was to dwell with his master for five years, the master to have the use of £20 during the term of the apprenticeship. Later in the century the costs of a clothmaking apprenticeship could be higher. Stephen Love, a well-off Goudhurst clothier who died childless in 1575, left his nephew and godson £40 'to see him brought up to the occupation of clothmaking'. Only £10 of the total was to pay for his schooling which would precede his apprenticeship.[10]

By the early sixteenth century clothiers were expected to be literate, and to have undertaken a substantial apprenticeship (although not necessarily the mid sixteenth-century legal norm of seven years). As apprentices they would learn the craft skills specific to clothiers (such as how to select, grade and dye wool) as well as a basic knowledge of broadcloth weaving, and perhaps also acquire a grounding in the business of clothmaking. If the few well-documented examples are typical, the young clothier's career began at fourteen or fifteen with a five- or six-year apprenticeship. Unpaid training ended by the age of twenty-one or twenty-two, when a young clothier might legally set up on his own. In many cases, however, young, unmarried clothiers worked as journeymen for established clothiers for several years before beginning their own clothmaking business – and households. Certainly in Cranbrook at the close of the century paid, resident journeymen figure regularly in the households of the most prominent clothiers. The majority of

---

[10] Pattenden (KAO PRC 32/15 fo. 31v); Spice (PRC 17/35 fo. 9v); Phillip (PRC 32/24 fo. 71); Love (PRO PROB 11/57/43).

journeymen recorded in the Cranbrook household lists seem to have been quite young men: their careers as employees of other men were limited to a few years before marriage. But inevitably, some men trained as clothiers found it difficult to establish themselves as independent manufacturers – or, having set up on their own, failed as entrepreneurs. Both categories of skilled men formed a pool of qualified labour which could be tapped by successful clothiers to expand their production at short notice.

How costly was it to gain a foothold on the first rung of the clothmaking career ladder? While there is little systematic evidence about the premiums demanded by master clothiers, it is likely that a well-connected and wealthy clothier expected a higher premium from his apprentices than did a struggling, first-generation clothmaker. Fees of £10 and more in Henry VIII's reign, and £25 or above in the later sixteenth century made an apprenticeship in clothmaking one of the most expensive of all crafts to learn outside of a major urban context. Indeed the cost of an apprenticeship ruled out a career in clothmaking for a large share of male teenagers in the Weald. The barrier of the apprenticeship premium reinforces the evidence about the landholding background of clothiers' fathers: poor men did not become clothiers. Families, of course, would not pay high apprenticeship premiums merely to ensure that their sons learned how to dye wool. The young man who served an apprenticeship under a successful clothier could be compared to the son of a minor gentry family who entered the service of a major county landowner. The ties of patronage, of business connections to be made, were equally if not more valuable than the specialized craft training. Naturally, existing ties of kinship and patronage were brought into play – along with hard cash – when parents sought a master for their son. In this way established family and business links were reinforced. Prominent clothiers, merchants and yeomen farmers sent their sons to serve apprenticeships under the tutelage of their business equals, or – as in so many Tudor relationships – to serve men whose status was slightly above their own. In this controlled, stepped fashion inter-generational social mobility was possible.

Not all clothiers took on apprentices from outside their immediate families, and many others retained just a single apprentice. The Cranbrook household lists of 1612 reveal a number of known clothiers without resident non-family apprentices. In fact apprentice training – and the economic benefits attached to their labour – was concentrated in the households of the wealthier clothiers. As early as 1473 Ralph Lynch, 'clothmaker', had at least two apprentices. The prosperous Biddenden clothier, John Ricard, left half a mark each to his three apprentices in 1551, and Francis Allard, one of Biddenden's clothmaking elite, assigned cash legacies to his three apprentices in 1592.[11] There was no craft organization to limit the number of apprentices a master might keep in order to restrain the better-off masters from using their economic position to the detriment of the less well-off members. London

---

[11] KAO PRC 17/2 fo. 206v; PRO PROB 11/35/19; 11/79/9.

gilds attempted to do just that: there was a constant battle within the Clothworkers' Company to limit the richer householders of the handicraft to two (and occasionally three) apprentices.[12] The clothmaking elite of Cranbrook, by the end of the sixteenth century, normally retained at least three apprentices (as well as one or two journeymen). About a dozen clothier households in the parish contained three or four servants specifically noted as apprentices amongst the lists made between 1608 and 1612. Walter Taylor – whose chattels were appraised at over £2,200 in 1613 – kept four apprentices as well as two resident journeymen in 1611. John Holden's household at Milkhouse in Cranbrook in 1612 included two apprentices and four journeymen, and John Sharpe's household in Cranbrook Town in 1608 contained eleven communicants, among them four apprentices.[13]

Given the nature of cloth production in the Weald, the wealthier a clothier was, the more profitable it would be to recruit additional resident labour. The more capital a clothier could deploy, the more raw material he could buy. Profits could be increased both by processing more wool and by speeding up the turnaround time between the purchase of raw materials and the disposal of the finished cloth. Both strategies demanded increased labour inputs; hence more unpaid labour – the apprentices – and possibly more paid workers, the journeymen. The costs of maintaining an extra apprentice or two would have been marginal for wealthy clothiers who already maintained large households. And apprentices even in the earliest years of their training would have been able to tackle the simpler but time-consuming tasks normally carried out on the clothmaker's own premises: sorting and washing wools, for example. By the same token, the marginal cost of retaining a second apprentice to a small-scale clothier who was producing no more than a few cloths at any one time would have been prohibitively high. Thus – in contrast to urban production – an unregulated apprenticeship system in the Weald worked to the advantage of the richer manufacturers.

Apprenticeship, of course, provided more than a structured system of craft education. It was at the same time an ingredient in the social cement that bound together members of the clothmaking trade. But all clothiers were not equal. Social, business and kinship networks existed throughout the period, but rich, well-established clothiers belonged to certain networks, while the small fry generated their own. Horizontal solidarities – that is, class – mattered more than any collective solidarity among all clothiers. Solidarity of the latter form occasionally made an appearance; when, for example, national political and economic problems pitted provincial clothmakers against the merchant oligarchy of London. But those occasions were few and far between. In normal times the social distance between

[12] Clothworkers' Company, *The Ordinances of the Clothworkers' Co.*, iii (1881), ordinances of 1532, no. 17; of 1587, nos. 54, 59; Clothworkers' Co. MS. 'Court Orders, 1536–58', e.g., fo. 242v.

[13] KAO P100/28/1; Taylor: PRC 28/5 fo. 469. Other examples include the households of Jn. Bennitt, Thos. Colvill, Jn. Holden, Jn. Hovenden, Robt. Hovenden, Thos. Rowe, another Jn. Sharpe at Golford Quarter, Ric. Sharpe, Thos. Sheffe, Jn. Weller, Steph. Weller.

wealthy clothmaking families and the small-scale clothiers – 'middling people' for lack of a better label – was maintained by a variety of personal and business relationships which united social equals.

The social links between the family of the master and that of the apprentice were often mirrored in clothiers' matrimonial ties. Many such ties are invisible to the historian because so many records fail to record a wife's maiden name. But when clothier families are well documented, and pedigrees can be assembled, it is clear that intermarriage between the economically successful was commonplace. William Lynch of Cranbrook (d. 1539), one of the wealthiest clothiers of his generation, arranged the marriage of his eldest daughter Elizabeth to Peter, the son of Alexander Courthop (d. 1525), another prominent Cranbrook clothmaker. Peter's younger brother William, also a clothier, married a daughter of John Sharpe (d. 1543), another wealthy Cranbrook clothier. Sharpe's two other daughters were married to Jerome Courthop (a nephew of Peter and William) and Richard Brickenden, a member of yet another major Cranbrook clothmaking family. Ties of marriage also linked the Courthops of Cranbrook with the Shorts of Tenterden, the Jordans of Cranbrook and the Gibbons of Rolvenden, all prosperous clothmaking families. The Gibbons were already connected to one of the most prominent Henrician clothmakers, John Fleet of Biddenden (d. 1558), through the marriage of Robert Gibbon, (d. 1565), to John Fleet's daughter Alice. A daughter of Peter Short (d. 1561) was also married to Simon Henden, one of the leading Benenden clothiers of the Elizabethan period. And marriage ties led to career associations: in 1595 Richard Jordan of Cranbrook, clothier, willed the interest on a £600 portion to his cousin, 'now my servant', Thomas Short.[14]

Marriage and apprenticeship ties visibly demonstrated the social and economic hierarchies among clothiers. Equally revealing are the ties of friendship and mutual trust implied by the choice of feoffees, executors and overseers. Such links hint at association in trade, but since no Wealden clothiers' business papers have survived we can only hypothesize that such relationships existed. The surviving wills of clothiers almost always contain the testator's executor(s) and, in a majority of wills, the names of overseers to assist the executor(s). Clothiers – by and large – tended to appoint close kin as executors but chose overseers from wider circles of acquaintance and kinship. In these choices they acted similarly to Wealden testators in other occupational groups. Clothiers were quite likely to appoint other clothiers – who were often near neighbours – as their overseers. And, since so many clothiers were related to one another through marriage, relatives who were also clothiers figure prominently in their nominations of both executors and overseers. Edward Bathurst of Staplehurst (d. 1559) named three executors: his wife, his brother Robert (who was a clothier) and James Buckhurst, also a Staplehurst clothier.

---

[14] Lynch (PRO PROB 11/27/34); Sharpe (KAO PRC 17/27 fo. 78); Courthop (PRC 32/30 fo. 510); Short (PRO PROB 11/44/28; 11/70/28); Jordan (PROB 11/87/15); Gibbon (PRC 17/34 fo. 14; PROB 11/48a/13); Fleet (PROB 11/42a/14).

His sole overseer was another Staplehurst clothmaker, 'my trusty friend' Matthew Medehurst. In a similar fashion the wealthy Cranbrook clothier Edmund Colvill (d. 1596) named his son executor, and appointed as overseers his father-in-law Thomas Russell and his brother-in-law Richard Jordan: both were clothiers.[15] Gervase Bigge, a Cranbrook clothier who died in 1568 without a direct heir, appointed his brother and the brother's son as executors, but named two prominent local clothiers who were not close relatives, Richard Brickenden and Edward Jordan, as overseers. In addition Bigge asked yet another member of the Cranbrook elite, Thomas Sheffe, to collect the profits of his lands until a nephew reached twenty-two and a marriage portion had been paid to a niece.[16]

Even if the clothier did not have an on-going business relationship with the man whom he appointed as overseer, the overseer who shared his trade would be able to supervise the deceased's business. The wealth of a clothmaker was mainly tied up in raw material at different stages of manufacture: another clothier could oversee the completion of production and the sale of the dead man's assets. And, if a clothier's widow carried on her husband's business, a clothier-overseer would have been equally useful. In their choices of men for such positions of trust, it is apparent that the better-off clothiers always selected men as wealthy as themselves; the less wealthy clothiers, in contrast, often chose richer clothiers as overseers – a publicly more prestigious position – but almost never as executors. In a similar vein, a number of wealthy clothiers appointed prominent local figures as overseers. Such cases amounted to public recognition of an existing patron–client relationship between the local notable and the clothier. At least four of Cranbrook's most prominent clothiers asked the Cranbrook landowner and rising civil servant, John Baker, to act as their overseer; while Tenterden's biggest clothier at mid-century, Peter Short, named the borough's leading citizen (who was also a local landowner), Edward Hales, as his overseer.[17] The numerous kinship and business relationships, which often are only visible at the time of a clothier's death, would have been crucial at the beginning of a clothmaker's independent career and probably useful throughout his years as a manufacturer. It is to the *business* of clothmaking that I now want to turn.

The cottage industry which produced woollens in the Kent Weald has been described in chapter 6. It examined the stages of manufacture that were carried out

[15] Bathurst (PRO PROB 11/43/32); Colvill (PROB 11/87/23). Other examples of clothier-kin in the wills of Fras. Allard (1592: PROB 11/79/9), Wm. Austen (1551: PROB 11/34/31), Wm. Barrentine (1572: PROB 11/54/43), Thos. Coucheman (1514: PROB 11/18/2), Thos. Dence (1585: PROB 11/68/36), Robt. Holden (1594: PROB 11/91/17), Robt. King (1586: PROB 11/69/42), Jn. Ricard (1551: PROB 11/35/19) and Alex. Sharpe (1585: PROB 11/68/48).

[16] PRO PROB 11/51/4. Other examples of the choice of a close relative plus a local clothier: wills of Sim. Lynch (1500: PROB 11/12/14), Wm. Milles (1558: PROB 11/42b/10) and Robt. Stace (1561: PROB 11/45/13).

[17] Cranbrook clothiers Ric. Barre (1538), Wm. Lynch (1539), Steph. Draner (1539) and Ric. Sheffe (1557): PRO PROB 11/27/30, 34; 11/39/34. Short: PROB 11/44/28.

in outworkers' own homes. The business relationships between the domestic workers and the clothiers have also been investigated. It was shown that thousands of men and women were 'employed' by capitalist clothiers in a mixture of full- and part-time work, and that a crucial element in a manufacturing entrepreneur's success lay in his capacity to retain large numbers of outworkers during certain periods of the year – while maintaining permanently only a small core of paid workers. The cardinal importance of the clothmaker's ability to make use of, even manipulate, the local labour market must be borne in mind throughout this chapter. It helps to explain the economic success of the region's relatively small elite of large-scale clothiers, who probably numbered no more than twenty to thirty men even at the peak of the industry's prosperity in the Elizabethan period.

Clothiers – like other skilled artisans – made use of a highly specialized craft training in their businesses. But they were also buyers and sellers of commodities – and of labour. What distinguished clothiers from most other small-scale producers was their command of capital. The 'mystery' of clothmaking depended as much on the entrepreneurial skills of a clothier as on his special knowledge of dyeing wool. Clothiers bought and sold in several markets, and without start-up capital they could not be master clothiers.

At the hypothetical beginning of a clothier's independent business life, capital had to be invested in two things: the first – but of least significance – were the tools and equipment needed to carry out the few stages of clothmaking which clothiers and their servants did themselves. They usually included one large copper and one lead vessel, as well as a variety of other vats and 'tonnes', used both to wash and to dye wool in the clothier's 'workhouse' or 'dyehouse'. In addition most clothiers possessed hurdles and a tenter on which to dry and stretch broadcloths. Finally, most clothiers would have needed weights and scales, and baskets and boards (on trestles) with which to sort wool. Basic equipment like this features frequently in clothiers' wills: Robert Wood of Lenham (d. 1502) left his son Edmund,

my leads and tonnes that I occupy to dye colours in at the day of my departing out of this world, forthwith all the implements belonging to the same craft of dyeing.

'Fixed' capital of this kind is frequently valued in clothiers' inventories, although in some cases appraisers seemed to have treated basic clothmaking equipment as part of the deceased's workhouse rather than as personal property. In the Elizabethan period the typical value of a clothmaker's workhouse equipment plus hurdles and a tenter was £10–£15. The clothmaking equipment of a petty clothier in the kersey district in 1579 was valued at under £5, but that was lower than most valuations. Even very wealthy clothiers do not appear to have owned much more equipment than the average clothmaker. In 1539 the copper, vats and tonnes owned by the wealthiest clothier in Cranbrook, Stephen Draner, were appraised at £11, equivalent to between £20 and £25 in the 1560s or 1570s.[18] Clothmaking equipment,

---

[18] Wood: KAO PRC/17/8 fo. 240v; equipment under £5: Barth. Pargate of Hothfield (PRC 10/9 fo. 363, of £27 total); typical early Elizabethan valuations of £10 (PRC 10/9 fo. 328v, of £136 total);

therefore, amounted to only a very small part of the value of a clothier's personal property. Whether a young clothier inherited dyehouse equipment (and many did) or had to purchase it when he set himself up, the cost of equipment was not the main financial hurdle to overcome. Far more significant in the economic calculations of most clothiers was their investment in raw materials.

A wide variety of commodities went into the manufacture of broadcloth and kerseys, very little of which was produced by clothiers themselves. Clothmakers bought raw materials in a variety of markets, some local but others national or even European in scope. Some commodities were obtained in simple cash transactions; others involved barter and commercial credit. The clothiers' search for raw materials is of interest both because it was a key facet of their business, but also because of the development of economic links between clothmakers and others which the need for such commodities engendered. We shall see that the lion's share of most clothiers' capital was deployed in the purchase of raw materials.

Firewood was of prime importance to clothmaking. Fuel was needed to heat the vats and coppers used in the dyeing process. Wood was the one raw material in relative abundance within the Weald itself. Clothiers, depending on their individual economic circumstances, obtained the necessary firewood either from woodland which they themselves owned or leased, or purchased it from nearby woodland owners. As was emphasized in chapter 2, gentry landowners in the Weald owned extensive woodland. In the region encompassing Cranbrook, Goudhurst and Biddenden it is likely that they sold far more wood to local clothiers than to the ironmakers of the Weald. In 1552, for example, Thomas Hendley of Cranbrook sold wood worth more than £175 to a score of local buyers, mainly clothiers. But woodsales on that scale by a single landowner were exceptional; the £23 spent by John Sharpe, clothier, in 1552 brought him all the firewood (but probably excluding mature oaks) from three and a half acres of forest in one bargain. By the 1570s there was considerable pressure on wood reserves, and the competing demands of ironmasters and clothiers had become a hot political issue. Surveys claiming that a majority of former woodland in the central Weald had been felled since 1550 probably emanated from clothmaking circles, and cannot be taken at face value. But their appearance shows that wood had become a limited and valuable commodity by the 1570s.[19]

Most substantial clothiers obtained wood from their own lands, as well as buying it from other landowners. Depending on the scale of their business, clothiers needed to have considerable quantities of wood on hand at their premises. The probate inventories of clothiers regularly record stocks of firewood. Thomas Grenell, a

---

£12 (PRC 10/9 fo. 233, of £194 total), about £14 (Gervase Gibbon of Benenden owned 2 workhouses: PRC 10/9 fo. 311 of £586 total); £10 (PRC 10/12 fo. 309, of £212 total); Draner (PRO PROB 2/525 of about £800 net).

[19] KAO U 1044/F1 p. 116. Surveys of woods felled: PRO SP 12/93 fo. 148. See chapter 5, p. 127 above.

wealthy Hawkhurst clothier, had wood at his workhouse worth £10 at the time of his death in 1573; that amounted to eighty loads. The appraisers of the goods of John Courthop, the Cranbrook clothier (d. 1574), noted that he owned wood 'standing on the lands of Thomas Sheffe', ready to be cut, worth £30. And Thomas Wells, a Biddenden clothier, had a stock of wood valued at £25 at his death in 1601.[20] Clothiers of this stature normally kept on hand wood alone worth more than their fixed plant. And major clothiers also owned woodland property. One of Cranbrook's leading clothiers, Alexander Courthop, mentioned several pieces of woodland in his 1525 will. Another well-off Cranbrook clothier, Alexander Coucheman (d. 1550), left a modest estate of about fifty acres to his two sons, but that included a wood of twenty-three acres. And Peter Courthop, Alexander's third son – and a clothier – owned at least sixty acres of woodland out of a total estate of about 240 acres. After his death in 1567, the appraisers counted £35 worth of wood among his goods, including wood worth £20 'standing upon other men's ground' that he had bought but not yet felled, and sixty loads each at his mansion house and his workhouse. Almost two generations later, Alexander Courthop, 'gent.' – formerly an active clothier – died leaving ninety-two acres of woodland, along with 290 acres of other land. One well-documented wood in Cranbrook, Foxrege, was owned by at least three families of clothiers in succession: Lynch, Hovenden and King.[21]

Examples could be multiplied. But that clothiers should have owned woodland is not surprising when it is recalled that most medium-sized freehold estates in the Weald included parcels of woodland. Like other landowners, clothiers were anxious to preserve their young trees – so that their woods could be regularly cropped, but never exhausted. They were also aware that once in a generation or so there could be a major felling to raise capital. Thus the Benenden clothier Robert Everenden (d. 1591) advised his executors to 'sell out of my wood called Holnes Wood to the value of £100'. But, that done, they were instructed to put up enclosures around the wood ' for the preservation of the springs and sheets' and not allow cattle to graze there for six years.[22]

Wool was the most important raw material for Wealden kerseys and broadcloths – as it was for almost all English textiles in the sixteenth century. Kentish clothiers obtained their supplies from a bewildering array of sources, some relatively close at hand, others much more distant and invariably more expensive. The Weald – unlike several clothmaking regions in England – was not a commercially significant wool producing region. As has been pointed out, Wealden pastoral husbandry emphasized beef over sheep production. Many Wealden farms carried small numbers of sheep, but mostly they kept cattle for the most practical of reasons: Wealden pasture was not well suited to sheep. But there were a number of long-

[20] KAO PRC 10/7 fos. 70, 123v; 10/30 fo. 483.
[21] KAO PRC 32/14 fo. 100; 17/27 fo. 19; PRC 28/1 fos. 115v–116; PRO Wards 7/12 nos. 66, 11; C 142/693 no. 7; PROB 11/27/34; 11/81/24. [22] PRO PROB 11/77/22.

established sheep-growing districts within thirty kilometres of the central Weald. Farmers on the hill pastures of the North Downs in Kent and on the South Downs in Sussex traditionally raised sheep alongside their crops of wheat and barley. Further north lay the Thames estuary marshes, where sheep had been raised in large numbers for centuries. And, closer to hand, was Romney Marsh, where local graziers raised and fattened sheep, and where Wealden landowners and commercial farmers often owned or leased marsh grazing for their own stock. The marshland was said to be rich enough to carry three sheep to the acre – far more than most Wealden or Downland pasture land. By the late seventeenth century, if not earlier, Kent was one of the two largest wool-producing counties in England, although Kent wool was considered relatively coarse.[23]

Clothiers did not have to look far afield to acquire much of the wool they required. They could buy wool from their farming neighbours who kept some sheep, from Wealden landowners who maintained sheepflocks on the Marsh, or from the big graziers who lived in Romney Marsh themselves. Robert Gibbon of Rolvenden (d. 1594) had sheep worth £26 on the Marsh, while Thomas Austen of Benenden (d. 1599) owned £50 worth of sheep in Romney Marsh, as well as £20 worth of wool there. Fifty pounds in sheep amounted to about 180 ewes and lambs.[24] The easternmost part of the Weald included marshland in several parishes, notably Tenterden and Wittersham, and the Marsh proper is only about ten kilometres from Tenterden Town. At least one clothier had to look no further than his own brother for wool. Simon Henden, one of Benenden's leading clothmakers, bought wool from his brother William of Tenterden in the 1580s; at William's death Simon owed him £12 for sixty-two quarters of wool. When Robert Courthop of Dymchurch (in the Marsh) died in 1566, his inventory listed 207 sheep and fifty-five lambs. His biggest debtor was the Biddenden clothier Richard Allard. Similarly, the wealthy Cranbrook clothier John Courthop (d. 1574) owed Richard Knatchbull of Mersham, gent., as much as £81 for eleven 'packs' of wool.[25]

And if relatives, friends and neighbours could not satisfy their requirement for wool from nearby marshes, Wealden clothiers could obtain the wool needed for coarse and ordinary quality cloths from sources which were not very distant. The normal clip of Kent and Sussex was probably large enough to meet the great majority of Wealden clothmakers' requirements. When they looked further afield for wool, it was mainly to obtain the finer quality wools not on sale locally. The normal arrangements are exemplified by the woolsales of the Roberts family of Boarzell in Ticehurst, Sussex (a cadet branch of the Roberts's of Glassenbury in Cranbrook) to Wealden clothiers. Surviving household accounts for the 1570s record a number of modest sales to Cranbrook clothiers, men who were probably

---

[23] Joan Thirsk (ed.), *The Agrarian History of England & Wales, iv 1500–1640* (Cambridge, 1967), pp. 56–7, 59–61; Peter Bowden, *The Wool Trade in Tudor and Stuart England* (1962), pp. 39–40.
[24] KAO PRC 10/23 fo. 78; PRC 28/3 fo. 315.
[25] KAO PRC 10/14 fo. 71v; PRC 10/2 fo. 85; PRC 10/7 fo. 123v.

known personally by the Roberts's. All the sales occurred in June or July, and the larger of them would have included about seven or eight tods of wool each (about 200 pounds). These purchases would have met only a small part of the annual needs of large-scale clothiers. They must have made many such local bargains – in addition to the wool they bought from further afield.[26] The richer clothiers, who were likely to buy wool worth several hundred pounds every year, were in a good position to bargain with Kent and Sussex graziers and farmers. They may have contracted to purchase the total wool clip of a number of farmers in a given year, in other words to forestall the market, whether or not they intended to re-sell the wool.

The majority of the Weald's clothiers did not turn to the national wool market for supplies. Operating on the basis of limited capital inputs, and with a full-time workforce of two or three people, they were not buying raw materials in large enough quantities to arrange purchases from wholesale wool dealers in London or from major graziers outside their own region. Most master clothiers had to purchase their wool (and other raw materials) locally. Neighbouring farmers might provide for most of their needs, but even the minor producers of broadcloth had to supplement the coarse, local wools with wool of better quality. Hence any clothier who attempted to manufacture export quality cloth needed to buy some wool from middlemen: either wool dealers in nearby market towns like Maidstone or Ashford or from merchants or rich clothiers in the Weald itself.

A minority of clothiers in the region did not manufacture high quality broadcloth. Most of these were kerseymakers, who produced the narrow-width, cheaper quality cloth for domestic consumption. The concentration of this branch of the Kent textile industry in a few parishes in the north of the Weald and in adjacent Chartland parishes suggests that such men chose to dwell near their wool supplies, and were much less reliant on middlemen for their raw wool or yarn. By the sixteenth century there is little evidence of kerseymaking in the central Wealden parishes where broadcloth was king. Most clothiers in the Weald proper, however, made broadcloth, and therefore required a variety of wools. Much had to be bought from non-producers. The smaller operators might turn to three main classes of suppliers: professional wool dealers or broggers, local general merchants, and rich clothiers who also acted as wool dealers within their own neighbourhood as a profitable sideline to their clothmaking business. Evidence of the purchasing habits of the smaller clothiers is largely missing. Wool broggers, who feature so strongly in contemporary pamphlets and parliamentary legislation, are hard to find in the Weald.[27] The lists of debts in probate inventories rarely record the occupations of debtors or the reasons for specific debts. If there were specialized wool broggers, or

---

[26] Robert Tittler (ed.), *Accounts of the Roberts Family of Boarzell, Sussex* (Sussex Rec. Soc., 71), pp. 120, 130, 138.

[27] On wool dealers see Bowden, *Wool Trade*; see, e.g., the 1551 act regulating the trade in wool: 5 and 6 Edw. VI, c. 7.

yarn merchants, operating in the Weald – as they did in the West Riding of
Yorkshire – they left little evidence of their trade. Wool dealers do not appear
among the many hundreds of probate inventories and wills examined for this study.
This does not rule out the possibility that specialized wool dealers travelled through
the Weald to sell in fairs and markets. Small-scale clothiers could have bought wool
from specialist dealers in Maidstone.

   Within the Weald, however, two other classes of suppliers predominated:
general local merchants and wealthy clothiers acting as middlemen suppliers of
wool and dyestuffs to their poorer rivals. Again, evidence of individual transactions
is hard to find, but circumstantial evidence as well as common sense point in that
direction. Large quantities of wool were purchased in London by Cranbrook's
leading clothiers, either from London-based wool wholesalers, or from provincial
wool dealers or major wool producers themselves who negotiated deals in the
capital. A 1615 apologia by wool dealers arguing against government legislation
prohibiting the re-sale of wool, speaks of the wools grown in Shropshire,
Staffordshire and Worcestershire as being partly consumed in Worcester but more
of them being used in Gloucestershire, Devon and Kent.[28] Undoubtedly much of
the wool bought by the major clothiers in London or directly from distant producers
was intended for their own use. But there was little in practice to prevent them from
re-selling wool to neighbouring clothiers – at a profit. In theory non-Londoners,
such as Kent clothiers, should have bought wool in London's public markets, from
London freemen. But both provincial graziers and wholesale wool dealers are
known to have dealt directly with Kentish clothiers in London. In January 1556, for
example, a London informer denounced William Courthop of Cranbrook for the
purchase of three packs of 'foreign' wool (i.e., not owned by a citizen of London).
The fine alone came to £8. Earlier, in 1531, William Netter of Cranbrook was
engaged in business dealings with a William North of Ellington, Huntingdonshire,
who was most probably a wool dealer. They met in London.[29]

   The re-sale trade in wool is partially revealed in penal informations brought in the
court of Exchequer over infractions of the statutes regulating the sale of wool. There
is normally no other evidence to corroborate the informer's story. A typical case is
the information that Matthew Medehurst, a Staplehurst clothier, bought 200 tods
of wool (at 16s. per tod) in Bedfordshire in 1565, which he subsequently kept in his
house, contrary to 5 & 6 Edw. VI, c. 7. Medehurst apparently acted against the
provision in the act which prohibited the retention of wool for more than a year
without making cloth from it. In another case the wealthy Cranbrook clothier
Alexander Weller was informed against for wool dealing at Maidstone in 1590, it
being alleged that he bought more wool than was necessary for his own use.[30] The
assumption of the legislators and the informers in cases like these was that clothiers

[28] PRO SP Dom. Jas. I/ 80 no. 13, quoted in George Unwin, *Industrial Organization in the 16th and 17th Centuries* (1904), p. 188.   [29] Corp. of London R. O., Book of Fines fo. 126v; KAO U55/B1.
[30] PRO E 159/349 Rec. Hil. rot. 136; /398 Rec. Hil. rot. 134.

who purchased wool in large quantities like wool dealers *were* wool dealers. At this point the distinction between merchant and manufacturer becomes most blurred.

The best evidence of large-scale purchases of wool as well as dyestuffs is to be found in the customs records of coastwise shipping between London and Rochester. In the half year from Easter to Michaelmas 1566, for example, about 30,000 pounds of wool was entered in the Rochester port books as coming from London and destined for Maidstone. Most of this wool was owned by a small number of Cranbrook clothiers: John and Peter Courthop, John and William Coucheman, John King and John Holden. Five sarplers (about 5,000 pounds) were the property of John Leeds of Leeds (near Maidstone) and another seven were owned by the Cranbrook merchant Thomas Sheffe. The account for 1570 shows a similar pattern: large consignments of wool shipped from London by Thomas Sheffe, Peter and William Courthop and by Richard Allard, the prosperous Biddenden clothier. In 1580 a total of thirty-two sarplers of wool (about 32,000 pounds) was sent via Rochester to the Weald between June and September by just three men: Sheffe, the wholesale merchant, and two clothiers, Robert King of Cranbrook and John Leeds.[31] Much of the non-local wool used by Wealden clothiers was thus brought into the region by major clothiers and the few wholesale merchants living in the Weald.

The capitalist clothiers and the merchants were also suppliers of the other crucial raw materials for the Wealden textile industry: dyestuffs and oil. Both groups bought dyestuffs and train oil from London import merchants. 'Seville oil' came from Spain, woad from southwestern France and madder and alum from the Low Countries. A variety of other dyestuffs (some of New World origin) were purchased by English merchants in the Netherlands: brazil, copperas, indigo, greenweed and cochineal. During the half year Easter to Michaelmas 1566 the Cranbrook clothier John King shipped from London, via Rochester, six to eight pipes of oil, two 'vats' and six 'casks' of madder, seventy bales of woad, three bags of alum, a quantity of soap, two vats of copperas and a parcel of brazil. About half a dozen men in all, including the Cranbrook clothiers John King, John and Peter Courthop, John and William Coucheman and William Love, imported from London in that half year about 330 bales of woad (over 6,500 pounds), twenty-five vats or casks of madder, twenty to twenty-five pipes of oil, seven or eight vats of copperas, about twenty bags or casks of brazil and eight bags of alum. Most of their shipments combined dyestuffs with raw wool.[32] Clothiers also might obtain supplies of dyestuffs from London merchants to whom they sold their cloth. Payment for Kent broadcloth could be in the form of goods as well as money: in 1526 the Biddenden clothier Matthew Horden sold two cloths to Thomas Howell, Draper of London, for £8 13s. 4d. The payment was to be £5 13s. 4d. in ready money and one bale of woad. Two years later another clothier, John Bigge of Goudhurst, sold Howell a russet broadcloth for £5 16s. 8d., of which £2 15s. was to be paid in woad.[33]

[31] PRO E 190/638/4, 11; E 190/641/12.   [32] PRO E 190/638/4 fos. 5, 5v, 6 and *passim*.
[33] Drapers' Co., London MS. C/AL 1 fos. 39v, 64v-65.

The handful of large-scale general merchants resident in the Weald – but not the clothiers – also imported dyestuffs and oil directly. Their imports reached the Weald via the port of Rye, from where they exported limited quantities of Kentish and other cloths to the Netherlands and to France. In the 1560s Wealden merchants were buying dyestuffs at Antwerp. Later they turned to the French ports, especially Rouen. In the year ending Michaelmas 1567, for example, Thomas Ruck and William Hider (both of Cranbrook), Edmund Roberts of Hawkhurst and Herbert Roberts of Tenterden imported oil and dyestuffs valued by customs officials at about £475 through Rye.[34] In the 1570s Thomas Ruck and Richard Lyne of Cranbrook were the most important Wealden merchants using the port of Rye, where another major importer was Richard Portreve, merchant of Rye. He was almost certainly the brother of Thomas Portreve, mercer of Cranbrook. The Portreves had been successful businessmen in Cranbrook since the late fifteenth century, if not earlier.[35] Significant quantities of dyestuffs passed through the port of Rye, but most dyestuffs used by the Weald's clothiers came from London by the same route as high quality wool: down the Thames, via the port of Rochester and up the Medway to Maidstone.

Ordinary Wealden clothmakers *could* obtain all the dyestuffs they required from local sources – although at higher prices than the major clothiers paid. Their bulk purchases gave the leading clothiers a competitive advantage over their less well-off local rivals. And that position was in turn attributable to their command of capital reserves beyond the scale of small master clothiers. But the capitalist clothiers were always in competition with the handful of Wealden merchants who could also supply the smaller clothiers with dyestuffs and wool, presumably on credit. The probate inventories of Thomas Portreve, senior and junior, mercers of Cranbrook, dated 1580 and 1581, are not especially detailed, but they show that each had shop goods on hand worth in excess of £200 (out of total movables of £477 and £558 respectively).[36] The 'mere merchant' Thomas Ruck was considerably richer. His movables were appraised at £1,856, on a par with the elite merchants in many provincial cities. In his warehouse were six Kent broadcloths, worth about £85, which he had probably purchased from minor local clothiers for later re-sale on the London market. But his warehouse was bulging with the dyestuffs needed by the clothmakers of the Cranbrook area: train oil worth £16, thirty-five bags of woad valued at £113, three and a half tons of brazil (value £112) and lesser amounts of madder and copperas.[37]

[34] PRO E 190/737/24.
[35] Will of Thos. Portreve (1490): PRO PROB 11/8/33; of Walt. Portreve, mercer (1548): KAO PRC 17/26 fos. 52v, 172v; cloth of Jas. Portreve seized at Blackwell Hall (1550): PRO E 159/330 Rec. Mich. rot. 173; inventory of Thos. Portreve (1580): KAO PRC 10/11 fo. 120v.
[36] KAO PRC 10/11 fo. 120v; 10/10 fo. 87.
[37] KAO PRC 21/6 fo. 460. On provincial merchants see Alan Dyer, *The City of Worcester in the Sixteenth Century* (1973), p. 85 and W. G. Hoskins, 'The Elizabethan Merchants of Exeter' in S. T. Bindoff *et al.* (eds.), *Elizabethan Government and Society* (1961).

The dyestuffs held by Thomas Ruck, the merchant, were far in excess of the stocks maintained by even the wealthiest clothiers. Since dyestuffs were available locally at almost any time, most clothiers held quite small amounts. Stephen Draner, the richest Cranbrook clothier of the 1530s, owned dyestuffs worth just £27 at his death in 1539. At the same time, his stock of completed broadcloths (thirty-one in all) amounted to £183.[38] Draner was not exceptional: the inventories of most working clothiers show only small stocks of raw material other than wool, in proportion to the total value of their goods. Typical of the lesser clothmakers was William Colliar of Marden (d. 1566) who had £20 worth of wool and prepared cloth in stock, but only £2 10s. in oil and dyestuffs, out of chattels worth £137 in all. Or Amos Spencer of Biddenden (d. 1594) who owned wool valued at £21, two ready-made cloths worth £30, but just £5 13s. in dyestuffs and oil. His inventory total was £75. Wealthier clothiers maintained larger stores of dyestuffs, but usually they were worth only a fraction of the value of their stocks of wool and cloth. Peter Courthop of Cranbrook (d. 1567), one of a dozen or so major Wealden manufacturers of his generation, held dyestuffs valued at £21 as well as £15 worth of oil for preparing wool – far more than a great majority of local clothiers. But at the same time he held over 500 tods of wool (raw and dyed) valued at £550 plus ready-made cloths worth £186 (out of a total inventory of nearly £1,800). At the end of the century Alexander Sheffe of Cranbrook (d. 1601) – another major operator – had dyestuffs worth £41; but his seventeen prepared cloths came to over £250, from a total inventory of £570 exclusive of debts due him.[39]

Clothiers, whatever the scale of their business, organized the production of broadcloth along very similar lines. If we set aside the differences in capital resources – and the ability of some clothiers to operate as middlemen as well as clothmakers – there was much in common between the big operators like the Courthops, the Sharpes and the Wellers and the small fry like William Collier and Amos Spencer. Some clothiers appear to have undertaken a bit of weaving on their own premises, using their own full-time workforce. Looms appear in a small minority of clothiers' wills and inventories. But this combination of trades was in the main limited to the kerseymakers. Not even the richest clothiers ever operated weaving sheds with multiple looms – along the lines of John Winchcomb of Newbury, even without the romantic exaggeration of Thomas Deloney.[40] Neither is there evidence of clothiers hiring out looms to weavers to use in their own houses.

The crucial, non-artisanal skill of the clothier was to organize other specialized workers to manufacture cloth, using his own raw materials. Division of labour lay at the heart of commercial broadcloth production in the Wealden district. Clothiers also needed a limited knowledge of the skills of all their specialized outworkers,

[38] PRO PROB 2/525.
[39] KAO PRC 10/2 fo. 106v; 10/23 fo. 324; 28/1 fo. 113; 28/4 fo. 33.
[40] 'The Pleasant Historie of Jacke of Newburie', in *The Works of Thomas Deloney* (ed. F. O. Mann, 1912), p. 20.

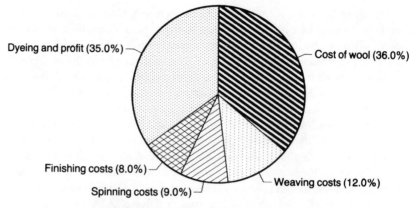

Figure 7.1a Clothier's costs and profits: coarse cloth, £10 wholesale, 1560s

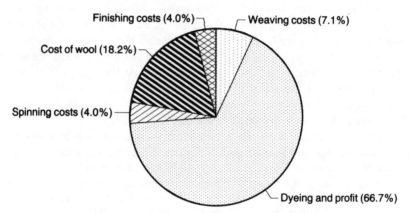

Figure 7.1b Clothier's costs and profits: fine cloth, £20 wholesale, 1560s

both to maintain quality control (which mattered to the London merchants who were their customers) and to obtain the highest level of production for the lowest possible wages. The clothier's special task was to ensure that his raw materials passed through the several stages of production as efficiently as possible, while maintaining a minimum quality standard and a flow of finished goods which correlated with probable market demand.

They also had to be canny enough businessmen to balance the probable differences in the profit margins of manufacturing different quality and colour cloths against the differences in the costs of raw material and production. Figure 7.1 shows that the mark-up on 'fine' cloths was disproportionately high. Clothiers' inventories reveal that wealthier clothiers always produced a sizeable amount of fine quality cloths, while the small fry did not. Men with liquidity could more easily bear the costs of better quality wool, more expensive dyes and slightly higher weaving rates.

Table 7.1 Clothiers' tax ratings compared to all taxpayers

Assessment	All taxpayers	Active clothiers
1524/5		
£1 in wages/goods	32%	None
£2–3 goods/wages & up to £1 19s land	31%	None
£4–10 goods & £2–6 p.a. land	24%	28.5%
£11–19 goods & £7–19 p.a. land	7%	16.5%
£20–29 goods/land	2.5%	14.5%
£30 or more in goods or land	3.5%	40.5%
Totals	1,396 taxpayers	42 clothiers
1543/4		
£1–2 goods; £1 land	37.5%	None
£3–4 goods; £2 land	15.5%	2%
£5–9 goods; £3–8 p.a. land	20.5%	7%
£10–19 goods; £9–19 p.a. lands	10%	19%
£20–29 goods	9%	17%
£20 or more, lands; £30 goods or more	7.5%	55%
Totals	1,447 taxpayers	69 clothiers

Sources: 5 Weald 100s in 1524/5 (PRO E 179/125/324); 6 Weald 100s in 1543/4 (PRO E 179/124/256, 259).

But they realized greater profits per cloth. Those with more capital to begin with could expect to earn disproportionately larger profits. Of course, all independent clothiers had to oversee the production process, and all clothiers needed some understanding of the wholesale market for cloth on which their prosperity rested. But there was, nevertheless, a qualitative difference between the clothmaking enterprises of the many small master clothiers and those of the few dozen major manufacturers operating at any one point in the sixteenth century.

The small masters of the Wealden industry might be labelled 'petty commodity producers' – or even 'handicraft' producers. Engels's remark that 'these small employers are neither genuine proletarians...nor genuine bourgeois',[41] could be applied to the petty clothiers as well as to the well-off master weavers. In comparison with most of their neighbours – the family farmers, shopkeepers and ordinary skilled craftsmen – even the lowest-ranking clothier in the Weald was relatively well-off. This is clearly demonstrated by comparing clothiers' tax assessments with those of all taxpayers in the central Wealden hundreds. Small master clothiers owned their own tools and raw materials, usually employed permanently one or two workers beyond their own immediate family, and were typically freeholders. Most manufactured a commodity that was destined for sale in

[41] F. Engels, *The Condition of the Working Class in England* (1969 edn), p. 226.

distant markets. Hence, they could not be lumped together with the many rural handicraft workers who produced goods for immediate re-sale to local customers. We do not find in the Weald the third and poorest sort of clothiers described in the pamphlet *Reasons to Prove the Convenience of Buying and Selling of Wool* of 1615 as such clothiers that have not stock enough to bestow, some in wool and some in yarn, and to forbear some in cloth as the rich clothiers do ... they buy but little or no wool, but do weekly buy their yarn in markets, and presently make it into cloth and sell it for ready money, and so buy yarn again.[42]

On the other hand, it is doubtful if the smaller Wealden clothiers were wholly independent in their economic dealings with the small class of large-scale clothmakers, or if the small masters regularly sold their finished cloth direct to the London wholesalers. It is likely that many small masters in the Weald depended on their wealthier colleagues in the trade both as middleman suppliers of raw materials and as wholesale buyers of their cloth. Obtaining raw materials in appropriate quantities – and perhaps on credit – was a fundamental part of all clothmakers' businesses; but it was also one of the criteria which distinguished the petty producers from the truly 'capitalist' entrepreneurs. In the case of the former, the cost of obtaining raw materials was a factor which limited – or even reduced – their potential profits from making cloth. In the case of the big operators, the control of raw materials had the opposite effect: it could generate extra earnings, above the profits of manufacturing.

The supply of raw materials is related intimately to the clothiers' role in organizing production itself. The scale of a clothier's output and the degree to which he had unstinted access to raw materials are two sides of the same coin. Is it possible to measure and compare the scale and size of clothiers' businesses? The sources are by no means ideal, nor are they available for all clothiers. But some useful indicators exist. First, there is a sample of clothiers who died after 1565 and whose personal estates are valued in probate inventories. The numbers are not large – just forty-seven between 1565 and 1599 – considering that there were several hundred clothiers in business during those four decades. The values of clothiers' chattels put them at the top of the ladder of occupational groups (ignoring the gentry) in the Elizabethan Weald, but many among them could by no stretch of the imagination be called wealthy (see table 7.2).

The mean value of clothiers' inventoried chattels was about £116 for the thirty-five-year period. But almost half the clothiers had total personal estates worth £100 or less when they died. Admittedly the overall average would have been much higher if the personal estates of very wealthy clothmakers whose wills were proved in the Prerogative Court of Canterbury could be taken into account. But there is no doubt that the industry had a long, impecunious tail of small masters whose capacity to operate independently must have been marginal at best. It is difficult to imagine how a clothmaker could run his own business with much less than £100 in

---

[42] Quoted in Unwin, *Industrial Organization*, p. 235.

Table 7.2 *Distribution of clothiers' estates, 1565–99*

Under £40	£40–60	£60–100	£100–200	£200–500	Over £500
7 (15%)	2 (4%)	13 (28%)	15 (32%)	6 (13%)	4 (8%)

circulating capital. But a few certainly seemed to have done. Some of the 'clothiers' with very small personal estates at their deaths were most likely either retired or journeymen still employed by others. Three out of five clothiers owned personal goods in the range £60 to £200: the average or 'typical' clothier was by no means a rich man, except in the company of husbandmen and tailors. Only a fifth of the clothiers with inventories could be called wealthy: the inventories of just ten men with chattels worth over £200 between 1565 and 1599 were enrolled in Canterbury diocesan courts. They – and many of the clothiers whose estates were handled by the provincial court – made up the elite of large-scale capitalist clothiers. Between forty and fifty clothiers left wills to be proved in the Prerogative Court of Canterbury; but not all of them were among the top rank of the region's clothmakers. But if about two dozen such men are added to the ten with high value probate inventories from the diocesan courts, the Elizabethan elite of Wealden clothiers adds up to no more than thirty or forty individuals! The great majority of clothmakers were either just scraping a living or were prosperous in a way not unknown to the better-off weavers, shopkeepers or farmers. To get some idea of the wide range of economic status between the relatively poor and the most successful clothiers, a few individual cases can be cited.

Dozens of small master clothiers worked in the Weald during the sixteenth century. Some can be identified from their wills; others are represented by probate inventories. Most are noticeably absent from the lists of clothiers fined for deficiencies in their cloth at Blackwell Hall. What stands out in all of this documentation is the small scale of their clothmaking businesses. In most cases, too, their clothmaking was combined with farming. A comparison of the values of their trade goods with their farming goods shows that in many cases clothmaking was a seasonal rather than a full-time pursuit. Thomas Cornell of Marden (d. 1553) identified himself as a clothier in his will, yet he says almost nothing about his textile business. One of his three overseers was a Merchant Taylor of London, another was a shearman, but there is nothing else about clothmaking. But the will makes clear that Cornell was a farmer and small property owner: we are told that his lands are worth £14 6s. 8d. per annum, aside from a piece of woodland in the process of sale. This is confirmed by his subsidy rating in 1545 of £7 per annum in lands, a not inconsiderable assessment. His farming and landowning interests were at least as important to Thomas Cornell as his clothmaking.[43]

---

[43] PRO PROB 11/36/6; E 179/124/259.

Not until the Elizabethan period is there much evidence of the scale of clothiers'
manufacturing operations. Before that small-scale clothiers can be identified in the
subsidy rolls with quite low assessments, and equally from the minimal legacies in
their wills. But there is little else to go on. The survival of probate inventories after
1565 improves the situation. Only a few inventories of independent master
clothiers survive with personal goods valued at less than £80. Most have chattels
worth at least £80–£100. Yet Christopher Champion of Biddenden (d. 1592) left
goods which indicate that he was both a farmer and a clothier, but which totalled
just £43! His trade goods do not include clothmaking equipment – probably he
leased a dyehouse – but did include one finished 'coarse' broadcloth, valued at £7
10s., and fifty-four quarters of wool (forty-eight already dyed and six of raw wool)
worth £15 10s. He was owed £2 14s. by others. His small farm had three acres in
crop, and presumably pasture for his three cows, a calf and one mare (worth in all
about £12). The circulating capital of Champion's clothmaking enterprise totalled
less than £25, which amounted to no more than three cloths in various stages of
production at any one time. His lifestyle can only have been very basic: his
household goods and apparel were worth only £6.[44]

The personal estate of Matthew Thorpe, clothier of Bethersden (d. 1571), shows
the same combination of clothmaking with farming practised on a very small scale
by Christopher Champion. In Thorpe's case, however, the farm was a good deal
more valuable than the textile business. Of a total inventory worth £72, Thorpe's
farm goods came to over £41 (or 57 per cent). His livestock included about 100
sheep and lambs, and must have supplied wool for his clothmaking. His trade goods
were valued at just over £20 (or 28 per cent of all chattels) and included seven
remnants of finished cloth (£4 13s.), eighty-five quarters of raw wool (£11 10s.) and
various dyestuffs (£2 7s.). Although Thorpe had no finished, full-sized broadcloths
in stock, there was wool sufficient for three or four. The capital devoted to the
clothmaking business suggests that he might have up to four cloths in production
at one time. Thorpe's inventory (made in June) cannot tell us how seasonal his
clothmaking operation was: did he have four cloths in production throughout the
year, or did he only produce four or eight cloths each winter and spring?[45]

Even if clothiers like Thorpe produced as few as eight cloths per year, they
nevertheless had a real impact on local labour markets. If Thorpe put out the wool
for four cloths to four full-time spinners simultaneously, fourteen weeks would have
passed before he could have distributed the yarn to his weavers; and then repeated
the process by distributing wool for another four cloths. In practice it may have
been normal to put out dyed wool to a larger number of spinners – starting at
regular intervals – to speed up this stage of clothmaking and to guarantee a more
even flow of production. And, if Thorpe monopolized the time of a local
broadweaver, his eight cloths would have taken between four and five months to

[44] KAO PRC 10/25 fo. 35.   [45] KAO PRC 10/5 fo. 219v.

complete, with the finishing processes still to follow. Yet on the evidence of his inventory alone, Matthew Thorpe probably devoted more of his energies to his farm than to his textile business.

A different balance between farming and clothmaking is suggested by the inventories of John Spratt of Biddenden (d. 1581) and Thomas Scranton of Staplehurst (d. 1565). Spratt's chattels came to £97 in all, but he was assessed at just £3 in goods in 1572. His farm may not have been as large as Thorpe's – his livestock were worth under £10 – but he was growing about four acres of winter wheat at the time of his death. But his clothmaking operation seems to have been in full swing in January when the inventory was made. He held over 100 quarters of raw and dyed wool (£20 13s.), enough for perhaps four full broadcloths, and the prepared yarn for one blue cloth (£13). He also held a stock of three finished cloths of different colours (valued at £27 in all). Spratt's trade goods (about £62 in all) were worth 64 per cent of his entire personal estate; the farm was small beer in comparison. Spratt could process the raw materials for about eight cloths at one time, which, when finished, would sell for over £70. Thomas Scranton's personal wealth was given as £131, some years before Spratt's chattels were appraised. But he too was an active clothier whose farm was merely a sideline. Indeed Scranton's farm was mainly a livestock enterprise. The farm goods were valued at £25 in all (less than a fifth of his total inventory), whereas the goods connected with his cloth manufacturing amounted to over £70. Scranton's inventory (drawn up in January) included almost no finished cloth, but over 200 quarters of raw and dyed wool (about £50), and four cloths in yarn (total value £20). Scranton held, early in the new year, the raw materials for about a dozen broadcloths, most of which had not yet been spun into yarn. He was well into middle age when the inventory was compiled: his first marriage occurred in 1543, and he was already assessed at £30 in goods in 1544/5. Scranton's turnover was probably considerably larger than Spratt's. Although Scranton's stock of cloth and raw material at one time was not much larger than Spratt's, the former's business was much less likely to have slowed down or ceased in certain seasons.[46]

Unfortunately we remain in the dark about the annual outputs of small-scale clothiers like Thorpe and Spratt, and even of the not-so-small operators like Scranton. The traditional, received wisdom is that most cloth manufacture ceased during the summer months, and peaked between Christmas and the late spring. But there is not enough evidence to demonstrate that this was invariably the case. Labour might have been hard to find during the height of the harvest season. But the extraordinary labour requirements of Wealden harvests were considerably less than in most mixed farming and cereals regions. Thus the seasonal rhythm of Wealden cloth manufacture may have been more steady than might at first be

[46] Spratt: KAO PRC 10/10 fo. 297 (new p. no. 734); Scranton: PRC 10/4 fo. 49; PRC 17/39 fo. 323v; PRO E 179/125/273 *sub* Cranbrook 100.

imagined. Scranton, the Staplehurst clothier, already had four cloths 'in yarn' by January (approximately a third of his total raw material supply at that point), and a Smarden clothier, John Williams (d. 1567), had more wool already washed, dyed and spun than in any other form – by November. The master clothier Amos Spencer, referred to earlier, had already completed 'two fine cloths' by the time of his death in December 1594; and John Spratt, mentioned above, held three finished broadcloths in January when he died. The clothmaking business of these typical small- and medium-scale clothiers appears to have carried on during most of the year, even though all of them – except Spencer – ran a farm themselves.[47]

The impression given by the inventories of small-scale clothiers is that both their capital invested in clothmaking and their annual turnover were quite limited. Most inventories show that small clothiers died without substantial trade debts due to them. They did not have sufficient capital to extend credit to the buyers of their cloth, and must have sold their finished cloths for ready money, or in part by barter for raw materials, or for payment within very short periods. The capital they deployed could be very little: the basic clothier's equipment would have come to about £10 or £12, and enough wool and dyestuffs to make a handful of cloths would have come to well under £40. Then there was the money needed to pay outworkers' wages before the cloths were sold, say another £10 or £12. By this estimate, it would have been possible to operate as an independent master clothier with an initial investment of little more than £60. Naturally, the output of such small manufacturers would also have been quite limited. Most small masters were probably responsible for no more than ten or twenty broadcloths per year, or an equivalent combination of broad and narrow-list cloths. At an average wholesale price of £10 per cloth in the 1570s, the value of most clothiers' production was less than £200 per year. Most of the petty clothiers of the Elizabethan Weald are not represented by a probate inventory or a will, and none could be put forward as examples of the newly-sophisticated entrepreneurship of 'proto-industrial' capitalism. The small master clothiers represent the 'lower class' of early capitalist production; a class of independent producers whose business operations were not very different from those of their predecessors a hundred years before. As a class, they were likely to be as involved in farm work as they were in clothmaking. And yet, in the sixteenth century, they were operating within a fundamentally different economic environment. There was indeed a huge gap between small masters like those just described and the wealthiest rank of clothiers. But the space was not vacant.

Wealthier manufacturers, who could deploy capital sums of several hundred pounds each were, by the middle of the sixteenth century, responsible for a large part of the region's growing cloth output. Clothiers of this rank were likely to own personal

---

[47] KAO PRC 10/4 fo. 49; 10/4 fo. 160; 10/23 fo. 324; 10/10 fo. 297 (p. 734).

goods appraised at £200 or more – if they were still in business when the inventory was made. They were also likely to be employers of non-family labour: an apprentice or two, and one or more journeymen. The Staplehurst clothier, James Buckhurst (d. 1587), falls neatly into this middling category of manufacturers. There is no inventory for Buckhurst (his estate was handled by the prerogative court) and he may well have been retired by 1587, when he was buried as an 'ancient householder'. He married a young widow in 1548, and is first recorded as a clothier in 1555. Broadcloths of his were fined for minor infractions at Blackwell Hall in London in 1561–2 and 1575–6. In 1563 his household included seven servants. There were five male servants, a substantial clothmaking workforce. Buckhurst was rated at £25 in goods in 1571/2, one of the four highest assessments in Marden hundred, and at the time of his death could afford to leave cash legacies totalling £450. He owned lands in the four adjacent parishes of Staplehurst, Frittenden, Headcorn and Sutton Valence, as well as property in Romney Marsh. There is no direct evidence about Buckhurst's cloth output, but it probably was quite substantial during the 1560s and 1570s, during which time his cloths were sold directly on the London market and he was able to build up his landed estate by cash purchases.[48]

An exceptionally informative will provides more insight into the clothmaking business of another middle-ranking clothier, John Bawden of Horsmonden, who died a relatively young man in 1564. Although there is no inventory, Bawden's will recites in detail his current assets and debts. It is unclear if he owned any land, but Bawden calculated that his personal estate was worth about £320. This was composed of debts due totalling about £100 (including £76 owed by four named Londoners) and the rest in stock in trade. At the time of his death, in March, two of his finished cloths,'green medlies', were at Blackwell Hall, 'with the clerk's man'. Three other cloths were at the fulling mill at Loose, two broadcloths were at the weaver's and the coloured wool for two more cloths were in the hands of two spinners. Bawden also noted that he had dyed wool sufficient for seven more cloths and half a finished cloth at home. This amounts to sixteen cloths either ready for sale or in the process of manufacture. As late as March Bawden still had in stock the wool for seven cloths, and four other cloths were at least several weeks short of completion. At the same time Bawden himself owed over £80, including over £7 to three different spinners, several pounds in wages to two weavers, £3 to the fuller Edward Coucheman and an unknown amount to a local shearman for 'dressing four cloths'. Even this very specific information cannot tell us Bawden's annual cloth output, his annual turnover or his profit. It's likely that he produced annually at least two or three times the number of cloths he had in various stages of production at any one point: an estimated output of forty to sixty broadcloths per annum. At £8 to £10 per cloth (to the London wholesalers), Bawden's annual turnover would have

---

[48] PRO PROB 11/71/58; as 'clothier' in 1555 will: KAO DRb/Pwr 11 fo. 320; subsidy: PRO E 179/126/423; Stapleh. parish register; household: KAO PRC 43/13/31.

come to £350 or £450. Bawden's will was that of a well-off man. He appointed his wife executor, and named three substantial local men as overseers. He left 2 marks to the local poor, half a mark each to 'my five servants' and portions of 100 marks each to his three underage sons. In the few years before his death he regularly sold cloths on the London market: at Blackwell Hall cloths of his were fined in both 1560–1 and 1561–2.[49] Little or nothing is known about Bawden's background: he was certainly not a member of a well-known clothmaking family. But his obvious prosperity in 1564 suggests that it was then possible for a trained clothier, without much capital at the outset, to accumulate considerable wealth in less than a decade in the trade.

A dispute about the ulnage payable on 'long' broadcloths, which reached the Exchequer in 1612, provides a third, detailed example of a medium-sized Wealden clothmaking business. The deputy ulnager for Kent sued Richard Sharpe, a Cranbrook clothier since the 1590s, for refusing to pay an extra one and one-half pence – above the normal four and one half pence – for each of his 'long' Kents. Depositions by the ulnager's deputies reveal the number of cloths he produced during the thirty-two months between Michaelmas 1607 and Whitsun 1610. In this period of comparative prosperity for the English textile trade, Sharpe submitted 171 cloths for sealing: an average of over five per month or about sixty-four long broadcloths per year. There was very little seasonal variation: in the half-year Lady Day to Michaelmas (25 March to 29 September) 1609 Sharpe had thirty-two cloths sealed; in the following half-year, which covers the winter months, the total was thirty-four. His output during the previous two half-year periods was much the same. Sharpe's cloths were usually longer than the statutory minimum for Kent broadcloths: thirty-two instead of twenty-eight yards. Cloths of that length would have sold for at least £10 and £12 apiece at the end of the sixteenth century, perhaps slightly more in the boom years of the early seventeenth century. Hence Sharpe's average output was worth about £700 or £750 per year. To spin the yarn for his sixty-four long cloths would have taken about two dozen spinners around 250 days each year. The yarn would have kept four broadweavers busy for about the same 250 days per year. Richard Sharpe, unlike William Bawden, was a member of a wealthy clan of Cranbrook clothiers, well established by the reign of Henry VIII. He was one of several sons of John Sharpe (d. 1580), one of the parish's leading Elizabethan clothmakers, and was already among the twenty highest-rated taxpayers in Cranbrook hundred in 1598. Having served as an assessor of church rates for the parish three times in the early 1600s, he was Constable of Cranbrook Hundred in 1612. The 1608 Easter Book for Cranbrook records that his household included two journeymen, two apprentices, two maids and several of his own children.[50]

[49] PRO PROB 11/47/15; Horsmonden register; PRO E 159/350 Rec. Hil. rots. 329, 331.
[50] Case: PRO E 134/10 Jas. I/Mich. 18; KAO P 100/28/1: 1608 at Plusshingherst; also Cranbrook register and churchwardens' accounts at KAO; subsidy: PRO E 179/127/516.

Evidence of Sharpe's real wealth when he was at the height of his prosperity, probably between 1604 and 1614, is unfortunately lacking. He was almost certainly well into retirement when he died in 1633. Although Richard Sharpe was not among the elite of the region's capitalist clothiers at the end of Elizabeth's reign, clothmaking certainly provided him with a substantial income, well above that of the many petty clothiers of the Weald. His business was undoubtedly based on substantial capital inputs, widespread use of credit and direct sales in the London wholesale market.

Selling cloth to buyers who were not the ultimate consumers of their product was a part of every clothier's business. A small part of the Weald's textile output was destined for local and native consumption: the coarse quality broadcloths and most kerseys. But most broadcloth was produced for distant – and especially – overseas markets. In neither branch of the Wealden woollen trade, however, is there any evidence of clothiers selling small quantities of their cloth directly to individual consumers. Clothmakers sold their product to a wide variety of middleman dealers and merchants. Retail woollendrapers in the small market towns of the Weald itself or elsewhere in Kent certainly kept stocks of cloth made in the Weald. Their inventories, however, suggest that only the wealthy urban drapers purchased whole broadcloths. The inventories of retail woollendrapers and general shopkeepers reveal only small quantities of broadcloth in stock: they must have purchased their cloth from wholesale merchants or substantial woollendrapers in nearby market towns like Maidstone, Ashford or Tenterden.[51] If small-scale Wealden clothiers chose not to sell their broadcloths in London – and there are large numbers of identified Elizabethan clothiers who do not turn up on the Blackwell Hall lists – they could offer them to the urban drapers from Maidstone, Ashford or Tenterden, to the few large-scale wholesale merchants in the Weald or to their local competitors – the capitalist clothiers of the region. Merchants like Thomas Sheffe of Cranbrook (d. 1520), Thomas Ruck of Cranbrook (whose 1583 inventory shows a stock of six finished broadcloths and a total personal estate of £1,856) or Thomas Sheffe II of Cranbrook (d. 1604) were potential buyers of local broadcloths, especially if they were willing to pay in ready money or in basic raw materials.[52] In turn they disposed of the cloth either to provincial woollendrapers or sent it for sale to London alongside the cloth of local manufacturers. The third possible outlet for

---

[51] Inventories of major urban drapers: Thos. Amee of Hythe (1568), KAO PRC 28/2 fo. 36; Walt. Shetterden of Sandwich (1571), PRC 10/5 fo. 286; Jn. Banks of Ashford (1579), PRC 10/10 fo. 29v; Jn. Day and Hen. Badcock (both 1582) of Tenterden, PRC 10/10 fo. 251v; 10/13 fo. 17; Thos. Barming of Faversham (1594), PRC 10/20 fo. 439; Chris. Scott of Canterbury (1568), PRC 21/1 fos. 25–32. Drapers in the Weald (except in Tenterden) were all small fry: Edw. Huggins of Goudhurst (1570), PRC 10/5 fo. 231; Ric. Water of Staplehurst (1580), PRC 10/10 fo. 214; Wm. Wilcock of Biddenden (1580), PRC 10/11 fo. 49; Geo. Duncke of Hawkhurst (1591), PRC 10/19 fo. 126v; Jn. Eddenden of Cranbrook (1588), PRC 10/17 fo. 279.

[52] Thos Sheffe: KAO PRC 32/13 fo. 16; Thos Ruck: PRC 21/6 fo. 460; Thos Sheffe, II: see his wholesale wool purchases: PRO E 190/641/12 fos. 1v, 3v, E 190/639/3 fo. 3v; rated at £30 per annum in lands, 1572: PRO E 179/126/423.

small manufacturers – who needed immediate payment for their cloth in order to carry on production – were their richer rivals in clothmaking. The evidence that the large-scale clothiers of the Weald were also middlemen buyers of locally produced cloth is purely circumstantial, but convincing. First, they had sufficient capital at their disposal to purchase and hold stocks of finished cloths. Second, they maintained large stocks of basic raw materials, which might be bartered for petty clothiers' finished cloths. And finally, they had regular commercial links with the men who exported most of the region's broadcloth production, the London cloth merchants. Among the businessmen in the Weald, only the handful of major wholesale merchants and the middling and wealthy clothiers were in a position to trade directly to London, given the terms of trade.

In their normal transactions with the London wholesalers, provincial clothmakers received payment for their goods in arrears. Half a year might pass between the delivery of cloths to the London buyer and his final payment to the clothier for a consignment of cloths. Such terms applied irrespective of whether the cloths were first sold at London's public market, Blackwell Hall, or their sale had been agreed between the clothmaker and a London merchant some months before. In both cases, the country clothier extended credit to the London wholesaler. As has been stressed in chapter 6, credit relationships occurred at every level of the clothmaking business. Clothiers may have purchased all or part of their raw materials on credit. Spinners and weavers extended credit to their employers, the clothiers, by accepting wages in arrears and clothworkers also appear to have accepted payment for their finishing tasks in arrears. Much of this is obvious from the references to debts owed in clothiers' wills, or in the few extant administrators' accounts.[53] Clothiers were obliged to do the same for their customers.

The most successful clothiers were those who could afford to carry their customers' debts. Clothmakers without sufficient capital to offer credit to the overseas merchants could not deal successfully on the London market, where the best prices for their cloth could only be obtained by offering delivery before payment. The extent of credit given by clothiers to cloth dealers can be seen in two main sources: the wills and inventories of clothiers, and in Chancery suits between London merchants and provincial clothiers. Wealthy clothiers who died while still in business were invariably owed money by Londoners who had already taken delivery of their cloths. This can be shown in the early prerogative court inventory of Stephen Draner, the leading Cranbrook clothier who died in 1539, in the detailed will of the Horsmonden clothier John Bawden (d. 1564), and in many diocesan probate inventories of the Elizabethan period.[54] What distinguishes the wealthiest

---

[53] See e.g. debts owed by clothier John Bawden (1564): PRO PROB 11/47/15; and the administrator's account for Alex Dence (1601): KAO PRC 21/16 fos.150–3v.

[54] PRO PROB 2/525; PROB 11/47/15 and PROB 11/77/26; KAO PRC 28/1 fos. 112–15 (P. Courthop); PRC 21/4 fo. 83 (P. Courthop, 1579); PRC 28/2 fo. 48 (R. Courthop, 1568).

clothmakers was the scale of their trade debts. The bigger operators in the late sixteenth-century Weald were delivering finished cloths worth several hundred pounds or more to their customers, and being paid three to six months later.

The wealthier clothiers also appear to have sold bigger consignments to individual London merchants. About 1515–18, the prosperous Cranbrook clothier Richard Barre sold sixteen broadcloths worth about £4 apiece to Thomas Maynard, Grocer of London, in one transaction. When, after many months without payment Barre sued Maynard in the London Sheriffs' Court, the latter replied with a bill in Chancery which admitted that he had already sold the cloths 'beyond the sea' and not yet paid Barre, but claimed that three cloths were defective and had had to be sold cheap. Later bills in Chancery by London merchants tell the same story: in the mid 1530s the London Merchant Taylor Richard Allen and the Cranbrook clothier Richard Courthop were involved in litigation arising from Allen's purchase the previous Christmas of about fifteen cloths for £100. Again, the customer claimed that several cloths were defective and refused to pay the full amount. Another example comes in a Chancery suit of the late 1550s: William Courthop, clothier of Cranbrook, alleged that he was owed £332 by Thomas Wygg, Clothworker of London; that Wygg was joined in a bond to pay Courthop £232 by another clothworker, Thomas Ormeston; and that the payment – in three instalments – had not been made. In one case of the 1550s the Benenden clothier William Foule had only received £8 of the £12 purchase price of a broadcloth sold to a London merchant two years before![55] In terms of the many thousands of bargains agreed between Kent clothiers and London merchants, the few that ended in the courts were almost negligible. But they do reveal the normal terms of trade which inevitably advantaged the wealthier clothier over his poorer local rivals. The rich clothier tended to sell his wares in advance of delivery to London, to sell them in larger quantities and probably for a better price than was obtainable by the small masters. He was therefore in a position to plan ahead and spread his production more evenly through the year. As a consequence he was probably better able to recruit and retain sufficient skilled outworkers without whom he could not make cloth. Thus the operation of the national cloth market – in which credit played such a large role – favoured the existing large-scale clothiers of the Weald and other clothmaking regions.

Who were the clothmaking elite and what made their businesses different from those of the clothiers we have already examined? A small number of rich clothmakers – living in Cranbrook and just two or three other parishes – dominated the local cloth industry. Both in terms of the volume and of the complexity of their businesses, this upper class of highly capitalized cloth manufacturers made the

[55] Barre: PRO C1/427/40; Ric Courthop: C1/719/15; Wm Courthop: C1/1420/44–8 and C 78/13 no. 3; Wm Foule: C1/1341/71. Other cases at C1/746/23 and C1/1301/76.

economic running in the era of early capitalism. As early as the 1520s, a small elite of extremely wealthy clothiers was apparent. In 1524/5 a handful of clothiers were taxed on personal wealth of at least £60; in most cases they each paid more in tax than local gentlemen. In the four central Wealden hundreds with extant subsidy rolls, six Cranbrook clothiers were rated on £100 or more, but only two gentlemen were assessed at £100 or above. In the next highest category – persons rated at £60 in goods or the equivalent in annual landed income – there were ten taxpayers: three gentry, five clothiers and two whose occupation is uncertain. The Cranbrook clothmaking elite was headed by Stephen Draner (rated at £300 in goods), three members of the Courthop clan (two at £200, one at £133 in goods), William Lynch (£160 in goods) and John Sharpe (£100 in goods). Rated at £60 in goods were the clothiers Richard Barre, Richard Bigge and Laurence Coucheman.[56] The Coucheman, Courthop, Lynch and Sharpe families produced clothiers throughout the century. They were joined by other widely ramified clothmaking clans, several of whom were active by the 1520s (the Hovendens of Cranbrook or the Gibbons of Rolvenden, for example). A few names disappeared from the trade in each generation: Richard Barre had no sons and the sons of Stephen Draner dropped out of the industry. But there was no predictable pattern of social mobility in which the sons of successful clothiers deserted trade and set up as gentlemen: the Courthops had the resources to do so in Henry VIII's reign but did not. Movement into the ranks of the gentry, however, become more common towards the end of the sixteenth century: notable examples include the Gibbon, Lynch and Allard families.

The wealth of the clothmaking elite was qualitatively as well as quantitatively different from anything seen in the Kent Weald before the sixteenth century. The remainder of this chapter analyses the fortunes of the top-rank clothiers. It examines first the nature and scale of their clothmaking businesses; and second, shows how manufacturing was one of a number of diverse sources of income. In doing so, we learn more about the nature of rural capitalism in the sixteenth century.

There is no direct evidence about the clothmaking business of the Courthops of Cranbrook, who were, as early as the 1520s, the wealthiest clan of manufacturers in the region. In that decade two generations of Courthops were active in the cloth trade. Clothmaking was not a trade to which parents conventionally assigned the younger son, or, for that matter, the eldest either. It was common for several brothers to work as clothmakers, but it is by no means clear if they traded in partnership. Small-scale and medium-sized clothiers frequently left their dyehouses – or their clothmaking equipment – to several sons.[57] Wealthier clothiers didn't

---

[56] The gentry were represented by Vincent Finch at £200 goods, George Guildford, Esq. at £100 per annum in lands, Steph. Scott at £80 in goods, Anne Culpeper at £57 in goods and Thos. Wilford at £50 per annum in lands. John Lachynden (£60 g.) and William Hamond (£80 g.) were probably clothiers. Missing from the rolls were the region's wealthiest landowners Edward and Henry Guildford, members of the royal household. PRO E 179/125/324.

[57] KAO PRC 17/18 fo. 51v; other examples: Jn. Atherst of Bidd. (1534): PRC 32/16 fo. 24; Wm. Day of Benen. (1527): PRC 17/17 fo. 278.

have to divide up the dyehouse; they and their sons could easily afford one each.[58] Wealthy clothiers seem to have operated from one central workhouse, even if they owned several. Clothiers' dyehouses were usually attached, or adjacent to, their dwelling houses. It was normal for independent, married clothiers to head their own households; ideally they would also conduct business from their own workshop. The only scope for family partnerships – though there is no direct evidence of them – would have been in the ownership of a fulling mill, the purchase of raw materials and in the sale of finished cloth. In all of these, the clothmaking businesses of several brothers would have profited from the benefits of scale. It may well be that the large raw material purchases made by a number of very wealthy Cranbrook clothiers were made on behalf of several associated clothiers. However, the evidence of fines imposed on faulty cloths at Blackwell Hall from the 1550s to the 1570s suggests that clothier-kin normally traded on their own accounts: cloths are never recorded as the property of more than one man, and there are often entries of cloths owned by different brothers (or uncle and nephew, or even father and son) in the same year or within a year or two of one another.

The business operations of the small elite of Wealden clothiers can be gauged from a closer analysis of several who are represented by detailed wills and inventories. The earliest example is Stephen Draner of Cranbrook, a contemporary of the second generation of Courthops to figure among the elite. Draner's subsidy assessment – £300 in goods – was the highest in the Weald in 1524/5. A good deal can be established about his career and business dealings. He was certainly the first of his family to rise to real wealth. His father is unknown, but he may have been the nephew of a certain Thomas Draner of Cranbrook (d. 1506), whose modest will he witnessed. An earlier John Draner of Cranbrook died in 1463 leaving a small freehold estate in Cranbrook and two other parishes to two daughters. The Draners lived in reasonable prosperity in Staplehurst from the 1530s onwards, but the surname disappeared from Cranbrook after mid-century.[59]

Stephen Draner, 'clothman' of Cranbrook, is first heard of in London in 1512–13, as a business associate of Richard Harman, a Cranbrook merchant. According to a case brought in Chancery years later – when Harman was in trouble for importing Tyndale's New Testament into England – Draner was acting as surety for Harman in the purchase of thirty-six fine cloths from a Suffolk clothier. In 1529 the clothier alleged that he was still owed £65 out of the original £140 agreed by Draner and

---

58 For example, Peter Courthop (1563 will: KAO PRC 32/30 fo. 510); Steph. Roger of Bidd. (1554 will: PRC 17/29 fo. 66); Robt. Bigge of Cranb.(1532 will: PRO PROB 11/25/4); Jas. Buckhurst of Stapleh.(1584 will: PROB 11/71/58); and John King (late of Cranbrook) w/three dyehouses (1591 will: PROB 11/81/24).

59 A John Draner (d. 1463) was wealthy enough to ask for a burial in church (KAO PRC 17/1 fo. 128); Thos. Draner (d. 1506) with five sons but not including a Steph. (PRC 17/10 fo. 239). Draners at Staplehurst incl. descendants of that Thos. including Michael (d. 1585), a well-off butcher and Robt. (d. 1589), a prosperous farmer. Two of Steph's sons were rated to the subsidy in Cranbrook in 1544: Thos. at £50 per annum in lands and Wm. at £26 per annum in lands.

Harman.[60] In 1512 Draner made the first of what was to be a long list of land acquisitions; about a dozen survive as final concords alone. He first appears in a local will in 1513, and in 1518 John King of Cranbrook refers to Stephen's eldest son John as 'my godson'.[61] In 1520 Draner gave £40, the second highest amount, to the Cranbrook church building fund, and the following year he and Alexander Courthop were made overseers of the estate of John Davy, a Cranbrook merchant.[62] Two years later came the £300 subsidy assessment. Draner was described about 1530 in a Chancery bill as 'a man of great substance as well in lands as in goods'.[63] By the early 1530s Draner was on friendly terms with two Kentish men who were rising quickly in the Crown service. John Baker and Christopher Hales brought Draner into the circle of Thomas Cromwell, the King's councillor. Stephen was almost certainly the 'Master Draner' who visited St Osyth's abbey on Cromwell's behalf in 1532, and in January 1534 Christopher Hales wrote to Cromwell to remind him to procure Draner's commission as Escheator for Kent, as it was late. Even so, such important connections also brought demands: in 1536 Draner was down to provide ten soldiers to oppose the rebels, the same contribution as several middle-ranking Kent gentlemen. Just three years later Draner made his will. His sole overseer was to be 'my trusty and well-beloved friend, John Baker, Esq., the King's general attorney'.[64]

Stephen Draner was probably at least fifty years old when he died, but he seems still to have been in the clothmaking business. In fact he was in London when the will was drawn up: one of the witnesses was John Askew, Draper of London, who owed Draner £200. Draner's inventory was completed in February 1540 and shows a gross personal wealth of £1,300. Against that he owed debts to named creditors of about £400 (including £42 to Cranbrook clothier Simon Lynch) and a rounded figure of £30 was due to spinners and weavers. His net worth was almost £900, a sum which would put his personal estate among the very wealthiest estates covered by our probate inventory sample for the years 1565–99 (and which in real terms would have been worth two to three times the 1539 value). Unfortunately there is almost nothing to compare with Draner's estate before the late sixteenth century. The composition of Draner's personal wealth exemplifies the difference between the small and medium-scale clothiers and those who can be called 'capitalist clothiers'. Draner's good debts came to over £865 (66 per cent of the gross total), and were owed by a combination of London merchants and local borrowers. The Londoners owed trade debts of about £500: at least three were members of the Drapers'

---

[60] PRO C1/668 nos. 56–7.

[61] Fines: PRO CP 25(2) 19/105 no. 14; 20/118 no. 44; 20/119 no. 16; 21/122 no. 22; 21/129 nos. 40, 50, 52–5, 58; 21/131 no. 51. Sold a messuage and 25 acres to John Baker (1519), KAO U24/T288; exec. of Ric More of Cranb. asked to sell two pieces of land to Draner, 1519: PRC 17/14 fo. 106v. Overseer in 1513: PRC 17/12 fo. 189. King: PRC 17/13 fo. 234.

[62] *Annals of Cranbrook*, p. 50; Davy: KAO PRC 17/15 fo. 121.　　　[63] PRO C1/647 nos. 2–3.

[64] *LP*, v, no. 1636; vii, no. 11; xi, App. 8; will written 29 August 1539: PRO PROB 11/27/34.

Company.[65] The local debtors included well-known clothiers such as Thomas Bathurst, John Courthop, Richard Holden, Thomas Woodgate, and the Cranbrook merchant Thomas Harman. But it is impossible from the inventory alone to know if such debts were personal borrowings or if they related directly to Draner's clothmaking business. The rest of Draner's chattels were made up of trade goods worth about £270 (21 per cent), cash and plate valued at almost £70 (5 per cent), livestock worth about £15 and household goods valued at around £80 (6 per cent).[66]

The great majority of Draner's personal estate – around 90 per cent – was made up of cash, debts and his stock in trade as a clothier. The contrast with the inventories of lesser clothiers is stark. Draner's warehouse was full of completed broadcloths: a stock of twenty-eight cloths valued at almost £185. He had wool in store priced at £39, sufficient perhaps for half a dozen ordinary broadcloths. The dyestuffs and oil on hand were valued at £32 alone. It would be nice to know if all twenty-eight cloths were of Draner's own making, or if he had purchased them from small-scale local clothiers. But if they were his own production, his business had completed twenty-eight full cloths by February, and might be expected to produce double or treble that number before the following autumn. Hence one might estimate an annual output of eighty-five to 100 cloths at this late stage of Draner's clothmaking career, when he may have been more active as a royal official and landowner than as a clothmaker. At the height of Draner's career as a clothier – in the 1520s – he was probably producing several hundred cloths each year. The inventory ignores freehold land altogether. And Draner had been buying land in many Kent parishes from early in his career as a clothier. Sadly, his will makes no mention of the land he left to his four sons so the dimensions of his landed estate are unknown. There are hints that it was substantial, though not as valuable as the biggest gentry estates. First, in 1544 the subsidy commissioners for Cranbrook Hundred assessed two of Draner's sons at £50 and £26 per annum in lands. In the same year Thomas Roberts, Esq. of Cranbrook was rated at £50 per annum. Secondly, Stephen's eldest son John Draner died in 1567 leaving an estate of almost 600 acres, part of which he inherited.[67] By the 1530s, if not earlier, Stephen Draner the clothier was becoming Stephen Draner the landowner – but without retiring from clothmaking.

The wealthiest clothiers were all landowners. Capitalist clothmakers financed their manufacturing businesses in part from the rents paid by their tenants. At the same time these early capitalists invested part of the profits of their businesses in houses

---

[65] Edmund and John Askew and Richard Poynter: see A. H. Johnson, *History of the Drapers' Co.*, ii, pp. 72, 82, 470.

[66] PRO PROB 2/525. The gross total given on the document reads £1,406 11s., but it seems to include several desperate debts, which are normally excluded here.

[67] PRO E 179/125/273; C 142/146 no. 116.

and farms which could be leased out. A good example of this symbiosis between estate building and business success is the career of the Cranbrook merchant Thomas Sheffe (d. 1604). He inherited a modest freehold estate in Cranbrook from his clothier father, but by the time of his death he owned almost a thousand acres in the Weald and in Romney Marsh.[68] Less spectacular – and less detailed – stories can be discovered about several wealthy clothiers. Alexander Courthop's 1524 will apportions a number of messuages and many pieces of land in Cranbrook and two other parishes among his four sons. Only rarely is the acreage given, but in many cases Courthop describes the parcels as 'two pieces of land bought of Thomas Taylor' or 'four pieces bought of Gervase Karkeregge'. The will also mentions that Courthop's eldest son John was to enjoy the lands that Alexander had already given him. The Courthop estate at this point was probably little more than 100 or 150 acres in all – much of it leased out – but it typifies the steady accumulation of small parcels of land engaged in by the richer clothiers.[69]

The continuing success of the established clothmaking families in the middle and later years of the century can be read in the evidence generated by the deaths of Alexander Courthop's third son Peter, of Stephen Sharpe and of Alexander Dence. Peter Courthop was probably the wealthiest clothier in the Weald when he died in 1567, aged about sixty-two. A probate inventory appraised his gross personal wealth at almost £1,800. The will he made in 1563, before the deaths of several of his sons, left cash legacies alone worth £575. And several inquisitions *post mortem* show that he owned about 240 acres of land in Cranbrook and Biddenden – probably a good deal more than had his father.[70] Peter's estate was grouped around four messuages, three of which included a dyehouse. Woodland accounted for sixty out of 241 acres in all. And, according to his will, Peter Courthop had purchased three of the messuages during his own lifetime. His prosperity as a manufacturer underwrote his estate building, and by his later years the reverse was also the case. An analysis of the inventory reveals the scale and nature of his business activities: cash and debts due made up 47 per cent of his chattels, and his stock in trade (in raw materials and cloth) came to a further 44 per cent of his goods. Breaking down the trade goods into notional cloths shows that in November 1567 he held eleven fully finished cloths, a further five cloths at the fulling mill, three cloths 'in yarn', six cloths in dyed wool, and undyed wool enough for about 120 cloths. The stock suggests a yearly output of several hundred broadcloths. And, like Stephen Draner, a major proportion of Peter Courthop's wealth was in the form of trade debts.

Stephen Sharpe, son of Laurence Sharpe, clothier (d. 1552), and Alexander Dence, son of Richard Dence, clothier (d. 1561), were leading members of the Cranbrook

---

[68] Ric. Sheffe's will (1557): PRO PROB 11/39/34; Thos. Sheffe's IPM: Wards 7/37 no. 11.

[69] KAO PRC 32/14 fo. 100. Courthop's feoffees were Baron Jn. Hales, Jn. Baker, Chris. Hales, Nic. Tufton, gent., the clothiers Giles Andrew and Ric. Bigge and Thos. Davy, merchant.

[70] Will w/witnesses Walt Hendley, gent. and three leading clothiers of Cranb. and Bidd.: Hen. Allard, Ric. Besbiche and Ric. Taylor: KAO PRC 32/30 fo. 510; inventory: PRC 28/1 fos. 112–15; IPMs: PRO Wards 7/12 fos. 66, 11.

clothier elite who died within six months of one another in 1573 and 1574. They shared a good deal in common – too much according to one informer of 1561, who accused Dence of suspect behaviour with Sharpe's wife – including a desire to be buried in style within Cranbrook church, and the ownership of a sizeable landed estate. Both men died in their mid 50s and both are represented by a will and an inquisition *post mortem*. The latter confirm what is suggested by the 1572 subsidy roll, where Sharpe is rated at £28 per annum and Dence at £30 per annum in lands: both owned substantial freehold estates. Sharpe's holdings lay mainly in Cranbrook but included lands in Goudhurst and Horsmonden. None is valued in the inquisition or in his will – it was all held in socage – but he was receiving rent from about twenty different tenants! His estate was of the order of 200 acres, and included a messuage and lands in Cranbrook called 'Sharpeys', perhaps part of his inherited family estate. Dence's inquisition and prerogative court of Canterbury will suggest a man of great prosperity and superior local connections. Though married, he had no surviving children, and left much of his wealth to local charities. His executives were the clothiers (and his relatives) Francis Hartrege and Alex Weller. He chose the vicar of Cranbrook and the parish oligarchs Peter Courthop and Thomas Sheffe as his overseers. Dence left legacies to relatives among most of the leading clothmaking families. Lands which Dence valued at over £37 per annum were left to his widow for her lifetime, then to two cousins. Lands worth £24 per annum would endow the 'Alexander Dence Alms House', and other properties were left to increase the endowment of Cranbrook school. According to his inquisition, Dence held lands in Cranbrook, Hawkhurst, Goudhurst and Frittenden, and about fifty acres in Romney Marsh: most of the property was occupied by thirty tenants. Exceptionally, the jurors reported a reasonably credible value for Dence's estate: about £145 per annum.[71]

Alexander Dence's landholdings were clearly more valuable than most of his fellow clothiers, including Stephen Sharpe's; but a good deal less extensive than the estates of leading local squires like Richard Baker, Walter Roberts or Alexander Culpeper. The Sharpe and Dence estates represent the economic design of most successful Wealden clothiers of the period: to enlarge – out of the profits of clothmaking – a small, inherited freehold estate into a larger, rentier estate. The rents from the latter helped expand the textile business, and the successful clothier-landowner rarely deserted manufacturing for the life of a petty squire. Perhaps their consciousness of mid sixteenth-century inflation and of the vagaries of the Elizabethan cloth market gave men like Courthop and Dence added insights into the dynamic material world around them. Certainly in the last few decades of the sixteenth century and the early decades of the next, the Wealden textile industry

---

[71] Sharpe: will (KAO PRC 17/42 fo. 16v); IPM (PRO C 142/164 no. 78); 1563 deposition as age forty-six (CCL X.10.10 fo. 12); wife and Alex. Dence (CCL X.1.3 fo. 74v). Dence: will (PRO PROB 11/56/20); IPM (C 142/169 no. 91); first rated to subsidy, Cranbrook 100, 1543/4; 1572 subsidy (PRO E 179/126/423 *sub* Cranbrook 100).

produced a number of prosperous clothiers who could command wealth greater than all but a handful of major gentry landowners. Unfortunately we have no well-documented equivalent of Stephen Draner for the last Elizabethan generation. Without realistic tax assessments or inventories from the prerogative court of Canterbury, we have to rely on the diocesan probate inventories to judge the scale of the major capitalist manufacturers' businesses at the end of our period. Which excludes many of the most successful entrepreneurs of the late sixteenth and early seventeenth centuries.

Clothiers' inventories proved in the local courts suggest that the most successful were coping well with inflation. In 1579 Peter Courthop, junior of Cranbrook, the nephew of Peter Courthop discussed above, died while still in his twenties. Yet his personal estate was already worth £855! His stock in trade was valued at £435 (51 per cent) and his recoverable debts came to over £340 (40 per cent). When he died in November he held in stock ten finished cloths (£113), seven more in yarn or at the spinners (£71) and enough raw or dyed wool to produce fifty to sixty broadcloths (£220).[72]

The inventories of the biggest clothmakers at the beginning of the seventeenth century show no reduction in the scale of their businesses. Thomas Wells of Biddenden died in 1601 with about £920 in personal property: debts of £449 (49 per cent), stock in trade of £295 (32 per cent) and a medium-sized farm (£42 or 4.5 per cent). Alexander Sheffe, clothier of Cranbrook, died in 1601 leaving chattels worth about £760. These included debts due of £190 (25 per cent) and trade goods of £423 (56 per cent). When he died he held seventeen finished broadcloths which his fellow clothiers who acted as appraisers valued at £255 alone.[73] The wealthiest clothiers' inventories of the years just prior to the Cockayne disaster record substantially higher totals than any in the sixteenth century, and hint at the scale of wealth of the richest Wealden clothiers whose wills were proved in London in the early 1600s. Walter Taylor of Cranbrook (d. 1613) had chattels worth about £2,200, made up of debts and cash worth £922 (42 per cent), stock in trade of £1,100 (50 per cent) and a substantial farm (3 per cent). Taylor had two workhouses in operation when he died and a stock of twenty-six finished cloths (£355). John Sharpe (living in Staplehurst but of the Cranbrook clothmaking family) also died in 1613 and left a personal estate valued at £2,689. His cash, plate and good debts came to over £1,400 (54 per cent), his stock in trade totalled £920 (34 per cent), and his farm goods alone (£135 or 5 per cent) were worth more than the total estate of most Wealden farmers.[74]

The large-scale capitalist clothiers of the Weald coped successfully with inflation,

---

[72] KAO PRC 21/4 fo. 83.
[73] KAO PRC 10/30 fo. 483; Sheffe: PRC 28/4 fo. 33 and PRC 21/16 fos. 150–3, where his widow claims she's paid over £500 in debts owed by Alex Sheffe.
[74] KAO PRC 28/5 fos. 469, 442.

competition and changes in market demand for textiles throughout the later sixteenth century. Their relative prosperity continued into the second decade of the next century. The commercial crisis which overtook the English textile industry from 1614 marked the end of more than a century of prosperity for the region's top manufacturers. The broadcloth industry of the Weald, unlike several other regional economies, never recovered from the collapse in overseas demand in the 1620s. Yet throughout the ups and downs of the cloth industry in the second half of the sixteenth century, wealthy Wealden clothiers managed to combine the various strands of their businesses and investments to produce increasing individual prosperity. They did so by making the best use of their initial advantage, the control of some liquid capital. What set them apart from the many small-scale master clothiers was their ability to manipulate the credit mechanisms on which the textile industry depended so as to increase their own output. Crucial to their business success were their non-industrial profits. Throughout the period the most successful clothiers were also farmers and rentier landowners. The profits of clothmaking were regularly supplemented by the profits of agriculture and, more importantly, the profits of the lands and houses they rented out. Their mercantile activities – as middlemen dealers in raw materials and in smaller producers' cloths – also contributed significantly to their overall balance sheets. These additional sources of revenue and capital enabled the leading Cranbrook clothiers to organize clothmaking on a scale far above that of their lesser rivals. They were in a position to dominate local labour markets, to profit from the purchasing and marketing needs of their poorer local competitors and to deal with the London wholesale merchants from a position of financial independence. The demand for high quality Wealden broadcloth – which made Kentish cloths among the most expensive on the market – meant that the major capitalist clothmakers of the Weald were not dominated by metropolitan capital during the sixteenth century. The local Wealden industry was characterized by economic hierarchies which separated most textile workers from a small number of independent clothmakers, and in turn exhibited enormous differences in wealth and economic independence between the petty manufacturers and the wealthy clothier elite. At the close of the sixteenth century the prospects for continued prosperity were good: the local industry was able to support dozens of small-scale clothmakers and master weavers in comparative prosperity, and a limited number of capitalist entrepreneurs in great wealth. Entrepreneurship appeared to be working.

The Weald and 'proto-industrialization'

The proto-industrialization model advanced by Mendels, Wrightson and Levine, and others relied – for its empirical foundations – on seventeenth- and eighteenth-century examples. In France, to cite one important instance, the migration of textile production from towns to the countryside began in the sixteenth and seventeenth centuries, several hundred years later than the same transformation occurred in England.[1] From about 1600 a wide variety of economic and demographic evidence survives with which to study the evolution of rural industry – and to test the model. In particular, after 1600 – both for England and for many regions of Continental Europe – there are data available to examine the links between rural industry and demographic change. But the proto-industry under the spotlight here traces its origins back to the fourteenth century. English rural clothmaking was established in all the major regions it was ever to thrive in *before 1500*: the West Country, East Anglia, West Yorkshire and the Kent Weald. Woollen manufacture was flourishing in all these areas for half a dozen generations before the parish register era began in 1538. Little evidence is available to study the origins and early growth of the characteristic English proto-industry – woollen textiles. The applicability of the model to sixteenth-century England has to be assessed on evidence drawn from an era when rural cloth production was already commercially successful, rather than from throughout its development. The object of this concluding chapter is to compare the experience of the Weald – and in passing that of other English regions

---

[1] Franklin Mendels, 'Proto-industrialization: the First Phase of the Industrialization Process', *Journ. Econ. Hist.* 32 (1972); 'Agriculture and Peasant Industry in 18th Century Flanders', in W. N. Parker and E. L. Jones (eds.), *European Peasants and their Markets* (1981); *Industrialization and Population Pressure in Eighteenth-Century Flanders* (New York, 1981); D. Levine, *Family Formation in an Age of Nascent Capitalism* (1977); P. Kriedte, H. Medick and J. Schlumbohm, *Industrialization before Industrialization* (1981); Rudolf Braun, 'Early Industrialization and Demographic Change in the Canton of Zurich', in Charles Tilly (ed.), *Historical Studies of Changing Fertility* (1978); Pierre Deyon, 'Variations de la production textile aux XVIe et XVIIIe: Sources et premières resultats', *Annales E. S. C.*, 18 (1963); Philip Benedict (ed.), *Cities and Social Change in Early Modern France* (1989), pp. 27, 31, 146.

of early manufacturing – with the model of rural, proto-industry suggested by Mendels and others.

It will also be necessary to say something about *de*-industrialization, because manufacturing in the Weald – as in many other English proto-industrial regions – did not evolve neatly from 'proto' industry to factory industry. Rather, proto-industry in the seventeenth-century Weald stalled – and then disappeared altogether. There is not scope to move beyond the chronological limits of this study in order to provide a narrative of the Kentish cloth industry's demise in the seventeenth century. Nevertheless, this conclusion will suggest some reasons for the failure of the Wealden textile industry, in circumstances not dissimilar to those which obtained in at least one other English clothmaking region during the 'general crisis of the seventeenth century'. In a study of the Kent Weald it is surely just as important to ask why rural manufacturing failed as to ask why it developed in the first place. To begin with, it is possible to identify a checklist of circumstances and conditions which provided the seedbed in which rural industry developed, or which at least appear to coincide with successful rural manufacturing in the sixteenth-century Weald. This same list of questions can be asked about other proto-industrial regions to discover if the circumstances which obtained in the Weald were common to all or most regions of rural manufacturing. In this way the general applicability – and usefulness – of at least the first part of the proto-industrialization model may be tested. The key questions or headings identified in the present investigation can be broken down as follows:

1 Topography and soil type
2 Date of permanent settlement
3 Type of agrarian regime
4 Pattern or structure of landholding and settlement type
5 Prevailing inheritance customs
6 Local availability of (?skilled) labour for non-agrarian employment
7 Rates of family formation and population growth
8 Natural resources (including access to raw materials)
9 Access to appropriate markets
10 Availability of capital to finance rural industry

The reader will rapidly recognize how much these headings are linked together in chains of causation and explanation. The interacting factors are dissociated only for heuristic reasons – in the individual chapters of this study, for example. But the proto-industrialization model forces us to look more holistically at historical circumstances and evidence.

Thus the geography of a region heavily conditions the types of human settlement and agricultural regimes which can succeed. Just as important, the prevailing topography and soils influenced the date of permanent settlement and the degree of seigniorial control over land and farming. Local access to minerals used in industry (coal, iron ore, fuller's earth, etc.) as well as the availability of water power in the form of fast-running streams are also a function of local geography – not open to human manipulation. The nature of settlement patterns, the structure of landholding and the prevailing type of agriculture in turn heavily influenced the rate of family formation and the level of population growth – and the local pool of labour available to would-be manufacturing employers. Local customs of inheritance were probably much influenced by differences in soil fertility and agricultural productivity, the density of settlement and the strength of manorial authority. Inheritance customs, in turn, had a direct influence on rates of family formation and therefore on the labour supply. But equally important to an understanding of the origins of cottage industry, inheritance customs had a strong effect on the pattern of landholding and the size of farms. The cross-linkages proliferate each time one 'factor' or another is examined.

In many ways the Kent Weald was a model proto-industrial *pays*. The Weald was a typical 'wood-pasture' region – like almost all the sixteenth-century proto-industrial areas (West and South Yorkshire, the clothing region covering East Somerset, West Wiltshire and parts of Gloucestershire, the Black Country and the major clothing area straddling the Essex–Suffolk border). In geographical terms it was part of the upland or highland zone of Britain – whereas many other wood-pasture *pays* were not. In geological terms the Wealden clays were generally unproductive soils compared to the rest of Kent and much of Sussex. Because of its topography and geology the Weald was settled at a much later date than the remainder of southeastern England. It remained predominantly wooded – without being a royal forest – until the high middle ages. The Weald was only permanently settled during the population 'boom' of the twelfth and thirteenth centuries. This was significantly later than was the case for most wood-pasture districts of England outside of the far north and far southwest. When it was settled, land in the Weald was held in severalty, and large, nucleated settlements were rare. The prevailing form was the hamlet of a handful of enclosed farms. Because of its infertile land, settlers had to be offered extremely advantageous terms by the Weald's aristocratic overlords. The result – at least to begin with – was a patchwork of individually held small farms, paying negligible ground rents and owing few or no labour services to their 'lords '. This pattern of free tenures and low outgoings encouraged the multiplication of small farms and an active land market. At the same time, the free alienation of holdings and the economic ups and downs of the fifteenth and early sixteenth centuries permitted the accumulation of larger than subsistence holdings by a minority of Wealden families.

Seigniorial authority was also weak in the Weald because lordship over land was so fragmented. Relatively weak aristocratic power seems to be another one of the common factors linking many proto-industrial regions. Weaker feudal authority seems to have gone hand-in-hand with more fragmented landownership, early enclosures and larger numbers of freeholders and smallholders. To use the language of the eighteenth and nineteenth centuries, proto-industrial areas were more likely to lie in regions of 'open' than of 'closed' parishes. 'Open' parishes are especially typical of forest regions – and of former forest regions like the Weald. Such regions were the home of industry and craft production well back into the middle ages, especially those based on raw materials available in the forest: wood (charcoal) and iron.[2]

In terms of farming regimes too, the Weald was a model proto-industrial area. As described in chapter 4, farming was heavily tipped in the direction of pastoral husbandry. This was also the case in many other proto-industrial areas: the clothmaking regions of the West Country clothing region, West Yorkshire and the valleys of the Stour and the Colne in Essex and Suffolk; and the metalworking districts of South Staffordshire, the Arden district and South Yorkshire.[3] Kent Weald farms usually had twice as many acres of pasture as arable, and the bulk of their grazing land supported cattle. To the extent that Wealden farms produced surpluses, their marketable 'crop' was cattle. Their arable fields were divided almost equally between wheat, and oats and pulses. They grew very little barley. When the Weald is considered as part of the wider southeastern region, consisting of Kent, Sussex and Surrey, it obviously formed a distinct interior (or 'upland') zone which exported certain commodities and imported others from the surrounding Lowland zone of both Kent and Sussex. In one sense, the model of two, interdependent agricultural zones described by Mendels is discernible in the two zones described here. But the two southeastern zones (inner Weald and surrounding Lowlands) did not function reciprocally in quite the way suggested by Mendels's model. In reality these zones exchanged *agricultural* surpluses between one another: the Weald exported cattle (and possibly some dairy products) and imported barley, while the Lowland zones (for example North Kent) imported beef and exported barley to the Weald. Parts of the inner, Wealden zone did indeed concentrate on craft production – as in Mendels's model – which was exported, but in the case of the Weald its manufactured commodities were produced mainly for distant markets. Only a small share of Wealden cloth production was destined for sale in its associated agricultural zone of intensive cereal production.[4]

[2] E.g., Jean Birrell, 'Peasant Craftsmen in the Medieval Forest', *AgHR*, 17 (1969).

[3] Joan Thirsk, 'Industries in the Countryside', in F. J. Fisher (ed.), *Essays in the Economic and Social History of Tudor and Stuart England* (1961); K. G. Ponting, *The Woollen Industry of South-west England* (1971); G. D. Ramsay, *The Wiltshire Woollen Industry in the Sixteenth and Seventeenth Centuries* (Oxford, 1943); Herbert Heaton, *The Yorkshire Woollen and Worsted Industries* (1920); George Unwin, 'The History of the Cloth Industry in Suffolk', in his *Studies in Economic History* (1927); E. M. Carus-Wilson, 'The Woollen Industry before 1550', in *VCH, Wiltshire*, iv; Marie B. Rowlands, *Masters and Men in the West Midlands Metalware Trades* (Manchester, 1975); Pauline Frost, 'Yeomen and Metalsmiths: Livestock in the Dual Economy of South Staffordshire', *AgHR*, 29 (1981); David Hey, 'The Origins and Early Growth of the Hallamshire Cutlery and Allied Trades' in John Chartres and David Hey (eds.), *English Rural Society, 1500–1800* (1990); V. H. T. Skipp, 'Economic and Social Change in the Forest of Arden, 1530–1649', in *AgHR*, Suppl. to vol. 18 (1970).

[4] Franklin Mendels, 'Seasons and Regions: Agriculture and Industry during the Process of Industrialization', in Sidney Pollard (ed.), *Region und Industrialisierung* (Gottingen, 1980); on the notion of dividing the southeast into interior and coastal fringe zones see Peter Brandon and Brian Short, *The South East from AD 1000* (1990), esp. chapter 1.

Although Gullickson has clearly shown that early modern rural industry could develop successfully in affluent, cereal-growing areas,[5] the experience in England is that almost without exception rural manufacturing developed in pastoral farming regions. On the other hand, by no means all wood-pasture areas supported proto-industry. Gullickson's other key point – that *subsistence* farming and proto-industrialization do not invariably go hand in hand – is borne out by the Kent evidence cited in chapters 2 and 4. Though the Weald may have been a region of subsistence farmers in the central middle ages, by the later fifteenth century – when Wealden clothmaking was rapidly expanding – farm sizes were extremely het-erogeneous. The region supported many large yeoman farms, numerous 'peasant' farmers and a growing number of smallholders – for whom waged labour on neighbouring farms or earnings from cottage industry were essential.

The prevailing inheritance customs in the Kent Weald may also have favoured the growth of cottage industry. But its importance cannot be heavily stressed because 'gavelkind' custom applied throughout Kent, not just in the Weald. Only the more limited argument – that inheritance custom was one of a number of factors which in a specific local context encouraged proto-industry – can be advanced. Gavelkind custom favoured the expansion of rural industry because it permitted the free alienation of all or any part of an estate held in gavelkind, without the consent of either potential heirs or overlord. Lands held in gavelkind were also partible among male heirs. Such customs would have had positive – though indirect – consequences for the establishment of rural industry. In the first place partible inheritance encouraged the establishment of families by *all* sons of landholders because all sons received a share of the family holding (or cash portions in lieu). In regions of impartible inheritance younger sons may have been relatively less likely to establish families. In the Weald, partible inheritance probably led to relatively higher rates of family formation and thus to more rapid population growth. Everything else being equal, rapid population growth favoured cottage industry by providing industrial employers with larger local pools of available labour. Secondly, gavelkind customs indirectly encouraged cottage industry by promoting both the fragmentation of holdings and the greater availability of smallholdings for purchase or to lease (chapter 2 above). The effect of both tendencies was to multiply the numbers of families who had – or could acquire – *some* land: but not enough to be self-sufficient without supplementary earnings from by-employments or agricultural wage labour. Gavelkind custom, of course, also permitted the opposite de-velopment: it made it easier for the enterprising, the ambitious or the lucky to build up their estates because it engendered a more active land market. The fragmentation of holdings caused by gavelkind custom acted to multiply the numbers of potential workers for cottage industry, while the build-up of larger estates facilitated by the

---

[5] Gay L. Gullickson, 'Agriculture and Cottage Industry: Redefining the Causes of Proto-Industrialization', *J.EcH*, 43 (1983).

same custom promoted capital accumulation and the appearance of men who might invest in rural manufacturing. Needless to say, cottage industry did not appear everywhere there was partible inheritance!

Demographic trends and patterns have been seen as crucial to the operation of proto-industry by almost all the contributors to the debate. Does the evidence from the Weald support or undermine their arguments? The answer cannot be a simple one because the proto-industrialization model itself is unsure whether cottage industry was the *cause* or the *consequence* of high population density and rapid population growth. All that the writers on proto-industrialization appear to be sure about is that cottage industry and regions of dense population go together. Or, put the other way, cottage industry seems *not* to have developed in regions with both surplus land and sparse populations.

The Weald was relatively sparsely populated in the high middle ages. Before the region's population could multiply to the levels it had reached in other parts of lowland England the prolonged demographic reverse of the fourteenth and early fifteenth centuries struck. There is little evidence of clothmaking in the Weald before the late fourteenth century. It appears, therefore, that domestic textile production, organized by putting-out clothiers, was established in the Kent Weald at a time when the region was *less* densely populated than surrounding regions. However, the paucity of evidence about local population trends in the fifteenth and early sixteenth centuries is a problem for all historians of this first period of proto-industry. What is known about English textile production and textile exports indicates that the rural cloth industry was established during the period of high population before the plague of 1348/9, but expanded most rapidly in the late fourteenth and early fifteenth centuries – during an era not notable for population pressure in rural areas.[6] Industry in the Weald was established somewhat later than, for example, the West Country undyed broadcloth region. Almost the whole early history of Wealden industry took place during the period of demographic decline or stagnation after 1348. At what point in the fifteenth century demographic stagnation was transformed into demographic advance in the Weald is not clear at all. It is certainly possible that the 'long sixteenth century' of rising population began earlier in Wealden clothing parishes than in the country in general. The earliest local evidence, wills and then parish register data from the 1540s – described in chapter 3 – shows that the population of the Kent Weald – especially in its central, clothing parishes – was growing rapidly by the early sixteenth century.

[6] Chapter 5 above and see also *VCH, Kent*, iii (1932), chapter on 'Industries', some of whose assertions about the early Kentish cloth industry must be treated sceptically; also H. L. Gray, 'The Production and Exportation of English Woollens in the Fourteenth Century', *EHR*, 39 (1924); A. R. Bridbury, *Medieval English Clothmaking* ( ); Herbert Heaton, *Yorkshire and Woollen Industry*; E. H. Carus-Wilson, 'The Woollen Industry before 1550'; E. M. Carus-Wilson and Olive Coleman, *England's Export Trade, 1275–1547* (1963), esp. p. 138–9; John Hatcher, *Plague, Population and the English Economy, 1348–1530* (1977).

The region's population, therefore, was high and growing at a time when English cloth production and exports were accelerating towards their sixteenth-century peaks – in the second quarter of the century. The Wealden population appears to have grown both through natural increase and through immigration from other parts of the county and from Sussex. Demographic growth and high local population densities seem to have been the *consequence* rather than the cause of proto-industrialization in the Weald. None of the evidence suggests that late fifteenth-century clothiers setting up business in the Weald found a region pullulating with poverty-stricken 'subsistence' farmers. On the other hand, even before 1500, landholdings in the Weald were subject to regular fragmentation and therefore the area would have contained a growing population of smallholders. Thus a region might have a substantial number of 'land-poor' smallholders – a potential proto-industrial workforce – and yet not be a 'subsistence farming' region in any conventional sense. The Weald was certainly one such region.

One strand of the proto-industrialization hypothesis is sustained by this case study of the Weald: thriving rural manufacturing does indeed appear to have fostered further demographic growth. Clothmaking parishes in the Weald were typically more densely populated and growing more rapidly than other Wealden parishes by the 1560s. If it was access to cheap or unsettled land that attracted immigrants into the still partially forested Weald in the fourteenth century, by 1500 migrants were lured there by the prospects of obtaining employment in clothmaking *and* cottages at low rents with or without a smallholding. The central Weald, clothmaking parishes were also growing through 'natural increase' during the later sixteenth century. The age at first marriage of women in the sample textile parishes was exceptionally low, and the birth intervals recorded in those same parishes tended to be relatively short – compared to contemporary national data sets. Notwithstanding the understandable scepticism of Houston and Snell, there was a clear link between the economic character of the 'clothing parishes' in the Weald and age at first marriage for women.[7] In *all* of the clothing parishes there was a net surplus of baptisms over burials between about 1560 and 1600.

All these indicators of rapid demographic growth come from the second half of the sixteenth century, *after* the period of brisk expansion of the traditional English woollen industry. Without parish registers, it is impossible to know if the population of proto-industrial districts was growing as rapidly before 1550 as after, or the relative contributions of migration and indigenous demographic growth to that expansion. Immigration probably played a more important role in the late fifteenth and very early sixteenth centuries than it did after 1550. In the latter half of the fifteenth century the burgeoning Wealden textile industry acted as a 'pull' factor in attracting inward migration. A hundred years later the Weald was densely

---

[7] R. A. Houston and K. D. M. Snell, 'Proto-industrialization?' *Hist.J,* 27 (1984); R. A. Houston, *The Population History of Britain and Ireland, 1500–1750* (1992), p. 84.

populated – yet still growing by 'natural' increase – while the local broadcloth industry was no longer expanding. The parish registration data analysed in chapter 3 in fact suggests that more people were emigrating from the proto-industrial parishes – than moving into them – by 1600. The region's population never became wholly dependent on cottage industry: the proto-industrialization model's worst scenario – of an increasingly landless, proletarianized workforce, rendered totally dependent on capitalist employers by the sheer weight of their own numbers – did not materialize in the early modern Weald. Emigration seems to have acted as a regulator which limited population growth in the most densely populated industrialized parishes. This outcome was not repeated in every English proto-industrial region: where the demand for a district's manufactured commodities held firm, the labour supply continued to grow even as the workforce became increasingly dependent on cottage industry. The examples that come to mind here include the West Yorkshire woollen and worsted districts and the Leicestershire hosiery region.[8]

Yet another factor in the equation of successful proto-industrialization was natural resources. Three crucial resources were available to the clothiers and ironmasters of the Weald: fast-flowing streams, abundant wood for fuel and, finally, certain minerals crucial to manufacturing woollens and iron. Thirty years ago Joan Thirsk justifiably cast doubt on traditional geographical explanations of industrial location – which over-emphasized natural resources and good communications links with ports and markets as the key reasons for the development of industry. Our assessment of the factors which gave rise to Wealden industry has similarly given greater weight to economic, agrarian and social circumstances. Nevertheless, it remains notable that cottage industry frequently *did* emerge in wooded regions with plentiful water supplies and close to key minerals. The location of early ironmaking and metalware industries did indeed have a great deal to do with access to seams of iron ore, to wood which could be converted into charcoal to fuel furnaces and to water to drive hammer mills.[9] The presence of all three did not guarantee the establishment of ironmaking or ironworking in a given region. Or that, once established, it would continue indefinitely in such a region. The demise of Wealden iron – *before* either its fuel or its mineral resources were exhausted – certainly demonstrates that factors other than natural resources influenced industrial location. But for several centuries the production of cloth and iron in the Weald profited from the plentiful local supplies of water and wood. Local, of course, has to

---

[8] Heaton, *Yorkshire Woollen and Worsted Industry*; Pat Hudson, 'From Manor to Mill: the West Riding in Transition' in M. Berg, P. Hudson and M. Sonenscher (eds.), *Manufacture in Town and County before the Factory* (1983); Hudson, 'Proto-industrialisation: the Case of the West Riding Textile Industry', *History Workshop*, no. 12 (1981); David Levine, 'The Demographic Implications of Rural Industrialization', *Social Hist.*, 2 (1977); Levine, *Family Formation in an Age of Nascent Capitalism* (1977).

[9] See chapter 5 above and H. R. Schubert, *History of the British Iron and Steel Industry* (1957); Ernest Straker, *Wealden Iron* (1931); G. Hammersley, 'The Charcoal Iron Industry and its Fuel', *EcHR*, 2nd ser., 26 (1973); Henry Cleere and David Crossley, *The Iron Industry of the Weald* (Leicester, 1985).

be taken very loosely. In the case of the Wealden textile industry, one important mineral – fuller's earth – was to be found not within the Weald but a few miles to the north in Boxley. And, as Thirsk rightly pointed out, the East Anglian textile industry operated profitably for centuries with fuller's earth imported from Kent.[10]

Similar suspicion is needed about the allegedly decisive importance of fast-moving streams to the rural textile industry. Decades ago E. M. Carus-Wilson asserted that English rural clothmaking could be traced to an 'industrial revolution' in the thirteenth century: the substitution of water-powered fulling mills for hand fulling. In her words,

With the invention of the fulling mill, water power was becoming a decisive factor in the location of the [cloth] industry, and it began to concentrate on the swift, clear streams of the north and west, in remote valleys beyond the bounds of chartered towns.[11]

However, Carus-Wilson's model not only failed to encompass the two most important rural woollen districts of the sixteenth century (Wiltshire–Somerset–Gloucestershire and East Anglia); it also over-rated the significance of fulling mills. As has been shown in chapter 6, very few fulling mills were required to process thousands of broadcloths. Though there were throughout the sixteenth century several fulling mills *in* the Weald itself, much of the region's cloth was processed by mills in the Maidstone area. In fact the most profitable sites for fulling mills in Kent did not always become clothmaking centres. Broadcloth was a valuable enough commodity to be carried a few miles to be fulled.

Water was, nevertheless, a crucial component of clothmaking, and the industry was unlikely to be found in regions *without* dependable streams. Water was needed both for washing the raw wool and for dyeing it. A good water supply was therefore a necessary (if not a sufficient) factor in locating rural clothmaking. Even more than for clothmaking, water was an indispensable resource for the Wealden ironmasters. Indeed most of the remains of the sixteenth- and seventeenth-century iron industry consists of ponds and other waterworks constructed to provide a consistent supply of water to drive their mills.[12] The combination of local iron ore and numerous small streams flowing into narrow valleys meant that the Weald was the ideal location for the improved blast furnace technology imported from fifteenth-century France. The same combination was to be found in almost all other early modern ironmaking districts; as was one other key component of both iron and textile manufacture: wood.

The crucial importance of wood to fuel the manufacturing processes carried out by clothiers and ironmasters alike is highlighted by their perennial competition for this valuable resource. The clothiers were already petitioning against the

---

[10] Robert H. S. Robertson, *Fuller's Earth: a History of Calcium Montmorillonite* (Hythe, 1986); Thirsk, 'Industries in the Countryside', p. 72.

[11] E. M. Carus-Wilson, 'An Industrial Revolution of the Thirteenth Century', *EcHR*, 11 (1941), reprinted in *Essays in Economic History*, i (1954), p. 52.

[12] Straker, *Wealden Iron*; Cleere and Crossley, *Iron Industry of the Weald*.

ironmasters' allegedly insatiable appetite for wood during the early 1570s. Two bills were introduced in Parliament in 1581 against the erecting of ironworks and for the preservation of woods, and yet another bill was initiated in the Commons 'for the maintenance of clothing in the parish of Cranbrook and within eight miles of the same' in 1593. More than a generation later – in 1637 – Cranbrook clothing interests complained to the privy council that the ironmaster and royal gunfounder, John Browne, was cornering the local timber market, due to which 'the ancient trade of clothmaking is likely to fall into decay'.[13] Given the fact that fuel accounted for around two-thirds of the cost of converting ore to bar-iron, it is hardly surprising that – after the Weald – the major sites of iron production should have been the Forest of Dean and South Wales.[14] Clothiers also consumed wood in large quantities – especially to heat their dyevats – although their fuel costs made up a much smaller proportion of manufacturing costs than it did for ironmaking. But they didn't *need* to use wood, at least according to the certificate of a London dyer (presumably procured by John Browne), who testified in 1637 that wool and cloth could be dyed using 'sea coal' as well or better than with wood.[15]

The location of the Weald, more than almost any comparable district, also made it an ideal proto-industrial region. It had the advantage of easy access to markets for its products. Its primary market was London, which could be reached quickly by packhorses and wagons directly from the Weald, or by a combination of land transport to anchorages on the Medway and coasting vessels to the capital. Supplies of better-quality wool and of imported dyestuffs could be obtained by clothiers by the same routes. Wools of lesser quality could be purchased easily from North and South Downs farmers in Kent and Sussex and from Romney Marsh. The region's cloth reached the market at Blackwell Hall within a day or two. Wealden iron may have taken a few more days, but it arrived in its prime market much more rapidly than iron produced in South Wales, Gloucestershire or the West Midlands. No other sixteenth-century manufacturing region had such rapid access to the metropolis, and this should have given Wealden commodities a comparative advantage over those of other districts.

Finally there is the issue of access to capital. As many historians have pointed out, pre-factory industry – and even early factories – required much smaller initial capital inputs than modern manufacturing industry. It was shown in chapter 7 that Wealden entrepreneurs never required vast sums to set up as putting-out clothiers, and that such men were able to raise sufficient capital from family resources alone. Only ironmaking demanded major capital inputs, and these in general came from

---

[13] Certificate of wood consumed by ironmaking and clothmaking, 1573–4: PRO SP 12/93 fo. 148; complaint of 1575 about the decay of the cloth trade in Kent: SP 12/106 no. 49; 1581 bills: *Journals of the House of Commons*, i, pp. 120–5, and HMC, *13th Report*, App. Pt. 4, pp. 75–6; 1593 bill: HMC, *3rd Report*, App. p.7; 1637: *Cal. State Papers, Domestic*, 1637, pp. 290–1.

[14] Hammersley, 'The Charcoal Iron Industry'; D. C. Coleman, *Industry in Tudor and Stuart England* (1975), pp. 42–3; Schubert, *History of the British Iron and Steel Industry*.

[15] *Cal. State Papers, Dom.*, 1637, p. 514.

two sources: the savings of the ironmasters and their families, and the investments of local gentry and noble landowners. The latter specialized in fixed capital investments – the ironworks themselves – and often provided the land on which the furnaces, forges and waterworks were sited. Their extensive landholdings were also a key source of timber supplies needed by Wealden ironmasters. The ironmasters themselves raised their own circulating capital, to buy raw materials and pay wages.

Capital investment from London seems to have had relatively little importance in financing Wealden industry, with the exception of a few major ironworks. We know that the royal gunfounder, John Browne, had recourse to the London capital market in the early seventeenth century and that he more than once found himself unable to repay his creditors. But John Browne's gunfounding and ironmaking operations were exceptionally large, and by no means typical of Wealden ironmaking.[16] In raising capital Wealden entrepreneurs – who were more frequently than not landowners and rentiers themselves – had no special difficulties and probably a number of advantages over manufacturers in other parts of England.

The list of circumstances and 'factors' which favour or encourage the development of cottage industry suggest that the Weald was a 'natural' – even predictable – location for proto-industry: a tick can be entered in the 'affirmative' box for almost all the relevant points. The 'fit' between the Weald and the 'model' list of factors leading to proto-industrialization is close indeed. But so too was it for a number of other sixteenth-century centres of cottage industry. Northeast Lancashire was an upland region of pastoral agriculture, abundant common land, fragmented holdings, secure customary tenures and weak manorial lordship – which experienced rapid demographic growth in the late sixteenth and early seventeenth centuries. According to John Swain, the only thing it lacked in reproducing Joan Thirsk's model of a region ripe for cottage industry was the custom of partible inheritance. Therefore he rules out partible inheritance as a significant precondition for proto-industrialization, or a crucial cause of the enlarged local labour supply. Swain argues that the key to the development of cottage industry was fragmentation of landholdings, and the increasing demand for part-time employment which fragmentation engendered.[17] Yet it can hardly be denied that partible inheritance fostered the fragmentation of family holdings where that custom prevailed.

The history of textile manufacture in the West Riding of Yorkshire – one of the few proto-industrial regions later to industrialize – suggests there is room for debate on another dimension of rural industrialization, its economic organization. Pat Hudson has argued that there is a correlation between areas of poorer land and weak lordship, and the development of clothmaking on a putting-out basis. Her

---

[16] Art. in supplementary volume of the *DNB* and *Cal. State Papers, Dom.*, 1634–5, p. 385.
[17] John T. Swain, *Industry before the Industrial Revolution: North-East Lancashire, c. 1500–1640* (Manchester, 1986).

example is the Yorkshire worsted industry. By contrast, areas of stronger seigniorial authority (which tended to be situated on better soils) resulted in cottage industry organized by small-scale, independent producers who worked up their own raw materials – not 'true' proto-industry according to some definitions. Yet the proto-industrial clothmaking of northeast Lancashire was also not organized by putting-out capitalists, even though the region was one of weak manorial authority. The organization of rural clothmaking by petty producers – rather than by putting-out employers – also characterized the cloth industry of rural North Wales around 1600.[18] Clothmaking in Kent conformed more closely to Hudson's model, however. Broadcloth production developed in a region of extremely weak lordship and poor soils, and was most definitely controlled by putting-out capitalists. At the same time, kerseymaking evolved in the region of better soils and stronger manorial organization to the north of the Weald – and was in the hands of small, independent clothiers, not dissimilar to the kerseymakers of the Halifax district.

Yet another hole in the apparently seamless fabric of the proto-industrial model is exposed when historians attempt to specify the topography most adaptable to cottage industry. Two categories have been proposed most frequently by historians: (1) wood-pasture regions and (2) hilly or forested, 'upland' *pays*. The former label defines a region by reference to the agricultural systems adopted by its human inhabitants, while the latter refers to the natural landscape itself. But the territory covered by the two categories is by no means identical. Wood-pasture systems evolved in many different topographical situations – not exclusively in hilly or forested, 'upland' landscapes. Early modern, English rural clothmaking was to be found primarily in wood-pasture regions of one sort or another. But some of these proto-industrial regions were hilly and/or forested upland districts – the Weald, northeast Lancashire, parts of the West Riding – but others were most definitely not. The two dominant centres of sixteenth- and seventeenth-century rural clothmaking – the main West Country undyed broadcloth region of northwest Wiltshire, north Somerset and southern Gloucestershire, and the coloured cloth region of the Stour valley on the Suffolk–Essex border – had wood-pasture farming systems like the Weald. But neither lay in upland or forested regions. Rural clothmaking also developed in certain fertile districts of lowland Lancashire, as well as in the cereal-growing pays de Caux in Upper Normandy.[19]

Two other notable conditions, however, are shared by the otherwise disparate regions of rural manufacturing. The first was emphasized by Thirsk in 1961: old enclosures and weak manorial structures.[20] Both the 'upland' or 'forested' regions of proto-industry like the Weald, and the two larger broadcloth centres which grew

[18] Pat Hudson, 'Proto-industrialization'; Swain, *Industry before the Industrial Revolution*; Walton, 'Proto-industrialisation'.

[19] John K. Walton, 'Proto-industrialisation and the First Industrial Revolution: the Case of Lancashire', in Pat Hudson (ed.), *Regions and Industries* (1989); Gullickson, 'Agriculture and Cottage Industry'.

[20] Thirsk, 'Industries in the Countryside', pp. 74–6.

up in 'lowland', river valleys in the West Country and in the Stour valley were areas of enclosed farms and relatively weak lordship. The two circumstances tended to evolve hand-in-hand. In quite different landscapes, this socio-economic framework was favourable to rural industry. In part this was because it permitted or encouraged population growth through in-migration. But, equally important, it encouraged the proliferation of small farmers and of petty freeholders, creating a social structure that also appears to have been a crucial pre-condition of successful proto-industry.

The second factor that appears to characterize most proto-industrial regions was the need for non-agricultural employment – sometimes seasonal, in other cases throughout the year – by a regional population that was too large for the prevailing structures of agriculture and landholding to sustain. The nature of agriculture in such regions need not be identical. Gullickson is right to stress that 'large-scale cottage industry could and did spread in regions of commercial cereal agriculture'; but it did so only if the region contained a class of under-employed cottagers![21] Cottage industry, therefore, was far more *likely* to spread in wood-pasture regions than in champion districts. 'Landlessness' is another way of describing a relatively abundant labour supply in an early modern, rural context. Fragmentation of holdings, the 'crucial factor' suggested by Swain, resulted in 'landlessness', which Gullickson points to as one of just two 'distinguishing features' of proto-industrial regions. Non-agricultural work might be seasonal – and engaged in by all members of a family at times of reduced demand for farm work – or it might be supplemental work performed by certain persons in the household throughout the year. Finally, in certain regions of 'mature' proto-industry, non-agricultural work came to be the primary employment of most of the family.

One powerful criticism of the proto-industrialization concept itself is that it is used to describe almost any non-agrarian work performed in the countryside. When the term is used this loosely, there appears to have been no end of 'proto-industrial' regions. Between areas where indigenous raw materials were converted into 'manufactured' commodities for local markets by independent artisans, and regions where putting-out capitalists organized the domestic production of their own raw materials primarily for sale in distant markets, or even districts where both forms of manufacturing took place side by side, proto-industrialization seems to have been absent from only a minority of the English countryside!

A typical case might be that of the five parishes, formerly part of the Forest of Arden, whose economic and social evolution has been convincingly analysed by Victor Skipp.[22] In the course of the seventeenth century – and in response to a burgeoning population – a wide variety of non-agrarian artisanal employment developed in the district. The jobs spread across the spectrum of manufacturing and craft trades – from weaving to metalwork to the wood and leather trades – and tended increasingly to be full-time rather than the by-employments of small farming

---

[21] Gullickson, 'Agriculture and Cottage Industry', p. 848.
[22] V. Skipp, *Crisis and Development* (Cambridge, 1978).

families. Skipp – wisely – makes no claims about proto-industrialization for this district. But by some definitions the Arden parishes might be labelled proto-industrial. What is absent in Arden is the concentration in a small area of a large number of specialized rural workers engaged in the production of manufactured commodities for non-local markets – the likes of which could be found in the Black Country during this period.[23]

The widespread lack of precision in describing well-established rural manufacturing or cottage industry has made it all the more difficult to explain its origins. The most convincing explanations for the 'rise' of proto-industry during the sixteenth to eighteenth centuries – population pressure, landlessness and the attractiveness of the consequent rural labour 'surplus' to urban capital – can hardly serve equally as credible explanations for the advent of rural clothmaking in the fourteenth and fifteenth centuries.

Such problems with the proto-industrialization model are, in principle at least, manageable. If a narrower, more precise definition of proto-industrialization is adhered to – one that limits its use to regions of relatively intense, capitalist manufacturing of commodities for distant markets – then the notion will remain useful if only for comparative, descriptive purposes. It is the second stage of the model – how proto-industrialization leads to industrialization – that remains most troublesome. For the majority of proto-industrial regions, historians need to explain de-industrialization rather than the successful transition to modern industry. That objective is especially apposite to our case study of the Weald. For if Wealden Kent was one of England's older proto-industrial regions, it was also the first to de-industrialize. It is the relatively early demise of cottage industry in the Weald as much as its appearance in the first place that may offer useful pointers to students of the proto-industrialization debate.

The chronology of industrial decline in the Weald is relatively well known and not in contention. The lingering decline of the Wealden broadcloth industry – which lasted from the 1620s to the 1670s – was due in part to difficulties faced by all regions which produced heavy woollens. The Wiltshire undyed broadcloth trade reached its zenith in the early decades of the seventeenth century, after which it decayed, to be replaced by the production of lighter, coloured 'Spanish' cloths.[24] The same pattern – a decline in demand for the region's traditional broadcloth in the first half of the seventeenth century, offset by rising production of the region's 'New Draperies' – obtained in the East Anglian textile districts.

The Kent broadcloth industry – like the rest of the English export trades – enjoyed its last boom decade in the years after the 1604 peace treaty with Spain. It

---

[23] E.g., Marie B. Rowlands, *Masters and Men in the West Midland Metalware Trades before the Industrial Revolution* (Manchester, 1975).

[24] G. D. Ramsay, *The Wiltshire Woollen Industry in the 16th and 17th Centuries* (1943); K. G. Ponting, *A History of the West of England Cloth Industry* (1957), esp. chapters 4–5.

was hit hard by the general slump in Dutch demand for English woollens associated with the Cockayne 'project' of 1614–16. Cloth production may have begun to recover by 1620, only to be dealt another severe blow by the trade and currency crisis which struck all of northern Europe about 1621. It was noticed in chapter 6 how Kentish broadcloth was unusually hard hit by the collapse in European markets by 1622.[25] Production recovered by the mid 1620s, only to be thrown into confusion again by another trade crisis in 1630–1. The 'recovery' after each successive export crisis was to a lower level of production and sales than the previous one. The central reality was that the most important markets for fine Kentish broadcloth – in Germany and central Europe – were severely disrupted by war, and not likely to revive even after the Peace of Westphalia in 1648. Limited production of traditional Wealden broadcloth continued until the end of the century and beyond. A few wealthy clothiers persevered into the Restoration period, but their numbers are minuscule compared to the numerous successful clothiers of the Elizabethan and early Jacobean eras.[26] The reality of industrial decline was reflected in a 1673 petition from Benenden – once at the heart of the broadcloth region – which complained of the 'great and general poverty in respect of the trade of clothmaking within the said parish'; and in the report of the rector of Biddenden in 1683 that the parish was 'not so populous now as formerly when the clothing trade there flourished'.[27] Contemporary complaint of economic decay and demographic decline is supported by Husbands's recent analysis of relative change between 1524/5 and the 1670s among a large sample of English communities. He found that by the Hearth Tax era Wealden communities had lost both population and aggregate taxable wealth relative to England as a whole.[28]

The iron industry of the Weald – always more prominent in Sussex than in Kent – went into a similar, though not quite terminal, decline in the seventeenth century. Against the background of an overall decrease in the relative importance of Wealden iron production and expanding output from the Midlands and South Wales, the Kent iron industry survived because the Crown found it convenient to produce ordnance there. Even in wartime, in 1653, there were just seven active furnaces in Kent (compared to twenty-nine remaining in Sussex). By the early eighteenth century the Kent iron industry was reduced to three furnaces and one forge, producing ordnance. Hardly any iron for peacetime uses was being produced in the Weald by the late seventeenth century.[29]

Why, then, did this successful, well-situated region disappear from the map of proto-industrial pioneers? And drop out long before the rise of the factory system in certain proto-industrial areas? The answers are by no means simple ones. Not

[25] See p. 159 above.
[26] See inventories of John Buckland of Staplehurst (1664) and John Barrett of Biddenden (1696): KAO PRC 27/16/10 and 27/34/69.
[27] Reports quoted in C. W. Chalklin, *Seventeenth Century Kent* (1965), pp. 121–2.
[28] Chris Husbands, 'Regional Change in a Pre-Industrial Economy', *J. of Hist. Geography*, 13 (1987), pp. 352, 354. [29] Chalklin, *Seventeenth Century Kent*, pp. 130–2.

only have historians been less interested in de-industrialization than in industrialization, but when they have tried to explain the failure of proto-industry to evolve into modern industry no single answer has met with general satisfaction. A number of solutions to this problem have been advanced for the Weald. Each will be examined in turn, before an alternative explanation is suggested. Throughout this study the Wealden cloth industry has been seen as the crucial proto-industry of the Weald. By the same logic, its demise must be seen as the main event of the region's de-industrialization.

The question of Kent's failing seventeenth-century industries was tackled many years ago by D. C. Coleman. His thesis was taken up and expanded by C. W. Chalklin in the 1960s, who cited the following reasons for the decline of traditional Kentish woollens: increased competition from Continental clothmakers; political disruptions to the industry because of the Thirty Years War abroad and the civil wars and interregnum at home; the emigration of skilled textile workers from the Weald to Europe (including the 2,000 workers said to have gone to the Palatinate in 1616); competition for labour from the expanding dockyards and from fruit- and hop-growing in mid Kent; and finally, the high cost of labour which made Kent broadcloth uncompetitive. It is the last reason – high relative labour costs – suggested first by Coleman, that Chalklin thinks the most important.[30] There is certainly much to recommend itself in Chalklin's long list of possible causes of industrial decline. But of them, the notion that Wealden textiles collapsed because of inflated labour costs is least convincing. For one thing, the same period witnessed the rise of successful worsted, silk and threadmaking industries in Sandwich, Canterbury and Maidstone – which Chalklin helpfully describes.[31] For another, it is likely that wages were falling in real terms – not rising – during the crisis decades between 1615 and 1645 or 1655. This explanation also fails to see the collapse of Continental demand for Kentish broadcloth as part of the wider changes in the structure of European textile markets. The emigration of workers away from the Weald is more consequence than cause of the decline of Wealden cottage industry. It is arguable that Chalklin's least favoured reasons for industrial decline – disruption of Continental markets and increased production of woollens in central Europe – are in fact the most convincing.

A strikingly different explanation of the Weald's industrial decline – influenced by recent theories of dependency and under-development – has been proposed by Brian Short. In his view, the Weald was – as late as the seventeenth century – an under-developed region. Its proto-industry can be seen as a form of what students of the Third World now call 'dependent capitalist development'. In Short's account the Wealden entrepreneurs were a 'clique', 'guided by national or international market forces', whose businesses were 'externally controlled and increasingly

---

[30] Chalklin, *Seventeenth Century Kent*, pp. 115–23; and citing D. C. Coleman, 'The Economy of Kent under the Later Stuarts', unpublished Ph.D thesis, University of London, 1951, pp. 153–4.

[31] Chalklin, *Seventeenth Century Kent*, pp. 123–9.

dependent on national, metropolitan and international forces'.[32] Short describes the Weald as a region whose industries were heavily dependent on metropolitan capital and whose agriculture was backward and starved of capital investment. In the course of the seventeenth century, according to Short, external capital – for wider national reasons – was withdrawn from Wealden industries and de-industrialization inevitably followed. At the same time, Short rejects the general explanation offered by Mendels and others for the de-industrialization of proto-industrial regions: at certain times there is a 'comparative advantage' for a region to switch from cottage industry to food production, especially when the former proto-industrial region has comparatively easy access to an expanding urban market. 'Wealden farming did not oust manufactures', asserts Short, because, 'Wealden farming could not compete with the returns to be gained from industry'.[33]

There is much food for thought in Short's theoretically informed interpretation of the Weald's industrial decline. It has the merit of seeing the industries of the region as part of a wider economic structure. The bulk of the Weald's cloth output was eventually sold to Continental buyers (chapter 6). The great majority of the region's iron production was likewise destined for non-local markets. From the start the Weald was tied into wider trading networks. But of course, this could be said of all true proto-industrial regions: those that evolved into centres of modern industry as well as those that did not. The same point – that Wealden producers were tied to non-local buyers – could be made about the meat producers of the Weald. The prosperity of their industry too was in a sense 'dependent' on external forces.

In the end, Short's model is unconvincing because it attempts to force sixteenth- and seventeenth-century reality into the straitjacket of modern dependency models. More particularly, it wrongly assumes that Wealden industry was heavily reliant on external capital – without giving any evidence of such dependency. Detailed study of the Wealden cloth industry, and of its entrepreneurs, shows that clothiers rarely, if ever, benefited from metropolitan investment. In fact, *they* extended credit to the London wholesalers. The capital necessary for their clothmaking businesses came from family and neighbours, from the retained profits of clothmaking, from their farming and leasing businesses and occasionally from their own mercantile activities within the Weald. The situation is more complicated in the case of the Wealden iron industry. With the cost of an iron furnace and its necessary waterworks amounting to at least £500, the capital required to establish and operate an ironworks usually derived in part from local Wealden landowners and in part from the ironmasters themselves. Investment from outside the region was the least important source of capital for the typical ironmaking business.

If Wealden manufacturing was not then the victim of outside capitalists'

[32] Brian Short, 'The De-industrialisation Process: a Case Study in the Weald, 1600–1850', in Pat Hudson (ed.), *Regions and Industries* (1989), quotations from pp. 162, 164.

[33] Short, 'De-industrialisation', p. 172.

withdrawing their investments, what killed off the region's apparently flourishing industries? In particular, why did the Wealden broadcloth industry – which by 1600 had enriched scores of local entrepreneurs and which still employed so many thousands of others – disappear within two generations of the export boom of 1604–14?

The key to this problem can be found by comparing the course of developments in the Wealden woollen industry with trends in clothmaking elsewhere in England. In almost every major region except the Weald, clothiers responded to overseas competition and wavering foreign and domestic markets by modifying the commodities they produced. A summary description of the English woollen industry as a whole would be very simple:

Clothiers reacted to reduced foreign demand for traditional broadcloth by diversifying their products, and especially by increasing production of the 'New Draperies', or other new fabrics. As a result the overall volume and value of English woollen cloth sold abroad rose during the seventeenth century.

Historians have frequently illustrated the details of this general model for East Anglia and for the West Country. In both cases local clothiers modified their own products. Nothing of the sort occurred in the Kent Weald. Here clothiers stuck to their traditional, high-quality – and high-cost – broadcloth through difficult times, perhaps thinking that there would always be a market for the finest quality broadcloth. By the Restoration prospects were thin indeed, but Wealden clothiers failed to read even the most obvious of signs. Their industry kept contracting – until it disappeared.

Only if the whole county of Kent is taken as a unit is the more usual scenario of English textile development reproduced. For a Kentish 'New Draperies' industry *was* established in the late sixteenth century, not in the traditional clothmaking region, but in East Kent towns. By the mid seventeenth century a diverse range of woollen and worsted cloths which could compete successfully in Continental Europe with the traditional, dyed in the wool broadcloth of the Weald was available. The makers of Salisbury and Worcester woollens too – like the traditional Kent clothiers – suffered heavily from the competition of the cheaper, coloured 'Spanish' cloths of Somerset and Wiltshire. And, like the Wealden textile industry, commercial clothmaking there declined. The message is not difficult to interpret, nor unique to the seventeenth century. The decay of rural clothmaking had little to do with level of wages clothiers paid their outworkers: we have seen that wages represented only a minority of their costs of production. And it had even less to do with the withdrawal of external finance, since Wealden clothiers had never relied on outside investment. The capitalist clothmakers of the Kent Weald failed because they failed as entrepreneurs. The clothiers themselves, of course, rarely faced bankruptcy or poverty. As their industry declined some simply turned to commercial farming, while others leased out their lands to local farmers. Even if Brian Short is correct in insisting that there was little capital invested in agricultural improvements on Wealden farms, investment in land and in livestock was the natural, local alternative to clothmaking. Thus, in a sense, Mendels's model of comparative advantage applies to the seventeenth-century Weald. At a time when markets for their traditional *manufactured* commodities seemed to be in decline, the metropolitan market for their *agricultural* commodities continued to grow. For many Wealden 'entrepreneurs' it was easier to withdraw from clothmaking altogether than to take risks in developing new products. The financial losses they might suffer by closing down their clothmaking businesses were minimal, and they could quite quickly transfer their capital into land or commercial livestock farming for the increasing appetite of a growing metropolis – or both!

How well then does the proto-industrialization 'model' compare with the 'empirical reality' of Wealden manufacturing from the fifteenth to the seventeenth centuries? The answer depends upon whether the historian chooses to test proto-industrialization as a rigid, predictive model of long-term historical change, as little more than fascinating historical speculation, or simply as a description of some of the linkages revealed by the evolution of early capitalist manufacturing in the countryside. As a comparative model, proto-industrialization is most convincing in its description of the social and demographic impact of fully developed cottage industry. It is less persuasive as an all-embracing explanation of how rural manufacturing came to develop where it did between the fifteenth and the eighteenth centuries. And it is equally incapable of suggesting any guidelines as to which proto-industrial centres would be transformed into 'modern' industry, and which would not. Or even of predicting in which regions rural industry would diversify and thereby endure for considerable periods of time; or instead – like the Weald of Kent – flourish for a few centuries and then vanish, leaving only traces for historians to pick over.

Bibliography

Note: Place of publication is London, unless otherwise cited.

A. Principal Manuscript Sources

Corpus Christi College, Cambridge
MS 122 (1563 Visitation of Canterbury diocese)

Cambridge University Library
Hengrave Hall Deposit MSS. 78/ 1–2

Canterbury Cathedral Library
Parish Registers of Shadoxhurst and Wittersham
Bishop's Transcripts for parishes of Frittenden and Smarden
Depositions in ecclesiastical courts: X.10.7–21; X.11.1 and PRC 39

East Sussex Record Office, Lewes
Dyke (Hutton) MSS

British Library, London
Add. MSS. 33,899; 34,154; 42,715 (Wotton estate survey);
Cotton. MSS. Titus B.1; Vesp. F.xii
Harl. MSS. 280 (1603 Communicant Survey); 594 (1563 Visitation of Canterbury diocese);
    Harl. Roll Y.4

Clothworkers Company, London
Court Orders, 1536–58

Corporation of London Record Office
Book of Fines

Drapers' Company, London
Queen Elizabeth's College MSS. H/Add. MS. C/AL 1

Public Record Office, London
C1–3 Chancery Proceedings   C 54 Close Rolls
C 66 Patent Rolls   C 78 Decree Rolls
C 142 Inquisitions Post Mortem   CP 25 Feet of Fines

E 101 Accounts
E 150 Inquisitions Post Mortem
E 179 Lay Subsidy Rolls
E 315 Miscellaneous Books
KB 9 Ancient Indictments
PROB 2 Probate inventories
PROB 11 Prerogative Court of Canterbury Enrolled Wills
REQ 2 Proceedings, Court of Requests
SC 2 Court Rolls
SC 11–12 Rentals and Surveys
SP 1, 12, 14, 16 State Papers
STAC 1–9 Proceedings, Court of Star Chamber
Wards 4 Schedules and Extents
Wards 7 Inquisitions Post Mortem

E 134 Depositions
E 159 Memoranda Rolls
E 190 Port Books
E 318 Particulars for Grants
LR 2 Miscellaneous Books

SC 6 Receivers' Accounts

Wards 5 Feodaries' Surveys
Wards 9 Miscellaneous Books

Kent Archives Office, Maidstone
Parish Registers (original) of Bendenden, Biddenden, Brenchley, Chiddingstone (microfilm only), Cowden, Cranbrook, Goudhurst, Hadlow, Halden, Headcorn, Horsmonden, Hunton, Lamberhurst, Newenden (printed copy only), East Peckham, Pembury, Penshurst, Pluckley, Rolvenden, Tenterden and Woodchurch. [Registers of Bethersden, Edenbridge, Hawkhurst, Marden, Sandhurst, Speldhurst, Staplehurst, Tonbridge and Yalding consulted in respective parish churches.]
Other parochial records:
PRC 43/13/41: Staplehurst household communicant list, 1563/4
P100/28/1: Cranbrook household communicant lists, 1608–12
P289/5/1: Pluckley parish rates
TR904: Chiddingstone parish rates
Wills (enrolled) for Rochester diocese in DRb/Pwr; Canterbury diocese PRC 17 and PRC 32
Probate inventories (Canterbury diocese): PRC 10/1–29; PRC 21/1–16; PRC 28/1–4
Canterbury Archdeaconry Court Act Books: PRC 3
Estate and Family Papers:
U24 U31 U38 U47 U49 U71 U78 U86 U106 U180 U195 U200
U249 U280 U282 U301 U350 U383 U409 U442 U455 U513
U514 U660 U705 U708 U769 U787 U789 U813 U814 U908
U934 U1000 U1006 U1024 U1044 U1050 U1061 U1094 U1220
U1299 U1406 U1408 U1450 U1475 U1513 U1542 U1823 U1996
U2087 U2026 U2140 U2315
TR 1295 Browne MSS.
Quarter Session Records: esp. QM/SRc; QM/SR; QM/SI

Bodleian Library, Oxford
Tanner MS. 240 (1569 Visitation of Canterbury diocese)
MS. Top. Kent c.11–12 (Twysden papers)

Nottingham University Library
Middleton MSS.

B. Printed Primary Sources

Accounts of the Roberts Family of Boarzell, Sussex, ed. Robert Tittler, Sussex Record Soc., 71 (1977–9)

Archdeacon Harpsfield's Canterbury Visitations (1556–8), Catholic Record Soc., 45–6 (1950–51)
Calendar of Patent Rolls, Edward VI–Elizabeth I, 16 vols. (1924–74)
Calendar of Quarter Sessions Records, 1574–1622 and *Calendar of Early Quarter Session Rolls, 1596–1605*, ed. Kent Archives Office
Deloney, *The Works of*, ed. F. O. Mann (1912)
Household and Farm Inventories in Oxfordshire, 1550–90, ed. M. A. Havinden (Oxfordshire Record Soc., 1965)
The Inrichment of the Weald of Kent, 1625 (attrib. to Gervase Markham)
Lambarde, William, *A Perambulation of Kent* (first published 1576), (1826)
Letters and Papers, Foreign and Domestic, of the Reign of Henry VIII, 21 vols. (1862–1932) (abbreviated to *LP*)
The Ordinances of the Clothworkers' Company, published by the Clothworkers Co. of London (1881)
The Registers of Staplehurst, 1538–1695, ed. J. S. F. Chamberlain, 4 vols. (Canterbury, 1907–14)
Rye Shipping Records, 1566–1590, ed. Richard Dell, Sussex Record Soc., 64 (1965–6)
Sidney Ironworks Accounts, 1541–1573, ed. D. W. Crossley (Camden Soc., 4th ser., 15, 1975)
A Survey of the Manor of Wye, ed. H. E. Muhlfeld (New York, 1933)
Tudor Royal Proclamations, ed. Paul L. Hughes and James F. Larkin (3 vols., 1969)

C. Secondary Sources

Allison, K. J., 'An Elizabethan Village Census', *BIHR*, 36 (1963)
Avery, David, 'Male Occupations in a Rural Middlesex Parish', *Local Population Studies*, 2 (1969)
Baines, Edward, *Account of the Woollen Manufacture of England* (1858), ch. 1
Baker, A. R. H., 'The Field Systems of Kent', unpublished Ph.D thesis, University of London, 1963
Baker, A. R. H. and R. A. Butlin (eds.), *Studies in Field Systems in the British Isles* (1973) 'Changes in the Later Middle Ages', in H. C. Darby (ed.), *New Historical Geography of Britain* (1974)
Benedict, Philip (ed.), *Cities and Social Change in Early Modern France* (1989)
Beresford, M. W., 'The Common Informer, the Penal Statutes and Economic Regulation', *EcHR*, 2nd ser., 10 (1957)
Beresford, M. W. *Lay Subsidies and Poll Taxes* (1963)
Berg, Maxine, Pat Hudson and Michael Sonenscher (eds.), *Manufacture in Town and County before the Factory* (1983)
Berry, William, *Pedigrees of the Families in the County of Kent* (1830)
Bindoff, S. T. (ed.), *The House of Commons, 1509–58* (1982)
Birrell, Jean, 'Peasant Craftsmen in the Medieval Forest', *AgHR*, 17 (1969)
Bowden, Peter, *The Wool Trade in Tudor and Stuart England* (1962)
Brandon, Peter and Brian Short, *The South East from AD 1000* (1990)
Braun, Rudolf, 'Early Industrialization and Demographic Change in the Canton of Zurich', in Charles Tilly (ed.), *Historical Studies of Changing Fertility* (1978)
Brent, C. E., 'Rural Employment and Population in Sussex between 1550 and 1640', *Sussex Archaeological Collections*, 114 (1976)
The Rural Economy of Eastern Sussex, 1500–1700, East Sussex Records Office (1978)
Bridbury, A. R., *Medieval English Clothmaking*
Carus-Wilson, E. M., 'The Woollen Industry before 1500', in *VCH, Wiltshire*, iv (1959)

Carus-Wilson, E. M., 'An Industrial Revolution of the 13th Century', *EcHR*, 11 (1941)
Carus-Wilson, E. M. and Olive Coleman, *England's Export Trade, 1275–1547* (1963)
Chalklin, C. W., 'The Rural Economy of a Kentish Wealden Parish, 1650–1750', *AgHR*, 10 (1962)
Seventeenth Century Kent (1965)
Clark, Peter, 'The Migrant in Kentish Towns, 1580–1640', in P. Clark and Paul Slack (eds.), *Crisis and Order in English Towns* (1972)
Clarkson, Leslie A., 'The English Leather Industry in the 16th and 17th Centuries', unpublished Ph.D. thesis, University of Nottingham (1960)
'The Leather Crafts in Tudor and Stuart England', *AgHR*, 14 (1966)
Proto-Industrialization: the First Phase of Industrialization? (Economic History Soc., 1985)
Cleere, Henry and David Crossley, *The Iron Industry of the Weald* (Leicester, 1985)
Coleman, D. C., 'An Innovation and its Diffusion: the "New Draperies"', *EcHR*, 2nd ser., 22 (1969)
Industry in Tudor and Stuart England (1975)
Cornwall, Julian, 'Farming in Sussex', *Sussex Archaeological Collections*, 92 (1954)
'The People of Rutland in 1522', *Trans. Leicestershire Archaeological and Historical Soc.*, 37 (1961–2)
Wealth and Society in Early Sixteenth Century England (1988)
Cox, Nancy and Jeff, 'Probate Inventories: the Legal Background', *Local Historian*, 16 (1984)
'Valuations in Probate Inventories', *Local Historian*, 16 and 17 (1985, 1986)
De Vries, Jan, *European Urbanization, 1500–1800* (1984)
Detsicas, Alec and Nigel Yates (eds.), *Studies in Modern Kentish History* (Maidstone, 1983)
Deyon, Pierre, 'Variations de la production textile aux XVIe et XVIIIe: Sources et premières resultats', *Annales E. S. C.*, 18 (1963)
Dobson, Mary, 'Marsh Fever – the Geography of Malaria in England', *J. of Historical Geography*, 6 (1980)
Drake, Michael, 'An Elementary Exercise in Parish Register Demography', *EcHR*, 2nd ser., 14 (1962)
Du Boulay, F. R. H., 'Denns, Droving and Danger', *Arch Cant*, 76 (1961)
The Lordship of Canterbury (1966)
Dyer, Alan, '"The Bishops" Census of 1563: its Significance and Accuracy', *Local Population Studies*, 49 (1992)
Everitt, Alan, *Continuity and Colonization: the Evolution of Kentish Settlement* (Leicester, 1986)
Fieldhouse, R., 'Social Structure from Tudor Lay Subsidies and Probate Inventories', *Local Population Studies*, 12 (1974)
Finlay, Roger, *Population and Metropolis: the Demography of London, 1580–1650* (Cambridge, 1981)
Forbes, Thomas R., *Chronicle from Aldgate* (1971)
Friis, A., *Alderman Cockayne's Project and the Cloth Trade* (1927)
Frost, Pauline, 'Yeomen and Metalsmiths: Livestock in the Dual Economy of S. Staffordshire', *AgHR*, 29 (1981)
Furley, Robert, *A History of the Weald of Kent*, 2 vols. in 3 (1871–4)
Gallois, R. W., *British Regional Geology: The Wealden District* (1965)
Goose, Nigel, 'Household Size and Structure in Early Stuart Cambridge', *Social History*, 5 (1980)
Goring, Jeremy, 'Wealden Ironmasters in the Age of Elizabeth', in E. W. Ives *et al.* (eds.), *Wealth and Power in Tudor England* (1978)
Gottfried, Robert, 'Bury St Edmunds and the Population of Late Medieval English Towns', *Journal of British Studies*, 20 (1980)

Gould, J. D., 'The Trade Depression of the Early 1620s', *EcHR*, 2nd ser., 7 (1954–5)
The Great Debasement (1970)
'Cloth Exports, 1600–1640', *EcHR*, 2nd ser., 24 (1971)
Gray, H. L., 'The Production and Exportation of English Woollens in the 14th Century', *EHR*, 39 (1924)
Greatorex, Irene, 'Seasonality and Early Modern Towns', unpublished Ph.D. thesis, CNAA (Thames Polytechnic), 1992
Gullickson, Gay L., 'Agriculture and Cottage Industry: Redefining the Causes of Proto-Industrialization', *J.EcH*, 43 (1983)
Gutmann, Myron, *Toward the Modern Economy: Early Industry in Europe, 1500–1800* (Philadelphia, 1988)
Hall, A. D. and E. J. Russell, *Agriculture and Soils of Kent, Surrey and Sussex* (1911)
Hammersley, G. F., 'The Charcoal Iron Industry and its Fuel', *EcHR*, 2nd ser., 26 (1973)
Hasted, Edward, *The History and Topographical Survey of the County of Kent*, 2nd edn, 12 vols. (1797–1801)
Hatcher, John, *Plague, Population and the English Economy, 1348–1530* (1977)
Heaton, Herbert, *The Yorkshire Woollen and Worsted Industry* (1920)
Hey, David, 'A Dual Economy in S. Yorkshire', *AgHR*, 17 (1969)
'The Origins and Early Growth of the Hallamshire Cutlery and Allied Trades', in John Chartres and D. Hey (eds.), *English Rural Society, 1500–1800* (1990)
Hoskins, W. G., 'The Elizabethan Merchants of Exeter', in S. T. Bindoff *et al.* (eds.), *Elizabethan Government and Society* (1961)
Houston, R. A., *The Population History of Britain and Ireland, 1500–1750* (1992)
Houston, Rab and K. D. M. Snell, 'Proto-industrialization?', *Hist.J*, 27 (1984)
Howell, Cicely, *Land, Family and Inheritance in Transition* (Cambridge, 1983)
Hudson, Pat, 'Proto-industrialization: the Case of the West Riding Textile Industry', *History Workshop*, 12 (1981)
'Landholding and the Organization of the Textile Manufacture in Yorkshire Rural Townships' in Maxine Berg (ed.), *Markets and Manufacture in Early Industrial Europe* (1991)
(ed.), *Regions and Industries* (1989)
Husbands, Chris, 'Regional Change in a Pre-Industrial Economy', *J. Historical Geography*, 13 (1987)
Johnson, A. H., *History of the Worshipful Company of Drapers*, 5 vols. (Oxford, 1914–22)
Jones, D. W., 'The "Hallage" Receipts of the London Cloth Markets, 1562–1720', *EcHR*, 2nd ser., 25 (1972)
Jones, E. L., 'The Agricultural Origins of Industry', *Past & Present*, 40 (1968)
Kain, Roger J. P. and Hugh C. Prince, *The Tithe Surveys of England and Wales* (1985)
Kenyon, G. H., 'Kirdford Inventories', *Sussex Archaeological Collections*, 93 (1955)
Kerridge, Eric, *The Agricultural Revolution* (1967)
Kriedte, Peter, Hans Medick and J. Schlumbohm, *Industrialization before Industrialization* (1981)
Laslett, Peter, *The World We Have Lost – Further Explored* (1983)
Laslett, Peter and Richard Wall (eds.), *Household and Family in Past Time* (Cambridge, 1972)
Lennard, R. V., 'English Agriculture under Charles II', *EcHR*, 4 (1932–4)
Levine, David, 'The Demographic Implications of Rural Industrialization', *Social History*, 2 (1977)
Family Formation in an Age of Nascent Capitalism (1977)
Mann, Julia de L., *The Cloth Industry of the West of England from 1640 to 1880* (1971)
McIntosh, Marjorie K., 'Servants and the Household Unit in an Elizabethan English Community', *J. of Family History*, 9 (1984)

Medick, Hans, 'The Proto-Industrial Family Economy', *Social History*, 1 (1976)
Mendels, Franklin, 'Proto-industrialization: the First Phase of the Industrialization Process', *J.EcH*, 32 (1972)
   'Seasons and Regions: Agriculture and Industry during the Process of Industrialization' in Sidney Pollard (ed.), *Region und Industrialisierung* (Gottingen, 1980)
   'Agriculture and Peasant Industry in 18th Century Flanders', in W. N. Parker and E. L. Jones (eds.), *European Peasants and their Markets* (New York, 1981)
Overton, Mark, *A Bibliography of British Probate Inventories* (University of Newcastle upon Tyne, 1983)
Patten, John, 'Changing Occupational Structure in the E. Anglian Countryside', in H. S. A. Fox and R. A. Butlin (eds.), *Change in the Countryside* (1979)
Perry, R., 'The Gloucestershire Woollen Industry, 1100–1690', *Trans. Bristol & Gloucestershire Archaeological Soc.*, 66 (1947)
Phelps-Brown, E. H. and Shiela Hopkins, 'Wage-rates and Prices: Evidence for Population Pressure in the 16th Century', *Economica*, 24 (1957)
Pile, C. C. R., *Cranbrook: A Wealden Town* (Cranbrook and Sissinghurst Local Hist. Soc., 1955), p. 24
Pilgrim, J. E., 'The Cloth Industry in Essex and Suffolk, 1558–1640', unpublished M. A. thesis, University of London, 1938
Ponting, K. G., *A History of the West of England Cloth Industry* (1957)
   The Woollen Industry of South-west England (1971)
Ramsay, G. D., 'The Distribution of the Cloth Industry in 1561–2', *EHR*, 57 (1942)
   The Wiltshire Woollen Industry in the 16th and 17th Centuries (1943)
   'Industrial Discontent in Elizabethan London: Clothworkers and Merchant Adventurers in Conflict', *The London J.*, 1 (1975)
   The English Woollen Industry, 1500–1750 (1982)
Riden, Philip (ed.), *Probate Records and the Local Community* (1985)
Roberts, B. K., 'Medieval Colonization in the Forest of Arden', *AgHR*, 16 (1968)
Roberts, M. F., 'Wages and Wage-earners in England', unpublished D. Phil thesis, 1981
Robertson, Robert H. S., *Fuller's Earth: a History of Calcium Montmorillonite* (Hythe, 1986)
Rollison, David, *The Local Origins of Modern Society: Gloucestershire, 1500–1800* (1992)
Rowlands, Marie B., *Masters and Men in the West Midlands Metalware Trades* (Manchester, 1975)
Schofield, R. S., 'Parliamentary Lay Taxation, 1485–1547', unpublished Ph.D thesis, University of Cambridge, 1963
   'The Geographical Distribution of Wealth in England, 1334–1649', *EcHR*, 2nd ser., 18 (1965)
   'Taxation and the Political Limits of the Tudor State' in Claire Cross et al. (eds.), *Law and Government under the Tudors* (1988)
Schubert, H. R., *History of the British Iron and Steel Industry* (1957)
Sheail, John, 'The Regional Distribution of Wealth in England as indicated in the Lay Subsidy Returns of 1524/5', unpublished University of London thesis, 1968
Sheail, John, 'The Distribution of Taxable Population and Wealth in England during the early Sixteenth Century', *Trans. Institute of British Geographers*, 55 (1972)
Short, Brian, 'The De-industrialisation Process: a Case Study of the Weald, 1600–1850' in Pat Hudson (ed.), *Regions and Industries* (1989)
Skipp, Victor, 'Economic and Social Change in the Forest of Arden', *AgHR*, Supplement, 18 (1970)
   Crisis and Development: an Ecological Case Study of the Forest of Arden, 1570–1674 (Cambridge, 1978)

Slack, Paul, 'Mortality Crises and Epidemic Disease in England, 1485–1610', in Charles Webster (ed.), *Health, Medicine and Mortality in the Sixteenth Century* (1979)

Smith, R. B., *Land and Politics in the England of Henry VIII* (1970)

Spufford, Margaret, *Contrasting Communities* (Cambridge, 1974)

'The Limitations of the Probate Inventory' in John Chartres and David Hey (eds.), *English Rural Society, 1500–1800* (1990)

Straker, Ernest, *Wealden Iron* (1931)

Supple, Barry, *Commercial Crisis and Change in England, 1600–1642* (1959)

Swain, John T., *Industry before the Industrial Revolution: North-East Lancashire, c.1500–1640* (Manchester, 1986)

Tawney, A. J. and R. H., 'An Occupational Census of the Seventeenth Century', *EcHR*, 5 (1934)

Teesdale, Edmund B., *Gunfounding in the Weald in the 16th Century*, Royal Armouries Monograph 2 (1991)

Thirsk, Joan, *English Peasant Farming: the Agrarian History of Lincolnshire from Tudor to Recent Times* (1957)

'Industries in the Countryside', in F. J. Fisher (ed.), *Essays in the Economic and Social History of Tudor and Stuart England* (Cambridge, 1961)

'Horn and Thorn in Staffordshire: the Economy of a Pastoral County', *North Staffordshire J. of Field Studies*, 10 (1969)

Horses in Early Modern England (University of Reading, 1978)

'Plough and Pen: Agricultural Writers in the Seventeenth Century', in Trevor Aston *et al.*, (eds.), *Social Relations and Ideas: Essays in Honour of R. H. Hilton* (1983)

England's Agricultural Regions and Agricultural History, 1500–1750, (1987)

The Agrarian History of England and Wales, iv, 1500–1640 (Cambridge, 1967) and *v, 1640–1750* (Cambridge, 1985)

Unwin, George, *Industrial Organization in the 16th and 17th Centuries* (Oxford, 1904)

'The History of the Cloth Industry in Suffolk' in his *Studies in Economic History* (1927)

Wall, Richard, 'Regional and Temporal Variation in English Household Structure from 1650' in John Hobcraft and Philip Rees (eds.), *Regional Demographic Development* (1977)

'The Age at Leaving Home', *J. of Family History*, 3 (1978)

Wallenberg, J. K., *The Place Names of Kent* (Uppsala, 1934)

Walton, John K., 'Proto-industrialisation and the First Industrial Revolution: The Case of Lancashire', in Pat Hudson (ed.), *Regions and Industries* (1989)

Webster, Charles (ed.), *Health, Medicine and Mortality in the Sixteenth Century* (1979)

Witney, K. P., *The Jutish Forest: a Study of the Weald of Kent from 450 to 1380 A. D.* (1976)

Wooldridge, S. W. and Frederick Goldring, *The Weald* (1953)

Wright, S. J., 'A Guide to Easter Books and Related Parish Listings', *Local Population Studies*, 42, 43 (1989)

Wrightson, Keith and David Levine, *Poverty and Piety in an English Village: Terling, Essex* (1979)

Wrigley, E. A. and R. S. Schofield, *The Population History of England, 1541–1871: a Reconstruction* (Cambridge, 1981)

'English Population from Family Reconstitution: Summary Results, 1600–1799', *Population Studies*, 37 (1983)

Yelling, James, 'The Combination and Rotation of Crops in E. Worcestershire, 1540–1660', *AgHR*, 17 (1969)

'Probate Inventories and the Geography of Livestock Farming: E. Worcestershire, 1540–1750', *Trans. Institute of British Geographers*, 51 (1970)

Zell, Michael, 'Church and Gentry in Reformation Kent', unpublished Ph.D. thesis, University of California, Los Angeles, 1974

'The Exchequer Lists of Provincial Clothmakers fined in London during the Sixteenth Century', *BIHR*, 54 (1981)

'The Mid-Tudor Market in Crown Land in Kent', *Arch Cant*, 98 (1981)

'The Social Parameters of Probate Records in the Sixteenth Century', *BIHR*, 57 (1984)

'Families and Households in Staplehurst, 1563–4', *Local Population Studies*, 33 (1984)

'A Wood-Pasture Agrarian Regime: the Kentish Weald in the 16th Century', *Southern History*, 7 (1985)

Index

Tudeley (14), 21, 30, 35, 86, 125

Wealth, inventoried and taxable, 136–52
  geographical distribution of, 139–50
  See also under Trades; Farms and farming;
    Textile industry

Wittersham (38), 61–2, 86, 202
Woodchurch (37), 12, 34, 59, 61, 86

Yalding (17), 14, 34–5, 45, 62, 86, 154–5, 188

Cambridge Studies in Population, Economy
and Society in Past Time

Titles available in paperback are marked with an asterisk.